Dyslexia
Integrating Theory and Practice

The Editors

Margaret Snowling, a cognitive psychologist, is Principal of The National Hospital's College of Speech Sciences, London. She has been involved in research and clinical work with dyslexic children for some 15 years and has published widely in the field. Dr Snowling is chairman of the British Dyslexia Association Psychology Committee.

Michael Thomson, a child psychologist, is Joint Principal of East Court School for Dyslexic Children. Formerly, as a lecturer in psychology at Aston University, he undertook research and clinical work with dyslexic children. His many publications include a series of adventure stories for children. Dr Thomson is a member of the Board of Studies of the British Dyslexia Association.

Dyslexia
Integrating Theory and Practice

Edited by

MARGARET SNOWLING and MICHAEL THOMSON

Selected papers from the Second International Conference of the British
Dyslexia Association 'Meeting the Challenge', Oxford, 1991

W

Whurr Publishers Ltd
London and New Jersey

First published 1991 by
Whurr Publishers Ltd
19b Compton Terrace, London N1 2UN, England

Reprinted 1992, 1993, 1996 and 1998

British Library Cataloguing in Publication Data
International Conference of the British Dyslexia
Association (2nd 1991)
  Dyslexia: integrating theory and practice.
  I. Title   II. Snowling, M.J.   III. Thomson, M.E.
  371.91

  ISBN 1-870332-47-4

Photoset by Scribe Design, Gillingham, Kent
Printed and bound in Great Britain by Athenæum Press Ltd, Gateshead, Tyne & Wear

Contributors

Marjorie Anderson, Department of Psychology, University of St Andrews, Scotland, UK

Zvia Breznitz, Department of Psychology, Queen's College, New York, USA

Gordon D.A. Brown, Cognitive Neurocomputational Unit, Department of Psychology, University College of North Wales, Bangor, UK

Steve J. Chinn, Mark College, Highbridge, Somerset, UK

Ann Cooke, Dyslexia Unit, University College of North Wales, Bangor, UK

John C. DeFries, Institute of Behavioral Genetics, University of Colorado, Boulder, USA

Drake D. Duane, Institute for Developmental and Behavioral Neurology and Professor, Arizona State University, Arizona, USA

Lynne Duncan, Department of Psychology, University of St Andrews, Scotland, UK

Linnea C. Ehri, Division of Education, University of California, Davis, USA

Nick Ellis, Department of Psychology, University College of North Wales, Bangor, UK

Usha Goswami, Department of Experimental Psychology, University of Cambridge, UK

Anne Henderson, Dyslexia Unit, University College of North Wales, Bangor and St David's College, Gloddaeth Hall, Llandudno, UK

Margaret Hubicki, British Dyslexia Association Music and Dyslexic Working Party, UK

Rhona Johnston, Department of Psychology, University of St Andrews, Scotland, UK

Virginia Kelly, Learning Disabilities Clinic, School of Education, University of Southampton, UK

Cynthia Klein, ALBSU National Development Project, Language and Literacy Unit, Southwark College, London, UK

Elaine Miles, Dyslexia Unit, University College of North Wales, Bangor, UK

Tim R. Miles, Professor Emeritus of Psychology, University College of North Wales, Bangor, UK

José Morais, Laboratoire de Psychologie experimentalle, Université libre de Bruxelles, Belgium

Jane Oakhill, Laboratory of Experimental Psychology, University of Sussex, UK

Jeanne Reilly, Fairley House School, London, UK

Georgina Rippon, Department of Psychology, University of Warwick, UK

Arlene W. Sonday, Fairleigh Dickinson University, Teaneck, Texas and Hamline University, St Paul, Minnesota, USA

Joy Stackhouse, National Hospital's College of Speech Sciences, London, UK

Keith E. Stanovich, Department of Psychology, Oakland University, Rochester, Michigan, USA

John F. Stein, University Laboratory of Physiology, Oxford, UK

Jane Taylor, Independent Handwriting Therapist, Weymouth, Dorset, UK

Michael Thomson, Joint Principal, East Court School for Dyslexic Children, Ramsgate, UK

Patience Thomson, Fairley House School, London, UK

Frances L. Watson, Cognitive Neurocomputational Unit, Department of Psychology, University College of North Wales, Bangor, UK

Bill Wells, National Hospital's College of Speech Sciences, London, UK

Colin R. Wilsher, College Visiting Fellow, Department of Psychology, University College of North Wales, Bangor, UK

Nicola Yuill, Cognitive and Computing Science, University of Sussex, UK

Acknowledgements

The papers included in this collection were selected from a large number of papers submitted for the Second International Conference of the British Dyslexia Association 'Meeting the Challenge'. We would like to thank Harry Chasty and our colleagues on the Conference Organizing Committee for their support. We thank all the contributors who met our harsh deadlines and are most grateful to Charles Hulme, Sue Boase, Bill Watkins and Jane Sugarman for editorial assistance. Sarah Alleemudder provided unflagging secretarial support, without which we could not have completed the volume – our special thanks to her.

Maggie Snowling and Michael Thomson
January 1991

Contents

Chapter 6

Chapter 7

Chapter 8

Part III: The definition, nature and prevalence of dyslexia

Chapter 9

Chapter 10

Chapter 11

Chapter 12

Part IV: Intervention: theoretical and practical issues

Chapter 13

Chapter 22

Chapter 23

Chapter 24

Chapter 25

Chapter 26

Chapter 27

Chapter 28

Index

Editorial

In April 1989, the First International Conference of the British Dyslexia Association brought together practitioners and academics from a wide range of disciplines under the theme 'Meeting Points'. A multi-professional sharing of knowledge resulted. In response, the theme for the Second International Conference is 'Meeting the Challenge'. This book, *Dyslexia: Integrating Theory and Practice*, presents selected papers from this Conference, papers which we feel reflect some of the changes in the field during the last 2 years and provide authoritative overviews signalling the future of research and practice.

The first section (Part I) is devoted to the biological bases of dyslexia where perhaps the most exciting area of research is in the genetics of reading disability. This is reviewed by John DeFries focusing on data from the Colorado Family Reading and Twin Studies. The influential DeFries and Fulkner method for estimating heritability of traits is described, and its application to the measures of reading pioneered by Olson and colleagues discussed. Arguably, one of the most significant findings is that estimates for the heritability of the phonological component of reading are higher than for the orthographic component. It is this aspect which commonly causes most difficulty for dyslexics.

Drake Duane presents an overview of neurological issues in dyslexia, including magnetic resonance imaging (MRI), EEG and neuroanatomical findings which support variation in the structure and function of the dyslexic nervous system. Two important points are made. First, correlated behaviours may reflect shared brain mechanisms. Hence, reading disorders are frequently associated with oral language disorders, a point picked up later by Stackhouse and Wells. Secondly, coexisting disorders may provide markers for developmental disorders. Thus, dyslexia coexists with attention deficit–hyperactivity dysfunction in one-third of cases and psychiatric disorders, e.g. conduct disorders and depression, are frequent.

It may be important to elucidate coexisting behaviours further in order to determine fully the mechanism of genetic influence, a point taken up by Tim Miles in his chapter on the prevalence of dyslexia.

John Stein introduces the topic of vision and language from a physiological perspective. He then reviews the work of his group suggesting visual deficits in dyslexia. Their finding that there is an increased incidence of individuals who have problems with binocular vergence control among dyslexics and that these dyslexics benefit from the occlusion of one eye (by patching) has proved highly controversial (Bishop, 1989). The more recent work of this group has attempted to show a direct link between these visual problems and the pattern of reading performance exhibited by those individual dyslexics so affected. Although their findings are preliminary, future work needs to be directed along these lines if the relationship between visual deficits and dyslexia is to be validated.

The final paper by Georgina Rippon describes a pilot study on the use of brain electrical activity mapping (BEAM) and its correlation with other laterality measures in a group of dyslexics. The emphasis was on within-group comparisons and, even within the small sample studied, there were heterogeneous patterns of lateralisation in brain electrical activity. Interestingly, these correlated with performance on the Annett Pegboard – an independent measure of laterality. Although preliminary, this study presents an interesting avenue of new research on cortical function and dyslexia.

The second section of the book (Part II) on the normal development of literacy provides an important backdrop to dyslexia research and practice. Linnea Ehri describes children passing through a stage when they are emergent readers to enter a 'decoding stage' before becoming fluent and passing on to a 'reading to learn stage'. Knowledge of this should guide teaching practice and would, no doubt, be endorsed by Elaine Miles, who urges that teachers need to be encouraged to teach reading and spelling skills to children according to the stage of development which they have reached. Ehri elaborates her theory by focusing on the development of sight word reading and spelling system knowledge – both crucial components of the acquisition of literacy. Ehri's theory has parallels with the theory of literacy development forwarded by Uta Frith in the UK and mentioned by other contributors to the Conference (Frith, 1985). Thus, the child begins reading using partial visual cues: 'visual cue reading'. He or she then moves into a phase of phonetic cue reading (where letter–sound correspondences are important for lexical access) and, finally, a phase of 'cipher-sight reading' is reached when readers can recognise words as wholes and retrieve their pronunciation. Roughly, these stages correspond to Frith's logographic, alphabetic and orthographic phases and are paralleled by changes in children's spelling performance from 'pre-phonetic' through 'semi-phonetic' to phonetic and culminating in the use of within-word patterns which recur across words.

Nick Ellis's work is broadly consistent with this framework. He presents data from longitudinal studies showing that reading initially proceeds 'wholistically' whilst spelling is dependent on explicit phoneme segmentation skills. Spelling and segmentation together then influence reading producing an 'alphabetic' strategy. A review of his earlier work on dyslexia is consistent with the view that, classically, dyslexics find it difficult to pass to an alphabetic phase of literacy development.

José Morais takes up in detail the role of phonological awareness in literacy. His position, and that of his colleagues in Brussels, is that phoneme segmentation skill (as opposed to other types of phonological awareness, such as rhyming ability) is a consequence of exposure to alphabetic literacy. Thus, the claim of this group is that awareness of speech at the level of the phoneme is not a prerequisite of literacy, as sometimes believed by practitioners, but a consequence of it. Moreover, the acquisition of phonological awareness and grapheme–phoneme correspondences is intimately related. This is precisely the argument articulated from a different starting point by Ellis: at the beginning of literacy acquisition, there is a major causal influence from knowledge of simple correspondence rules to conscious phonemic ability; later on, conscious phoneme awareness leads to knowledge of complex correspondences.

Usha Goswami puts forward a different view of phonological awareness and its relationship with reading and spelling development. First, she reviews research indicating that syllables can be divided into onset and rime units. The onset of the syllable corresponds to the initial consonant or consonant cluster whilst the rime refers to the vowel and the succeeding consonant or consonants. Children find it easier to divide syllables into onsets and rimes than into phonemes. Like Morais, Goswami claims that phonemic awareness is a consequence of literacy development whereas awareness of onset and rimes precedes reading and may have important effects on it. Specifically, she presents evidence that children can use analogies between words which they are taught to read and new words with which they are presented, at an early stage of development. Moreover, there is a significant relationship between their ability to make rhyme analogies (in reading) and rhyme judgements even when controlling for general verbal ability and phoneme deletion performance. Similarly, analogies may be used early in the development of spelling. Thus, Goswami de-emphasises the use of spelling–sound knowledge in early reading and spelling development and focuses instead upon the use of larger units, such as rime-analogies. Children's awareness of these may be linked with their awareness of the rhyming relationships between spoken words.

The research on literacy development has important implications for theory and practice in dyslexia. All of the contributors to the book are agreed that phonological awareness has important effects on learning to read and spell. The view that dyslexics' reading and spelling problems are associated with difficulties in phonological awareness is widely held. However, for theoretical reasons, the attempt to train phoneme awareness as a prerequisite for literacy appears to be misguided; rather, training in phoneme awareness might usefully parallel training in spelling–sound correspondence and spelling itself. Alternatively, training in the segmentation of onsets and rimes (an easier task) might allow the child to capitalise upon analogies between written words (e.g. beak, peak) both for reading and spelling.

Some 10–20 years ago, there was much debate about the use of the term 'dyslexia' and the aetiology of the 'dyslexic' syndrome. Definitional issues still abound, but the debate is now more focused, mainly centring on whether or not IQ is relevant in the definition of reading disability. A recent international meeting of the Association of Child Psychology and Psychiatry of Great Britain found academics and clinicians to be divided on this controversial issue. Here, Keith Stanovich discusses the theoretical and practical implications of discrepancy definitions of reading disability where actual reading attainment is below the level expected, given the child's age and IQ; his points are tightly argued and, in particular, alert us to the difficulty of holding to such a definition when IQ itself can be affected (i.e. depressed) as a consequence of reading difficulty.

Tim Miles is understandably cautious about the definition of dyslexia but, nonetheless, argues that it is possible to arrive at estimates of the prevalence of dyslexia by allowing different criteria for its definition and different criteria for underachievement in reading. Importantly, Miles does not equate specific reading difficulty and dyslexia. Instead he views failure on items from the Bangor test (developed to diagnose dyslexic difficulties) as indicative of dyslexia. These include problems with the sequence of the months of the year and with verbal short-term memory. By implication, the discrepancy definition of dyslexia is not central to his view. Here he describes data from over 12 000 children in the National Cohort Study analysed by himself and Mary Haslum. These data suggest a prevalence of dyslexia of between 2 and 4 per cent.

The papers by Johnston, Anderson and Duncan, and Brown and Watson, represent some of the recent attempts by cognitive psychologists to elucidate dyslexic reading behaviour. Although it is widely held that dyslexics have phonological difficulties affecting their ability to read non-words, Johnston and her colleagues point out that there have been a number of failures to replicate this finding. They speculate that one reason may be individual differences among dyslexics and explore this question by comparing subgroups who differ in their relative strengths and weaknesses. Contrary to the prevailing view that dyslexics are not subject to visual processing difficulties, Johnston et al. view such problems as significant, at least in the way in which they modify the reading strategies which individual dyslexics have at their disposal. Thus, dyslexics who score well in relation to reading age-matched controls on an Embedded Figures Test have an advantage over those who have difficulty, given similar levels of phoneme segmentation ability in the two groups. The children with good visual skill read irregular words better (perhaps because of their visual distinctiveness), but their non-word reading was more seriously impaired – as though their visual skills were not conducive to the development of phonological reading strategies. Although this study is preliminary in nature and the subgroup samples are very small, it represents an important step towards elucidating the ways in which the pattern of strength and weakness in individual dyslexic children interacts with the demands of learning to read (Snowling, 1987).

Brown and Watson introduce the use of connectionist models to the study of dyslexia. This is an exciting new theoretical development in the field. Connectionist models can simulate complex behaviours yet depend upon the interaction between many simple elements. They offer the possibility of formulating computationally explicit models of cognitive processes which have a number of attractive properties. These models show learning and also degradation when damaged. The skills and knowledge they represent are not all-or-none attributes – the models show incremental improvements in performance with training and gradual decreases in performance in response to damage (removal of units or connections between units in the models). Ultimately, a proper under-standing of the reading impairments in dyslexia will depend upon explicit models of the reading process. Connectionism represents the most promising avenue to the development of such models at the moment. The chapter by Brown and Watson represents an interaction between basic and applied research, bringing together some of the latest work in the cognitive psychology of reading with studies of dyslexia.

The second half of the book (Parts IV–VI) addresses intervention. A clear message for practitioners and theoreticians alike is delivered by Joy Stackhouse and Bill Wells who debate whether the speech disordered and the reading disordered are one and the same population. Through two single case studies, the similarities between two children, one presenting with spoken language and one with written language difficulties, are elucidated. Both children have problems in metaphonological tasks and have been forced to rely on visual skills for the development of reading. These data encourage the closer collaboration of speech and language therapists with teachers in the management of spoken and written language difficulties.

Elaine Miles takes up the issue of subtypes of dyslexia and in a paper primarily directed to teachers, warns against the distinction between auditory and visual dyslexia. In a useful review, she reminds us that many so-called visual deficits may be the result of linguistic deficiencies. Moreover, developmental differences between dyslexics may at least partly account for the way in which they perform on tests of auditory and visual processing. Teachers should not stress any particular modality during teaching but should recognise that both reading and spelling are multisensory activities which support each other and interact. Her message also has theoretical significance – any theory of dyslexia must account for the ways in which processing strengths and weaknesses may impact on the course of development in different ways at different stages.

From the biological perspective, Colin Wilsher discusses the question of whether medicinal treatment of dyslexia is advisable. He begins with a critical review of studies on the use of megavitamins, antihistamines, applied kinesiology and psychostimulants. He then focuses on the use of nootropics, for example piracetam. A number of methodologically sound studies from different centres have produced evidence that the use of nootropics can lead to improvements in reading comprehension and prose reading (based on the Gray Oral Reading Test). The mechanism of the drug action is not explicated although there is a suggestion that it may work by increasing attentional resources.

Jane Oakhill and Nicola Yuill review research focusing on children who are not dyslexic but who have specific problems with reading comprehension (in the case of their own work, as diagnosed by poor performance on tests of listening comprehension). They also report two experiments describing techniques which led to an improvement in reading comprehension. The techniques described may well be applicable to dyslexics. In particular, they may benefit from instruction in the higher order comprehension skills involved in interpreting text and in ways of making inferences, both during reading for pleasure and in formal comprehension exercises. Another interesting element of the paper is the use of imagery in the development of comprehension skills. Many dyslexics have particularly good skills in visual imagery which may well be a source of strength.

The chapter by Zvia Breznitz also focuses on comprehension, reporting some experimental investigations of normal and dyslexic children. In these studies, the subjects were asked to modify their reading rate in slow and fast paced conditions. In the fast condition, text appeared on a computer screen all at once and then gradually disappeared. In the slow condition, text appeared on the screen word by word. Subjects read the text and then answered questions about it. The results were counterintuitive; in three experiments, speeding up novice readers improved reading comprehension. Of interest in this paper was the notion that fast reading allowed a more efficient use of memory skills or perhaps reduced distractibility.

The final chapter in the section on empirical studies of intervention (Part V), by Michael Thomson, is the latest in a series of his papers evaluating teaching techniques. This paper compares the use of simultaneous oral spelling and visual inspection as a means of teaching spelling to dyslexics and comparing them with a control group of normal readers. Of particular interest is the finding that dyslexics benefit mainly from simultaneous oral spelling whereas the controls learn with both techniques. The implications are that a general remedial approach to teaching may be appropriate for some children but dyslexics respond to specific remedial techniques designed to circumvent their weaknesses.

The book ends with a digest of papers focusing on practical teaching skills (Part VI). We had many papers describing teaching methods submitted to the Conference. Owing to space limitations, it was not possible to include them all. Regrettably, we decided to exclude those which described local authority policies and teaching provisions in general terms. We have selected a number of papers which we felt offer some new insights into teaching. First, whilst there has been an enormous amount of work on the assessment and treatment of literacy skills in dyslexia. very little work has focused on mathematics. The paper by Steve Chinn is a welcome overview of the sorts of procedures that might be involved in the assessment of mathematical difficulties in dyslexia. It incorporates guidelines originating from the British Dyslexia Association Subcommittee on Mathematics. The paper by Anne Henderson follows and examines some aspects of teaching mathematics.

As dyslexia has become widely recognised, there are increasing numbers of books, programmes and courses describing the structured multisensory teaching of reading and writing skills. Less commonly addressed are the 'higher order' skills which dyslexics require when studying for examinations or during ordinary school work. The paper by Patience Thomson introduces the idea of teaching these at an early level to primary school pupils. Topics include the transfer of oral to written work, mapping skills, memory organisation, descriptive writing and group teaching. She makes the important point that many study skills are enhanced by teaching in groups and also have important links with communication skills. The paper by Virginia Kelly is aimed at secondary school students. Her paper covers reading for study purposes, handling data, note-taking and displaying of work. Particularly interesting is the adaptation of some of De Bono's work for use with dyslexics. Of course, this would be a help for all students, but details for use with dyslexics will be helpful for many teachers who are dealing with secondary school pupils.

Closely linked to study skills at the secondary level are the development of teaching programmes for adult dyslexics and college students. The paper by Arlene Sonday examines the application of teaching basic skills to American college students and on examination allowances ('accommodations'). Cynthia Klein discusses how to set up a learning programme for adult dyslexics. Some of her views are controversial, for example she claims that many dyslexics do not find spelling syllable by syllable very easy and that they should be taught using the 'look, cover, write, check' method. However, she emphasises the point that, when teaching adults, it is very important to find out the particular strategy and learning style that best suits the individual student.

The next paper, by Ann Cooke, addresses an issue which is of fundamental importance in increasing awareness of dyslexic children in the classroom, i.e. the transfer from individual remedial lessons, perhaps at a remedial centre, to everyday classroom work. It is too easy to assume that structured teaching will be automatically generalised. This paper provides a timely reminder of the issues involved and provides suggestions as to how remedial and class teachers can liaise most successfully in the interests of the child. Examples of particular teaching techniques are provided by Jeanne Reilly and Jane Taylor. From the perspective of speech therapy, Jeanne Reilly discusses the development of speaking and listening skills using tape-recorders. Jane Taylor focuses on handwriting from a practical perspective. She introduces the interesting idea that pupils can improve their performance by being encouraged to monitor and evaluate their own handwriting. Developing awareness of skill and of ways in which it might be improved is a teaching strategy that also can effectively be used in other curriculum areas.

The final paper, by Margaret Hubicki, in Part VI is an extremely novel contribution. It focuses upon the difficulties that dyslexic children may have in learning music. The paper provides an introduction to the topic as well as discussing some practical issues.

References

BISHOP, D.V.M. (1989). Unstable vergence control and dyslexia – a critique. *British Journal of Ophthalmology* 73, 223–235.

FRITH, U. (1985). Beneath the surface of developmental dyslexia. In: K.E. Patterson, J.C. Marshall and M. Coltheart (Eds), *Surface Dyslexia.* London: Routledge & Kegan Paul.

SNOWLING, M. (1987). *Dyslexia: A Cognitive–Developmental Perspective.* Oxford: Basil Blackwell.

Maggie Snowling and Michael Thomson
January 1991

Part I
Biological Bases

Chapter 1
Genetics and Dyslexia: An Overview

J.C. DeFRIES

The fact that dyslexia tends to cluster in certain families has been known for many years. For example, in 1905, C.J. Thomas, Assistant Medical Officer (Education), London County Council, described the familial nature of 'congenital word-blindness' as follows:

> In this connection it is to be noted that it frequently assumes a family type; there are a number of instances of more than one member of the family being affected, and the mother often volunteers the statement that she herself was unable to learn to read, although she had every opportunity. (p. 381)

Over the years, familial transmission for dyslexia has been well documented, and a number of different modes of inheritance have been proposed to account for this familiality. For example, in the sample of 112 families included in Hallgren's (1950) classic study of dyslexia, 88% of the probands (the index cases through which other family members were ascertained) had one or more relatives who were also affected. Based on results of statistical genetic analyses that are relatively crude, by present-day standards, Hallgren concluded that the transmission of dyslexia in these families followed an autosomal dominant mode of inheritance, i.e. inheritance of a single copy of a specific allele (a form of gene) is sufficient to cause dyslexia (Plomin, DeFries and McClearn, 1990). However, there are several reasons to question the validity of Hallgren's hypothesis. [For an excellent critical review of the early literature concerning genetics and dyslexia, see Finucci (1978).] First, both parents were unaffected in 17% of the families of probands. If dyslexia is due to an autosomal dominant allele, at least one parent of each dyslexic child should also be affected. Secondly, although test data were available from probands and some family members, diagnoses of adults were based largely upon interview data. Thirdly, a casual reading of Hallgren's case studies suggests a preoccupation with familial transmission. Hallgren seemed to be reluctant to diagnose a child as being dyslexic unless another member of the family was also affected. Such a bias, if present, could have yielded a sample of families with a disproportionate number of cases of parent–offspring transmission.

Subsequently, Symmes and Rapoport (1972) attempted to account for the higher prevalence of 'unexpected reading failure' in males than in females by proposing that the condition may be caused by a recessive allele carried on the X chromosome. Females have two X chromosomes (in addition to 22 pairs of autosomes), whereas males have one X and a smaller Y chromosome. Therefore, for the condition to be expressed in females, a recessive allele must be present on both X chromosomes; however, in males, a recessive allele on their single X chromosome would be sufficient to cause the condition. Consequently, sex-linked recessive disorders (e.g. color blindness) are more prevalent in males than in females. If dyslexia were due to a sex-linked recessive allele and the frequency of this allele were 0.1 in the general population, then the expected prevalence of dyslexia in males would be 0.1, whereas it would be only $(0.1)^2 = 0.01$ in females. Parent–child resemblance for sex-linked characters also differs as a function of gender. Fathers transmit their only X chromosome to their daughters, and sons receive their only X chromosome from their mothers. In contrast, mothers and daughters each share one of their two X chromosomes, and fathers and sons share no X chromosomes. Thus, for conditions influenced by an X-linked recessive allele, father–daughter resemblance should approximate mother–son resemblance, both of which should exceed mother–daughter resemblance, and father–son resemblance should be negligible. Results of more recent family studies of reading disability have failed to provide evidence for this X-linked recessive hypothesis (e.g. DeFries and Decker, 1982).

Finucci et al. (1976) reported the first family study of reading disability in which relatives, as well as probands, were administered an extensive psychometric test battery. Although the sample of probands was rather small (15 males and 5 females), considerable evidence for familiality was obtained; 34 of 75 first-degree relatives were also diagnosed as being reading disabled. In the 16 families of probands in which both parents were tested, 13 had one or both parents affected. Thus, 81% of the probands had at least one affected parent, a proportion very similar to that previously reported by Hallgren (1950). However, because various patterns of inheritance appeared to be present in these 20 pedigrees, the authors concluded that reading disability is genetically heterogeneous.

Colorado Family Reading Study

Our first attempt to assess the etiology of reading disability, the Colorado Family Reading Study, was initiated in 1973. The primary objectives of that study were as follows:

1. To construct a short battery of tests that differentiates children with a diagnosed reading disability from matched controls.
2. To assess possible deficits in parents and siblings of affected children.
3. To study the transmission of reading disability in families of affected children.

Reading-disabled children were ascertained by referral from personnel of local school districts in Colorado using the following criteria for selection: 7.5–12 years of age; reading performance equal to or less than one-half of that expected on the basis of age and grade level (e.g. a child in the fourth grade who is reading at or below the second grade level); IQ of 90 or above; and living at home with both biological parents. School records were reviewed to ensure that the selection criteria were met and that the children had no serious emotional problems or uncorrected deficits in auditory or visual acuity. After the families of the reading-disabled children had been scheduled for testing, prospective control families were contacted. Control children were matched to reading-disabled children on the basis of age (within 6 months), gender, school and home neighborhood. Except for reading level, which was equal to or greater than grade placement, each control child also met the proband selection criteria. Parents and siblings (7.5–18.0 years of age) of proband and control children were also tested. Families were middle class and the primary language spoken in the home was always standard American English.

Although the design of the Colorado Family Reading Study (Figure 1.1) is very simple, it facilitates a number of interesting comparisons. In

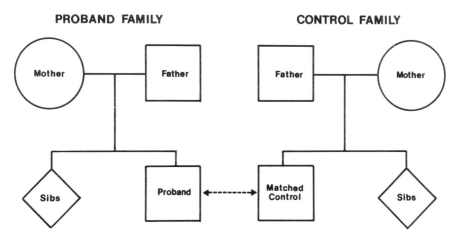

Figure 1.1 Design of the Colorado Family Reading Study. [From Genetic aspects of reading disability: The Colorado Family Reading Study (p. 258) by J.C. DeFries and S.N. Decker, 1982, *Reading Disorders: Varieties and Treatments*, edited by R.N. Malatesha and P.G. Aaron, New York: Academic Press. Copyright © 1982 by Academic Press. Reprinted by permission.]

addition to the obvious comparison of probands vs matched controls, we can compare the performance of the first-degree relatives (brothers, sisters, fathers and mothers) of reading-disabled children to that of the relatives of controls. To the extent that reading disability is heritable, relatives of reading-disabled children should manifest at least some deficits on measures of reading performance.

During the 3-year project, 125 probands, their parents and siblings, and members of 125 control families were administered an extensive psychometric test battery. The total number of subjects tested in these 250 families was 1044, the most extensive family study of reading disability conducted to date. It is interesting to note that this referred sample of

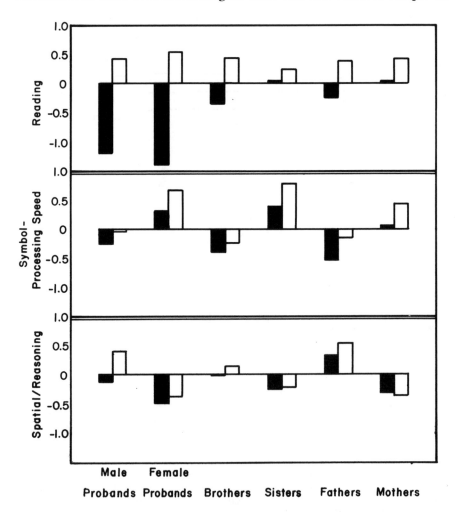

Figure 1.2 Average composite scores of probands (solid bars), controls (open bars) and their first-degree relatives tested in the Colorado Family Reading Study. [Data from Decker and DeFries, 1980.]

reading-disabled children included 96 boys and 29 girls, a gender ratio of 3.3:1.

Test descriptions and average test scores for the various groups included in the Colorado Family Reading Study were previously reported by Foch et al. (1977) and DeFries et al. (1978). In this brief review, only average composite scores will be presented.

Individual scores on eight tests administered to all subjects in the study [Reading Recognition, Reading Comprehension, Spelling and Mathematics subtests of the Peabody Individual Achievement Test (Dunn and Markwardt, 1970); Coding Subtest Form B of the Wechsler Intelligence Scale for Children – Revised or WISC-R (Wechsler, 1974); the Colorado Perceptual Speed Test; Primary Mental Abilities Spatial Relations (Thurstone, 1963); and the Nonverbal Culture Fair Intelligence Test (Institute for Personality and Ability Testing, 1973)] were age adjusted and subjected to principal component analysis with Varimax rotation (Nie et al., 1975). Three readily interpretable components adequately accounted for the pattern of correlations among the eight tests (Decker and DeFries, 1980). The first component (general reading performance) correlated most highly with Reading Recognition, Reading Comprehension and Spelling. A second component, termed 'symbol-processing speed', correlated most with the Colorado Perceptual Speed Test and WISC coding. The third component (spatial/reasoning) correlated most with Nonverbal Intelligence and Spatial Relations. Based upon the results of this principal component analysis, three composite scores were computed for each subject, one representing each of the three ability dimensions.

The average principal component scores of reading-disabled boys and girls, their matched controls, and the first-degree relatives of both the probands and the controls are depicted in Figure 1.2. These composite scores have been standardized to have a grand mean of zero and a standard deviation of one; thus, negative scores indicate average performance below the mean of all family members in the study. An unweighted means analysis of variance with unequal subclass numbers was employed to assess the significance of family type (probands vs controls), gender and their interaction. [Resulting F-values were reported by Decker and DeFries (1980).]

Although the difference between probands and controls is significant ($P < 0.05$) for each of the three composite measures, the difference for reading (about 1.8 standard deviations, on average) is substantially larger than that for the other measures. Significant gender differences in the proband and control groups are in the expected direction, with boys obtaining higher average spatial scores and girls obtaining higher average scores on symbol-processing speed.

The difference between siblings of probands and siblings of controls is significant for the reading and symbol-processing speed measures.

Moreover, there is a significant interaction between family type and gender for reading, with brothers of probands being more impaired than sisters of probands. With regard to the sibling data, significant gender differences are also present (and in the expected direction) for the symbol-processing speed and spatial measures.

The pattern of significant main effects for the parental data exactly parallels that for siblings. Again, the largest difference between parents of probands and parents of controls is for the reading measure. Fathers of probands also tend to be somewhat more affected than mothers of probands, but this difference is not large enough to result in a significant interaction between family type and gender.

The reading and symbol-processing speed deficits of siblings and parents of probands depicted in Figure 1.2 conclusively demonstrate the familial nature of reading disability. Consequently, these family data were subjected to various genetic analyses. As predicted by the sex-influenced polygenic threshold model, relatives of reading-disabled girls were found to be at higher risk for reading problems than relatives of reading-disabled boys (DeFries and Decker, 1982). Tests for major-gene influence were also undertaken, but with mixed results. For example, variances of reading performance scores obtained by relatives of probands were significantly greater than those for relatives of controls, in accordance with a major-gene hypothesis. However, little or no evidence was obtained to support the hypothesis that reading disability is caused by a recessive allele carried on the X chromosome. Furthermore, when data from families of male probands were subjected to complex segregation analysis, no evidence was obtained for autosomal major-gene influence (Lewitter, DeFries and Elston, 1980). On the other hand, when data from families of female probands were analysed, a hypothesis of single-gene, recessive inheritance could not be rejected. Based on a comparison of various test statistics, Lewitter, DeFries and Elston (1980) argued that the failure to reject the recessive-allele hypothesis was not due to the small number of female probands in the study. Thus, results of this segregation analysis of family data also suggested that reading disability may be genetically heterogeneous.

Genetic Linkage Analysis

The first credible evidence that reading disability may be caused by a major gene linked to a specific chromosome was reported by Smith et al. (1983). Nine families in which there was apparent autosomal dominant transmission for reading disability (namely, a history of reading disability occurred in three successive generations) were selected for study. Each of 84 family members included in these nine families was administered a test battery to detect reading problems and to ensure that the disability was limited to reading and spelling. Children were diagnosed as affected if they had a reading level at least 2 years below expected grade level and a full-scale IQ greater than 90. Adults were diagnosed using self-reports if there was a discrepancy between test results and a history of reading problems. It is of special interest to note that each of the nine probands for these families was male, but that the gender ratio in their 41 affected relatives was 1.16 males to each female.

Smith et al. (1983) subjected the resulting pedigree data to linkage analysis. LOD scores were computed to assess the possibility of linkage between the hypothesized allele for reading disability and various genotype and chromosomal markers. LOD is an abbreviation for logarithm to the base 10 of the odds, where the 'odds' is a ratio of conditional probabilities, i.e. the probability of co-transmission between the character and a marker, given linkage, divided by the probability of co-transmission given independent assortment. Therefore, a LOD score of 0 indicates that the two events are equally likely, whereas a LOD score of 3 indicates a probability ratio of 1000:1 in favor of linkage. A negative LOD score indicates that the ratio of probabilities is less than one, and thereby provides evidence against linkage. LOD scores were computed for each family, assuming various possible linkage relationships, and then summed across families.

Smith et al. (1983) reported co-transmission between reading disability and a marker on chromosome 15 that yielded a LOD score of 3.2. However, about 70% of this total score was due to transmission in only one of the nine families, and another family had a large negative score.

Subsequently, Smith et al. (1990) augmented their sample to include a total of 250 individuals in 21 informative families. In addition to the markers used in their previous analysis, family members were also typed for DNA markers. With the inclusion of these additional families, the maximum LOD score for linkage to chromosome 15 was reduced to 1.3. However, as shown in Figure 1.3, LOD scores for individual families ranged from over +2.0 to less than −2.0. These recent results suggest that only about 20% of the families of probands manifest apparent linkage to chromosome 15. Therefore, to the extent that reading disability is heritable, it must be due to one or more major genes at other chromosomal locations, or possibly to the combined effects of several genes. Current studies by Smith and her colleagues are also using markers on chromosome 6 to search for other possible genetic linkages. As depicted in Figure 1.3, results of these initial studies suggest that some families manifest apparent linkage of reading disability to chromosome 15 but not 6, whereas others show possible linkage to chromosome 6 but not 15.

Although a number of different genetic models have been proposed to account for the familial nature of reading disability, there is no consensus at this time regarding a particular mode of inheritance. If there is a major

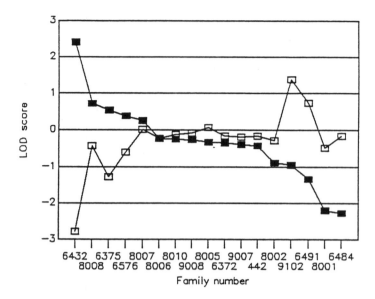

Figure 1.3 LOD scores for markers on chromosomes 15 (■) and 6 (□) in families of reading-disabled children. Families are ordered according to decreasing LOD scores for chromosome 15. [From Colorado Reading Project: An update by J.C. DeFries, R.K. Olson, B.F. Pennington and S.D. Smith, 1991, *The Reading Brain: The Biological Basis of Dyslexia*, edited by D.B. Gray and D. Duane, Parkton, Maryland: York Press. Copyright © 1991 by York Press. Reprinted by permission.]

gene linked to chromosome 15 that causes reading disability, its frequency must be rather low. Perhaps most cases of dyslexia are caused by several genes with relatively minor, but cumulative, effects. Twin studies can be used to localize such quantitative trait loci, as well as to assess both genetic and environmental etiologies.

Twin Studies

Previous twin studies of dyslexia used a comparison of concordance rates in identical (monozygotic, MZ) and fraternal (dizygotic, DZ) twin pairs as a test for genetic etiology. A pair is concordant if both members are affected, but discordant if only one member manifests the condition. Because MZ twins are genetically identical, whereas DZ twins share only half of their segregating genes on average, a greater MZ than DZ concordance provides evidence for a genetic etiology.

The concept of concordance is very simple; however, its estimation depends upon the manner in which the sample of twins has been ascertained (DeFries and Gillis, 1990). For example, if 'truncate selection' has been employed such that both members of the pair could be ascertained as probands, then 'probandwise' concordance rates should be computed. Because previous twin studies apparently ascertained samples in this manner, probandwise concordance rates will be reported in this brief review.

Concordance rates in previous twin studies

Zerbin-Rüdin (1967) reviewed data from six case studies of twins with 'congenital word-blindness', a Danish twin study, and six pairs of twins included in Hallgren's (1950) family study. As shown in Table 1.1, the probandwise concordance rates in this sample of 17 MZ and 34 DZ twin pairs are 100% and 52%, respectively.

Table 1.1 Probandwise concordance rates for reading disability

Study	Number of pairs		Percentage concordance	
	Identical	Fraternal	Identical	Fraternal
Zerbin-Rüdin (1967)	17	34	100	52
Bakwin (1973)	31	31	91	45
Stevenson et al. (1987)	14–19	27–42	33–59	29–54
Colorado Reading Project	101	114	70	43

Bakwin (1973) ascertained same-sex twin pairs through mothers-of-twins clubs and obtained reading history information via parental interviews, telephone calls and mail questionnaires. In the resulting sample of 676 children, 31 pairs of MZ twins and 31 pairs of DZ twins each included at least one member with 'a reading level below expectation derived from the child's performance in other school subjects' (p. 184). As shown in Table 1.1, the probandwise concordance rates in these MZ and DZ twin pairs are 91% and 45%, respectively.

More recently, Stevenson et al. (1984, 1987) reported results from the first twin study of reading disability in which the subjects were administered standardized measures of intelligence, reading and spelling. Twins were diagnosed for reading or spelling handicap ('backwardness' or 'retardation') using various diagnostic criteria, and resulting probandwise concordance rates ranged from 33% to 59% for MZ twin pairs and from 29% to 54% for DZ pairs. Thus, although concordance for pairs of MZ twins exceeds that for DZ twins in each of these three previous twins studies of reading disability, considerable variation exists among the results of the individual studies.

Colorado Twin Study

Because of a paucity of well-designed twin studies of dyslexia, a twin study was initiated in 1982 as part of the on-going Colorado Reading Project

(Decker and Vandenberg, 1984; DeFries, 1985). A psychometric test battery which includes the WISC-R (Wechsler, 1974) or Wechsler Adult Intelligence Scale – Revised (WAIS-R; Wechsler, 1981) and the Peabody Individual Achievement Test (PIAT; Dunn and Markwardt, 1970) is being administered to MZ and DZ twin pairs in which at least one member of each pair manifested a school history of reading problems and to a comparison group of twins with a negative school history. Data from the PIAT Reading Recognition, Reading Comprehension and Spelling subtests are used to compute a discriminant function score for each member of the pair, employing discriminant weights estimated from an analysis of data obtained from an independent sample of 140 reading-disabled and 140 control non-twin children tested during an earlier phase of the project. Twin pairs are included in the proband sample if at least one member of the pair with a positive school history of reading problems is also classified as affected by the discriminant score, and has a Verbal or Performance IQ score of at least 90, no diagnosed neurological, emotional or behavioral problems, and no uncorrected visual or auditory acuity deficits.

In order to determine zygosity of twin pairs, selected items from the Nichols and Bilbro (1966) questionnaire are administered. If zygosity is doubtful, analyses of blood samples are also employed. Twin pairs are all reared in middle-class homes, speak standard American English and range in age from 8 to 20 years at the time of testing.

To date, a total of 101 pairs of MZ twins, 73 pairs of same-sex DZ twins and 41 pairs of opposite-sex DZ twins meet the criteria for inclusion in the proband sample. In contrast to referred samples in which the gender ratio is typically three or four males to each female, the numbers of male and female probands in the current twin sample are 149 and 156, respectively. Because female MZ pairs are often over-represented in twin studies (Lykken, Tellegen and DeRubeis, 1978), the observed gender ratio of 0.93:1 in this proband sample may be due to a differential volunteer rate of male and female MZ twin pairs. In fact, the gender ratio in the sample of MZ probands (0.78:1) is somewhat lower than that for either same-sex or opposite-sex DZ probands (1.23:1 and 1.08:1, respectively). However, none of these gender ratios approaches that typically reported for referred samples. A lower gender ratio in a research-identified sample of non-twin, reading-disabled children was also recently noted by Shaywitz et al. (1990). Thus, the preponderance of males typically found in referred samples of reading-disabled children is probably due, at least in part, to ascertainment bias.

As indicated in Table 1.1, probandwise concordance rates of MZ and DZ twin pairs included in the Colorado Reading Project are 70% and 48%, respectively. Although the difference between these MZ and DZ concordance rates is not large, it nevertheless confirms the previous evidence for at least some genetic etiology of reading disability.

Multiple regression analysis of twin data

A comparison of concordance rates in identical and fraternal twin pairs is an appropriate test of genetic etiology for categorical variables such as presence or absence of a disease state; however, dyslexic subjects are ascertained because of deviant scores on continuous measures such as reading performance (Figure 1.4). For such characters, a comparison of

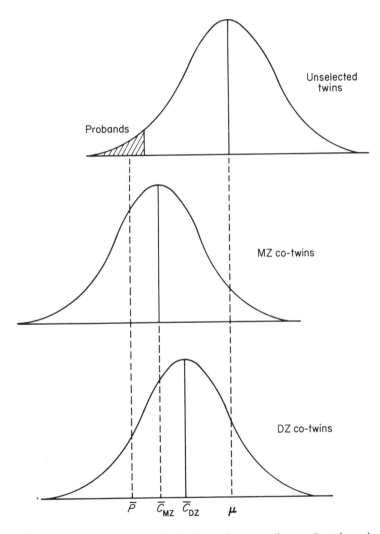

Figure 1.4 Hypothetical distributions for reading performance of an unselected sample of twins, and of the identical (MZ) and fraternal (DZ) co-twins of dyslexic probands. The differential regression of the MZ and DZ co-twins towards the mean of the unselected population (μ) provides a test of genetic etiology. [From Evidence for a genetic aetiology in reading disability of twins by J.C. DeFries, D.W. Fulker and M.C. LaBuda, 1987, *Nature* **329**, p. 537. Copyright © 1987 by Macmillan Journals Ltd. Reprinted by permission.]

co-twin means yields a more powerful test of genetic etiology (DeFries and Fulker, 1985, 1988).

When MZ and DZ probands are selected because of deviant scores on a continuous measure, the scores of their co-twins are expected to regress towards the mean of the unselected population. However, to the extent that the deficit of probands is due to heritable influences, this regression towards the mean should differ for MZ and DZ co-twins. MZ probands and co-twins share all of their genes, whereas DZ probands and co-twins share only half of their segregating genes on average; thus, if dyslexia has a genetic etiology, the scores of DZ co-twins should regress more towards the mean of the unselected population. Consequently, if the means of the MZ and DZ probands are equal, a t-test of the difference between the means of the MZ and DZ co-twins would provide a sufficient test for genetic etiology. However, a multiple regression analysis of selected twin data provides a more general, statistically powerful and flexible test.

In 1985, David W. Fulker and I formulated two multiple regression models for the analysis of selected twin data: (1) a basic model in which the partial regression of co-twin's score on the coefficient of relationship provides a statistically powerful test for genetic etiology, and (2) an augmented model that provides indices of the extent to which individual differences within the selected group are due to heritable and to shared-environmental influences. These two models are as follows:

$$C = B_1 P + B_2 R + A \qquad (1)$$

and

$$C = B_3 P + B_4 R + B_5 PR + A \qquad (2)$$

where C is the co-twin's score, P is the proband's score, R is the coefficient of relationship ($R = 1.0$ for MZ twin pairs and 0.5 for DZ twin pairs), and PR is the product of proband's score and relationship. Inclusion of the interaction term in the augmented model causes the expectations for the coefficients of P and R to differ from those estimated from the basic model; thus, their coefficients have different subscripts.

It was shown that B_1, the partial regression of co-twin's score on proband's score, is a measure of average MZ and DZ twin resemblance, whereas B_2 estimates twice the difference between the MZ and DZ co-twin means after co-variance adjustment for any difference between the MZ and DZ proband means (DeFries and Fulker, 1985). Therefore B_2 was advocated as a test of significance for genetic etiology. Furthermore, it was demonstrated that B_3 and B_5 provide direct estimates of the proportion of variance due to environmental influences shared by members of twin pairs (c^2) and heritability (h^2), respectively.

It was also noted that h_g^2 (a measure of the extent to which the deficit of probands is due to heritable influences) could be estimated from the results of fitting the basic model to selected twin data. Moreover, it was suggested that a comparison of h_g^2 and h^2 could be used to test the hypothesis that the etiology of extreme scores differs from that of variation within the normal range. The deviant scores of probands could be due to a major gene effect or to a gross environmental insult, for example, whereas individual differences within the normal range may be due to multifactorial influences. If this is the case, then h_g^2 and h^2 may differ in magnitude. However, if probands are merely the lower tail of a normal distribution of individual differences, then h_g^2 should equal h^2. More recently, it was shown that a simple transformation of twin data prior to regression analysis facilitates a direct estimate of h_g^2, as well as a test of the hypothesis that the etiology of extreme scores differs from that of individual differences within the normal range (DeFries and Fulker, 1988). When each score is expressed as a deviation from the mean of the unselected population and then divided by the difference between the proband and control means, $B_2 = h_g^2$ and $B_4 = h_g^2 - h^2$.

To illustrate this methodology, the basic and augmented models were fitted to the discriminant score data of probands and co-twins included in the current Colorado sample. In a manner analogous to that used for computation of probandwise concordance, data from concordant pairs were double entered for these analyses. The average scores of the MZ and DZ probands and co-twins for this composite measure of reading performance are presented in Table 1.2. These data are standardized and expressed in standard deviation units from the mean of 432 control individuals (members of twin pairs with a negative school history for reading problems). From this table it may be seen that the probands are highly selected. The average scores of the MZ and DZ probands are both over 2.5 standard deviations below the mean of the comparison group. In addition, it may be seen that the MZ co-twins have regressed only 0.22 of a standard deviation on average towards the control mean, whereas DZ co-twins have regressed 0.86 of a standard deviation on average. Thus, when the basic model was fitted to these data, $B_2 = -1.34 \pm 0.30$ ($P < 0.001$). When the same model was fitted to transformed discriminant

Table 1.2 Mean discriminant scores of 101 pairs of identical twins and 114 pairs of fraternal twins in which at least one member of each pair is reading disabled[a]

	Probands	Co-twins
Identical	-2.74	-2.52
Fraternal	-2.65	-1.79

[a]Expressed in standard deviation units from the mean of 432 control individuals.

function data, $B_2 = h_g^2 = 0.49 \pm 0.11$ ($P < 0.001$). Thus, results of this analysis suggest that about one-half of the deficit of probands, on average, is due to heritable influences.

When the augmented model was fitted to the transformed discriminant function data, $B_5 = h^2 = 0.75 \pm 0.35$ ($P < 0.01$, one-tailed) and $B_3 = c^2 = 0.11 \pm 0.27$ ($P > 0.25$). Thus, individual differences within the probands are highly heritable, whereas environmental influences shared by members of twin pairs are not an important source of variance. More importantly, the estimates of h_g^2 and h^2 are rather discrepant (0.49 and 0.75, respectively), suggesting that probands are not merely the lower tail of a normal distribution of individual differences. However, the difference between these two genetic parameter estimates is not significant ($B_4 = -0.26 \pm 0.37, P > 0.25$). Thus, a larger sample of twins is required to test this hypothesis more rigorously. Because this hypothesis has relevance to important issues in the field of learning disabilities, such as the specificity issue recently articulated by Stanovich (1986) and Foorman (1989), additional testing of dyslexic twins is clearly warranted.

Discussion

The multiple regression analysis of selected twin data is a highly flexible methodology. The basic model can be easily extended to include other main effects and interactions (Cohen and Cohen, 1975) in order to test for differential etiology as a function of group membership. For example, Geschwind (1981) speculated that girls may be less affected than boys 'by certain environmental influences, such as the quality of teaching, social class differences, or outside pressures within society' (p. xiv). More recently, Harris (1986) suggested that twin analyses should be conducted separately for males and females because the etiology of reading disability may differ as a function of gender. However, by fitting an extended regression model that includes gender as a dummy variable (e.g. boys and girls are coded +0.5 and −0.5, respectively) to data from both males and females simultaneously, the hypothesis of differential etiology as a function of gender can be tested directly (DeFries, Gillis and Wadsworth, 1990).

In this manner, data from probands of ostensible subtypes could also be analysed simultaneously to assess the validity of alternative topologies. For example, an extended basic model could be fitted to data from reading-disabled twins with or without attention deficit–hyperactivity disorder. Results of such analyses could help clarify the nature of the relationship between these two associated disorders (Silver, 1990).

Age adjustment can be accomplished easily by including age of proband as a co-variate in the multiple regression model. Moreover, by including the product of age and the coefficient of relationship in an extended basic model, Stevenson et al.'s (1987) hypothesis that genetic factors are less important as a cause of reading problems in older children can be tested (Wadsworth et al., 1989). In a similar manner, the relevance of IQ to the definition of learning disabilities (Siegel, 1989; Torgesen, 1989) could be assessed by testing for differential etiology as a function of general cognitive ability level.

In addition to these 'univariate' applications of the multiple regression analysis of selected twin data, in which co-twins' scores for some measure are predicted from probands' scores for the same measure, 'bivariate' analyses are also possible. In the bivariate case, probands are selected for some character (X) and co-twins are measured for a different character (Y). When the basic model is fitted to such data, the resulting estimate of 'bivariate h_g^2' is a function of the genetic co-variance between the two variables. For example, Richard K. Olson and colleagues recently undertook an analysis of measures of word recognition, phonological coding and orthographic coding in our sample of reading-disabled twins (DeFries et al., 1990). Resulting estimates of univariate h_g^2 for word recognition (0.54 ± 0.08) and phonological coding (0.54 ± 0.10) were found to be somewhat higher than that for orthographic coding (0.28 ± 0.11). When a bivariate model was fitted to the data in which co-twins' scores for either phonological coding or orthographic coding were predicted from word recognition scores of probands, a very interesting pattern of results was obtained. The resulting estimate of bivariate h_g^2 for word recognition and phonological coding (0.81 ± 0.14) is substantially higher than that between word recognition and orthographic coding (0.27 ± 0.18). This result suggests that the genetic etiology of deficits in word recognition may be due largely to heritable influences on phonological coding.

This hypothesis was recently tested employing confirmatory factor analysis (Gillis et al., 1990). A factor model was fitted to Reading Recognition, phonological coding and orthographic coding data from 86 pairs of MZ twins and 73 pairs of DZ twins in which at least one member of each pair is reading disabled, and separately to data from 92 pairs of MZ and 59 pairs of DZ twins in the control sample. Resulting estimates of h^2 for word recognition, phonological coding and orthographic coding were 0.59, 0.43 and 0.05 in the proband sample, and 0.35, 0.52, and 0.20 in the controls. Estimates of the genetic correlation between word recognition and phonological coding were 0.81 and 0.68 in the proband and control samples, respectively, whereas those between word recognition and orthographic coding were 0.45 in both samples. The genetic correlation between phonological coding and word recognition is significantly larger than that between orthographic coding and word recognition ($P < 0.005$) in the proband sample, and the difference is marginally significant ($P < 0.10$) in controls. Thus, these results also suggest that the genetic etiology of reading disability is largely due to heritable variation in phonological coding.

Concluding Remarks

Although results of twin and family studies reviewed in this chapter provide compelling evidence for a genetic etiology of reading disability, the mechanism of genetic influence has not yet been elucidated. Consequently, a linkage analysis of data from fraternal twin pairs tested in the Colorado Reading Project was recently initiated. Employing a variant of our multiple regression analysis of twin data, scores of DZ co-twins are predicted from probands' score and relationship at various marker loci. In this manner, an attempt will be made to assess the extent to which the reading performance deficit of probands is due to major genes and/or quantitative trait loci (Lander and Botstein, 1989).

In conclusion, research on genetics and dyslexia is currently a very active area of investigation. In addition to providing information pertaining to etiology, genetic analyses are being employed to test hypotheses that are relevant to a number of important issues in the field of learning disabilities.

Acknowledgements

This work was supported in part by a program project grant from NICHD (HD-11681), and the report was written while J.C. DeFries was supported by a University of Colorado Faculty Fellowship. The invaluable contributions of staff members of the many Colorado school districts which participated in our research, and of the twins and their families, are gratefully acknowledged. I also thank Jacquelyn J. Gillis and Sally J. Wadsworth for statistical analyses and Rebecca G. Miles for expert editorial assistance.

References

BAKWIN, H. (1973). Reading disability in twins. *Developmental Medicine and Child Neurology* **15**, 184–187.

COHEN, J. and COHEN, P. (1975). *Applied Multiple Regression/Correlation Analysis for the Behavioral Sciences.* Hillsdale, NJ: Lawrence Erlbaum Associates.

DECKER, S.N. and DeFRIES, J.C. (1980). Cognitive abilities in families of reading-disabled children. *Journal of Learning Disabilities* **13**, 517–522.

DECKER, S.N. and VANDENBERG, S.G. (1985). Colorado twin study of reading disability. In: D.B. Gray and J.F. Kavanagh (Eds), *Biobehavioral Measures of Dyslexia*, pp. 123–135. Parkton, MD: York Press.

DeFRIES, J.C. (1985). Colorado reading project. In: D.B. Gray and J.F. Kavanagh (Eds), *Biobehavioral Measures of Dyslexia*, pp. 107–122. Parkton, MD: York Press.

DeFRIES, J.C. and DECKER, S.N. (1982). Genetic aspects of reading disability: The Colorado Family Reading Study. In: R.N. Malatesha and P.G. Aaron (Eds), *Reading Disability: Varieties and Treatments*, pp. 255–279. New York: Academic Press.

DeFRIES, J.C. and FULKER, D.W. (1985). Multiple regression analysis of twin data. *Behavior Genetics* **15**, 467–473.

DeFRIES, J.C. and FULKER, D.W. (1988). Multiple regression analysis of twin data: etiology of deviant scores versus individual differences. *Acta Geneticae Medicae et Gemellologiae* **37**, 205–216.

DeFRIES, J.C., FULKER, D.W. and LaBUDA, M.C. (1987). Evidence for a genetic aetiology in reading disability of twins. *Nature* **329**, 537–539.

DeFRIES, J.C. and GILLIS, J.J. (1990). Etiology of reading deficits in learning disabilities: Quantitative genetic analysis. In: J.E. Obrzut and G.W. Hynd (Eds), *Advances in the Neuropsychology of Learning Disabilities: Issues, Methods and Practice*. Orlando, FL: Academic Press.

DeFRIES, J.C., GILLIS, J.J. and WADSWORTH, S.J. (1990). Genes and genders: A twin study of reading disability. In: A.M. Galaburda (Ed.), *The Extraordinary Brain: Neurobiologic Issues in Developmental Dyslexia*, in press. Cambridge, MA: MIT Press.

DeFRIES, J.C., SINGER, S.M., FOCH, T.T. and LEWITTER, F.I. (1978). Familial nature of reading disability. *British Journal of Psychiatry* **132**, 361–367.

DeFRIES, J.C., OLSON, R.K., PENNINGTON, B.F. and SMITH, S.D. (1990). Colorado Reading Project: An update. In: D.B. Gray and D. Duane (Eds), *The Reading Brain: The Biological Basis of Dyslexia*, in press. Parkton, MD: York Press.

DUNN, L.M. and MARKWARDT, F.C. (1970). *Examiner's Manual: Peabody Individual Achievement Test*. Circle Pines, MN: American Guidance Service.

FINUCCI, J.M. (1978). Genetic considerations in dyslexia. In: H.R. Myklebust (Ed.), *Progress in Learning Disabilities*, Vol. 4, pp. 41–63. New York: Grune & Stratton.

FINUCCI, J.M., GUTHRIE, J.T., CHILDS, A.L., ABBEY, H. and CHILDS, B. (1976). The genetics of specific reading disability. *Annals of Human Genetics* **40**, 1–23.

FOCH, T.T., DeFRIES, J.C., McCLEARN, G.E. and SINGER, S.M. (1977). Familial patterns of impairment in reading disability. *Journal of Educational Psychology* **69**, 316–329.

FOORMAN, B.R. (1989). What's specific about specific reading disability: An introduction to the special series. *Journal of Learning Disabilities* **22**, 332–333.

GESCHWIND, N. (1981). A reaction to the conference on sex differences and dyslexia. In: A. Ansara, N. Geschwind, A. Galaburda, M. Albert and N. Gartrell (Eds), *Sex Differences in Dyslexia*. Towson, MD: Orton Dyslexia Society.

GILLIS, J.J., DeFRIES, J.C., OLSON, R.K. and RACK, J.P. (1990). Confirmatory factor analysis of reading performance and process measures in the Colorado Reading Project. *Behavior Genetics* **20**, in press.

HALLGREN, B. (1950). Specific dyslexia ('congenital word-blindness'): A clinical and genetic study. *Acta Psychiatrica et Neurologica Scandinavica*, Suppl. **65**, 1–287.

HARRIS, E.L. (1986). The contribution of twin research to the study of the etiology of reading disability. In: S.D. Smith (Ed.), *Genetics and Learning Disabilities*, pp. 3–19. San Diego: College-Hill Press.

INSTITUTE FOR PERSONALITY AND ABILITY TESTING (1973). *Measuring Intelligence With Culture Fair Tests: Manual for Scales 2 and 3*. Champaign, IL.

LANDER, E.S. and BOTSTEIN, D. (1989). Mapping Mendelian factors underlying quantitative traits using RFLP linkage maps. *Genetics* **121**, 185–199.

LEWITTER, F.I., DeFRIES, J.C. and ELSTON, R.C. (1980). Genetic models of reading disability. *Behavior Genetics* **10**, 9–30.

LYKKEN, D.T., TELLEGEN, A. and DeRUBEIS, R. (1978). Volunteer bias in twin research: The rule of two-thirds. *Social Biology* **25**, 1–9.

NICHOLS, R.C. and BILBRO, W.C. (1966). The diagnosis of twin zygosity. *Acta Genetica et Statistica Medica* **16**, 265–275.

NIE, N.H., HULL, C.H., JENKINS, J.G., STEINBRENNER, K. and BENT, D.H. (1975). *Statistical Package for the Social Sciences*, 2nd edn. New York: McGraw-Hill.

PLOMIN, R., DeFRIES, J.C. and McCLEARN, G.E. (1990). *Behavioral Genetics: A Primer*, 2nd edn. New York: Freeman.

SHAYWITZ, S.E., SHAYWITZ, B.A., FLETCHER, J.M. and ESCOBAR, M.D. (1990). Prevalence of reading disability in boys and girls. *Journal of the American Medical Association* **264**, 998–1002.

SIEGEL, L.S. (1989). IQ is irrelevant to the definition of learning disabilities. *Journal of Learning Disabilities* **22**, 469–478.

SILVER, L.B. (1990). Attention Deficit–Hyperactivity Disorder: Is it a learning disability or a related disorder? *Journal of Learning Disabilities* **23**, 394–397.

SMITH, S.D., KIMBERLING, W.J., PENNINGTON, B.F. and LUBS, H.A. (1983). Specific reading disability: Identification of an inherited form through linkage analysis. *Science* **219**, 1345–1347.

SMITH, S.D., PENNINGTON, B.F., KIMBERLING, W.J. and ING, P.S. (1990). Familial dyslexia: Use of genetic linkage data to define subtypes. *Journal of the American Academy of Child Psychiatry*, in press.

STANOVICH, K.E. (1986). Cognitive processes and the reading problems of learning-disabled children: Evaluating the assumption of specificity. In: J.K. Torgesen and B.Y.L. Wong (Eds), *Psychological and Educational Perspectives on Learning Disabilities*, pp. 87–131. Orlando, FL: Academic Press.

STEVENSON, J., GRAHAM, P., FREDMAN, G. and McLOUGHLIN, V. (1984). The genetics of reading disability. In: C.J. Turner and H.B. Miles (Eds), *The Biology of Human Intelligence*, pp. 85–97. Nafferton, England: Nafferton Books Unlimited.

STEVENSON, J., GRAHAM, P., FREDMAN, G. and McLOUGHLIN, V. (1987). A twin study of genetic influences on reading and spelling ability and disability. *Journal of Child Psychology and Psychiatry* **28**, 229–247.

SYMMES, J.S. and RAPOPORT, J.L. (1972). Unexpected reading failure. *American Journal of Orthopsychiatry* **42**, 82–91.

THOMAS, C.J. (1905). Congenital 'word-blindness' and its treatment. *Ophthalmoscope* **3**, 380–385.

THURSTONE, T.G. (1963). *Examiners' Manual: Primary Mental Abilities*. Chicago: Science Research Associates.

TORGESEN, J.K. (1989). Why IQ is relevant to the definition of learning disabilities. *Journal of Learning Disabilities* **22**, 484–486.

WADSWORTH, S.J., GILLIS, J.J., DeFRIES, J.C. and FULKER, D.W. (1989). Differential genetic aetiology of reading disability as a function of age. *The Irish Journal of Psychology* **10**, 509–520.

WECHSLER, D. (1974). *Examiner's Manual: Wechsler Intelligence Scale for Children – Revised*. New York: The Psychological Corporation.

WECHSLER, D. (1981). *Examiner's Manual: Wechsler Adult Intelligence Scale – Revised*. New York: The Psychological Corporation.

ZERBIN-RÜDIN, E. (1967). Kongenitale Wortblindheit oder spezifische dyslixie (Congenital Word-Blindness). *Bulletin of the Orton Society* **17**, 47–56.

Chapter 2
Neurobiological Issues in Dyslexia

DRAKE D. DUANE

In the United States of America, the decade 1990–2000 has been designated 'The Decade of the Brain'. This joint congressional and presidential action, at the suggestion of the National Institutes of Neurological Disease and Stroke, will launch a concerted effort to unravel the mysteries of the central nervous system. Developmental disorders, among them dyslexia, have received special attention. Currently, four federally funded institutes are devoted to various biological issues in dyslexia. Three recently added institutes are devoted to the study of learning disabilities. One of these additionally is researching the pheno-menon of attention deficit–hyperactivity disorder (ADHD). Several project grants related to the biology of developmental disorders are now in progress. What I shall present in large measure reflects the research of these investigative centers.

Dyslexia, a condition of differential aptitude, offers an opportunity to examine the neurobiological substrate of aptitudes and behaviors other than reading. To gain the full measure of this opportunity, I shall comment on behaviors that are correlated with reading inefficiency, specifically oral language and visual perception. Further, there are conditions that co-occur with dyslexia in higher frequency than expected, specifically attention deficit–hyperactivity disorder (ADHD), disorders of vigilance and perhaps some psychiatric syndromes. Important new advances with respect to the biological characteristics of the dyslexic, including the anatomy and neurophysiology of the dyslexic nervous system, may provide insights into the genesis of a variety of aptitudes in our species.

Correlated Behaviors

Correlated behaviors may reflect shared brain mechanisms. For example, the high prevalence of delays in developmental speech milestones, inefficiencies in rhyming, difficulties in acquisition of the ability to name letters, awkwardness in attempts at phonemic segmentation in the first 6 years of life (Liberman et al., 1977; Bradley and Bryant, 1983) compounded by persistent difficulties in stressed oral speech such as rapid automated naming (Denckla and Rudel, 1976), and later still stumbling attempts at gaining proficiency with a second language (Dinklage, 1971), suggest that reading disorders (and perhaps spelling as well) share some of the properties of oral language development. Thus factors that shape competence in speech may be similar to those factors that direct competence in deciphering script. It should be recalled that physical insults to the nervous system in utero through to early puberty rarely, if ever, affect reading in isolation but commonly influence both reading and speech. These early-in-life, developmental conditions are never discrete localized insults to the nervous system but are rather more widespread. It is in adulthood that the mature nervous system may, from a lesion as tiny as a small coin, produce what is called 'global aphasia'.

In addition, it may not be by chance that the early acquisition of reading skills is performed aloud with the same oral rehearsal as the infant employs in practising the production of speech sounds. The motor theory of speech perception suggests that the production of speech sounds is an essential concomitant to the comprehension of speech sounds that are heard. Further, there is probably an anatomical structure or system crucial to that mechanism (Liberman and Mattingly, 1989). A similar structural-to-functional relationship may exist for early reading and the system may be anatomically juxtaposed to that for speech.

Despite the very strong correlation with oral language, there are children with reading difficulties who seem to have little or no problem in speech perception or speech production. These children commonly are motorically awkward, are inefficient in visual memory and are frustrated by tasks that psychologists call 'visual–perceptual'. These reasonably fluent-speaking children represent disorders of the non-language-dominant hemisphere. It seems that, as they mature, their decoding skills improve but they continue to miss the point of metaphor and are unaware of the emotional content of what they read. As children and young adults, they similarly miss the point of affective communication in voice and gesture from those around them (Weintraub and Mesulam, 1983; Voeller, 1986). All of this implies that, although the former group of speech-impaired children dominates the reading-disabled population, reading appears to be a quite complex behavior by which there is more than one means for someone to be inept. Furthermore, it is essential that we study more than the reading process if we are to understand the *individual* who suffers with reading disability.

Coexisting Disorders

Coexisting disorders may serve as markers of developmental processes producing the condition or marking the time in development when a common event resulted in two distinct disorders. An example of the latter would be the effect on fingerprints of events occurring in utero between the eleventh and nineteenth week of gestation. This may include a viral illness which befell the mother at, for example, 13 weeks producing an adverse effect on both brain development and dermatoglyphics (Sorenson-Jamison, 1990). In the former instance, Down's syndrome seemed to provide a potential link to Alzheimer's disease and perhaps genetic mechanisms for both due to the chromosomal aberration associated with Down's syndrome and the Down's phenomenon characteristically associated with premature decline in cognitive function. Furthermore, both were marked by neuropathological similarities to those seen in presenile and senile memory disturbance (Lai and Williams, 1989). However, it is also possible that the associations may simply be fortuitous or so obscure that the relationship may escape detection.

Attention deficit–hyperactivity disorder

Some United Kingdom researchers have expressed considerable reservation to the idea in the USA of ADHD, arguing that the label has been frequently misapplied to children who are anxious or depressed, or simply contentious. Nevertheless, cautious behavioural assessment reveals numbers of children in the USA (and probably elsewhere) whose nervous system dysfunction produces inefficient voluntary control of attention resulting in inefficient learning, weak memorization and/or motoric restlessness not attributable to social environment upheaval. When cautiously defined, three-quarters of such inattentive learners demonstrate calm and deliberate learning promoted by judicious use of medications.

The Learning Disabilities Institute at Yale University in the USA confirms that at least one-third of those suffering from carefully defined disorders of attention have coexistent learning problems, commonly in mathematics and occasionally in reading (Shaywitz et al., 1991). Furthermore, more than one-third of those with verified academic underachievement also demonstrate features of attention deficit–hyperactivity dysfunction. So high a prevalence raises the possibility of conjoint cause. The response to medication suggests that there are molecular and/or neurochemical factors in academic underachievement. Explication of that association may afford useful insights into learning, attention and memory in the general population.

Daytime somnolence

Beginning with the development of the learning disabilities assessment program at the Mayo Clinic in Rochester, Minnesota in the late 1970s and continuing with greater intensity with work at the Institute for Developmental and Behavioral Neurology in Scottsdale, Arizona, it is apparent that there is a high prevalence in developmental nervous system disorders of daytime somnolence (D.D. Duane, personal observations; L. Epcar and D. Duane, abstract submitted to the American Academy of Neurology). This may be the crucial determining factor in the so-called non-vigilance that is commonly observed in the ADHD population (Weinberg and Brumback, 1990), but it may also represent a separate manifestation of the mechanisms that underlie developmental learning disorders including those of reading. A recent study of 100 students evaluated for developmental disorders in Scottsdale revealed that 58% showed daytime non-alertness confirmed by a study known as pupillometry (Yoss, Moyer and Ogle, 1969). Although strongly associated with attention deficit–hyperactivity disorder, abnormal pupillometry occurred almost as frequently in the smaller group of students with reading disabilities in isolation (Table 2.1).

Table 2.1   Pupillometry in developmental disorders ($n = 100$)[a]

	Number	Abnormal pupillometry	
		No.	%
ADHD	50	31	62
ADHD + RD	24	15	62
RD	18	8	44
Other	8	4	50
Total	100	58	58

ADHD = attention deficit–hyperactivity disorder.
RD = reading disability.
[a]Mean age = 12.5 years (17–23 years); female:male = 17:83.

This approach provides a precise determination of whether an alerting compound is useful. By comparing pre- and postdose performance on cognitive measures, the dose at which effectiveness is achieved can be verified. Additionally, physiological studies known as the P300 (an evoked EEG potential) in our laboratory are strongly associated with attentional control disorder and to a lesser extent to reading disorder (Duane, 1991a).

Psychiatric disorders

Psychiatric disorders are known to be more prevalent in the reading-disabled population, specifically conduct disorder and depression (Rutter, 1974). Although these may represent the effects upon the spirit of school frustration, current investigation of the relationship between the brain and affect raise the possibility that the same biological mechanisms which induce reading disabilities may play a role in engendering psychiatric disorder (Duane, 1989). Our preliminary work (Duane, 1991b) in this regard suggests at least one similarity between individuals referred for neurological evaluation because of a possible brain mechanism producing the psychiatric syndrome. Contrasted with a group of children and young adults with developmental disorders, both populations demonstrate laterality quotients lower than the general population, i.e. the degree of right-handedness encountered in the developmental disorders and psychiatric disorders is less than that seen in a control group of neurological patients with either focal dystonia or minor neurological symptoms such as neck, back or head pain. More work is required, however, before any definite conclusion can be reached regarding the possible association.

Biological Features

Magnetic resonance imaging

A number of verified observations have been made with respect to the anatomy of the nervous system in reading disorders. At the clinical level, magnetic resonance imaging (MRI) has shown symmetry in the width of the posterior one-third of the cerebral hemispheres. This feature is strongest in those children who also have oral language difficulty in addition to reading difficulty (Hynd and Semrud-Clikeman, 1989). These findings positively correlate with postmortem investigations involving 10 dyslexics, 7 male and 3 female, studied at the Beth Israel Hospital in Boston by Dr A.M. Galaburda and his associates (Galaburda, Rosen and Sherman, 1989). In each instance, the upper surface of the temporal lobe called the temporal plane is of equal width on the two sides. Such symmetry is observed in less than 25% of the general population. That 10 consecutive nervous systems would demonstrate this property is a very low statistical probability. To what extent this symmetry is under direct genetic influence or reflects other events in fetal brain development is as yet unclear. Further, it is apparent that there are individuals with a symmetrical nervous system who show no obvious difficulty in reading (Filipek and Kennedy, 1991). Thus, symmetry is only one feature of the dyslexic nervous system.

Electroencephalography

Physiological measures with electroencephalography (EEG), but particularly with derivatives of the EEG through computer-assisted analysis of what is called the power spectrum, are suggestive of idiosyncratic physiological organization of the nervous system in those with reading disorders. The work of Frank Duffy and colleagues at Boston Children's Hospital has been crucial to this investigation (Duffy et al., 1980).

Nevertheless, it is safe to say that there is no physiological test which is diagnostic of dyslexia, but rather the findings represent physiological clues as to what may be the quirks of the dyslexic nervous system.

My own investigations in Arizona (Duane, 1991a) suggest the following:

1. A not uncommon frequency of low amplitude spikes in the routine EEG. This may explain why occasional nocturnal seizures or febrile fits may occur in those with a variety of developmental disorders including dyslexia.
2. A common pattern in those with reading disabilities that is also prevalent among those with left-handedness or weak right-handedness consisting of an asymmetry of the alpha distribution increased in the right posterior hemisphere as opposed to the left.
3. Among those with reading disability, a tendency for the localization of the P300 to be displaced from the left towards the right posterior hemisphere.

Let me again re-emphasize that none of these is diagnostic of dyslexia. However, these findings do not occur in high frequency in the general population. Thus, they represent additional data supporting variation in the structure and function of the dyslexic nervous system. It should also be borne in mind that these variations are subtle and are no more markers of 'disease' than is isolated handicap/retardation in reading a marker for general intellectual handicap (retardation).

Cerebral blood flow

At the metabolic level, studies of cerebral blood flow and PET scans suggest a reduction in the left posterior hemisphere during tasks of reading among those with reading disabilities. These abnormalities persist into adulthood as defined by a study at the Bowman Gray Medical Center in Winston-Salem, North Carolina, involving a group of adults who as children were diagnosed as dyslexic by Mrs June Orton (Wood et al., 1991).

Pathogenesis

Genetic mechanisms

Early on in the history of the description of dyslexia, British physicians noted the high prevalence of reading disorders in families (Hinshelwood, 1917). This raised the possibility of familial mechanisms, but the mode of inheritance was unclear. Today it is quite clear that among the mechanisms that may produce dyslexia are those linked to the human gene. This work is reviewed in Chapter 1. However, what is not clear is the extent to which these chromosomal anomalies explain the full spectrum of reading disability observed in the classroom, i.e. there may be non-genetic as well as genetic mechanisms which may produce reading problems. Indeed, future classifications of dyslexia may segregate on the basis of family history or genetic cause vs non-genetic or epigenetic mechanisms.

Epigenetic mechanisms

The existence of non-genetic factors in dyslexia has been suggested by the brain anatomy research of Galaburda which was initiated by the late Professor Norman Geschwind of the Harvard Medical School. This study, supported by the Orton Dyslexia Society in 1980 following a meeting at Airlie House, Virginia in 1978, in addition to describing the symmetry of the temporal plane referred to above, verifies two types of microscopic pathology observed in all seven males and two of the three female dyslexic subjects. These are: focal cortical dysgenesis, disarrays in the layered pattern at the brain's surface marked by (1) ectopias – cell rests at the surface – and (2) derangements of the layered pattern below these superficial cell clumps (Galaburda et al., 1985). The second involves fibromyelin plaques – tiny cortical scars – seen in one of the seven males and two of the three females. This change may represent the effects of blood vessel occlusion. These apparently minor changes of the surface of the brain seen on both sides, maximal left and more frontal than posterior, have a profound influence on the organization of the nervous system. Indeed, it is on this basis that the symmetry pattern of dyslexia may be generated, i.e. surface cell abnormalities that provoke unusual connections in the same and the opposite hemisphere. This may explain the unusual frequency of visual spatial ability among those with reading disabilities, i.e. not compensatory but rather a by-product of the developmental brain process producing dyslexic underperformance.

There have been three mechanisms postulated to account for these pathological phenomena (Galaburda, 1990): first, the male sex steroid testosterone as a direct provocator; secondly, autoimmine antibodies within the maternal circulation affecting brain development in the fetus; and thirdly, circulatory failure, if not on an autoimmune basis, then perhaps on the basis of reduction in maternal placenta perfusion in the perinatal period. Each of these hypotheses has its difficulties. The issue of gender has recently been debated in the USA. It is clear that the frequency of developmental disorders referred to physicians is strongly influenced not by academic achievement but by social conduct, i.e. students who are obstreperous in the classroom are more apt to be sent for psychological assessment and to receive special educational intervention in the USA, although a recent study suggested equal prevalence of reading disability among males and females in Connecticut (Shaywitz et al., 1990). The Isle of Wight Study (Rutter et al., 1976), a much more in-depth epidemiological study, confirmed a higher rate of reading disability among males. Pooling together these two data points would suggest that, although reading disability is more prevalent in boys than in girls, there is a tendency to overrefer boys either because of associated ADHD features which are more prevalent in males than females or because of male aggressiveness.

A further difficulty to the Galaburda immune hypothesis is the observation by Aldinolfi (1990) that maternal antibodies do not enter the fetal circulation. Thus, although higher rates of occurrence of antinuclear antibodies are observed in mothers of dyslexic offspring (Pennington et al., 1987), it is not clear whether the maternal antibodies in the mother's circulation themselves have a direct effect on brain development.

Finally, the fact that there are distinct micropathological patterns seen in male dyslexics as opposed to female dyslexics raises concern as to their specificity. Furthermore, it has been shown that in mutant mice similar cortical anomalies may occur without immune dysfunction (Nowakowski, 1988). Thus, it may be genes and only genes that produce cortical dysgenesis.

This can be summed up by saying that the abundant data collected so far clearly suggest biological mechanisms are at the root of dyslexia. Perhaps the end of this decade, the last decade of our millennium, will be the 'Decade of the Brain' for dyslexia and other developmental disorders.

References

ALDINOLFI, M. (1990). Maternal brain antibodies and neurological handicap. In: A.M. Galaburda, G.F. Rosen and G.D. Sherman (Eds), *The Extraordinary Brain: Neurobiological Issues in Developmental Dyslexia*, in press. New York: Plenum.

BRADLEY, L. and BRYANT, P.E. (1983). Categorizing sounds and learning to read – A causal connection. *Nature* **301**, 419–421.

DeFRIES, J.C., OLSON, R.K., PENNINGTON, B.F. and SMITH, S.D. (1991). In: D.B. Gray and D.D. Duane (Eds), *The Reading Brain: The Biological Basis of Dyslexia*, in press. Parkton, MD: York Press.

DENCKLA, M.B. and RUDEL, R.G. (1976). Rapid 'Automatized' Naming (R.A.N.): Dyslexia differentiated from other learning disabilities. *Neuropsychologia* **14**, 471–478.

DINKLAGE, K.T. (1971). Inability to learn a foreign language. In: G.B. Blaine Jr and C.C. McArthur (Eds), *Emotional Problems of the Student*, 2nd edn. New York: Appleton-Century-Crofts.

DUANE, D.D. (1989). Neurobiological correlates of learning disorders. *Journal of American Academy of Child and Adolescent Psychiatry* **28**, 314–318.

DUANE, D.D. (1991a). Biological foundations of learning disabilities. In: J.E. Obrzut and G.W. Hynd (Eds), *Neuropsychological Foundations of Learning Disabilities*. Orlando, FL: Academic Press.

DUANE, D.D. (1991b). Summary. In: D.B. Gray and D.D. Duane (Eds), *The Reading Brain: The Biological Basis of Dyslexia*, in press. Parkton, MD: York Press.

DUFFY, F.H., DENCKLA, M.B., BARTELS, P.H. and SANDINI, G. (1980). Dyslexia: Regional differences in brain electrical activity by topographic mapping. *Annals of Neurology* **7**, 412–420.

FILIPEK, P.A. and KENNEDY, D.N. (1991). Magnetic resonance imaging: Its role in the developmental disorders. In: D.B. Gray and D.D. Duane (Eds), *The Reading Brain: The Biological Basis of Dyslexia*, in press. Parkton, MD: York Press.

GALABURDA, A.M. (1990). The testosterone hypothesis: Assessment since Geschwind and Behan. *Annals of Dyslexia* **30**, 18–38.

GALABURDA, A.M., ROSEN, G.F. and SHERMAN, G.D. (1989). The neural origin of developmental dyslexia: Implications for medicine, neurology and cognition. In: A.M. Galaburda (Ed.), *From Reading to Neurons*. Cambridge, MA: MIT Press.

GALABURDA, A.M., SHERMAN, G.F., ROSEN, G.D., ABOITIZ, F. and GESCHWIND, N. (1985). Developmental dyslexia: Four consecutive patients with cortical anomalies. *Annals of Neurology* **18**, 222–233.

HINSHELWOOD, J. (1917). *Congenital Word-blindness*. London: H.K. Lewis.

HYND, G.W. and SEMRUD-CLIKEMAN, M. (1989). Dyslexia and brain morphology. *Psychological Bulletin* **106**, 447–482.

LAI, F. and WILLIAMS, S. (1989). A prospective study of Alzheimer Disease in Down Syndrome. *Archives of Neurology* **46**, 849–853.

LIBERMAN, A.M. and MATTINGLY, I.G. (1989). A specialization for speech perception. *Science* **243**, 489–494.

LIBERMAN, I.Y., SHANKWEILER, D., LIBERMAN, A.M., FOWLER, C. and FISCHER, F.W. (1977). Phonetic segmentation and recording in the beginning reader. In: A.S. Reber and D. Scarborough (Eds), *Reading: Theory and Practice*. Hillsdale, NJ: Lawrence Erlbaum Associates.

LUBS, H.A., DUARA, R., LEVIN, B., JALLAD, B., LUBS, M.-L., RABIN, M. et al. (1991). Dyslexia subtypes: Genetics, behavior and brain imaging. In: D.B. Gray and D.D. Duane (Eds), *The Reading Brain: The Biological Basis of Dyslexia*, in press. Parkton, MD: York Press.

NOWAKOWSKI, R.S. (1988). Development of the hippocampal formation in mutant mice. *Drug Development Research* **15**, 315–336.

PENNINGTON, B.F., SMITH, S.D., KIMBERLING, W.J., GREEN, P.A. and HAITH, N.M. (1987). Left-handedness and immune disorders in familial dyslexics. *Archives of Neurology* **44**, 634–639.

RUTTER, M. (1974). Emotional disorder in educational underachievement. *Archives of Diseases in Childhood* **49**, 249–256.

RUTTER, M., TIZARD, J., YULE, W., GRAHAM, P. and WHITMORE, K. (1976). Research report: Isle of Wight studies, 1964–1974. *Psychological Medicine* **6**, 313–332.

SHAYWITZ, S.E., SHAYWITZ, B.A., FLETCHER, J.M. and ESCOBAR, M.D. (1990). Prevalence of reading disability in boys and in girls. Results of the Connecticut Longitudinal Study. *Journal of the American Medical Association* **264**, 998–1002.

SHAYWITZ, B.A., SHAYWITZ, S.E., LIBERMAN, I.Y., FLETCHER, J.M., SHANKWEILER, D.P., DUNCAN, J.S. et al. (1991). Neurolinguistic and biologic mechanisms in dyslexia. In: D.B. Gray and D.D. Duane (Eds), *The Reading Brain: The Biological Basis of Dyslexia*, in press. Parkton, MD: York Press.

SMITH, S.D., KIMBERLING, W.J., PENNINGTON, B.F. and LUBS, H.A. (1983). Specific reading disabilities: Identification of an inherited form through linkage analysis. *Science* **219**, 1345–1347.

SORENSON-JAMISON, C. (1990). Dermatoglyphics of dyslexia. *Annals of Dyslexia* in press.

VOELLER, K.K.S. (1986). Right-hemisphere deficit syndrome in children. *American Journal of Psychiatry* **143**, 1004–1009.

WEINBERG, W.A. and BRUMBACK, R.A. (1990). Primary disorder of vigilance: A novel explanation of inattentiveness, daydreaming, boredom, restlessness and sleepiness. *Journal of Pediatrics* **116**, 720–725.

WEINTRAUB, S. and MESULAM, M. (1983). Developmental learning disabilities of the right hemisphere. *Archives of Neurology* **40**, 463–468.

WOOD, F., FELTON, R., FLOWERS, L. and NAYLOR, C. (1991). Neurobehavioral definition of dyslexia. In: D.B. Gray and D.D. Duane (Eds), *The Reading Brain: The Biological Basis of Dyslexia*, in press. Parkton, MD: York Press.

YOSS, R., MOYER, R. and OGLE, K.N. (1969). The pupillogram and narcolepsy. A method to measure decreased levels of wakefulness. *Neurology* **19**, 921–928.

Chapter 3
Vision and Language

J.F. STEIN

I believe that the time is now ripe to reconsider the widely held view that disordered visual perception has no part to play in the problems that face dyslexic children. The main reason is still the obvious one, namely that it is self-evident that reading requires the reader to be able to perceive small visual symbols accurately. This is why the classic descriptions of Hinshelwood, Morgan and Orton emphasised the importance of the visual system by their choice of descriptive terms such as 'word blindness' and 'strephosymbolia'. This is also why dyslexics and their teachers so often believe that it is the children's sight that is at fault.

It is a promising time to examine this matter further, because our understanding of vision has recently made great strides. Now visual neuroscience is even beginning to help to illuminate cognitive psychology. Indeed physiologists and psychologists concerned with dyslexic problems have even begun talking to each other! In this paper, therefore, I want: first to give a brief overview of some of the recent advances in visual physiology which are relevant to dyslexics' problems; secondly, to discuss recent experimental results which point clearly to many dyslexics having visual–perceptual impairments; thirdly, to show how they may be used to reinterpret the evidence that has been used in the past to discount visual–perceptual deficits; and finally to show how phonological and visual deficits are not mutually exclusive – they can happily coexist in the framework of hemispheric specialisation.

The Sustained and Transient Visual Systems

The standard clinical tests for basic visual disorders usually include: measuring visual acuity, usually using the Snellen chart; assessing the visual fields to exclude field defects; a simple check of colour vision, usually the Ishihara test; and making sure that eye movements to the six cardinal positions of gaze are full and equal. Most children with reading difficulties perform completely normally on these tests. What is more, children with serious abnormalities in these tests nevertheless usually learn to read perfectly well. Thus, we have to look at a higher level than the primary visual capacities assessed by these tests, which mainly depend upon the peripheral visual apparatus, for possible abnormalities that may help to explain the difficulties of dyslexics.

The recent advances which I believe are beginning to clarify these problems start with the distinction that can be made between large and small (magnocellular and parvocellular) ganglion cells in the retina (Perry, Oehler and Cowey, 1984). The parvocellular ones comprise 90% of the ganglion cells. Their responses are 'sustained' in time; they signal the colour and fine detail of objects, but not the timing of visual events. They project to the four parvocellular layers of the lateral geniculate nucleus.

The magnocellular ganglion cells carry relatively coarse spatial information about the mass of objects in the visual scene. Their responses are 'transient' (Enroth Cugell and Robson, 1966), so they signal more precisely the timing of visual events. They therefore play an important part in detecting the movements of objects, and ultimately their signals are used to control eye and limb movements made in relation to visual targets.

Even in the primary (striate) visual cortex, the parvo- and magnocellular streams are kept largely separate (Zeki and Shipp, 1988). From the striate cortex the parvocellular system passes through successive stages which are concerned with the processing of pattern, shape and colour in the prestriate cortex. This information is finally relayed laterally and inferiorally to the inferotemporal cortex, just behind the ear. It is thought that here matching takes place between these current images and stored templates of previously experienced objects; thereby visual recognition is achieved (Ungerleider and Mishkin, 1982).

The magnocellular pathway passes through different regions of striate and prestriate cortex, dorsally towards the posterior part of the parietal cortex (PPC) situated at the back of the crown of the head. Information about the rate and direction of movements of images across the retina are projected via this pathway to the PPC. Also signals about the movements of the eyes arrive here. Hence, the form of an object which is being inspected is analysed by the parvocellular pathway which projects to the inferotemporal cortex, whereas the movements of its images on the two retinae, together with the movements of the eyes, are projected to the PPC by the magnocellular system (Glickstein, 1991).

There is now good evidence that information about movements of images across the retina is put together in the PPC with signals about the movements of the eyes made by the observer, to determine whether it was the subject's eyes or the target which moved (Stein, 1989a). Since the position of the images of an object on the retina depends as much upon where the eyes are pointing, as upon its true location in the outside world, such association of retinal and eye movement signals is essential in order to determine precisely where an object is located with respect to the observer. The process by which these associations are achieved seems to be that of directing attention to particular targets. By this means a representation of the position of objects in the outside world is created in the PPC (Stein, 1991). Accurately locating targets in this way is, of course, also an essential prerequisite for aiming eye, limb or body movements towards them.

In humans it is the right PPC which seems to have become particularly specialised for this purpose; the homologous parts of the left parietal cortex have become specialised for the requirements of speech production and comprehension. These latter can be thought of as involving the direction of attention to the order of acoustic events in time.

It will not have escaped the reader's attention that the direction of attention in space is not only important for aiming eye movements but also for sequencing the spatial order of letters in a word (Stein, 1989a), whilst the direction of attention to the sequence of sounds in time is crucial for picking up important phonological differences (Tallal and Piercy, 1973). Both these skills are obviously important in reading.

As mentioned earlier, the parvocellular (sustained) system is most concerned with the visual analysis of fine detail. This can be quantitatively described as enhanced sensitivity to 'high' spatial frequencies (Cambell, 1974). But the parvocellular system is not attuned to rapid changes of light intensity in time. The magnocellular system, however, is highly sensitive to the rate of change of light intensity, whereas it has much lower spatial resolution, being only affected by coarse, low spatial frequencies (Breit-meyer, Levi and Hawerth, 1981).

The two systems are of course not entirely independent: there are numerous reciprocal interconnections between them. It seems that, functionally, these interactions are mainly inhibitory. The transient, low spatial frequency, magnocellular system inhibits the sustained, high spatial frequency, parvocellular processing stream, particularly at the end of each eye fixation. This inhibition may help the visual system to prepare for the next fixation. Otherwise, the visual persistence which is characteristic of the sustained system might smear the visual information gained from one fixation into the next during tasks such as reading.

The Transient System in Dyslexics

Using a number of different psychophysical techniques, Bill Lovegrove and his colleagues (Lovegrove, 1991) have gathered much evidence which demonstrates that dyslexic children have a relative impairment of their transient systems. At the low spatial frequencies characteristic of the transient system, the flicker fusion frequency is much lower in dyslexic children than in normal controls, their contrast sensitivity function is depressed, especially at these low spatial frequencies, and they exhibit significantly smaller visual evoked potentials over the occipital and parietal lobes over the low range of spatial frequencies. These differences are large and sufficiently reliable to discriminate individual children as dyslexic or otherwise just by means of these visual tests in the majority of cases. In fact, 75% of the dyslexic children who Lovegrove investigated showed a clearly reduced sensitivity of their transient systems.

Eye Movements in Dyslexics

The magnocellular (transient) system for analysing visual motion probably also plays a major role in the control of eye movements, particularly the opposite ('vergence') movements of the two eyes required to converge on near objects (Marr and Poggio, 1979). As described earlier, the PPC is the highest level of this system; this cortical area is responsible for the direction of attention and of eye and limb movements towards targets of interest. Patients with lesions in the right parietal cortex show delayed initiation of saccades towards the left, and the saccades tend to fall short of targets on the left (hypometria). They also have impaired smooth pursuit eye movements and they are inaccurate at localising targets, particularly as regards their distance; this is particularly marked on their left side. They exhibit striking disorders of vergence control, so they often have very impaired ability to fuse the images supplied by the two eyes. Hence they exhibit very reduced stereoacuity (Fowler et al., 1989). These symptoms are usually associated with the most common symptom of right PPC lesions, namely sensory inattention or 'neglect', the inability to attend to objects on the left-hand side. None of these visuospatial symptoms is common after lesions of the left PPC.

Over the last 10 years, we have been able to show that many dyslexic children show symptoms very similar to those of patients with right PPC lesions, although of course they are less severe (Stein, 1989b). Up to two-thirds of dyslexic children demonstrate unstable binocular control whether this is assessed by means of the Dunlop Test (Stein and Fowler, 1982) or by recording their vergence eye movements (Stein, Riddell and Fowler, 1988). Their stereoacuity is therefore reduced, because this depends on accurate vergence control and binocular fixation, as explained earlier. In addition, dyslexics' sense of visual direction is much less accurate than that of controls, whether they are matched for age or reading age. These impairments are particularly marked in the left hemifield (Riddell, Fowler and Stein, 1990) which clearly implicates the right hemispheres and probably the right PPC.

The link between these results and the findings of Bill Lovegrove is that, as mentioned earlier, the magnocellular transient system projects primarily to the PPC, and it is particularly concerned with vergence control. A vicious circle may therefore arise. The transient system of many dyslexic children fails to develop properly; this leads to impaired vergence control, which, in turn, feeds back to prevent normal maturation of the transient system, as this depends upon concomitant, properly synchronised development of accurate binocular fixation. We are currently attempting to test the hypothesis that impaired development of the transient system is caused by and contributes to inaccurate vergence control, by comparing the vergence responses of dyslexic and normal subjects to the low spatial frequencies that are dealt with by the transient system. These results will then be incorporated into a computer model of the vergence control system which we can then 'lesion' to see if we can simulate the impairments we find in dyslexics and right parietal patients.

Crowding

Another contribution to this study has been the discovery that many dyslexics have problems with 'crowding'. They show a much greater than normal susceptibility to peripheral distractors, when attempting to identify small visual targets (Geiger and Lettvin, 1987; Atkinson, 1991; Ruddock, 1991). These crowding effects confirm that these dyslexic children are unable to direct their visual attention to small visual targets reliably and accurately. This weakness may also be shown in more conventional tests for sensory inattention or neglect. When dyslexic children are asked to draw a clock (a common test for parietal neglect), they often draw them very distortedly, and some will draw all the figures on the right-hand side, leaving the left side completely empty. Likewise, if asked to cross out all the small stars in an array of large and small ones, many will tend to miss out a few stars on the left in this 'star cancellation task' (Halligan, Marshall and Wade, 1989). All these symptoms are highly reminiscent of those of patients with right PPC lesions.

Evidence against Visuospatial Impairments in Dyslexics

In the face of all this evidence that dyslexics do indeed show signs of visual–perceptual impairment, why is it still believed so strongly that dyslexics' vision is totally normal? Most of the evidence which speaks against a visual impairment has come from the use of standardised psychological tests of visuospatial ability. Typically these involve analysis of large pictures, and so they do not stress the temporal integration capacities or call upon the fine binocular control mechanisms that are required for reading (Willows, 1990).

In a very well-known series of experiments, however, Vellutino and his colleagues used letters from the Hebrew alphabet to investigate the possibility of visual–perceptual differences between disabled and normal readers. Neither group was familiar with Hebrew. Vellutino concluded that poor readers performed as well as normal readers in recognising, reproducing or associating these novel symbols with words (Vellutino et al., 1977). However, it has now become clear (Lyle and Goyen, 1975; Willows, 1990) that there is a developmental trend which has to be considered. Below the age of 8 the accuracy and response speed of most dyslexic children in recognising Hebrew letters is in fact inferior to that of normal readers, but these differences become much less marked in most children as they grow older. However, in a few dyslexics, significant impairments in visuospatial skills do persist. Most of Vellutino's work has been carried out with children over the age of 10, however, and hence his studies have missed the large differences in young children, and also those in the minority of older children, because they have been grouped together with the majority who no longer show large visuospatial impairments. This has been true of the work of most of the researchers who have denied the existence of visuospatial impairments in dyslexic children.

One problem which many people have is to understand how visuospatial impairments, such as those described earlier, could possibly be specific to reading. Why do dyslexics not display their visuospatial problems in their other activities? In fact they often do – they are notoriously clumsy and messy. Also their sense of the visual direction of small targets is deficient, as mentioned earlier. The point is that the visuospatial impairments which I have been describing are relatively subtle. Impairments of transient processing, fine binocular control or accurate direction of visual attention are not gross. They do not reveal themselves as clear reductions in visual acuity or ocular motility. The conditions under which they are tested must stress them in the same way as reading does. In fact this argument about specificity seems to me to be much more potent when applied to the phonological impairments that so many dyslexic children seem to have. Why do these not usually interfere with their ability to learn to speak?

Effects of Visuospatial Impairment in the Reading Process

A persuasive way of making the case that visuomotor impairments may be a contributory cause of reading difficulties is to show in detail how they can lead to reading errors.

This is what Piers Cornelissen, Sue Fowler and myself have been trying to do. On reviewing the kind of mistakes that those children, who had been diagnosed as having binocular instability on our tests, were making when they were attempting to read, we found that they tended to make a high proportion of attempts which were nonsense words – non-words. We thought that these children may suffer visual 'scrambling' when viewing text. Since their eyes move around uncontrollably due to their lack of vergence stability, they may experience temporary diplopia, which would cause letters foveated by one eye to be superimposed on different ones foveated by the other eye; also letters could appear to move from one position to another. Their binocular instability would therefore scramble the information presented to the reading process. If such children had mastered phonological rules fairly well, they would attempt to sound out what their visual system presented them with, and the result would be a nonsense word.

To test this hypothesis further, Cornelissen presented children with lists of words chosen in relation to their reading age so that they would make approximately 50% errors. The three lists were linguistically similar; the only difference between them was that they were printed in three different sizes. We postulated that making print smaller would tax the children with unstable binocular control, and cause them to make more non-word errors than stable children of similar reading age. The results strongly confirmed our hypothesis. Unstable dyxlexics made significantly more non-word errors when print size was reduced, whereas dyslexics with the same reading age, but stable binocular control, actually made less non-word errors under these conditions (Cornelissen et al., 1991). Thus, our research showed that a purely visual alteration led children, who had been identified as having unstable binocular control in a completely non-linguistic test, to make an increased number of non-word errors. These results support our hypothesis that the unstable fixation of many dyslexic children causes text to appear jumbled up, which makes it difficult for them to read. It is interesting to compare the similarities between these errors made by developmental dyslexics, and those made by patients with acquired dyslexia of the 'surface' type following brain damage (Marshall and Newcombe, 1973). Such patients show impaired recognition of graphemes, together with some malfunction of their grapheme-to-phoneme rules. Clearly, the former describes the reading of our 'visual' dyslexics.

Phonemic Segmentation

It is the phonological impairment of dyslexics that has received most attention recently, however, partly because this is easy to test for, whereas visual impairment is subtle and requires sophisticated equipment to demonstrate it. More persuasive, however, has been the tireless advocacy by Isabel and Alvin Lieberman of the view that dyslexics have poor stability to segment speech into phonemes, and that this explains their reading problems. This hypothesis makes good sense, it is easy to understand and it has received much experimental support (Bradley and Bryant, 1983; Lieberman, 1989; Olson et al., 1989; Snowling, 1989). As Al Lieberman puts it 'reading is hard because listening is so easy'. We speak by means of a continuous series of articulatory gestures which we learn by copying those around us; we do not have to be taught them explicitly. But the alphabetic principle is not so easily learned. In order to read we must learn to segment the continuous stream of sounds that we produce so easily when speaking, into separate phonemes, to match with their written version, graphemes. But these breaks are essentially arbitrary. They do not reflect the structure of speech. Therefore they have to be taught and learnt, and many children have difficulty in learning them.

There is therefore now very clear evidence, with which few disagree, that a major problem which dyslexic children face is deficient phonological skill. Quite often this problem is preceded by a history of difficulties with learning to speak such as lisping, stammering and late development of proper pronunciation. This lack of skill can therefore be attributed to an impairment of their speech processing system, their 'encapsulated phonological linguistic module'. This module is known to reside primarily in the left hemisphere, so it is natural to suspect and look for signs of left hemisphere damage in dyslexic children.

Hemispheric Specialisation

There is no analogous 'visual linguistic module' situated in the right hemisphere (Stein, 1991). Clearly, reading makes use not only of phonological but also of visual skills. It must be remembered, however, that reading is a cultural achievement which was only invented 2000 years ago, and only in the last 100 years has it been at all widespread. So it is much more likely that reading, like speech, was made possible by the prior evolutionary development of hemispheric specialisation for other purposes (Stein, 1988). It is probable that locating and memorising the position of landmarks require greater visual and ocular–motor precision than can easily be organised by communication between the hemispheres; consequently, visuospatial functions were the first to be gathered up in the right hemisphere. Signs of this can be discerned even in lower mammals (Webster, 1977). Later the left hemisphere was taken over for the development of accurate vocalisation. Hence the left hemisphere contains modules specialised for the production and comprehension of speech; these require precise sequencing of changes in sound frequency and amplitude in time.

Right hemisphere specialisation evolved for the accurate sequencing of locations in space – not for the purposes of reading, but for the much more basic function of finding your way home. Nevertheless, the requirements of reading were able to take advantage of the specialised processing systems that had evolved in the right hemisphere. But the precise binocular control and the accurate visual sequencing of small letters, which is essential for reading, make heavier demands on these right hemisphere functions than almost any other tasks undertaken by humans.

Further progress in understanding the aetiology of dyslexia will therefore probably come from perfecting better tests of hemispheric specialisation and of its disorders. These should enable us to clarify the genetic mechanisms which give rise to the two hemispheres' processing styles and the signs of altered function which result from their disorder (Annett, 1991). The results of neuroanatomical, CT, MRI, PET and brain electrical activity mapping (BEAM) studies have made it clear that most dyslexics suffer abnormalities in both hemispheres, particularly in the right and left posterior parietal areas (Galaburda, 1988). It is to be hoped these will soon be interpretable in terms of the altered physiological mechanisms which prevent successful reading. Presumably left-sided abnormalities give rise to the phonological coding problems of dyslexic children, and the right-sided abnormalities give rise to the visuospatial deficiencies, about which most of this chapter has been concerned.

Thus most dyslexics have both phonological and visuospatial impairments, and the two are tightly correlated, probably because they are consequences of the same genetic processes that control hemispheric specialisation. Since they so often occur together, they are very difficult to tease apart. Tests of phonology are well established and accepted, and they can account for much of the variance in reading ability in dyslexic children. However, if tests of visuomotor control are correlated with reading measures, they can also account for much of the variance. This does not necessarily mean, as is often assumed, that the visual correlation is merely an ephiphenomenon. It can, and probably does, mean that most dyslexics have both visuospatial and phonological problems.

Visual Impairments: Cause or Effect?

To persuade people that visuospatial impairments actually do cause difficulties with learning to read, further evidence is required. First it would be convincing to show that a group of pre-reading children with poor visual processing skills, but average phonological ones, nevertheless develop into children with reading disabilities. We are endeavouring to collect such evidence at the moment. The converse of this would be to show that children with good visual processing abilities progress to be good readers. We have found that this is indeed the case (Riddell, P., unpublished results).

Another way of convincing people that visuospatial deficiencies cause reading difficulties is to compare dyslexic children with younger normal readers. This is the so-called reading level match design, introduced by

Lynette Bradley and Peter Bryant in the 1970s. We have been able to show that young normal readers have far more stable ocular control than older dyslexics who had achieved the same reading level (Riddell, Fowler and Stein, 1990). This strongly suggests that the dyslexics' poor binocular control was a cause of their reading disability, rather than a consequence of it; after all the normal children could read at the same level as the dyslexics because they had normal binocular control, even though they were much younger.

The evidence from reading level matches does not rule out the possibility that it is not lack of binocular control per se that impedes a child's reading, but rather something connected with it, for example coexisting phonological problems. One way to show that visual impairment may be a specific cause of reading difficulties is to demonstrate in detail the way in which it gives rise to reading errors, as outlined earlier. But in the end, the most convincing evidence is to show that treatments which improve binocular control are followed by reading progress. This has been done in two studies (Stein and Fowler, 1981, 1985). Paradoxically, we have been able to show that treatment by means of monocular occlusion improves binocular stability. We have found that the children who gain stable binocular control by this means improve their reading significantly. This effect is independent of their IQ or initial reading age (Stein, 1989c).

Conclusions

In conclusion, in this chapter I have described how recent advances in our understanding of the information processing operations, which take place in the visual system for locating visual targets, force a re-evaluation of the view that dyslexic problems are purely linguistic and have nothing to do with the visual system. Most dyslexics have impaired development of the transient visual stream which dominates the control of eye movements, particularly the binocular adjustments that are needed to recover the third dimension of depth. Hence, dyslexics demonstrate unstable binocular control, poor stereoacuity and inaccurate judgements of visual direction. These lead to their experiencing diplopia and hence their tendency to superimpose letters on top of each other, and to missequence letters in a word. They therefore have a special propensity to make 'non-word' reading errors; these may be correct phonological interpretations of the scrambled material that their visual system presents them with. These effects of their perceptuomotor impairments on the reading process are analogous to those experienced by acquired 'surface' dyslexics.

When reviewing the evidence that has been adduced against the idea that dyslexics have visuoperceptual impairments, it is clear that the tests which have been employed have usually not taxed the same visual processing skills that are required for reading. When these have been stressed, differences between young (< 9 years old) dyslexics and controls do become apparent, although they are less evident in older age groups. However, the results from groups of older dyslexics do not exclude the possibility that a minority continue to show impairments, which would not show up in group studies.

The question of whether visual impairments are the cause or effect of reading difficulties has been addressed first by showing that visual impairments cause specific kinds of reading error, secondly by reading level matches, in which it has been shown that children with reading disorders have visual impairments whereas younger children with the same reading ability do not have these impairments, thirdly by means of longitudinal studies which show that the visual skills of preschool children may predict future reading ability, and finally and most powerfully, by investigating the effects of treatment. If a child's binocular instability can be remedied then reading may progress rapidly, implying that the visual impairment was a potent cause of his reading difficulties.

Finally, I have discussed the evidence that phonological and visuospatial impairments may coexist in many dyslexics. This is probably because dyslexic problems arise from disordered development of hemispheric specialisation in these children. Further understanding of the genetic mechanisms controlling specialisation of the right hemisphere for visuo-spatial skills and of the left for phonological/linguistic abilities should help us to unravel what goes wrong with dyslexics' hemispheric processing.

References

ANNETT, M. (1985). *Left and Right, Hand and Brain: The Right Shift Theory*. London: Lawrence Erlbaum Associates.

ATKINSON, J. (1991). Crowding effects in young children and dyslexics. In: J.F. Stein (Ed.), *Vision and Visual Dyslexia*, Vol. 13, *Vision and Visual Dysfunction*, in press. London: Macmillan.

BRADLEY, L. and BRYANT, P.E. (1983). Categorizing sounds and learning to read – a causal connection. *Nature* 301, 419–421.

BREITMEYER, B.G., LEVI, D.M. and HAWERTH, R.S. (1981). Flicker masking in spatial vision. *Vision Research* 21, 1371–1385.

CAMBELL, F.W. (1974). The transmission of spatial information through the visual system. In: F. Schmidt (Ed.), *Neurosciences 3rd Study Program*, pp. 95–105. Cambridge, MA: MIT Press.

CORNELISSEN, P., BRADLEY, L., FOWLER, M.S. and STEIN, J.F. (1991). What children see affects how they read. *Developmental Medicine and Child Neurology* in press.

ENROTH CUGELL, C. and ROBSON, J.G. (1966). The contrast sensitivity of retinal ganglion cells. *Journal of Physiology* 187, 519–552.

FOWLER, M.S., MUNRO, N., RICHARDSON, A. and STEIN, J.F. (1989). Vergence control in patients with lesions of the posterior parietal cortex. *Journal of Physiology* 417, 92P.

GALABURDA, A. (1988). The pathogenesis of childhood dyslexia. In: F. Plum (Ed.), *Language, Communication and the Brain*, pp. 127–137. New York: Raven Press.

GEIGER, S. and LETTVIN, J.Y. (1987). Peripheral vision in persons with dyslexia. *New England Journal of Medicine* **316**, 1238–1243.

GLICKSTEIN, M. (1991). Cortical visual areas and the visual guidance of movement. In: J.F. Stein (Ed.), *Vision and Visual Dyslexia*, Vol. 13, *Vision and Visual Dysfunction*, in press. London: Macmillan.

HALLIGAN, P.W., MARSHALL, J.C. and WADE, D.T. (1989). Visuospatial neglect. *The Lancet* **ii** 908–910.

LIEBERMAN, I.Y. (1989). Phonology and beginning reading. In: C. von Euler (Ed.), *Wenner Gren Symposium*, No. 511, pp. 207–221. London: Macmillan.

LOVEGROVE, W. (1991). Spatial frequency processing in normal and dyslexic readers. In: J. Stein (Ed.), *Visual Dyslexia*, vol. 13, *Vision and Visual Dysfunction*, in press. London: Macmillan.

LYLE, J.G. and GOYEN, J.D. (1975). Effect of exposure, speed and discrimination difficulty on visual recognition in retarded readers. *Journal of Abnormal Psychology* **84**, 673–676.

MARR, D. and POGGIO, T. (1979). A computational theory of human stereovision. *Proceedings of the Royal Society of London. Series B: Biological Sciences* **204**, 301–328.

MARSHALL, J.C. and NEWCOMBE, F. (1973). Patterns of paralexia – a psycholinguistic approach. *Journal of Psycholinguistic Research* **2**, 177–199.

OLSON, R.K., WISE, B., CONNERS, F., RACK, J. and FULKER, D. (1989). Specific deficits in component reading and language skills: Genetic and environmental influences. *Journal of Learning Disabilities* **22**, 339–348.

PERRY, V.H., OEHLER, R. and COWEY, A. (1984). Retinal ganglion cells that project to the dorsal lateral geniculate nucleus in the monkey. *Neuroscience* **12**, 1101–1123.

RIDDELL, P., FOWLER, M.S. and STEIN, J.F. (1990). Inaccurate visual localisation in dyslexic children. *Perception and Motor Skills* **70**, 707–718.

RUDDOCK, K.H. (1991). Visual search in dyslexia. In: J.F. Stein (Ed.), *Vision and Visual Dyslexia*, Vol. 13, *Vision and Visual Dysfunction*, in press. London: Macmillan.

SNOWLING, M. (1989). *Dyslexia – a Cognitive Developmental Perspective*. Oxford: Blackwell.

STEIN, J.F. (1988). Physiological differences between left and right hemispheres. In: F.C. Rose (Ed.), *Aphasia*. London: Whurr Wyke.

STEIN, J.F. (1989a). Representation of egocentric space in the posterior parietal cortex. *Quarterly Journal of Experimental Physiology* **14**, 583–606.

STEIN, J.F. (1989b). Visuospatial perception and reading problems. *Irish Journal of Psychology* **10**, 521–533.

STEIN, J.F. (1989c). Unstable vergence control and specific reading impairment. *British Journal of Ophthalmology* **73**, 49.

STEIN, J.F. (1991). Visuospatial sense, hemispheric asymmetry and dyslexia. In: J.F. Stein (Ed.), *Vision and Visual Dyslexia*, Vol. 13, *Vision and Visual Dysfunction*, in press. London: Macmillan.

STEIN, J. and FOWLER, S. (1981). Visual dyslexia. *Trends in Neuroscience* **4**, 77–80.

STEIN, J.F. and FOWLER, S. (1982). Diagnosis of dyslexia by means of a new indicator of eye dominance. *British Journal of Ophthalmology* **66**, 332–336.

STEIN, J.F. and FOWLER, M.S. (1985). Effect of monocular occlusion on visuomotor perception and reading in dyslexic children. *The Lancet* **ii**, 69–73.

STEIN, J.F., RIDDELL, P. and FOWLER, M.S. (1988). Disordered vergence eye movement control in dyslexic children. *British Journal of Ophthalmology* **72**, 162–166.

TALLAL, P. and PIERCY, M. (1973). Defects of non-verbal auditory perception in children with developmental aphasia. *Nature* **241**, 468–469.

UNGERLEIDER, L.S. and MISHKIN, M (1982). Two cortical visual systems. In: D.J. Ingle (Ed.), *The Analysis of Visual Behaviour*, pp. 549–586. Cambridge, MA: MIT Press.

VELLUTINO, F.R., STEGER, J.A., MEYER, B.M., HARDING, S.C. and NILES, C.J. (1977). Has the perceptual deficit hypothesis led us astray? *Journal of Learning Disabilities* **10**, 54–61.

WEBSTER, W. (1977). Hemispheric asymmetry in cats. In: S. Harnard (Ed.), *Lateralisation in the Nervous System*. New York: Academic Press.

WILLOWS, D.M. (1990). Visual processing in learning disabilities. In: B.Y.L. Wong (Ed.), *Learning about Learning Disabilities*. New York: Academic Press.

ZEKI, S.M. and SHIPP, S. (1988). The functional logic of cortical connections. *Nature* **335**, 311–317.

Chapter 4
EEG Topographical Mapping and Laterality Measures in Dyslexic Children

GEORGINA RIPPON

Introduction

Developmental dyslexia has been defined as: 'a disorder manifested by difficulty in learning to read despite conventional instruction, adequate intelligence and sociocultural opportunity. It is dependent upon fundamental cognitive disabilities which are *frequently of constitutional origin*' (own italics) (Waites, 1968). Neuropsychological and psychophysiological research has pursued the aim of identifying specific cortical dysfunction in dyslexics, with particular emphasis on the hypothesis that dyslexia is associated with inadequate or inappropriate lateralisation of function in the two cerebral hemispheres. A large body of research into this hypothesis exists, but the results are generally inconclusive and/or contradictory (Beaton, 1984; Bryden, 1988). A range of models has been proposed, generally based on the suggestion that performance on language-based tasks is impaired due to inadequate or inappropriate development of hemispheric specialisation for language functions (see Molfese and Segalowitz, 1988). Additionally, Witelson (1976) implicates anomalous bilateral representation of spatial functioning which interferes with normal left hemisphere specialisation for linguistic processing. This model suggests that anomalous lateralisation is more likely to be demonstrated in visual tasks. It is unusual in that it implicates dysfunction in processes other than linguistic as underlying reading difficulties.

One particular reason for the lack of clear-cut findings which presents itself is that researchers may not be dealing with a homogeneous population. Keefe and Swinney (1979) address this issue directly, using dichotic listening and divided visual field techniques. Their results suggest that at least two categories of dyslexic children can be identified: one type demonstrating left hemisphere deficits and the other right hemisphere deficits. Indirect evidence for heterogeneous lateralisation can be found in a study by Annett and Kilshaw (1984) who reported not only higher incidences of left and mixed handedness in a dyslexic population but also higher incidences of strong right handers. More recently, this finding has been extended by Annett and Manning (1990), showing that poor readers in a large sample of primary school children were more likely to be at the extremes of a distribution of right–left hand skill scores, i.e. strongly dextral or with mixed or left hand preference.

The heterogeneous nature of reading disorders has been acknowledged for some time among researchers interested in cognitive deficits in handicapped (backward) readers (Hynd and Cohen, 1983). One dichotomy which has been described concerns handicapped readers with mainly auditory problems (auditory–linguistic or dysphonetic dyslexia) as opposed to a second group with mainly visual problems (visuospatial or dyseidetic dyslexia) (Boder, 1973; Pirozzolo, Rayner and Hynd, 1983).

It is possible that different anomalies of cerebral lateralisation parallel differences between subtypes of dyslexia. Several workers have suggested that children with auditory–linguistic type problems demonstrate left hemisphere deficits, whereas children with visuospatial problems demonstrate right hemisphere deficits (e.g. Obrzut, 1988; Rourke and Fisk, 1988). Bakker et al. (Bakker, Teunissen and Bosch, 1976; Bakker, 1979; Bakker et al., 1980) propose two types of reading difficulty: type I is characterised by over-reliance on left-hemisphere processing, with reading errors indicating poor spatioperceptual analysis, whereas children with type II problems demonstrate an over-reliance on right-hemisphere processing. Their reading strategies indicate a continued application of an initially appropriate but subsequently inappropriate spatioperceptual analysis. Their right hemisphere is dominant and strongly specialised for spatial analysis.

If it is the case, as seems likely, that the reading-disordered population is a heterogeneous one, then any attempt to investigate the underlying processes which does not take this heterogeneity into account will produce the type of conflicting and contradictory results that are, in fact, characteristic of this research. This point is best expressed by Keefe and Swinney (1979): 'results suggest that the dyslexic population is heterogeneous with regard to cerebral lateralisation and that previous work treating it as homogeneous is most likely misleading. It appears important to both *carefully examine individual subject data in such studies* [own emphasis] and to consider the consequences of there being different types of cerebral lateralisation etiologies for what has been typically considered to be a homogeneous dyslexic population.'

Measurement of Anomalous Lateralisation in Dyslexia Research

Much neuropsychological research has employed indirect measures of cerebral lateralisation such as dichotic listening or divided visual field techniques. One problem with these techniques is that they require analysis of fairly simple stimuli, whereas many researchers have indicated that where differences between normal and dyslexic populations have been found it is related to the processing of relatively complex information. Satz (1976) carried out a comprehensive survey of such studies and concluded that they had little to contribute to an understanding of the link between cerebral dominance and reading disability.

One method of assessing an individual's laterality has arisen out of research into handedness (see Annett, 1985, for a review). Annett's research in this area makes use of the difference between left- and right-hand performances on a simple perceptuomotor task as an assessment of an individual's laterality. The task involves moving a row of small wooden pegs from one set of holes to another and is generally known as the Annett pegboard. Mean times for the right hand (R) are subtracted from mean times for the left hand (L), and the size of the L−R score taken as an index of the subject's 'sinistrality' (L<R) or 'dextrality' (L>R). Annett's work in this area indicates that an excess of dyslexics can be found at both the sinistral extreme of the L−R distribution and, more unexpectedly, at the dextral extreme. More recent findings have indicated that, in normal populations, 'strongly dextral' children do show more deficits in certain skills relevant to literacy, such as spelling (Annett and Manning, 1989, 1990). There are strong parallels with Bakker's findings here and the issue of dyslexic subtypes could well be of relevance. An obvious problem, however, is that a measure of hand skill is at best an indirect measure of cortical lateralisation.

Electroencephalography provides a direct measure of cortical activity and various studies have indicated the usefulness of this technique in investigations of developmental literacy problems (Hughes, 1982). However, early research in this area was initially limited to comparisons between relatively few electrodes (4–8) sited over areas whose relevance had been inferred from the nature of the difficulties associated with dyslexia. This meant that such work assumed the dysfunction to be located to relatively specific sites and it was not possible to investigate the interrelationship between activity over the whole cortex.

The problem of limited data collection was overcome by Duffy, Burchfiel and Lombroso (1979) using a technique known as brain electrical activity mapping (BEAM). BEAM techniques allow the simultaneous measurement of activity from many electrodes. Interpolation techniques are applied and enable the production of colour-coded topographical maps, giving an instantaneous on-line picture of the changing patterns of activity over the cerebral cortex. Duffy has applied BEAM techniques in dyslexia research (Duffy et al., 1980, 1988), has considered the issue of EEG differences between different types of dyslexia and has reported bilateral parietal and left temporal anomalies in children characterised by difficulties with sequential ordering in repetition tasks (Duffy et al., 1980).

Flynn and Deering (1989) employed mapping techniques to investigate differences between dyslexic children classified as dysphonetic, dyseidetic or mixed (Boder, 1973). One area of differentiation was in the left temporal–parietal region, where the dyseidetic group showed a significantly greater increase in theta activity during the above tasks. Flynn and Deering suggest this indexes an over-utilisation of an inappropriate left hemisphere processing strategy. This closely parallels similar suggestions by Bakker for his type II group. There are also strong similarities with Annett and Manning's (1989) 'strong dextrals'.

This study was an initial investigation of these issues and its exploratory nature must be emphasised. Employing the BEAM techniques mentioned above, cortical activity was measured in a small group of children with known reading difficulties while carrying out a range of tasks designed to emphasise either auditory or visuospatial processing. Following Keefe and Swinney (1979), the emphasis was on individual subject data and comparisons were made within the group, with particular emphasis on variations in lateralisation. Additionally, the correlation between the simple but indirect measure of functional lateralisation provided by the Annett pegboard and the more complex but direct measure provided by BEAM techniques was investigated.

Method

Subject population (Table 4.1)

There were 12 children (11 boys and 1 girl, age range 7;0–11;3) recruited through the Coventry branch of the Dyslexia Institute. Background information on some of the children was available from psychologist's reports provided with parents' permission. As part of the battery of tests, Raven's Coloured Progressive Matrices (Raven, Court and Raven, 1984) and Boder's Test of Reading/Spelling patterns (Boder, 1973) were administered.

Some comment should be made on the nature of the subject population. It could be said that this group is quite possibly not representative of the reading-disabled children who are recruited from remedial classes within the state educational system. Many of them were not receiving remedial support from their schools as the nature of their literacy problems was not felt to be sufficiently severe. However, their parents felt that the children had particular difficulties which merited help from the Dyslexia Institute. A common characteristic was evidence of difficulty with spelling, in some cases in the absence of severe reading difficulty or together with a reading difficulty that had responded to earlier remediation. Some children indeed

Table 4.1 Subject population – background details

	Warwick University Tests			Background Information from Dyslexia Institute Records					
	Age at testing (years)	Raven's Matrices Percentile	Boder	Age at testing (years)	WISC Verbal IQ	WISC Performance IQ	WISC Full IQ	Reading age (years)	Spelling age (years)
S1	8;7	75	Dyseidetic	6;3	119	111	118	7;0 (Acc) 7;10 (Comp)	6;5
2	10;3	10	Mixed	N/A	N/A	N/A	N/A	N/A	N/A
3	11;5	75	Mixed	11;5	114	112	115	12;6 (Acc) 12;6 (Comp)	11;0
4	11;3	25	Dysphonetic	9;6	140	112	129	11;3	9;4
5	7;9	75	Dyseidetic	N/A	N/A	N/A	N/A	N/A	N/A
6	9;3	10	Mixed	8;0	74	92	N/A	7;0	6;10
7	7;4	90	Dysphonetic	5;11	Very superior	Average	N/A	10;0	6;9
8	7;0	95	Dysphonetic	6;7	121	129	N/A	6;10 (Acc) 6;9 (Comp)	6;1
9	10;10	50	Dyseidetic	N/A	N/A	N/A	N/A	N/A	N/A
10	9;6	50	Dyseidetic	7;2	123	118	123	6;10 (Acc) 6;9 (Comp)	6;1
11	11;7	50	Dyseidetic	10;7	N/A	N/A	N/A	9;2 (Acc) 10;1 (Comp)	9;0
12	8;11	50	Dysphonetic	8;9	117	105	112	7;2 (Acc) 8;5 (Comp)	6;4

N/A = not available.
Acc = accuracy.
Comp = comprehension.

had reading ages in advance of their chronological age but, for example, showed spelling ages only consistent with or even behind their reading age. Handwriting problems were also commonly described. All were described as under-achieving in literacy skills in relation to their general level of intellectual functioning.

Apparatus and data analysis

EEG was monitored with a Neurosciences Series III Brain Imager from 28 scalp electrodes referenced to linked ears; electrode placements are derived from the International 10-20 system. The electrodes are mounted in an elasticated cap secured to the subject's head with elastic chin straps fastened to an elastic chest strap.

Raw EEG data were subjected to fast Fourier power spectrum analysis and colour-coded topographical maps produced. Numerical data were down-loaded for subsequent analysis. In this case, as individual differences were of interest, artefact-free individual average maps were generated for the information input phase for each of the four task conditions. Average left and right hemisphere measures were calculated using data from the FTC1/2, TCP1/2, CP1/2 and PO1/2 electrodes and laterality indices for each subject were calculated using the equation $(L-R)/(L+R)$. Data from this combination of electrodes provide an index of general hemispheric activity. Individual data would be inspected for areas of localised activity with reference to previous findings using this technique (Duffy et al., 1980; Flynn and Deering, 1989). The Brain Imager allows consideration of the five traditional bandwidths. Data from the beta-2 bandwidth will be presented here as an appropriate index of task-related responses (Ray and Cole, 1985).

Tasks involved

Assessment of functional laterality

Hand preference was assessed by asking the child to carry out a range of one-handed tasks and seeing which hand he used. This covered the normal tasks, such as writing and cleaning your teeth, and also more unusual ones such as which hand is at the top when you're using a broom.

Hand skill was assessed by means of a manual dexterity task – the Annett pegboard. Using alternate hands, the child has to move a line of pegs from one row of holes to another as rapidly as possible. This is repeated five times for each hand, and an average score for left and right hands calculated. A left–right score is also calculated to see how great the difference is between the two hands for this particular type of task. This score can then be compared with age-related norms taken from a large sample.

Assessment of cortical laterality

A battery of different tasks was used to investigate those most effective in demonstrating heterogeneity of cortical activity in the cortical population. For this chapter, results will be reported from two pairs of tasks selected to emphasise auditory and visual skills respectively, in an attempt to emphasise hemispheric differences in processing. The tasks were the following.

Digit span (from the Wechsler Revised Memory Scale)
The child is read number sequences of increasing length and after each sequence asked to repeat from memory. This was classified as an auditory test; the brain maps reported here are those taken while the child is listening to the sequence he or she then has to repeat.

Visual memory span (from Wechsler Revised Memory Scale)
The examiner touches coloured squares in sequences of increasing length and, after each sequence, the child is asked to repeat the performance from memory. This was classified as the visual equivalent of the digit span test; the brain maps reported here are those taken while the child is watching the examiner point to the squares.

Word span
The child is read lists of increasing length of either animal names or nonsense words and after each list has to repeat them from memory. The use of either meaningful (animal names) or non-meaningful (nonsense names) words was designed to determine whether children find it easier to deal with just sounds rather than when the sounds also carry meaning. The brain maps reported here are those taken while the child is listening to the lists.

Figural memory test (from Wechsler Revised Memory Scale)
The child looks briefly at two abstract designs and is then asked to identify them among a group of nine designs. This was used as the visual equivalent of the word span tests; the brain maps reported here are those taken while the child was looking at the designs.

Additional information

1. The Boder Test of reading spelling patterns was administered in the course of the session. Although it was not intended specifically to classify the children according to Boder's criteria, it was felt that the test would provide useful indices of 'dysphonetic' and/or 'dyseidetic' tendencies in the group.
2. Raven's Coloured Progressive Matrices were also administered as a non-verbal measure of general intellectual functioning.

Procedure

The child was brought to the university by his or her parent(s). The procedure was explained and then the testing session began. Parents were free to stay; all but one chose to leave the child and come back later. All the children were relatively familiar with assessment situations and settled down quickly. The laterality measures were taken first and then the child was prepared for brain imaging. This entails fitting the elasticated cap which holds the electrodes and then filling the electrodes with electrode jelly and ensuring good contact between scalp and electrode. This takes on average about 10 minutes and the children watched a video while it was going on or chatted to the experimenter. Baseline BEAM measures were taken first and then the experimental tasks were carried out with BEAM data being collected in parallel. The session took an hour to an hour and a half on average, with a short 'refreshment break' in the middle.

Results

Following Keefe and Swinney's exhortation to examine carefully individual differences, the preliminary data analysis here is mainly of a descriptive kind, with particular emphasis on individual differences in patterns of laterality.

Patterns of lateralisation

Hand preference

All the children were consistent right handers, none using their left hand for more than two of the items on the handedness questionnaire. It was reported that one child had only just settled into consistently using his right hand; his responses to the questionnaire were no different from the others.

Hand skill

Mean scores for the left and right hands were calculated and transformed into standardised scores for age, using right hand norms for both hands as in the study by Annett and Kilshaw (1984). The laterality index for standardised scores is calculated using R−L scores. Scores ranged from −4.00 to 105.17 with a mean of 25.51 and a standard deviation of 31.67. Within the group, there were several cases of 'strong dextrals', i.e. large differences between the hands arising from good right-hand scores and poor left-hand scores. Only one child showed faster left-hand than right-hand scores and a second gained equal scores with both hands.

BEAM measures

Grey scale versions of the coloured topographical maps are shown in
Figures 4.1–4.4. These grey scale versions are hand-drawn tracings of the
coloured maps produced by the brain imager. In each case, the top map
shows the pattern of activity over the whole cortex, with the anterior/
posterior, right/left orientation as shown. The lower map is that produced
when right-hemisphere activity is subtracted from left-hemisphere activity.
This can indicate which areas of the brain show asymmetrical activity, i.e.
left-dominant (L>R) or right-dominant (L<R), and where the activity is
symmetrical (L=R). Figures 4.1 and 4.2 give examples of left lateralised
activity in both auditory (Figures 4.1a and 4.2a) and visual tasks (Figure
4.2). Subject TS (Figure 4.1) shows indications of increased activity in the
left frontal regions whereas subject KG (Figure 4.2) shows greater
involvement in the left temporal regions.

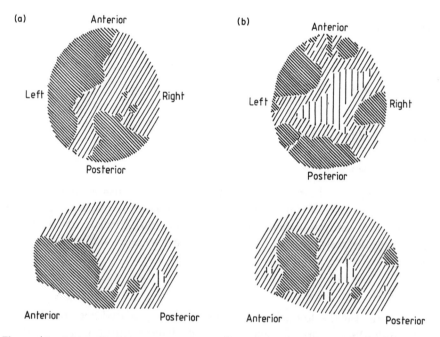

Figure 4.1 Subject TS. (a) Digit span test: grey-scale versions of individual subject's average
map showing EEG activity during an auditory task. The bilateral view (top) indicates activity over
the whole cortex, the lateral view (bottom) is of the map produced by subtracting right
hemisphere from left hemisphere activity. Top: $\boxtimes$ 40–60 μV; $\boxtimes$ 24–36 μV; $\boxplus$ 4–20 μV. (b) Figural
memory test: grey-scale versions of individual subject's average map showing EEG activity during
a visual task. The bilateral view (top) indicates activity over the whole cortex, the lateral view
(bottom) is of the map produced by subtracting right hemisphere from left hemisphere activity.
Top: $\boxtimes$ 20–30 μV; $\boxtimes$ 12–18 μV; $\boxplus$ 2–10 μV. For both (a) and (b) the key for the bottom figures
is $\boxtimes$ L>R; $\boxtimes$ L=R; $\boxplus$ L<R.

Table 4.2   Laterality indices: beta-2 activity in digit span (DS), visual memory span (VMS), word span (WS) and figural memory test (FMT), with standardised pegboard scores

	DS	VMS	WS	FMT	Pegboard R−L
S1	0.03	0.08	0.01	0.11	105.17
2	0.12	0.09	0.10	−	46
3	0.07	0.07	0.05	0.12	64
4	0.13	0.09	1.00	0.08	24
5	−0.05	0.08	−0.13	−	19
6	0.13	0.10	0.07	0.11	14
7	0.04	0.17	0.10	0.15	16
8	0.18	0.07	0.10	0.01	9
9	0.04	0.05	0.01	−0.05	8
10	0.03	0.04	0.06	0.00	5
11	−0.20	0.03	0.11	0.02	0
12	0.15	0.03	0.03	0.03	−4

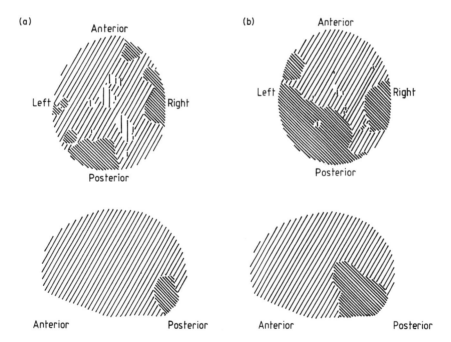

Figure 4.2   Subject KG. (a) Digit span test: grey-scale versions of individual subject's average map showing EEG activity during an auditory task. The bilateral view (top) indicates activity over the whole cortex, the lateral view (bottom) is of the map produced by subtracting right hemisphere from left hemisphere activity. (b) Figural memory task: grey-scale versions of individual subject's average map showing EEG activity during a visual task. The bilateral view (top) indicates activity over the whole cortex, the lateral view (bottom) is of the map produced by subtracting right hemisphere from left hemisphere activity. For (a) and (b), top: ▨ 20−30 μV; ▧ 12−18 μV; ▥ 2−10 μV; bottom: ▨ L>R; ▧ L=R; ▥ L<R.

As outlined above, EEG data were subjected to fast Fourier transform and subsequently converted to laterality indices for each subject. Laterality indices for the four tasks are shown in Table 4.2.

Data from the figural memory test were corrupted for two of the children; these were entered into subsequent calculations as missing data. Each child's brain maps were then classified according to whether they showed evidence of predominantly left hemisphere activity (laterality

Table 4.3   Frequency distribution of different patterns of EEG activity within the digit span (DS), word span (WS), visual memory span (VMS) and figural memory test (FMT)

Test	LH>RH	LH<RH	LH=RH
DS	6	2	4
WS	8	1	3
VMS	8	0	4
FMT	5	2	3

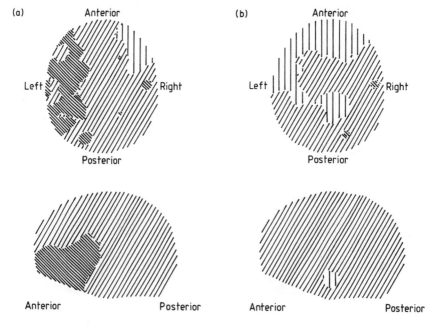

Figure 4.3   Subject EB. (a) Digit span test: grey-scale versions of individual subject's average map showing EEG activity during an auditory task. The bilateral view (top) indicates activity over the whole cortex, the lateral view (bottom) is of the map produced by subtracting right hemisphere from left hemisphere activity. (b) Figural memory task: grey-scale versions of individual subject's average map showing EEG activity during a visual task. The bilateral view (top) indicates activity over the whole cortex, the lateral view (bottom) is of the map produced by subtracting right hemisphere from left hemisphere activity. For (a) and (b), top: ▨ 20–30 μV; ▨ 12–18 μV; ▥ 2–10 μV; bottom: ▨ L>R; ▨ L=R; ▥ L<R.

index $> +0.05$), predominantly right hemisphere activity (laterality index 0.0 to -0.5) or bilateral activity (laterality index 0.0 to $+0.5$). The frequency distributions of these classifications as a function of the different tasks are shown in Table 4.3.

The unexpectedly high occurrence of predominantly left hemisphere activity in the visual tasks should be noted.

Correlation between neuropsychological and psychophysiological indices of laterality

Spearman rank correlations were carried out between the R–L pegboard scores and the laterality indices for the different tasks. The correlations for the auditory tasks were not significant (pegboard × digit span = 0.06; pegboard × word span = -0.045); the correlations for the visual tasks were significant (pegboard × visual memory span = 0.641; $P<0.05$, two-tailed; pegboard × figural memory test = 0.663, $P<0.05$, two-tailed).

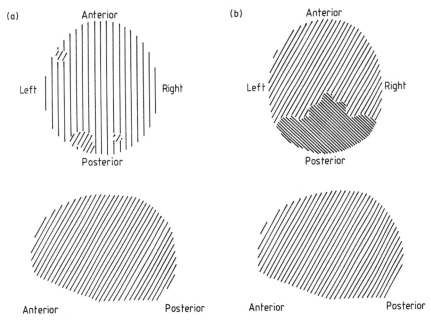

Figure 4.4 Subject DL. (a) Digit span test: grey-scale versions of individual subject's average map showing EEG activity during an auditory task. The bilateral view (top) indicates activity over the whole cortex, the lateral view (bottom) is of the map produced by subtracting right hemisphere from left hemisphere activity. (b) Figural memory task: grey-scale versions of individual subject's average map showing EEG activity during a visual task. The bilateral view (top) indicates activity over the whole cortex, the lateral view (bottom) is of the map produced by subtracting right hemisphere from left hemisphere activity. For (a) and (b), top: ▨ 20–30 μV; ▨ 12–18 μV; ▥ 2–10 μV; bottom: ▨ L>R; ▨ L=R; ▥ L<R.

The implication of these correlations is that, for the visual tasks at any rate, the greater the dextrality shown by subjects in the pegboard task, the more likely they were to show *left* hemisphere activity in the visual tasks. This can be demonstrated testing the frequency with which 'strong dextrals' (in this group individuals with R−L scores above the median) show predominantly left hemisphere activity in the visual tasks as opposed to the less strongly dextral. This is shown in Table 4.4.

Table 4.4 Distribution of 'strong' and 'weak' dextrals (as determined by pegboard) in left and right dominant patterns of EEG in the visual memory span test and the figural memory test

	L<R	L>R
Visual memory span test		
Strong dextrals	0	6
Weak dextrals	5	1
Figural memory test		
Strong dextrals	0	5
Weak dextrals	4	1

Chi-squared tests indicate that for visual memory span the distributions are significantly different ($\chi^2 = 5.48$, $P<0.02$, two-tailed) and those for figural memory test approach significance ($\chi^2 = 3.75$, $0.10<P>0.05$).

Intercorrelations between cortical activity in auditory and visual tasks

Spearman rank correlations were carried out between the laterality indices for the different tasks. There was a significant correlation between the two visual tasks ($r = 0.673$, $P<0.05$, two-tailed); there was no significant correlation between the auditory tasks or between the two auditory and visual tasks.

Discussion

The results of this small pilot study are consistent with previous findings in the literature. Individual average maps indicated subjects showing increased levels of frontal involvement (subject TS) and of temporal involvement (subject KG) (compare Duffy et al., 1980; Flynn and Deering, 1989). With respect to more generalised patterns of asymmetrical or symmetrical activity, heterogeneous patterns of lateralisation in brain electrical activity were observed, even in a population this small. These correlated significantly with pegboard performance. The pattern derived from one group of subjects gave evidence of marked left cerebral dominance. There were large hand differences on the Annett pegboard, arising from average or superior performances with the right hand, and depressed scores from the left hand. BEAM data revealed a preponderance of *left*-hemisphere activity particularly in the visual tasks (Figures 4.1 and 4.2).

It should be noted that the expected pattern of activity for the visual tasks would be right hemisphere preponderance or, as has been shown more recently, bilateral activity (Rippon, 1989,1990). The group described above appear to provide evidence for the 'over-reliance' on the left hemisphere claimed to be characteristic of individuals who are indexed as strongly dextral by the Annett pegboard (Annett and Manning, 1989).

The second group had smaller hand differences on the pegboard and could be described as weakly dextral or less strongly lateralised. The BEAM data corroborated these findings; EEG laterality indices generally indicated small L−R differences or bilateral activation. Figures 4.3 and 4.4 give examples of this characteristically symmetrical activity.

It is interesting that the variations in patterns of lateralisation emerged most clearly when considering the data from the visual tasks. Indeed, the preponderance of left hemisphere activity was greater in these tasks than in the auditory tasks. As mentioned earlier, most models concerning reading difficulties have concentrated on dysfunction in linguistic processing. An exception to this is Witelson (1976) who has suggested that reading problems may arise from anomalous specialisation for visuospatial skills. With respect to different patterns of lateralisation as a function of subtypes of reading disorder, the strong dextrals in this group show parallels with Bakker's type I dyslexics, who show an over-reliance on left hemisphere processing and poor visuospatial skills. It may be that this group of subjects has a higher incidence of literacy problems associated with visuospatial dysfunction which is being indexed by the anomalous patterns of cortical lateralisation. Flynn and Deering (1989) report higher levels of left hemisphere activity in their dyseidetic group and suggest that this may index an overuse of linguistic abilities rather than deficient visuo-spatial skills. There are also parallels with the finding of Annett and Manning (1990) of reading difficulties in children with strong right-hand and poor left-hand skills.

This suggestion of visuospatial difficulties as characteristic of this group is, to some extent, confirmed by results of the Boder test which was also administered during the testing session, showing a relatively high incidence of dyseidetic tendencies among this group (see Table 4.1). Boder (1973) reports that the dysphonetic subtype is more common. The unusual nature of this population was discussed above; it may be that children with dyseidetic problems are more likely to present with the spelling and handwriting difficulties characteristic of this group.

The lack of correlation between the laterality indices for the auditory and the visual tasks suggests that the children are not displaying a characteristic pattern of cortical activity whatever the task requirements, but a pattern which is specifically elicited by visual tasks. This is shown by the significant correlation between the two visual tasks. This may be an index of a tendency towards visuospatial difficulties shown by this group. A group which has evidence of strong auditory difficulties in the absence of visuospatial difficulties is currently being recruited to investigate whether their specific pattern of cortical activity relates more to auditory tasks than to visual tasks as in the group studied here.

The strong correlation between lateralisation indexed by pegboard scores and that indexed by EEG activity in visual tasks is particularly interesting. At a theoretical level it provides some validation for the link between functional and cortical, and for Annett's (1985) claims that strong dextrality as measured by hand skill is an index of strong left hemisphere specialisation. The existence of several subjects with this pattern of lateralisation in a dyslexic population could indicate the cost of an over-reliance on left hemisphere skills (Annett and Manning, 1989). At a practical level, it indicates that the pegboard could be a useful tool for screening large populations for different patterns of cortical lateralisation. Smaller groups of individuals displaying the more unusual extremes could subsequently be investigated in the laboratory using BEAM techniques.

Although on a small scale, this study has indicated the heterogeneous nature of lateralisation patterns within a dyslexic population. The possibility of some connection between variations in lateralisation and the particular nature of the children's difficulties is indicated by evidence of dyseidetic tendencies in this group paralleled by the lateralisation anomalies emerging most clearly during visual tasks. The relation between functional lateralisation as indexed by pegboard scores and cortical lateralisation as indexed by BEAM activity is of both methodological and theoretical significance. A follow-up study currently in progress comprises the recruiting from a large sample of reading-disabled children of one group with marked visual weaknesses and another with marked auditory weaknesses. This should enable us to investigate the implications of the current study in more depth. It is hoped that these and further studies will go some way towards resolving some of the conflicts and contradictions which remain in this potentially fruitful field of study.

Acknowledgements

Thanks are due to David Sleight and Sue Booth who helped in the data collection, and to Marian Annett for many fruitful discussions. Most of all, they are due to the children from the Coventry branch of the Dyslexia Institute who participated so cheerfully in the study and to their parents who agreed so readily to help.

References

ANNETT, M. (1985). *Left, Right, Hand and Brain: The Right Shift Theory*. London: Lawrence Erlbaum.

ANNETT, M. and KILSHAW, D. (1984). Lateral preference and skill in dyslexics: Implications of the Right Shift Theory. *Journal of Child Psychology and Psychiatry* **25**, 357–377.

ANNETT, M. and MANNING, M. (1989). The disadvantages of dextrality for intelligence. *British Journal of Psychology* **80**, 213–226.

ANNETT, M. and MANNING, M. (1990) Reading and a balanced polymorphism for laterality and ability. *Journal of Child Psychology and Psychiatry* **31**, 511–529.

BEATON, A. (1985). *Left Side, Right Side: A Review of Laterality Research*. London: Batsford.

BAKKER, D.J., TEUNISSEN, J. and BOSCH, J. (1976). Development of laterality reading patterns. In: R.M. Knights and D.J. Bakker (Eds), *The Neuropsychology of Learning Disorders*. Baltimore: University Park Press.

BAKKER, D.J. (1979). Hemispheric differences and reading strategies: Two dyslexias? *Bulletin of the Orton Society* **29**, 84–100.

BAKKER, D.J., LICHT, R., KOK, A. and BOUMA, A. (1980). Cortical responses to word reading by right- and left-eared normal and reading disturbed children. *Journal of Clinical Neuropsychology* **2**, 1–12.

BODER, E. (1973). Developmental dyslexia: A diagnostic approach based on three atypical reading-spelling patterns. *Developmental Medicine and Child Neurology* **15**, 663–687.

BRYDEN, M.P. (1988). Does laterality make any difference? Thoughts on the relation between cerebral asymmetry and reading. In: D.L. Molfese and S.J. Segalowitz (Eds), *Brain Lateralisation in Children: Developmental Implications*. New York: Guilford Press.

DUFFY, F.H., BURCHFIEL, J.L. and LOMBROSO, C.T. (1979). Brain electrical activity mapping (BEAM): a method for extending the clinical utility of EEG and evoked potential data. *Annals of Neurology* **5**, 309–321.

DUFFY, F.H., DENKLA, M.B., BARKELS, P.H. and SANDINI, G. (1980). Dyslexia: regional differences in brain electrical activity by topographic mapping. *Annals of Neurology* **7**, 412–428.

DUFFY, F.H., DENCKLA, M.B., McANULTY, G. and HOLMES, J.A. (1988). Neurophysiological studies in dyslexia. In: F. Plum (Ed.), *Language, Communication and the Brain*. New York: Raven Press.

FLYNN, J.M. and DEERING, W.M. (1989). Subtypes of dyslexia: Investigation of Boder's system using quantitative neurophysiology. *Developmental Medicine and Child Neurology* **31**, 215–223.

HUGHES, J.R. (1982). The electroencephalogram and reading disorders. In: R.N. Malatesha, and P.G. Aaron (Eds), *Reading Disorders: Varieties and Treatments*. London: Academic Press.

HYND, G.W. and COHEN, M. (1983). *Dyslexia: Neuropsychological Theory: Research and Clinical Differentiation*. New York: Grune & Stratton.

KEEFE, B. and SWINNEY, D. (1979). On the relationship of hemispheric specialisation and developmental dyslexia. *Cortex* **15**, 471–481.

MOLFESE, D.L. and SEGALOWITZ. S.J. (Eds) (1988). *Brain Lateralisation in Children: Developmental Implications*. New York: Guilford Press.

OBRZUT, J.E. (1988). Deficient lateralisation in learning-disabled children: Developmental lag or abnormal cerebral lateralisation? In: D.L. Molfese and S.J. Segalowitz (Eds),

Brain Lateralisation in Children: Developmental Implications. New York: Guilford Press.

PIROZZOLO, F.J., RAYNER, K. and HYND, G.W. (1983). The measurement of hemispheric asymmetries in children with developmental reading disabilities. In: J.B. Hellige (Ed.), *Cerebral Hemisphere Asymmetry: Method, Theory and Application*. Praeger.

RAVEN, J.C., COURT, J.H. and RAVEN, J. (1984). *Manual for Raven's Progressive Matrices and Vocabulary Scales*. London: H.K. Lewis.

RAY, W.J. and COLE, H.W. (1985). EEG alpha activity reflects attentional demands and beta activity reflects emotional and cognitive processes. *Science* **228**, 750–752.

RIPPON, G. (1989). Bilateral electrodermal activity: effects of differential hemispheric activation. *Journal of Psychophysiology* **3**, 65–73.

RIPPON, G. (1990). Individual differences in electrodermal and electroencephalographic asymmetries. *International Journal of Psychophysiology* **8**, 309–321.

ROURKE, B.P. and FISK, J.L. (1988). Subtypes of learning-disabled children: Implications for a neurodevelopmental model of differential hemispheric processing. In: D.L. Molfese and S.J. Segalowitz (Eds), *Brain Lateralisation in Children: Developmental Implications*. New York: Guilford Press.

SATZ, P. (1976). Cerebral dominance and reading disability: an old problem revisited. In: R.M. Knights and D.J. Bakker (Eds), *The Neuropsychology of Learning Disorders*. Baltimore: University Park Press.

WAITES, L. (1968). *World Federation of Neurology: Research group on developmental dyslexia and world illiteracy*. Report of Proceedings.

WITELSON, S. (1976). Abnormal right hemisphere specialisation in developmental dyslexia. In R.M. Knights and D.J. Bakker (Eds), *The Neuropsychology of Learning Disorders*. Baltimore: University Park Press.

Part II
The Normal Development of Literacy

Chapter 5
The Development of Reading and Spelling in Children: An Overview*

LINNEA C. EHRI

The question of how students learn to read has been addressed by researchers from three different perspectives: an instructional perspective, a disability perspective and a developmental process perspective. Some researchers have compared the effectiveness of different methods of teaching reading, e.g. phonics methods vs whole word or meaning emphasis methods (Chall, 1967; Feitelson, 1988). Some researchers have compared good and poor readers in order to identify underlying capabilities that distinguish them and account for learning difficulties (Vellutino, 1979; Snowling, 1980; Stanovich, 1980, 1986; Bryant and Bradley, 1985; Perfetti, 1985). Still others have focused on the cognitive–linguistic processes involved in learning to read, the course of development of these processes in normal readers, and what factors contribute to and enable their development (Ehri, 1980, 1987, 1991; Byrne, 1990; Goswami and Bryant, 1990; Gough, Juel and Griffith, 1990; Treiman, 1990). Although different, these three vantage points are not mutually exclusive. At some point, each must consider and incorporate the other to become a full account of reading acquisition. In this chapter, I will adopt a developmental process perspective.

Understanding the processes involved in learning to read turns out to be a complex task because reading entails a host of processes operating together in concert (Guthrie, 1973; Rumelhart, 1977). For example, as readers' eyes move across a line of text, they are picking up visual information about letters, words and sentences at the same time as they are mentally processing the information by computing the structure and meaning of the words and sentences, integrating this with information they have already read and their world knowledge to understand the text, and

---

*I wish to apologize to the many researchers who have conducted studies bearing on assertions about reading and writing development included in this chapter. Due to space limitations, there was room to mention only some of the relevant studies.

63

forming expectations about forthcoming text. Another reason why an account of reading acquisition processes is complex is that learning is influenced by many factors exerting an impact at many points along a lengthy course of development extending for several years, e.g. factors such as genetic endowment (Olson, 1985), the learner's knowledge of spoken language, the learner's experiences listening to text (Feitelson, Kita and Goldstein, 1986), the beginner's knowledge of letters and phonemic awareness (Share et al., 1984), the instructional methods received by the beginner (Chall, 1967), and how much the student practises reading (Stanovich, 1986). Although all these processes and causal factors are involved, a few can be singled out as central: those that are specific to reading, that are hardest for students with normal minds and experiences to learn, and that are essential for attaining reading competence. In this brief overview, I will concentrate on the essential processes and how they develop.

A Stage Theory of Learning to Read

To begin, let me outline how far the beginner travels in learning to read. Jean Chall (1983) has provided a way to conceptualize reading development in terms of stages. I will present a modified version of her view which distinguishes four stages: stage 0, a prereading or emergent reading stage; stage 1, an initial reading or decoding stage; stage 2, a fluency stage; and stage 3, a reading to learn stage. Adoption of a stage view means that readers must pass through and attain the capabilities at each stage in order to attain competence at the next stage.

The first *prereading or emergent reading stage* (stage 0) begins during the preschool years and lasts until children are able to read print independently. During this time, children learn to comprehend and produce spoken language. Those who are raised in a literate culture also learn much about the functions of written language as they participate in literacy events and as they observe literate members of the culture use reading and writing for various purposes (Goodman and Goodman, 1979; Holdaway, 1979; Clay, 1985; Mason and Allen, 1986). Prereaders listen to stories read to them in books and develop the ability to 'pretend' read those they have heard many times (Sulzby, 1985). They learn how to hold books, what print looks like, what a reading voice sounds like, and how stories are structured to include a setting, main characters, goals, conflicts, reactions and outcomes. Their vocabularies grow substantially from listening to stories. They learn to name and write alphabet letters. They learn nursery rhymes and they play rhyming games which enhances their awareness that language has words and sounds as well as meaning (Maclean, Bryant and Bradley, 1987; A. Hall, 1990, unpublished data). They read labels and signs in the environment such as 'stop' and 'McDonalds'

(Goodman and Altwerger, 1981; Masonheimer, Drum and Ehri, 1984; McGee, Lomax and Head, 1988). They practise writing by scribbling or copying print, or inventing their own spellings to label their drawings. Because children know much about print and reading, even though they cannot read print themselves at this stage, they are referred to as *emergent readers* (Teale and Sulzby, 1986).

Research indicates that emergent readers are ready to enter the next stage when they learn the shapes and names or sounds of most alphabet letters and when they acquire rudimentary awareness of sounds in words. The two best predictors of how well children succeed in reading during the next stage are letter name knowledge and phonemic segmentation skill (Share et al., 1984; Juel, Griffith and Gough, 1986). These are better predictors even than measures of intelligence and storing listening experiences. An experimental study by Lundberg, Frost and Petersen (1988) showed that prereaders, who were trained to segment speech into phonemes before they received any reading instruction, learned to read and spell better than control subjects who did not receive this training.

The next stage, stage 1, is the *initial reading or decoding stage* when students come to understand how the spelling system represents spoken language. They learn how letters symbolize phonemes and how to convert a sequence of letters into a pronounced word. They learn how to generate plausible spellings of words by writing the sounds they hear in the words. As their phonemic segmentation skill grows, they detect more sounds in words to represent with letters. As they learn to read more words, their knowledge about how sounds are symbolized in the conventional system grows. Direct structured teaching is more effective for ensuring that students learn how the spelling system works than leaving students to discover the system for themselves (Chall, 1967; Anderson et al., 1985; Adams, 1990).

During stage 1, students begin to build a sight vocabulary which they use to read simple text. When they come across unfamiliar words in their text reading, the better readers learn to look at letters to figure out words rather than ignore letters and guess words based on text already read (Biemiller, 1970). Because they are following the story line in their text reading, they anticipate subsequent meanings and learn to read in a way that integrates the words they encounter in print with the meanings of words they have already read.

Students move into stage 2, the *fluency stage*, during their second year of reading instruction. Attaining fluency involves becoming faster and more skilled at performing the various reading operations learned at stage 1: decoding unfamiliar words, reading known words with less effort and greater speed, coordinating word-reading operations with text comprehension processes more efficiently. It is important that the texts students read contain mostly words in their sight vocabularies and that the language and ideas in these texts are easy to understand. An important contributor to development at this stage is practice. Students' reading fluency grows not only from reading many different stories but also from reading and rereading the same stories. Rereading stories is thought to be helpful because the attention required for reading individual words diminishes with each rereading and hence increases the attention available for coordinating word reading with text comprehension processes (Samuels, 1979; Herman, 1985; Perfetti, 1985; Dowhower, 1987; Dewitz and Skilliter, 1989).

During the fluency stage, many words are added to students' sight vocabularies. Word attack skills grow as students receive more decoding instruction and as they recognize common spelling patterns in the sight words they learn to read (Venezky and Johnson, 1973). Students become able to read sight words, not only accurately but also automatically and rapidly, i.e. they develop the ability to look at familiar words and instantly recognize their pronunciations and meanings without expending any effort. In fact, students develop the ability to read sight words as rapidly as they can name single letters or digits, indicating that sight words are being processed as single units rather than letter by letter (Ehri and Wilce, 1983).

To understand what it means to recognize sight words automatically, imagine yourself staring at a row of object drawings such as a horse, a table, a tree, an apple. A distracting word is printed in the middle of each drawing, e.g. COW, CHAIR, ROSE, ORANGE. Your task is to name the pictures as rapidly as you can and ignore the words printed on them. Research shows that people who have learned to read the words automatically cannot ignore them. Naming pictures printed with distracting words takes longer than naming pictures printed with non-words, particularly if the words are semantically related to the pictures (Rosinski, Golinkoff and Kukish, 1975; Guttentag and Haith, 1978). Automatic word recognition skill has been observed in readers as young as the end of first grade and is a major contributor to the development of text reading fluency during stage 2.

Students move into stage 3, the *reading to learn stage*, when they gain sufficient skill performing the mechanics of reading. This enables them to read well enough to comprehend more difficult material whose ideas are unfamiliar. According to Chall (1983), this is the stage when students begin reading to 'learn the new' – new knowledge, new information, new thoughts, new experiences. Chall places this stage as emerging around the fourth year of reading instruction. This is when teachers expect students to acquire information in subject areas by reading text. The material read is more difficult than that read at the fluency stage. The ideas are less familiar, and the vocabulary may involve technical words whose meanings are unfamiliar.

Intelligence is more highly correlated with reading skill at this stage than at earlier stages (Singer, 1977). Students who have larger vocabularies, broader world knowledge and superior reasoning skills have a definite advantage in comprehending and remembering what they read at this stage. However, it is also the case that students who read extensively acquire larger vocabularies and more effective comprehension skills as a result of their reading practice (Stanovich, 1986). At this stage, the amount of reading that students do becomes a major determiner of differences that distinguish good from poor readers (Juel, 1988).

Now that I have provided a general overview of the course of reading development, I will take a closer look at the early period. Because reading development is closely related to spelling development during this time (Morris and Perney, 1984; Shanahan, 1984), I will also consider the course of spelling development.

The Early Stages of Learning to Read and Spell

When children begin reading print independently, their progress is governed primarily by the growth of two knowledge sources: their sight vocabulary and their knowledge of the spelling system (Ehri, 1991). With sight words stored in memory beginners are able to read unfamiliar text independently. With knowledge of how the alphabetic system works beginners are able to decode unfamiliar words. Also, it enables them to store sight words in memory. More will be said about this storage process later. Of course, beginners need to know the English language, how to interpret sentences and construct meanings from the text they read. However, among beginners who are competent speakers of English, differences in their success at stage 1 arise, not so much from differences in their knowledge of language and meaning, as from differences in their knowledge about print.

First, I shall examine beginners' knowledge about the spelling system as it develops from stage 0 to stage 2. The best view is provided by an analysis of the spellings that beginners invent and how these inventions change as children gain experience reading and writing. To invent spellings, children use their knowledge of letter names, letter sounds and print conventions to create plausible spellings of words whose correct forms are unknown. Several phases of development have been distinguished to reflect how much the child understands about the spelling system:* pre-phonetic

---

*In previous publications (Ehri, 1986, 1989), I have used different labels for two of these phases. In this paper, I have changed 'precommunicative' to 'pre-phonetic', and 'morphemic' to 'within-word pattern'. Margaret Hughes pointed out to me that the former is a misnomer because emergent readers intend their writing to perform a communicative function. Ed Henderson and his 'descendants' have persuaded me that within-word pattern is a more precise term than morphemic.

(stage 0), semiphonetic (between stage 0 and stage 1), phonetic (stage 1), and within-word pattern (stage 2) (Read, 1971, 1986; Henderson, 1981; Gentry, 1982; Morris and Perney, 1984; Ehri, 1986; Templeton and Bear, 1990).

The least mature spellings produced by emergent readers at stage 0 are *pre-phonetic* spellings. Children may spell by scribbling. Their scribbles may contain intersecting lines and curves characteristic of the writing system they have seen even though no letters are distinguishable (Harste, Burke and Woodward, 1982). Children may spell by stringing letters and numbers together. However, letters are not selected because they correspond to any sounds in the words being written. Examples of pre-phonetic spellings are: HS for 'quick', KO for 'muffin', A for 'hill'.

A major shift in spelling occurs when children realize that sounds in the names of letters correspond to sounds they detect in the pronunciations of words. This enables them to produce *semiphonetic* spellings. At first they symbolize the most salient sounds they hear, the first sound, or the first and final sounds in words. Letter names provide the basis for their selections, e.g. spelling 'while' as YL, 'eight' as AT, 'chicken' as HN (note how H contains 'ch' in its name). Consonants are represented more frequently than vowels because consonants begin and end most words and because many vowel sounds are not found in letter names.

As semiphonetic spellers gain more experience analysing print–speech relationships, they develop the ability to detect and spell more sounds in words. For example, in a 3-month period in first grade, the semiphonetic spellings of one child changed from KA for 'quick' symbolizing one correct sound to KWK symbolizing three sounds. Examples of other semiphonetic spellings are: 'party' spelt PT or PRD; 'stink' spelt SK or SEK.

Although children's letter choices may violate spelling conventions, they are nevertheless logical and indicate that learners are attempting to use what they know about letters to figure out how the spelling system works. Non-conventional choices such as Y for 'w' and H for 'ch' typically appear during the course of development, but subsequently disappear as learners discover that the conventional system works another way. For example, the spelling of 'wife' changed from YUF to WIF, the spelling of 'choked' from HK to CHOT in a 3–4 month period.

Spelling development takes a major step forward when children become able to produce phonetically complete spellings of words. At this point, children become wedded to the belief in one letter (or digraph) for every sound. The hardest part of this process is learning to segment pronunciations of words into their constituent phonemes (Liberman et al., 1977). Difficulty arises because there are no acoustic boundaries between sounds in speech. Rather sounds are continuous and are folded into each other and co-articulated (Liberman et al., 1977a). Students must learn to segment pronunciations into sounds at the level of phonemes. Phonemes which are hardest to detect are those appearing in the middle of syllables, those blended in consonant clusters (e.g. bl-, spr-, -nt, -mp), and schwa vowels in unstressed syllables (e.g. the sound symbolized by E in 'chicken').

Although beginners' phonetic spellings may include unconventional choices, these letter selections reflect a keen sensitivity to sound. For example, one child produced the following phonetic spellings: SDAP (stop), SDEC (stink), SBUJ (sponge). Her choice of voiced rather than voiceless letters, D rather than T, B rather than P, for the second phoneme in initial clusters, is phonetically accurate. If you tape-record these words and then splice off the first sound, you will hear 'dop' rather than 'top', 'bunj' rather than 'punj' because voicing onset begins during the second consonant rather than afterwards at the vowel (Reeds and Wang, 1961). Children detect this fact and represent it in their spellings (Treiman, 1985).

In the case of spelling short vowels whose conventional spellings are unknown, children may select the long vowel that is articulated most similarly to a short vowel, e.g. spelling 'fish' as FESH. Notice how your mouth shifts only slightly in producing short 'i' and long 'e' (i.e. contrast 'fish' vs 'feesh'). Children may spell short 'o' or short 'u' with the letter 'i', e.g. 'bunny' spelt BINE, 'top' spelt TIP. In saying the name of the letter 'i', they hear the short 'o' and 'u' sounds at the beginning and so choose 'i' as their spelling. These choices indicate phonetic sensitivity.

Although children's phonetic inventions may be unconventional at first, the conventional system works its way into their productions. They learn the correct letter symbols for short vowels. Their repertoire of symbols expands to cover sounds not found in any letter names, e.g. short vowels, digraphs TH and SH, hard G ('got'), /h/.

Learning about the conventional system serves to alter beginners naïve but correct phonetic intuitions when the conventional system represents the phonemes differently (Ehri, 1984). For example, as soon as beginners learn that initial consonant clusters are always spelt SP, never SB, SK but never SG, inventions which reflect awareness of the phonetic reality of initial /sb/ and /sg/ in words disappear (Treiman, 1985). Beginners correctly detect affricate sounds /ch/ and /j/ at the onset of words such as 'truck' and 'dragon' which they spell CHRUK and JRAGN (Read, 1971). However, they soon learn that affrication is not what the conventional system symbolizes but rather /tr/ and /dr/, so they shift to TR and DR in their spellings. With this, their awareness of affricate sounds in these words disappears. These examples show how spelling development during the phonetic phase involves learning to conceptualize phonemic segments in words in a way that optimizes the correspondence between phonemes detectable in pronunciations and letters in conventional spellings. The learner's initial insights persist if they agree with the conventional system but undergo modification if they do not. In this way, spellings work their way into the minds of beginning readers and writers.

Once students acquire a fairly complete understanding of conventional grapheme–phoneme relationships, they have the basis for distinguishing and learning *spelling patterns* that recur across words. Some tension is involved in shifting from phonemic spellings to word pattern spellings in which grapheme–phoneme relationships may be violated. For example, we observed children spell past tense morphemes correctly – 'watched' as WOCHED. However, when they were then shown phonetic spellings, such as WOCHT, they changed their minds, reasoning that because the latter sounded right, it must be right (Ehri, 1986).

Spelling with patterns includes learning long vowel spellings and the influence of final silent E. Whereas phonetic spellers write words such as 'seed' as CED, pattern spellers may write CEDE. Examples of other patterns to be learned are consonant doubling (e.g. taping vs tapping), -TION rather than -SHUN, -IGHT, morphemic spellings in which letters remain the same but sounds change in derived forms of words (e.g. sign, signature; medical, medicinal). Understanding the spelling regularities in multisyllabic words requires moving beyond phonetic spelling principles (Templeton and Scarborough-Franks, 1985). Examples of within-word pattern inventions are: RIDDING for 'riding', CHOCED for 'choked', CLINGCK for 'clink', and RISE for 'rice'.

Once students learn how to spell words phonetically by using conventional letter symbols, and once they learn about spelling patterns, they become much more accurate in spelling words correctly, not only because they have the knowledge to invent correct spellings, but more importantly because this knowledge makes it easier for them to store the correct spellings of specific words in memory. Even irregular spellings can be remembered more easily when students recognize how most of the letters are phonetically or morphemically regular (e.g. 'island' and 'sword' having all but one pronounced letter) (Ehri, 1989).

To summarize, beginners' knowledge of the spelling system evolves from a partial understanding of how salient sounds in words are symbolized with letters, to a complete understanding of how words are segmented into phonemes and how these segments are symbolized with letters in the conventional system. As students use their knowledge of the system to decode unfamiliar words and to store the spellings of specific words in memory for reading and writing, they become aware of spelling patterns that recur across words, and these patterns are added to their general knowledge about the system.

The Development of a Reading Sight Vocabulary

Before explaining how children use their knowledge of the spelling system to build a vocabulary of sight words, I need to say why I consider sight word reading to be a key component of the reading process and the most important form of word reading to explain. In reading English, readers' eyes are confronted with three types of structural units that make contact with their knowledge of language: letters, words and sentences. During the course of learning to read, the eyes come to favor written words as units. This is because words, unlike sentences, can be assimilated in one glance, and because written words correspond more reliably to specific spoken words than graphemes correspond to specific phonemes. Many years ago, Cattell (1886) found that readers could recognize a whole word as quickly as they could recognize a single letter, and in fact they could name a word faster than a letter, indicating that words are the favored units.

How do readers read words? Several ways have been distinguished (Ehri, 1991). Sight words are read by remembering how the words were read previously. Unfamiliar words are read by using knowledge of the spelling system to figure out the word's identity. This might involve converting letters into sounds and blending the sounds, or it might involve recognizing how unknown words are analogous to known words (Marsh et al., 1981; Goswami, 1986; Gaskins et al., 1988; Laxom, Coltheart and Keating, 1988). Words can be read by using context clues. A word's identity might be apparent from text preceding the word, for example, 'The snack bar at the movie theatre sells buttered _____'.

In order to read text effectively, readers need to be able to recognize most words by sight, i.e. by accessing stored representations of specific words in memory. Only a small proportion of words may be read by guessing from context, not only because most words cannot be guessed accurately but also because effective guessing requires accurate reading of 80–90% of the remaining words. Applying word attack skills to decode unfamiliar words works for a few words, but, if this approach is adopted with many words, text reading proceeds too slowly for comprehension to operate efficiently (Perfetti, 1985). Also, many studies indicate that readers do not apply word attack skills to decode the words they already know how to read (Gough, 1984).

In reading words by sight, mature readers do not rely on memory for non-alphabetic features of words such as their shape or length. On the contrary, they have full knowledge of the letters. Adams (1979) found that, if words were flashed very briefly, too briefly for subjects to see and rehearse the individual letters, adults could nevertheless report the letters accurately. Moreover, their performance was all or none. If the words were presented too briefly, no letters were recognized. If the words were presented just long enough to be recognized, letter recall was close to perfect. This contrasts with performance on nonsense words for which letter recall was gradual and increased with exposure duration rather than being all or none. These findings indicate that the information stored in memory and used to recognize words by sight is information about letters (Adams, 1990).

The Stages of Sight Vocabulary Development

Now I shall consider the course of sight word reading development. Three forms of sight word reading can be distinguished. They differ in whether or not letter–sound relationships are used to remember how to read the words, and in how completely the letter–sound relationships are represented in memory when they are used. These three forms of word reading correspond to the pre-phonetic, semiphonetic and phonetic phases of spelling development.

Emergent readers read words by selecting salient visual cues in or around words and associating these with the words in memory. The cues selected bear no relation to sounds in the word. Hence, they are like pre-phonetic spellings. We have called this visual cue reading or logographic word reading (Frith, 1985; Seymour and Elder, 1986; Ehri, 1990, 1991). Emergent readers might remember the shape of one of the word's letters, for example, the tail on the end of 'dog' written in lower case, or a logo accompanying the word, such as golden arches behind 'McDonalds'. However, this approach is not very effective for learning to read most English words. It is difficult to find features that are unique and distinguish one word from another (Gough and Hillinger, 1980; Gough, Juel and Griffith, 1990). Because associations between the visual features of words and their pronunciations and meanings are arbitrary, it is difficult to remember how to read the words.

When emergent readers learn about letters and can spell semiphonetically, they become able to remember how to read words by associating some of the letters seen in spellings with sounds detected in pronunciations of the words. We have called this phonetic cue reading (Ehri and Wilce, 1985; Ehri, 1987, 1991). It is like visual cue reading in that only one or a few specific cues, not the entire spelling, are selected and associated with the word in memory. However, it is different from visual cue reading in that the cues are *letters* which link the spelling to the pronunciation of the word. For example, beginners might remember how to read the word 'banana' by selecting the letters B and N and associating sounds in the names of these letters with sounds heard in the word's pronunciation. These associations are stored in memory and retrieved the next time the word is seen. Phonetic cue reading is more effective than visual cue reading because the associations between spellings and pronunciations are systematic rather than arbitrary and thus are easier to remember. However, because only some of the letters contribute to the associations, there is still room for confusion between similarly spelt words (e.g. horse and house, bump and blimp).

In one study examining the word reading skills of beginners, we found that stage 0 readers learned to read words more readily when there were distinctive visual cues available, even though none of the letters corresponded to sounds in the words (e.g. wBc to symbolize 'elephant'). In contrast, novice stage 1 readers learned to read words having letter–sound cues more easily (e.g. LFT to symbolize 'elephant') (Ehri and Wilce, 1985). This indicates that prereaders use salient visual cues whereas novice beginning readers are capable of using phonetic cues to remember how to read sight words.

When beginners learn how to segment words into all their constituent phonemes, and when they learn more about conventional ways of symbolizing sounds with letters, particularly vowel spellings, they develop the ability to read sight words by storing in memory complete associations between specific spellings and their pronunciations. We call this cipher sight word reading (Gough and Hillinger, 1980; Ehri, 1990). For example, cipher readers can recognize and remember how all of the letters in 'banana' correspond to sounds in the pronunciation. These correspond-ences provide the access route into memory enabling readers to look at the word and retrieve its specific pronunciation and meaning as a unitized whole. Two studies have shown that cipher readers remember the specific letters that they see in words rather than phonetically equivalent alternative letters (Ehri, 1980; Reitsma, 1983).

In comparing the sight word reading of phonetic cue readers and cipher readers (Ehri and Wilce, 1987a), we found that cipher readers were able to learn to read a set of 15 similarly spelt words perfectly, whereas cue readers were not. Cue readers confused words sharing similar letters, indicating that they were using partial letter cues to read the words. In recalling spellings of the words, cipher readers remembered more letters than cue readers except for initial and final consonants that were recalled well by both groups. Quite probably, initial and final letters were the cues that cue readers tried to use to read the words by sight.

To summarize, readers' knowledge of the spelling system enables them to form associations in memory in order to read words by sight. Prereaders at stage 0 have no knowledge of the alphabetic system so they remember salient visual features of words. Emergent readers on the verge of moving into stage 1 have semiphonetic knowledge of the system and can use partial letter–sound cues to remember how to read words. Stage 1 readers who have phonetic knowledge of the system can analyse spellings completely as symbols for the phonemic structure of pronunciations and can store these connections in memory to read words by sight.

I shall now consider what causes children to move from visual cue reading to phonetic cue reading, i.e. from stage 0 to stage 1. One proposal is that emergent readers become skilled at reading words logographically and that, in doing this, they discover how the letter–sound system works, and they move spontaneously into the alphabetic decoding stage. However, Byrne (1990) has conducted studies that raise doubt. He found that children do not become analytical about the alphabetic nature of print on their own simply by learning to read words with similar letters such as 'fat, bat, hat' and so forth. In order to shift into alphabetic word reading, emergent readers must gain access to a mental representation of speech at the level of phonemes and must learn how letters symbolize phonemes.

Masonheimer, Drum and Ehri (1984) studied emergent readers who were experts at reading environmental print. They found that, despite their expertise, these readers had not become analytical about letters in the signs they could read. When shown signs whose letters had been altered, for example 'Xepsi' for 'Pepsi', they read the sign as 'Pepsi' and failed to notice any problem, even when questioned about the possibility of a mistake. These findings raise doubt that acquiring environmental print expertise moves readers closer to stage 1 reading.

Another kind of experience that has been proposed to move logographic readers into alphabetic word reading is pretend reading practice in which readers learn to fingerpoint read stories that they have memorized (Holdaway, 1979). However, Morris (1983, 1990) found that success in this task required knowing how to segment and spell beginning consonant sounds in words. J. Sweet and L. Ehri (1990, unpublished data) found that success required having phonemic segmentation skill.

These findings indicate that emergent readers do not progress to phonetic cue reading as a result of practice reading words logographically. The problem is that there is nothing about logographic reading which entices readers to become analytical about print and to pay attention to letter units and their correspondence to sounds. In fact, the visual features attended to are antithetical because they involve a competitive way of organizing print cues and associating them with words in memory.

The way that movement from stage 0 to stage 1 occurs is by acquiring letter knowledge and rudimentary phonemic segmentation skill. As stated above, these are the two best predictors of reading achievement. Studies have indicated that teaching prereaders how to analyse language into phoneme-size units before they receive reading instruction helps them learn to read and spell (Lundberg, Frost and Petersen, 1988). Also, teaching beginners how to categorize and spell phonemes in words while they are learning to read facilitates reading and spelling development (Bradley and Bryant, 1983, 1985; Ehri and Wilce, 1987b; Uhry, 1989).

Treiman (1990) suggests that because beginners have an easier time dividing words into onsets and rimes than into phonemic segments (e.g. onsets are initial consonants in syllables, rimes are the vowel and what follows, as in 'b-at', 'bl-imp'), instruction should begin with these units. Wise, Olson and Treiman (1990) found that beginners who learned to read words by segmenting them into onset and rime subunits remembered how to read the words better than readers who segmented the words into other subunits, indicating that onset–rime segmentation benefits word reading. Goswami (1986) found that novice beginners could make use of onset–rime units to read unfamiliar words by analogy to known words, for example, reading 'peak' by analogy to 'beak'. However, L.C. Ehri and C. Robbins (1990, unpublished data) found that beginners' success at reading by rime analogies may require some decoding skill, enough to know how to blend the new onset with the known rime stem.

Although much more could be said about how beginners move into reading and spelling, my main point is that movement is not spontaneous if some critical ingredients are lacking.

Conclusions

To conclude, although I have focused on the cognitive–linguistic processes that are involved in learning to read, conclusions agree with those emerging from disability research and from instructional research. Students who have difficulty learning to read are almost always deficient in their knowledge about the spelling system and in their ability to read sight words effectively. Instructional methods which facilitate acquisition of reading skill during the early period are those that are effective in providing students with working knowledge of the spelling system. Learning to read takes time, practice, a prepared but maleable mind and instructional support. Emergent readers do not become fluent readers in a day, a week or even a year. They begin slowly and make many mistakes as they learn how to operate. However, their mistakes are common to all beginners; they reflect the kinds of processes that are emerging and changing with development, they supply observable signs of students' progress, and they provide important clues about how to tailor reading and writing instruction so that it is effective in moving learners along the course of development.

References

ADAMS, M. (1979). Models of word recognition. *Cognitive Psychology* **11**, 133–176.

ADAMS, M. (1990). *Beginning to Read: Thinking and Learning About Print*. Cambridge, MA: MIT Press.

ANDERSON, R., HIEBERT, E., SCOTT, J. and WILKINSON, I. (1985). *Becoming a Nation of Readers*. Washington, DC: The National Institute of Education.

BIEMILLER, A. (1970). The development of the use of graphic and contextual information as children learn to read. *Reading Research Quarterly* **6**, 75–96.

BRADLEY, L. and BRYANT, P. (1983). Categorising sounds and learning to read – A causal connection. *Nature* **301**, 419–421.

BRADLEY, L. and BRYANT, P.E. (1985). *Rhyme and Reason in Reading and Spelling*. Ann Arbor, MI: University of Michigan Press.

BRYANT, P. and BRADLEY, L. (1985). *Children's Reading Problems*. Oxford: Blackwell.

BYRNE, B. (1990). Studies in the unbiased acquisition procedure for reading: Rationale, hypotheses, and data. In: P.B. Gough, L.C. Ehri and R. Treiman (Eds), *Reading Acquisition*, in press. Hillsdale, NJ: Lawrence Erlbaum Associates.

CATTELL, J. (1886). The time it takes to see and name objects. *Mind* **11**, 63–65.

CHALL, J. (1967). *Learning to Read: The Great Debate*. New York: McGraw-Hill.

CHALL, J. (1983). *Stages of Reading Development*. New York: McGraw-Hill.

CLAY, M. (1985). *The Early Detection of Reading Difficulties*, 3rd edn. Auckland, New Zealand: Heinemann.

DEWITZ, P. and SKILLITER, M. (1989). *The Effects of Phoneme Awareness Training and Repeated Readings on Intermediate Grade Level Disabled Readers*. Paper presented at the meeting of the National Reading Conference, Austin, Texas, November 1989.

DOWHOWER, S. (1987). Effects of repeated reading on second grade transitional readers' fluency and comprehension. *Reading Research Quarterly* 22, 389–406.

EHRI, L.C. (1980). The development of orthographic images. In U. Frith (Ed.), *Cognitive Processes in Spelling*, pp. 311–338. London: Academic Press.

EHRI, L.C. (1984). How orthography alters spoken language competencies in children learning to read and spell. In: J. Downing and R. Valtin (Eds), *Language Awareness and Learning to Read*, pp. 119–147. New York: Springer Verlag.

EHRI, L.C. (1986). Sources of difficulty in learning to spell and read. In: M.L. Wolraich and D. Routh (Eds), *Advances in Developmental and Behavioral Pediatrics*, pp. 121–195. Greenwich, CT: Jai Press.

EHRI, L. (1987). Learning to read and spell words. *Journal of Reading Behavior* 19, 5–31.

EHRI, L.C. (1989). Movement into word reading and spelling: How spelling contributes to reading. In: J. Mason (Ed.), *Reading/Writing Connections*, pp. 65–81. Boston, MA: Allyn Bacon.

EHRI, L. (1990). Reconceptualizing the development of sight word reading and its relationship to recoding. In: P. Gough, L. Ehri, and R. Treiman (Eds), *Reading Acquisition*, in press. Hillsdale, NJ: Erlbaum.

EHRI, L. (1991). Development of the ability to read words. In: R. Barr, M. Kamil, P. Mosenthal and P. Pearson (Eds), *Handbook of Reading Research*, Vol. 2, pp. 383–417. New York: Longman.

EHRI, L.C. and WILCE, L.S. (1983). Development of word identification speed in skilled and less skilled beginning readers. *Journal of Educational Psychology* 75, 3–18.

EHRI, L.C. and WILCE, L.S. (1985). Movement into reading: Is the first stage of printed word learning visual or phonetic? *Reading Research Quarterly* 20, 163–179.

EHRI, L.C. and WILCE, L.S. (1987a). Cipher versus cue reading: An experiment in decoding acquisition. *Journal of Educational Psychology* 79, 3–13.

EHRI, L.C. and WILCE, L.S. (1987b). Does learning to spell help beginners learn to read words? *Reading Research Quarterly* 22, 47–65.

FEITELSON, D. (1988). *Facts and Fads in Beginning Reading: A Cross-Language Perspective*. Norwood, NJ: Ablex.

FEITELSON, D., KITA, B. and GOLDSTEIN, Z. (1986). Effects of listening to series-stories on first graders' comprehension and use of language. *Research in the Teaching of English* 20, 339–356.

FRITH, U. (1985). Beneath the surface of developmental dyslexia. In: K.E. Patterson, J.C. Marshall and M. Coltheart (Eds), *Surface Dyslexia*, pp. 301–330. London: Erlbaum.

GASKINS, I.W., DOWNER, M.A., ANDERSON, R.C., CUNNINGHAM, P.M., GASKINS, R.W., SCHOMMER, M. and the Teachers of Benchmark School (1988). A metacognitive approach to phonics: Using what you know to decode what you don't know. *Remedial and Special Education* 9, 36–41.

GENTRY, J. (1982). An analysis of developmental spelling in GNYS AT WRK. *The Reading Teacher* 36, 192–200.

GOODMAN, Y.M. and ALTWERGER, B. (1981). *Print Awareness in Preschool Children: A Working Paper. A Study of the Development of Literacy in Preschool Children.* Occasional Papers No. 4, Program in Language and Literacy, University of Arizona.

GOODMAN, K. and GOODMAN, Y. (1979). Learning to read is natural. In: L. Resnick and P. Weaver (Eds), *Theory and Practice of Early Reading*, Vol. 1, pp. 137–154. Hillsdale, NJ: Lawrence Erlbaum Associates.

GOSWAMI, U. (1986). Children's use of analogy in learning to read: A developmental study. *Journal of Experimental Child Psychology* **42**, 73–83.

GOSWAMI, U. and BRYANT, P. (1990). Rhyme, analogy and children's reading. In: P. Gough, L.C. Ehri and R. Treiman (Eds), *Reading Acquisition*, in press. Hillsdale, NJ: Erlbaum.

GOUGH, P.B. (1984). Word recognition. In: P.D. Pearson (Ed.), *Handbook of Reading Research*, pp. 225–253. New York: Longman.

GOUGH, P.B. and HILLINGER, M.L. (1980). Learning to read: An unnatural act. *Bulletin of the Orton Society* **30**, 180–196.

GOUGH, P., JUEL, C. and GRIFFITH, P. (1990). Reading, spelling, and the orthographic cipher. In: P. Gough, L. Ehri and R. Treiman (Eds), *Reading Acquisition*, in press. Hillsdale, NJ: Lawrence Erlbaum Associates.

GUTHRIE, J. (1973). Models of reading and reading disability. *Journal of Educational Psychology* **65**, 9–18.

GUTTENTAG, R. and HAITH, M. (1978). Automatic processing as a function of age and reading ability. *Child Development* **49**, 707–716.

HARSTE, J.C., BURKE, C.L. and WOODWARD, V.A. (1982). Children's language and world: Initial encounters with print. In: J. Langer and M. Smith-Burke (Eds), *Bridging the Gap: Reader Meets Author*, pp. 105–131. Newark, DE: International Reading Association.

HENDERSON, E.H. (1981). *Teaching Children to Read and Spell.* Dekalb, IL: Northern Illinois University Press.

HERMAN, P. (1985). The effects of repeated readings on reading rate, speech pauses, and word recognition accuracy. *Reading Research Quarterly* **20**, 553–564.

HOLDAWAY, D. (1979). *The Foundations of Literacy.* Sydney, Australia: Ashton Scholastic.

JUEL, C. (1988). Learning to read and write: A longitudinal study of 54 children from first through fourth grades. *Journal of Educational Psychology* **80**, 437–447.

JUEL, C., GRIFFITH, P.L. and GOUGH, P.B. (1986). Acquisition of literacy: A longitudinal study of children in first and second grade. *Journal of Educational Psychology* **78**, 243–255.

LAXOM, V.J., COLTHEART, V. and KEATING, C. (1988). Children find friendly words friendly too: Words with many orthographic neighbours are easier to read and spell. *British Journal of Educational Psychology* **58**, 103–119.

LIBERMAN, A., COOPER, F., SHANKWEILER, D. and STUDDERT-KENNEDY, M. (1967). Perception of the speech code. *Psychological Review* **74**, 431–461.

LIBERMAN, I.Y., SHANKWEILER, D., LIBERMAN, A.M., FOWLER, C. and FISCHER, F.W. (1977). Phonetic segmentation and recoding in the beginning reader. In: A.S. Reber and D.L. Scarborough (Eds), *Toward a Psychology of Reading*. Hillsdale, NJ: Lawrence Erlbaum Associates.

LUNDBERG, I., FROST, J. and PETERSEN, O. (1988). Effects of an extensive program for stimulating phonological awareness in preschool children. *Reading Research Quarterly* **23**, 263–284.

McGEE, L.M., LOMAX, R.G. and HEAD, M.H. (1988). Young children's written language knowledge: What environmental and functional print reading reveals. *Journal of Reading Behavior* **20**, 99–118.

MacLEAN, M., BRYANT, P. and BRADLEY, L. (1987). Rhymes, nursery rhymes, and reading in early childhood. *Merrill–Palmer Quarterly* **33**, 255–281.

MARSH, G., FRIEDMAN, M., WELCH, V. and DESBERG, P. (1981). A cognitive-developmental theory of reading acquisition. In: G.E. Mackinnon and T.G. Waller (Eds), *Reading Research: Advances in Theory and Practice*, Vol. 3, pp. 199–221. New York: Academic Press.

MASON, J. and ALLEN, J. (1986). A review of emergent literacy with implications for research and practice in reading. In: E.Z. Rothkopf (Ed.), *Review of Research in Education*, Vol. 13, pp. 3–47. Washington, DC: American Educational Research Association.

MASONHEIMER, P.E., DRUM, P.A. and EHRI, L.C. (1984). Does environmental print identification lead children into word reading? *Journal of Reading Behavior* **16**, 257–272.

MORRIS, D. (1983). Concept of word and phoneme awareness in the beginning reader. *Research in the Teaching of English* **17**, 359–373.

MORRIS, D. (1990). Concept of word: A pivotal understanding in the learning to read process. In: E. Henderson, S. Templeton and D. Bear (Eds), *Development of Orthographic Knowledge: The Foundations of Literacy*, in press. Hillsdale, NJ: Lawrence Erlbaum Associates.

MORRIS, D. and PERNEY, J. (1984). Developmental spelling as a predictor of first-grade reading achievement. *The Elementary School Journal* **84**, 441–457.

OLSON, R.K. (1985). Disabled reading processes and cognitive profiles. In: D. Gray and J. Kavanagh (Eds), *Behavioral Measures of Dyslexia*, pp. 215–267. Parkton, MD: York Press.

PERFETTI, C.A. (1985). *Reading Ability*. New York: Oxford University Press.

READ, C. (1971). Preschool children's knowledge of English phonology. *Harvard Educational Review* **41**, 1–34.

READ, C. (1986). *Children's Creative Spelling*. London: Routledge & Kegan Paul.

REEDS, J. and WANG, W. (1961). The perception of stops after S. *Phonetics* **6**, 78–81.

REITSMA, P. (1983). Printed word learning in beginning readers. *Journal of Experimental Child Psychology* **36**, 321–339.

ROSINSKI, R., GOLINKOFF, R. and KUKISH, K. (1975). Automatic semantic processing in a picture–word interference task. *Child Development* **46**, 247–253.

RUMELHART, D. (1977). Toward an interactive model of reading. In: S. Dornic (Ed.), *Attention and Performance*, Vol. 6, pp. 573–603. New York: Academic Press.

SAMUELS, J. (1979). The method of repeated readings. *The Reading Teacher* **4**, 403–408.

SEYMOUR, P.H.K. and ELDER, L. (1986). Beginning reading without phonology. *Cognitive Neuropsychology* **3**, 1–36.

SHANAHAN, T. (1984). Nature of the reading–writing relation: An exploratory multivariate analysis. *Journal of Educational Psychology* **76**, 466–477.

SHARE, D.L., JORM, A.F., MacLEAN, R. and MATTHEWS, R. (1984). Sources of individual differences in reading acquisition. *Journal of Educational Psychology* **76**, 1309–1324.

SINGER, H. (1977). IQ is and is not related to reading. In: S. Wanat (Ed.), *Issues in Evaluating Reading*. Arlington, VA: Center for Applied Linguistics.

SNOWLING, M. (1980). The development of grapheme-phoneme correspondence in normal and dyslexic readers. *Journal of Experimental Child Psychology* **29**, 294–305.

STANOVICH, K. (1980). Toward an interactive compensatory model of individual differences in the development of reading fluency. *Reading Research Quarterly* **16**, 32–71.

STANOVICH, K. (1986). Matthew effects in reading: Some consequences of individual differences in the acquisition of literacy. *Reading Research Quarterly* **21**, 360–406.

SULZBY, E. (1985). Children's emergent reading of favorite storybooks: A developmental study. *Reading Research Quarterly* **20**, 458–481.

TEALE, W. and SULZBY, E. (1986). *Emergent Literacy: Writing and Reading*. Norwood, NJ: Ablex.

TEMPLETON, S. and BEAR, D. (Eds) (1990). *Development of Orthographic Knowledge: The Foundations of Literacy*. Hillsdale, NJ: Erlbaum.

TEMPLETON, S. and SCARBOROUGH-FRANKS, L. (1985). The spelling's the thing: Knowledge of derivational morphology in phonology and orthography among older students. *Applied Psycholingustics* **6**, 371–389.

TREIMAN, R. (1985). Spelling of stop consonants after /s/ by children and adults. *Applied Psycholinguistics* **6**, 261–282.

TREIMAN, R. (1990). The role of intrasyllabic units in learning to read and spell. In: P. Gough, L. Ehri and R. Treiman (Eds), *Reading Acquisition*, in press. Hillsdale, NJ: Lawrence Erlbaum Associates.

UHRY, J. (1989). *The Effect of Spelling Instruction on the Acquisition of Beginning Reading Strategies*. Unpublished doctoral dissertation, Teachers College, Columbia University, New York.

VELLUTINO, F.R. (1979). *Dyslexia: Theory and Research*. Cambridge, MA: MIT Press.

VENEZKY, R.L. and JOHNSON, D. (1973). Development of two letter-sound patterns in grades one through three. *Journal of Educational Psychology* **64**, 109–115.

WISE, B., OLSON, R. and TREIMAN, R. (1990). Subsyllabic units in computerized reading instruction: Onset-rime vs. postvowel segmentation. *Journal of Experimental Child Psychology* **49**, 1–19.

Chapter 6
Spelling and Sound in Learning to Read

NICK ELLIS

This chapter provides an overview of my work on the development of reading and dyslexia and draws out implications for teaching. It presents the following arguments:

1. The most general information processing deficit in developmental dyslexia lies in phonological processing.
2. Studies of individual differences in reading development where intelligence is controlled generate patterns of associations which are essentially similar to those that arise from studies of developmental dyslexia.
3. An understanding of the development of reading can only come from longitudinal investigations of development itself, and such studies demonstrate typical sequences of interactive growth of related skills.
4. There is reciprocity in skill acquisition: a new skill invariably initially builds on whatever relevant abilities are already present; then, as it is used, it may well legitimise and make more relevant those same prior skills and so in turn cause their further development.
5. A key stage in the development of reading is the acquisition of an alphabetic strategy and the evolution of this skill can be traced from implicit phonological awareness through explicit phonological awareness to spelling and hence to reading itself. Finally it draws out implications for teaching practice.

Developmental Dyslexia as a Deficiency in Phonological Processing

When two letters of the same case are presented simultaneously and the child has to report whether they are the same (OO) or different (OB), dyslexic and control children do not differ either in the speed or in the accuracy with which they can perform this task. Also the dyslexic children or poor readers are no slower than age-matched controls when the letters, though different, are visually confusable (OQ, RP, EF, CG) (Ellis, 1981a,b). It seems unlikely, therefore, that dyslexic children have difficulty in dealing with the visual characteristics of letters as such. In contrast, when two letters of different case have to be adjudged same (Gg) or different (Gw, Gd) on the basis of name characteristics, the dyslexic children are reliably slower and more error prone than age-matched controls. It thus seems that dyslexic children have no extra difficulty in dealing with the visual aspects of letters as such, but that they show an impairment when the task demands the access and analysis of phonological features. This dissociation is similarly demonstrated in the study of Done and Miles (1978) who presented dyslexic subjects and age-matched controls with arrays of digits and afterwards made the correct digits available and asked the children to place them in the original order. At this task, where the stimuli were nameable, the dyslexic children scored considerably lower than the controls, but when non-verbal nonsense shapes were used as stimuli in place of digits the differences were minimal. Finally, when both groups had both been given 'paired associate learning', where names were learned for the nonsense shapes, the performance of the controls again became significantly superior.

This deficit in accessing phonological information is confirmed in the wide range of demonstrations of dyslexic children being slow in naming letters, objects, colours, digits, pictures, non-words and words (Ellis and Miles, 1981) and their difficulties in verbal short-term memory which are often taken as symptomatic of the syndrome.

These findings point to developmental dyslexia as a deficiency in phonological processing: developmental dyslexics are specifically impaired on tasks requiring access to or analysis of phonological material, but they provide no evidence for a comparable difficulty with concrete or visual material (Vellutino, 1979; Frith, 1981; Miles and Ellis, 1981).

Studies of Individual Differences in Reading Development

In 1979 we recognised that the then-current knowledge of reading (e.g. Gibson and Levin, 1975) came predominantly from studies carried out over some 50 years. During this time there had been considerable change in educational practice. Moreover, the studies had involved children of various ages, educational and cultural background. They had largely failed to take account of individual differences between children and, more seriously, had actually failed to say much about the *development* of reading. If we wish to study development we must do so directly. Only when the same persons are tested repeatedly over time does it become possible to identify developmental changes and processes of organisation within the individual. Cross-sectional studies which compare different groups of people at different stages of acquisition must always come a poor second when small but reliable changes with age are to be detected, and where teaching methods and teachers change with time. They also fail to tell us about the causes of development: a cross-sectional study may show an association between two phenomena, but only a longitudinal investigation can determine which came first.

Taking account of these criticisms, we embarked on a longitudinal study of the first 3 years of reading development (Ellis and Large, 1987, 1988). We followed a cohort of children and therefore could make a meaningful analysis of the changing nature of individual children's reading skill. We were also able to determine which skills promote reading development and which benefit from it, and the relative importance of different contributory skills.

A cohort of 40 children was assessed for their abilities on 44 variables. These measured as wide a range of information-processing skills as was practically possible. We measured general intelligence using the Wechsler Intelligence Scale for Children – Revised (WISC-R) (Wechsler, 1977), and also took measures of reading, spelling, vocabulary, short-term memory, visual skills, auditory–visual integration ability (e.g. letter-recognition, colour naming rate), auditory/language abilities including phonological awareness, language knowledge (grammar and syntax) and rote knowledge and ordering ability (reciting the days or counting forwards and backwards). The children were assessed on these measures each year, from 5 to 8 years of age. In the first of our reports (Ellis and Large, 1987), we extracted three groups at age 8 on the basis of reading and IQ scores. Group A showed a specific reading disability (high IQ, low reading), group B were good readers of similarly high IQ, and group C showed a more generalised reading deficit in that they were at the same level as group A in reading but their IQ scores were low. We then went back through the data available on the earlier development of these children.

The children with specific reading difficulties differed from their better-reading peers in terms of the relatively few variables which concerned phonological segmentation, short-term memory and naming. The children with generalised reading disability differed from their better-reading peers in almost every respect, but the strong discriminators concerned phonological processing. The children with specific reading disability differed from those with generalised reading disability in terms of intelligence and abilities which involve visual processing. These patterns of ability were broadly replicated at each age from 5 to 7 years of age.

Thus, rather few tests discriminated between children with specific reading disability and their age- and IQ-matched controls. These all concerned phonological processing, short-term memory or access to the names of visual material. The most important discriminators were the rhyming tasks which require implicit use of phoneme segmentation. The next strongest discriminator was auditory digit span, a most common finding in the developmental dyslexia literature (see Ellis and Miles, 1981, for a review). Following this came other tests of short-term memory for verbal material (auditory sentence span, auditory word span), and of phonological processing (sound blending, phoneme segmentation). We additionally found that the rate at which children can access the names of colours discriminated between the groups, and we confirmed the typical WISC-R profile of dyslexic children, the children having problems with Digit Span, Comprehension, Information and Coding subtests (Spache, 1976). The only discriminator which was not of a phonological type was visual serial ordering which squeezed in at the bottom of the list – a suitable placement because of the dispute over whether visual encoding problems fall out of group studies as being associated with dyslexia.

None of the other tests, the larger part of the battery, significantly discriminated between these groups – the children with specific reading problems did not show problems of visual processing, syntactic skills, rote knowledge or ordering.

'Reading' Changes in Nature in the Course of Development

We analysed our longitudinal study in several ways (Ellis and Large, 1988). At each year, we determined the associations between our many variables. The abilities which at one point in time were associated with later reading skill were charted for the whole group, for a subset of children who at 5 years of age started with no reading skill, and for another group of children who were progressing rapidly at 7 years of age. We used a statistical technique, cross-lagged correlation, to investigate causal paths. These analyses allowed us to chart the course of reading development and to focus on the ways in which the associated skills, such as spelling, reading, phonological awareness and syntactic knowledge, interact at different stages of development.

We found that the nature of reading skill changed rapidly during the first 3 years of acquisition. It began as an undifferentiated skill associated with knowledge of the letters of the alphabet, phonological awareness and visual, symbolic, short-term memory processes. It then changed in character, being associated with holistic pattern recognition skills. By 6 years of age, phonological awareness and verbal short-term memory processes were by far the strongest associates of reading. By 7 years of age, the better readers' skills were associated with analytical visual–perceptual analysis, the learning of new symbol–sound associations and sound-blending skill. Reading had become a multifaceted ability tapping a wide range of underlying skills – from language comprehension to analysis of the order of elements in a visual array – and different strategic blends of these abilities were now being used in different reading situations.

Reciprocal Interactions in the Development of Skills

This first longitudinal study allowed us to chart the interactions between different skills in the first 3 years in the development of reading. We identified the very different types of reading at different stages of development, and also some powerful reciprocal interactions in development. For example, we found from the *prereading* analyses that phonological skills promoted the acquisition of letter knowledge and that these two abilities, together with visual short-term memory, led to the development of reading. However, the *postreading* analyses indicated that, by this stage, reading promoted the acquisition of phonological skills and verbal short-term memory, and that the phonological skills in turn led to the development of visual short-term memory! (Ellis, 1990). The literature on this topic so far had tended to ask which direction of causality applied (e.g. Ehri, 1979; Bradley and Bryant, 1983; Bryant and Bradley, 1985; Bryant and Goswami, 1987). The answer is that both directions apply because a new skill invariably builds initially on whatever relevant abilities are already present; then, as the new skill is used, it may well legitimatise and make more relevant (Istomina, 1975) those prior skills and so in turn instigate their further development. Stanovich has persuasively argued the case for reciprocal relationships: 'In short, many things that facilitate further growth in reading comprehension ability – general knowledge, vocabulary, syntactic knowledge – are developed by reading itself' (Stanovich, 1986, p.364). Furthermore, 'interrelationships between the various subskills of reading and intelligence increase with age, *probably due to mutual facilitation*' (Stanovich, Cunningham and Feeman, 1984, p.278, my emphasis). In the evolution of our research we have used three metaphors for skill development: river and delta formation (see Hardy, 1965), pace-makers and followers, and symbiosis. They are all images of reciprocal interactions of elements over time. Such is the growth and development of skill.

This study also provided details about the move from early whole-word reading to a strategy that capitalises on grapheme–phoneme associations. We have shown in the first two sections that developmental dyslexics are particularly deficient in their phonological abilities, the very skills which are needed for learning these grapheme–phoneme associations. Therefore a finer-grained longitudinal study was needed to identify how phonological skills grow and become incorporated into the reading process.

The 'Finer-grained' Longitudinal Study

Although the importance of phonological awareness (PA) in the acquisition of reading had been established, causal pathways between the two abilities eluded clear definition (Shanahan and Lomax, 1986; Bryant and Goswami, 1987). Many and various factors might influence the co-development of phonological awareness and reading (see Chapter 7). Research which examines the relationship of phonological awareness to the emergence of literacy had often neglected spelling as an agent that independently influences and is influenced by phonological awareness and reading. Whilst it had been acknowledged that use of a phonological strategy plays a fundamental role in spelling before it becomes important in reading (Smith, 1973; Bryant and Bradley, 1980; Snowling and Perin, 1983; Juel, Griffith and Gough, 1986), comparatively little attention had been focused on the possible routes of interaction among reading, spelling and phonological skills. Correlational studies provided evidence of a strong relationship between early reading and spelling and between spelling and phoneme awareness. However, the form of causal connections could not be determined from correlations alone.

Theoretical analyses which assign spelling a major role in the development of phonological as well as reading skills include Chomsky (1977), Elkonin (1973), Lewkowicz (1980) and Ehri and Wilce (1987). In a three-phase model of reading acquisition, Frith (1985) proposes that an alphabetic or sound strategy is first utilised in spelling practice and later carried over to reading, which the child has previously approached using a logographic or visual strategy. Yet only a few studies have been designed to explore the manner in which spelling contributes to or benefits from phonological and reading skills, although Ehri and Wilce (1987) have recently demonstrated transfer of phonological strategy from spelling to reading.

In terms of educational practice, it is vital to explore how the early development of spelling and phonological awareness helps children across the threshold to literacy and thus a more detailed description of the interactive development of all three components – reading, spelling and phonological awareness – is required. Cataldo and Ellis (1988, 1990) and Ellis and Cataldo (1990) therefore adopted a longitudinal design to identify the early sequences of interactive development in reading, spelling and phonological awareness skills. We elucidate the early causal relations among these three variables by following the development of each skill in a group of children as they move from preliteracy through the beginning stages of learning to read and spell.

In this study, the early interactive developments of reading, spelling and phonological awareness are charted in a group of 28 children during their first 3 years in school. During this time the children were tested in reading and spelling real and nonsense words, phoneme segmentation and auditory categorisation at four intervals. The Wechsler Preschool Primary Scale of Intelligence (Wechsler, 1967; Saville, 1971) was included in the set of initial assessments. A test of phoneme segmentation was given as a measure of explicit phonemic awareness and a test of auditory categorisation was taken as a measure of implicit phonological awareness. The majority of the sample had only begun to attend school at the time the initial assessments were taken at the beginning of the school year when their mean age was 4;6 years. The children were retested at the end of their first school year, at the beginning of their second year and finally at the beginning of their third school year. Again statistical techniques (LISREL causal path analyses) were used to investigate the contribution of each ability to the subsequent growth of skill in word recognition, spelling and phonological awareness. The patterns of interaction among these three abilities provided a preliminary framework for mapping the early stages in the acquisition of literacy.

By broadening the phonological awareness–reading paradigm to include spelling, we were able to see a clearer picture of the early interaction among these abilities. There were three measured phases of development. Phase 1 spans the children's first year in school. Phase 2 charts the development from spring of the first school year to autumn of the second year. Phase 3 looks at development from the beginning of the second year in school to the beginning of the third year. During phase 1 spelling was found to be an important contributor to the early formation of reading. This pattern of influence was repeated more strongly in the second phase. The pronounced influence of spelling on reading contrasts with a negligible contribution of reading to spelling in both phases 1 and 2. Implicit PA initially predicted early attempts to read as well as to spell, but lost its influence on both reading and spelling in the following two phases. In contrast, explicit PA consistently predicted spelling in all three phases, the influence increasing over time. Explicit PA only emerged as a strong predictor of reading in phase 3.

The early transfer between reading and spelling appears to be unidirectional: knowledge gleaned from spelling is contributing to reading. Similarly, both implicit and explicit PA affect spelling development with explicit PA increasing its influence as the contribution of implicit PA diminishes. Later in the developmental sequence, explicit PA begins to contribute directly to reading. The pattern of interactions among abilities in phase 1 clarifies the different roles of implicit and explicit PA in the early formation of reading skill. Implicit information about the sound properties of words directly affects early reading attempts: explicit knowledge of phonemic content influences reading via spelling experience. The first evidence of the direct influence of explicit PA on reading occurs in phase 3, when explicit PA predicts ability to read non-words. In earlier phases, explicit PA does not influence reading directly but acts as the strongest predictor of spelling both real and nonsense words. In turn, spelling is the most consistent predictor of reading.

This early interactive sequence describes the pattern of growth from pre-alphabetic to alphabetic stage reading (Frith, 1985). The emergence of explicit PA as a significant predictor of reading marks entry into the alphabetic stage of reading. With increased reading experience, this early reading strategy is expanded; children can now read using partial phonetic cues accessed through constituent letters, or by using the similarity of the component letters of new words to component letters of other words they know. In this way novice readers evolve a strategy that they associate with the quickest route to reading real words for meaning. But when children are confronted with nonsense or new words in the absence of meaningful context, they may switch to an alphabetic approach. Here we see evidence of the selective use of strategies for different purposes. Children are able to shift from one reading strategy to another, depending on the demands of the task. Beginners attempt to read unknown words via a strategy of combining context, visual and phonetic cues and, only when this fails, switch to deciphering. Initially deciphering is used exclusively for reading unknown words when other strategies fail, but with practice children integrate this alphabetic approach into their repertoire of automatic reading strategies.

Models of reading and spelling *development* seek to explain the movement from one stage to the next. Our results describe the ways in which spelling acts as a mediator for the influence of explicit phonological awareness on reading. Children's very first efforts at reading are characterised by a visual or logographic strategy where letters are analysed for salient graphic cues to rapid word recognition; this is the pre-alphabetic stage. When a small number of pronunciations can be accessed in this manner, the child may embark upon a more advanced strategy of using associations between partial phonetic cues in the spoken word with letters in the printed version and subsequently utilise these associations to recognise the words. Children appear to use implicit PA to help them make these rudimentary sound analyses of pronunciation. In addition, spelling practice may contribute to the store of associations between the spoken words and letter–sound constituents in printed words. At first, spelling may encourage children to focus on the first letter of printed words and to begin to analyse this first letter, in the reading task, for phonetic cues to pronunciations. This may lead children to discriminate between stored pronunciations on the basis of the first letter of the printed word. As visual and phonetic cue strategies make increasing demands on the child's memory, the efficiency of this strategy decreases. Conversely, as the source of knowledge about letter–sound associates, and the relationships between letters in printed words and sounds in spoken words enlarge, the child is discovering that he or she can rely on the use of this knowledge for successful word recognition. Our studies report the idea that the transition from pre-alphabetic stage reading to alphabetic stage reading is facilitated by spelling. By employing explicit PA in spelling practice, the child gains familiarity with the alphabetic nature of writing and builds a reliable fund of information about letter–sound correspondences. Spelling affords the opportunity to forge a meaningful link between phonological awareness and letter–sound knowledge. This connection is a prerequisite to the development of phonological strategies in reading.

Conclusions and future research

These studies show how reading changes in nature as it is learned and that an important early stage in its development is the adoption of an alphabetic reading strategy. We trace the precursors of the phonological knowledge which forms the foundations of grapheme–phoneme reading back through spelling, through explicit phonological awareness and in turn to its source in implicit phonological awareness. We also report data pointing to phonological deficits in dyslexia and suggest that their reading and spelling development is limited by their prior failures to acquire this knowledge. As Frith (1985, p.324) says: 'Classic developmental dyslexia is the failure of alphabetic skills.'

There remains the need for further longitudinal studies which go back even further into early development. One promising example is that of MacLean, Bryant and Bradley (1987) who demonstrate the importance of children's early experience of nursery rhymes to their phonological awareness. The question that then arises is why, assuming developmental dyslexics receive equally such early exposure, they do not assimilate this knowledge. Then we must determine the neurological and genetic reasons which underlie this constitutional disability (see Chapters 1 and 2).

Whilst these studies help describe interactions in the development of phonological awareness, spelling and reading, they tell us little about the detailed mechanisms of interactive growth. A major remaining question concerns the process by which alphabetic knowledge both leads to and benefits from knowledge of the phonemic structure of the language. Gordon Brown and I are currently using powerful modelling techniques to explore this question (see Chapter 12). If we can simulate the development of alphabetic skills using computer modelling, then we will be a step closer to understanding the interaction of skills during development.

Implications for Teaching

Can our findings contribute to *The Great Debate* (Chall, 1967) concerning the 'best' ways of teaching reading? At the core of this debate vie methods based on look-and-say, phonics, spelling and meaning. Over the decades each has ascended and waned in almost predictably recurrent cycles.

The alphabet method, in spite of occasional protest, was almost universally used from the Greek and Roman times until some thirty years ago, and of course has not been discarded even yet. In this method the child learned first the names of the large and small letters and their order in the alphabet. This was task enough, uninteresting as it was to many, to keep them employed for some months, or even in some cases for a year or more. Then the combinations like *ab, eb, ib* were spelled out and pronounced, and then three-letter combinations like *glo, flo, pag*, etc., in all of which the early pages of the old spellers abounded. ... Spelling the word preceded its pronunciation, until it was well known. It was assumed that there was a necessary connection between naming the letters of a word and pronouncing that word.   (Huey, 1908, pp. 254–255)

Just how naming the letters was supposed to assist in pronouncing the word it is difficult to see. The value of practice in learning to spell doubtless had much to do with blinding centuries of teachers to its uselessness for the reading of words and sentences. However, in dealing thus constantly with the letters and their combinations, the pupil necessarily acquired a familiarity with *the sounds represented by each letter*, whether purposely these taught or not. And thus this method always combines something of phonics as well. ... The phonic method, used by the Jansenists in the Port Royal Schools, long neglected but advocated again by Thornton in 1790... *It is a spelling method, but the word is spelled by its elementary sounds and not by the letter-names. The word is slowly pronounced until its constituent sounds come into consciousness, and these sounds are associated with the letters representing them. Drill in this sound analysis trains the articulation, trains the ear and the ability to sound the letters of any new word, and gives the power to pronounce it by blending the sounds suggested.*   (Huey, 1908, p. 266, our emphasis)

In 1908, Huey decried the spelling methods which involve the names of letters, but he does acknowledge the advantages of training in phonics. Yet at the same time he equivocated and was concerned about teaching which concentrates on the 'mechanics' of reading:

It seems a great waste to devote, as at present, the main part of a number of school years to the mere mechanics of reading and spelling. The unreasoned and unreasonable devotion to our irrational English spelling in itself robs the child of probably two whole years of school life... the results too often show only mechanical, stumbling, expressionless readers, and poor thought-getters from what is read. The mechanical reading is thought to come from learning reading as mere word-pronouncing; the stumbling and hesitation, from the over-attention to form as against content, especially from the early and too constant analysis of the reading process in phonics.   (Huey, 1908, pp. 301–302)

In response to such criticisms, from the 1930s on, modal reading tuition was based on principles which:

include as major goals, *right from the start*, not only word recognition, but also comprehension and interpretation, appreciation, and application of what is read to the study of personal and social problems. ... Drill or practice 'in isolation' (i.e., apart from the reading of sentences or stories) should be avoided; instead, phonics should be 'integrated' with the 'meaningful' connected reading. In addition, the child should not isolate sounds and blend them to form words. Instead, he should identify unknown words through a process of visual analysis and substitution.

(Chall, 1967, pp. 13–15)

The pendulum followed its natural return in America in the mid-1950s with Flesch's (1955) popular *Why Johnny Can't Read* which challenged the then prevailing emphasis on sight—method teaching and which advocated a return to a phonic approach as the best, nay only, method to use in beginning instruction, and in Britain with the evaluation studies of Daniels and Diack (1956) which demonstrated a superiority of their 'phonic-word method' over the current mixed methods.

And again, two decades later, the position swung back away from phonics and spelling to Smith's 'psycholinguistics guessing game':

> Reading is not 'decoding to sound'.   (Smith, 1978, p. 83)

> Mediated word identification . . . strategies . . . include the use of phonics (spelling—sound correspondences). Attempting to decode isolated words to sound is unlikely to succeed because of the number, complexity, and unreliability of phonic generalisations. Phonic rules will help to eliminate alternative possibilities only if uncertainty can be reduced by other means, for example, if the unfamiliar words occur in meaningful contexts. Spelling—sound correspondences are not easily or usefully learned before children acquire some familiarity with reading.
> (Smith, 1978, p. 150)

> Of course, spelling is a problem, both in school and out, but it is a problem of writing, not of reading. . . .Knowing how to spell does not make a good reader because reading is not accomplished by the decoding of spelling. . . .I am not saying that knowledge of spelling is not important, only that it does not have a role in reading, and that undue concern with the way in which words are spelled can only interfere with a child's learning to read.   (Smith, 1978, p. 143)

Our present results lead us firmly to believe that Smith is wrong in these claims. They compel us to advocate a move back to methods of teaching reading which involve spelling and phonics. This direction is further reaffirmed by the accumulation of evidence from evaluative studies of differing teaching methods that phonic and spelling-pattern training is particularly effective. Thus Chall's (1967) exhaustive meta-analysis of the studies performed between 1910 and 1965 concludes:

1. A code (phonics) emphasis tends to produce better overall reading achievement by the beginning of the fourth grade than a meaning emphasis, with greater accuracy in word recognition and oral reading from the very beginning, and better vocabulary and comprehension scores by mid-second grade. With a code emphasis the child seems initially to read more slowly because of the greater emphasis on accuracy; however, by the third or fourth grade when he or she is more fluent his or her rate is equal to, or may ultimately exceed, that produced by a meaning emphasis.

2. Systematic phonics programmes which rely on direct teaching of letter—sound relationships are as successful as, or perhaps more successful than, programmes that rely on 'discovery' — the so-called

linguistic approaches that do not teach letter–sound correspondences directly.

We find, similarly, in Bradley and Bryant's training study (1983) that when children who were behind in reading at 4 and 5 years of age were trained on sound categorisation they showed greater improvements in reading over the next 2 years than those who were given semantic categorisation training. However, those children who were given sound categorisation and, with the help of plastic letters, were additionally taught how each common sound was represented by a letter of the alphabet, showed even greater improvement. Furthermore, less than 10 hours of such training spaced over 2 years led to these superiorities in reading being sustained through until the children were 13 years old (Bradley, 1989). We can conclude from these results that phonic training is particularly effective for individuals who are handicapped in reading and, furthermore, training in sound categorisation is even more effective when it is linked to spelling and involves an explicit connection with the alphabet.

Our findings concerning the growth of cognitive skills can explain these findings. Within a developmental context, explicit phoneme awareness initially appears to grow out of an implicit appreciation of the overall sound properties of words. Then explicit phonemic awareness is itself an important factor in the first stages of spelling development, emerging only later as a significant contributor to reading. The early influence of explicit phoneme awareness on spelling, in conjunction with the major contribution of spelling to beginning reading, indicates that experience in spelling promotes the use of a phonological strategy in reading. Thus training individuals in phonics and spelling will help them to become proficient readers. In saying this we are not advocating a return to Huey's 'mere mechanics of reading and spelling. The unreasoned and unreasonable devotion to our irrational English spelling', we are certainly not suggesting spelling by letter names; rather we promote the notion of reading programmes which include the wide range of goals from word attack skills, through comprehension to interpretation, and which are tailored to the needs of the particular child and particular stage (Frith, 1985; Ellis and Large, 1988) of reading development. However, we do believe that it is advisable for beginning readers and those who are backwards or specifically handicapped to be assisted in developing facility in dissecting a word's sound structure so as to foster symbol–sound and sound–symbol association. At times this must involve the direct teaching of these associations.

The final conclusion concerns the early identification of children at risk. The work of Bradley (1989) demonstrates that the younger the child, the more effective the remedial intervention. We do not need to wait until children are 7 or 8 years of age or older to identify that they are falling substantially behind in their reading development. Our present description of the growth of reading skill identifies its precursors as phonological skills and early spelling. We can therefore use young children's problems in these areas as indices predictive of risk of later reading delay.

Acknowledgements

I express grateful thanks to my co-workers: Alan Baddeley, Gordon Brown, Suzanne Cataldo, Barbara Large, Tim and Elaine Miles.

References

BRADLEY, L. (1989). *Specific learning disability: prediction – intervention – progress.* Paper presented to the Rodin Remediation Academy International Conference on Dyslexia, University College of North Wales, September, 1989.

BRADLEY, L. and BRYANT, P.E. (1983). Categorizing sounds and learning to read – a causal connection. *Nature* **301**, 419–421.

BRYANT, P.E. and BRADLEY, L. (1980). Why children sometimes write words which they do not read. In: U. Frith (Ed.), *Cognitive Processes in Spelling.* London: Academic Press.

BRYANT, P.E. and BRADLEY, L. (1985). *Children's Reading Problems.* Oxford: Blackwell.

BRYANT, P.E. and GOSWAMI, U. (1987). Phonological awareness and learning to read. In: J.R. Beech and A.M. Colley (Eds), *Cognitive Approaches to Reading.* Chichester: Wiley.

CATALDO, S. and ELLIS, N. (1988). Interations in the development of spelling, reading and phonological skills. *Journal of Research in Reading* **11**(2), 86–109.

CATALDO, S. and ELLIS, N.C. (1990). Learning to Spell, Learning to Read. In: P.D. Pumphrey and C.D. Elliott (Eds), *Children's Difficulties in Reading, Spelling and Writing.* Basingstoke: Falmer Press.

CHALL, J. (1967). *Learning to Read: The Great Debate.* New York: McGraw-Hill.

CHOMSKY, C. (1977). Approaching reading through invented spelling. In: L.B. Resnick and P.A. Weaver (Eds), *The Theory and Practice of Early Reading,* Vol. 2, Hillsdale, NJ: Erlbaum.

DANIELS, J.C. and DIACK, H. (1956). *Progress in Reading.* University of Nottingham: Institute of Education.

DONE, D.J. and MILES, T.R. (1978). Learning, memory and dyslexia. In: M.M. Gruneberg, P.E. Morris and R.N. Sykes (Eds), *Practical Aspects of Memory.* London: Academic Press.

EHRI, L.C. (1979). Linguistic insight: threshold of reading acquisition. In: T.G. Waller and G.E. MacKinnon (Eds), *Reading Research: Advances in Theory and Practice,* Vol. 1, New York: Academic Press.

EHRI, L.C. and WILCE, L.S. (1987). Cipher versus cue reading: an experiment in decoding acquisition. *Journal of Educational Psychology* **79**, 3–13.

ELKONIN, D.B. (1973). U.S.S.R. In: J. Downing (Ed.), *Comparative Reading.* New York: Macmillan.

ELLIS, N.C. (1981a). Information processing views of developmental dyslexia I–IV. *Dyslexia Review* **4**(1), 10–21 and **4**(2), 5–17.

ELLIS, N.C. (1981b). Visual and name coding in dyslexic children. *Psychological Research* **43**, 201–218.

ELLIS, N.C. (1990). Reading, phonological processing and STM: Interactive tributaries of development. *Journal of Research in Reading* **13**(2), 107–122.

ELLIS, N.C. and CATALDO, S. (1990). The role of spelling in learning to read. *Language and Education*, in press.

ELLIS, N.C. and LARGE, B. (1987). The development of reading: as you seek so shall you find. *British Journal of Psychology* **78**, 1–28.

ELLIS, N.C. and LARGE, B. (1988). The early stages of reading: A longitudinal study. *Applied Cognitive Psychology* **2**, 47–76.

ELLIS, N.C. and MILES, T.R. (1981). A lexical encoding deficiency I: experimental evidence. In: G.Th. Pavlidis and T.R. Miles (Eds), *Dyslexia Research and Its Applications to Education*. Chichester: Wiley.

FLESCH, R. (1955). *Why Johnny Can't Read and What You Can Do about It*. New York: Harper and Brothers.

FRITH, U. (1981). Experimental approaches to developmental dyslexia: an introduction. *Psychological Research* **43**, 97–110.

FRITH, U. (1985). Beneath the surface of developmental dyslexia. In: K. Patterson, M. Coltheart and J. Marshall (Eds), *Surface Dyslexia*. London: Erlbaum.

GIBSON, E. and LEVIN, H. (1975). *The Psychology of Reading*. Cambridge, MA: MIT Press.

HARDY, A. (1965). *The Living Stream*. London: Collins.

HUEY, E.B. (1908). *The Psychology and Pedagogy of Reading*. Cambridge, MA: MIT Press.

ISTOMINA, Z.M. (1975). The development of involuntary memory in preschool age children. *Soviet Psychology* **13**, 5–64.

JUEL, C., GRIFFITH, P.L. and GOUGH, P.B. (1986). The acquisition of literacy: a longitudinal study of children in first and second grade. *Journal of Educational Psychology* **78**, 243–255.

LEWKOWICZ, N.K. (1980). Phonemic awareness training: what it is and how to teach it. *Journal of Educational Psychology* **72**, 686–700.

MacLEAN, M., BRYANT, P. and BRADLEY, L. (1987). Rhymes, nursery rhymes and reading in early childhood. *Merrill–Palmer Quarterly* **33**, 255–281.

MILES, T.R. and ELLIS, N.C. (1981). A lexical encoding deficiency II: clinical observations. In: G.Th. Pavlidis and T.R. Miles (Eds), *Dyslexia Research and Its Applications to Education*. Chichester: Wiley.

SAVILLE, P. (1971). *A British Supplement to the Manual of the Wechsler Preschool and Primary Scale of Intelligence*. Windsor: NFER-Nelson.

SHANAHAN, T. and LOMAX, R.G. (1986). An analysis and comparison of theoretical models of the reading–writing relationship. *Journal of Educational Psychology* **78**, 116–123.

SMITH, F. (1973). Alphabetic writing – a language compromise? In: F. Smith (Ed.), *Psycholinguistics and Reading*. New York: Holt Rinehart & Winston.

SMITH, F. (1978). *Understanding Reading: A Psycholinguistic Analysis of Reading and Learning to Read*, 2nd edn. New York: Holt, Rinehart & Winston.

SNOWLING, M. and PERIN, D. (1983). The development of phoneme segmentation skills in young children. In: J. Sloboda (Ed.), *The Acquisition of Symbolic Skills*. London: Plenum Press.

SPACHE, G.D. (1976). *Investigating the Issues of Reading Disabilities*. Boston: Allyn and Bacon.

STANOVICH, K.E. (1986). Matthew effects in reading: Some consequences of individual differences in the acquisition of literacy. *Reading Research Quarterly* **XXI**, 360–407.

STANOVICH, K.E., CUNNINGHAM, A.E. and FEEMAN, D.J. (1984). Intelligence, cognitive skills, and early reading progress. *Reading Research Quarterly* **XIX**, 278–303.

VELLUTINO, F.R. (1979). *Dyslexia: Theory and Research*. Cambridge, MA: MIT Press.

WECHSLER, D. (1967). *Manual for the Wechsler Preschool and Primary Scale of Intelligence*. New York: The Psychological Corporation.

WECHSLER, D. (1977). *Wechsler Intelligence Scale for Children – Revised*. New York: The Psychological Corporation.

Chapter 7
Metaphonological Abilities and Literacy

JOSÉ MORAIS

The aim of this chapter is to examine the relationships between metaphonological abilities and literacy and it may be appropriate to begin by defining these two terms.

Literacy and the Acquisition of Literacy

Literacy will be taken here as the capacity to understand correctly the meaning of texts as well as the capacity to convey meaning in a written form. These are the functions of reading and writing respectively. Reading and writing are complex activities, which means that they include a variety of processes or operations on mental representations, until their respective end-products are attained.

Both reading and writing are language activities. It is reasonable to assume that they share many of their component processes and representations with the comprehension and production of oral language. Why is this a reasonable idea? It is reasonable because oral language largely precedes written language both in the history of our species and in ontogenetic development. Written language appeared about 2000 years ago, whereas human beings were speaking among themselves 60 000 years before that. As far as our children are concerned, they begin learning to read and write at the age of 2, 3 or even 4 years after they have developed the ability to say almost everything they need or want to say. Writing systems allow language to last far beyond echoes and, no matter how different they may be, they preserve the structures of oral language while giving them a new expression. Thus, reading and writing activities may be considered as secondary to the comprehension and production of oral language. If these known facts and ideas are recalled here, it is only to emphasise the necessity of distinguishing, among the processes used in reading and writing, those which have been acquired and consolidated for oral language from those which belong to literacy proper.

95

An analytical approach of reading and writing must disclose subgoals of these activities. Although the final goal is to understand or produce meaningful written language, there is a specific function of literacy which is to gain access to the pre-existing language and cognitive systems. The language and the cognitive systems are themselves intimately connected, especially at the level of the set of representations usually called the mental lexicon. Both syntactic structures and semantic networks are ways, although different ones, of combining or connecting words. Literacy provides a new form of word representation: it means adding orthographic representations to the pre-existing phonological and semantic representations of words. Specific algorithms (processes and representations) must ensure the specific computational problems of reading and writing, which are, respectively, to recover the phonology and the semantics of the word from its written expression, and to produce the written form of the word.

The acquisition of literacy consists mainly of the acquisition of these algorithms. Further language and cognitive improvements, beyond the beginning of literacy instruction, may indeed contribute towards making literacy activities more efficient. But, at least in the first stages, the main constraint is the capacity of the learner to make contact with the mental lexicon from the text, and to find the written word, spontaneously or under dictation, both precisely and rapidly enough to create favourable conditions for the operation of syntactic and semantic processes (analysis and integration in the case of reading, organisation and production in the case of writing). Success in the acquisition of the specific algorithms of reading and writing gives the child a very powerful way of processing information, and thus of acquiring knowledge, as well as developing sophisticated linguistic and metalinguistic devices.

Juel (1988) has illustrated quite convincingly this snowball effect in a longitudinal study. Groups of first-grade children characterised as good and poor comprehenders in reading were termed 'equally proficient' in listening comprehension (the ability to match pictures with orally presented stories) and oral production (telling a story about a picture). However, the good readers became progressively much better than the poor readers at these two tasks. Interestingly enough, performance in word recognition accounted for 44% of the variance in a test for the prediction of reading comprehension using a particular statistical method, after controlling for the influence of listening comprehension, whereas listening comprehension had no unique influence.

I shall come back to the relationship between the general function of literacy activities and their specific functions. For the sake of conciseness, and also because most of the available data concern reading ability, I will consider only the particular case of reading.

The literature usually shows a high degree of association (correlations from -0.5 to -0.8) between the scores of written story comprehension and the latency of single written word naming. A study by Lesgold, Resnick and Hammond (1985) has suggested that there may be an asymmetrical causal relationship in the development of these two abilities. The authors followed around 300 children from the first to the third grade and found that latency of word naming in the first grade was predictive of text comprehension in the third grade, but that the reverse relationship, i.e. between text comprehension in the first grade and naming latency in the third grade, was not obtained. Thus, rapidity in accessing word pronunciation seems to have an influence on the development of text comprehension ability rather than the reverse. Moreover, this pattern of results was found both for children learning to read according to a phonic method and for those learning to read according to a whole-word method. It raises two questions: one concerns the importance of access to word pronunciation in the improvement of reading ability and the other the ways by which word pronunciation is accessed.

Studies of written word recognition in adults have indicated that words can be accessed either by using a process of sequential phonological recoding or by assembling the letter string, which would be based, at least in part, on the knowledge of grapheme–phoneme correspondences. However, for most words, especially frequent ones, and certainly for highly irregular ones, such phonological mediation is not used; in this case, the orthographic representation corresponding to a word would be accessed on the basis of the abstract identities of letters or other word constituents. The main question that a theory of reading acquisition has to deal with is, of course, how these two routes of written word recognition are acquired.

The most promising cognitive theories of reading acquisition presented so far (Seymour and MacGregor, 1984; Frith, 1985; Stuart and Coltheart, 1988) agree on the following claims: first, visual processing of words, based on physical features (i.e. logographic reading) rather than on abstract identities (orthographic reading), is insufficient to allow recognition of the increasing number of words the beginning reader has to learn. Secondly, a mechanism of phonological assembly, based initially on the knowledge of simple grapheme–phoneme correspondence, and later incorporating the knowledge of contextual rules, must be acquired. Thirdly, this mechanism plays some crucial role in the acquisition of orthographic representations of words. Fourthly, in the very first years of reading acquisition, phonological assembly is predominant, but it is progressively replaced by orthographic reading.

One finding that illustrates this shift was provided by Doctor and Coltheart (1980). Rejection of a meaningless all-word sentence that sounds correct, such as 'I have know time', was obtained in 29.2%, 56.3% 68.8% and 81.3%, of 6, 7, 8 and 9 year olds respectively. Rejection of this kind of written sentence can only occur if the subject does not use a strict phonological decoding procedure. Thus, the resort to orthographic reading clearly increases with age (more plausibly, with reading experi-ence). It should also be remarked that this form of reading is already available in the younger children, although to a limited extent. Perhaps a more optimistic indication of this ability at this stage of reading acquisition is provided by the observation that second-graders can read correctly 75% of a corpus of irregular words (Backman et al., 1984).

If we consider again the idea that phonological decoding plays a crucial role in the development of orthographic reading, it is possible to think of a role in two non-exclusive ways. Phonological decoding gives the child the possibility of finding by him- or herself the pronunciation of words rarely or never seen before. Thus, the child can establish the association between a written word and its pronunciation as many times as he or she needs in order to become sufficiently acquainted with this word. According to this view, formerly put forward by Jorm and Share (1983), phonological recoding simply helps the child to consolidate the relation-ship between an orthographic representation and the corresponding pronunciation. It does not contribute in any significant way to the constitution of the orthographic representation itself. However, it is possible to figure out, as it seems to be the case in Seymour's model (compare, for instance, Seymour, 1987), that phonological decoding helps to establish a matrix of correspondences between phonological and orthographic units, without which the orthographic representation typical of the skilled reader can hardly be elaborated. In sum, there are two putative contributions of phonological decoding to the development of orthographic reading: one in which the final output of phonological decoding is associated with a separate orthographic representation, and the other in which the intermediate or partial outputs of phonological assembly intervene in the constitution of the orthographic (or pre-orthographic?) representations.

Distinguishing Phonological and Phonemic Awareness

A classic illustration of the development of phonemic awareness was provided by Liberman et al. (1974). They administered a syllable and a phoneme counting task to some children. For syllable counting, the children had to tap the table once for 'but', twice for 'butter' and three times for 'butterfly'. For phoneme counting, they had to tap once for 'u', twice for 'bu' and three times for 'but'. The results indicate that about half of the pre-schoolers (4 year olds) and the kindergarteners (5 year olds) could perform the syllable counting task successfully. In contrast, it was exceptional that a child at these ages succeeded in counting phonemes. Nevertheless, more than 70% of first-graders (6 year olds) showed no difficulty with either task. Thus, phonemic awareness seems to develop either between ages 5 and 6, or when authors declared that they could not disentangle the two interpretations, namely an effect of age and an effect of instruction, although they preferred the idea that instruction in reading was the critical variable.

One of the ways to disentangle these alternative interpretations is to examine whether illiterate adults are aware of phonemes. If phonemic awareness develops spontaneously as a consequence of cognitive matura-tion, then illiterate adults should demonstrate signs of phonemic aware-ness. But if it develops only when people learn to read and write, then illiterates should be unable to perform tasks requiring the awareness of phonemes. This test was carried out by our group (Morais et al., 1979). We showed that the great majority of Portuguese illiterate adults are unable either to delete the initial phoneme of an utterance, or to add one at the beginning of an utterance. By contrast, the great majority of people who had been illiterate during childhood, but who had attended literacy classes at adult age, were nearly perfect on the same tasks. We concluded from these results that development of phonemic awareness requires some specific experience not provided by primary linguistic activities, and that usually this critical experience is the acquisition of the alphabet.

A further study, by Read et al. (1986), showed that it may be a specific form of literacy that is associated with phonemic awareness. They found that Chinese adults who know the logographic representation of Chinese, but who have never learned an alphabet, were as poor as the Portuguese illiterate adults in the same phoneme deletion and addition tasks. Thus, the critical experience necessary to acquire phonemic awareness seems to be the learning of an alphabetic writing system.

This view is just the opposite of another view, defended for instance by Leroy-Boussion (1975) in France, which states that phonemic awareness is a prerequisite of reading acquisition, and that therefore children should be instructed in reading until they display some signs of phonemic awareness. Other authors, for instance the Oxford group (compare Bryant and Goswami, 1987; Bryant et al., 1989), think that the emergence of at least some form of phonemic awareness does not depend on instruction in the alphabetic code, but may arise gradually from other metaphonologi-cal abilities such as sensitivity to rhyme.

The disagreement between the positions of our group and of the Oxford one may in part be accounted for by terminological differences. However, these differences reflect conceptual differences and should not be underestimated.

It is important to distinguish clearly between the different forms of phonological awareness. One way to do this is to examine possible simple dissociations and, in particular, to verify which phonological properties people can be aware of without being aware of phonemes. It has been shown that both preliterate children and illiterate adults are able to make comparisons of phonological duration, to segment utterances into syllables and to appreciate rhyming relationships (compare for populations of illiterates, Morais et al., 1986; Kolinski, Cary and Morais, 1987; Bertelson et al., 1989). Moreover, the detailed examination of one illiterate poet (see Morais, 1990) shows quite convincingly that expertise in rhyming appreciation and production does not transfer to phonemic analysis at all.

The very fact that phonemic awareness is a highly specific form of phonological awareness is, of course, irrelevant for the demonstration that phonemic awareness depends on acquaintance with the alphabetic code. Thus, the critical question is 'can we find people who display clear signs of phonemic awareness and who, at the same time, have no knowledge of the alphabetic code?'. I and others say no. The Oxford group is among those who say yes in support of their position. These authors mention that some proportion of children, before they have been submitted to formal literacy instruction in school, obtain above-chance scores in phonemic awareness tasks. There are, however, two objections to this argument. First, most children in our times learn the phonemic counterparts of letters either at home or in kindergarten. Indeed, the critical factor is not whether the child attends the primary school, but whether he or she has received some information about the alphabetic code. Stuart and Coltheart (1988) found a very strong positive correlation between phonemic analysis ability and letter-to-sound correspondence knowledge in kindergarteners. Children who have been told the sounds of letters and who begin using these letters to spell a few words may display signs of phonemic awareness, even while they are still totally unsuccessful at word-reading tests.

The second objection to the above-mentioned argument is that the children may have developed a strategy that, although not relying on phonemic awareness, may cope with a so-called phonemic awareness task. Content et al. (1986) have found that prereaders may acquire, from corrective feedback, some ability which enables them to delete the initial consonant of an utterance. Later on, Content, Morais and Bertelson (1987) found that this ability is not transferable to a test in which a few items have to be classified according to whether they do or do not share the same initial consonant. Further observations suggested that what prereaders may acquire from corrective feedback in the deletion test is simply a technique of finding the first vocalic sound of the utterance as an attack point for the answer. More recently, L. Scliar-Cabral, L. Nepomuceno and J. Morais (unpublished data) have examined one case of an illiterate adult who seems to behave in the same way. We tested, in Brazil, a sample of more than 20 illiterate people on the initial consonant deletion task. We provided no corrective feedback and no training trials. The task was conveyed to the subjects by means of examples. We could not obtain a single correct response from any of the subjects, with the exception of a woman who, surprisingly, scored more than 50% correct. All the information we could collect about this woman seems to indicate that she had never been taught the alphabetic code. However, it would probably be a mistake to credit her with phonemic awareness. As a matter of fact, she was completely unable to perform a test of deletion of the initial segment when this was a syllabic vowel as in /afu/. Interestingly, most of the responses were repetitions; the subject tended to favour the same strategy, i.e. to begin with a vocalic sound, in both deletion tests. This led to a pattern of results, namely relatively good performance in consonant deletion, but a complete failure in vowel deletion, which we had never observed before in illiterate populations. Moreover, when tested on the classification of utterances according to the initial consonant or vowel, this 'exceptional' subject displayed the usual near chance-level score of illiterates. In conclusion we must be cautious in the interpretation of occasional good scores in so-called phonemic awareness tasks. Given that at least some of these tasks can be accomplished without the awareness of phonemes, it is important both to make a correct analysis of the demands of each task and, if possible, to compare performance obtained on several tasks.

The idea that children do not represent phonemes consciously as separate entities or concepts before they learn the alphabetic code is, at the very least, plausible. What reason could they do it for? What other function besides alphabetic literacy could phonemic awareness be indispensable to? Those who believe that phonemic awareness develops in children before they receive any instruction on the phonemic counterparts of letters should attempt to answer such questions.

Phonemic Awareness and the Knowledge of Grapheme–Phoneme Correspondences

We come back to the idea, developed in the first section, that a procedure of phonological assembly, which is based on the knowledge of grapheme-to-phoneme correspondence, is essential to the acquisition of reading in an alphabetic writing system. No one doubts that this knowledge of grapheme–phoneme correspondence requires explicit attention to graphemes, and at the very beginning attention to their concrete realisation, i.e. letters. Likewise, why should it be doubted that it also requires explicit attention to phonemes and, before that, attention to the phonological constituents of speech, because these provide the material for the conceptual derivation of phonemes? Some people might say that the acquisition of the knowledge of grapheme–phoneme correspondence is a case of implicit learning, i.e. without any consciousness of correspondence, at least of the simplest ones, between graphemes and phonemes. But we shall assume for a while that everybody rejects this idea, so that we can push the next question a step further and test an even stronger claim. If the knowledge of grapheme–phoneme correspondence can only be acquired by paying attention to both graphemes and phonemes, does this mean that knowledge can only be acquired through explicit instruction of the correspondence?

Byrne (1988) has provided data which suggest that phonemes are not spontaneously derived from sequences of symbols that represent them. He presented preliterate children with two-symbol sequences representing a CVC, and with the name of each sequence. Examples were such that in each sequence the first symbol corresponded to the initial C and the second to the VC. In a later phase, a correct choice between two new names of sequences would have indicated that the subjects had extracted the phonemic value of the first symbol. However, responses were at guessing level, and a further experiment involving both syllables and phonemes showed that the difficulty was specifically at the phonemic level. Moreover, additional training on the segmental structure of these names was ineffective. Correct choice between two new names required both phonemic training and the learning of symbol–sound correspondences. The clear implication of this study is that, without explicit instruction on the alphabetic code, i.e. of grapheme–phoneme correspondence, both phonemic awareness and reading novel material are hardly attainable, or perhaps impossible.

Further evidence, this time coming from a natural setting, has recently been obtained by J. Alegria, J. Morais and G. D'Alimonte (unpublished data). The aim of the study was to examine whether first-graders who learn to read without being informed explicitly of the alphabetic code, i.e. who learn to read according to a whole-word method, do develop phonemic awareness. We found a very small proportion of children who obtained good scores both on initial phoneme deletion and on a reading test. However, as mentioned above, the difficulty with the interpretation of these sorts of data is that we also need information about the instruction provided at home. Having questioned the parents of those children, we learned that the children had been taught the sounds of letters at home. This suggests, consistent with Byrne's (1988) findings, that the acquisition of phonemic awareness requires not only alphabetic literacy instruction but also explicit instruction on the alphabetic code.

Now, whatever the role of phonemic awareness in the acquisition of the grapheme–phoneme correspondence knowledge, this knowledge could also be attained in an implicit, unconscious way, through the information that the whole-word reader has about more global (either word-level or syllable-level) correspondence between the written words and their spoken names. In one experiment of the above-mentioned study (Alegria, Morais and D'Alimonte, unpublished data), we found a minority of children who were able to read pseudo-words whilst being unable to delete the initial consonant of an utterance intentionally. However, these results were probably unreliable, because these subjects, all from a highly literate milieu, were also relatively poor in syllable deletion. This led us to suspect that the use of pseudo-words in the deletion test may have prevented us from assessing correctly the real competence of these children in phonemic analysis. In a further experiment, in which the stimuli used for the deletion test were all real words, we did not find a single subject who, if able to read pseudo-words, would have been poor on deletion of the initial consonant. Thus, as with Byrne's (1988) results, ours argue against the idea that the knowledge of grapheme–phoneme correspondence is acquired in an implicit way.

The child who receives explicit information about the sounds of letters, for instance [pə] for 'p', is probably led to compare these sounds with other sounds ([pe, pε, pa] etc.), not only because they bear some phonological similarity, but also because the same letter is found in other clusters of letters (in French orthography, 'pe', 'pai', 'pa' etc.). This may be the first step to the analysis of speech into phonemes.

On the way from impressions of phonological similarity to phonemic conceptual analysis, the child is helped by the fact that, in some clusters of letters, the final letter (or letters) represents a sound that he or she can hear and pronounce in isolation. Of course, this makes the relationship between the recurring initial letter and what seems to make the sounds [pe, pε, pa] similar even more intriguing to the child. The pupil may not overlook the teacher's efforts to pronounce the stop consonant without a vowel. These efforts may induce an imitative behaviour, which in turn may have a positive effect in the discovery of the phoneme. Indeed, the child may discover some articulatory invariant in his or her own pronunciation of [pə, pe, pε, pa]. This articulatory invariance presumably helps the child to locate the phonetic component that makes all those short utterances sound strangely similar. The redundancy of auditory and articulatory cues, and their correspondence with a letter, allow the child to elaborate an abstract category which, intuitively, may seem perceptual, but actually is conceptual.

Even when the child has acquired a set of phonemic concepts, some problems both in conscious phonemic analysis and in literacy activities may remain. For instance, a child who has elaborated the concepts of /p/ and /l/ may not be able to transcode the perceptual representation of [ple, plε, pla] etc., into a sequence of abstract categories that include those two phonemes. Thus, in a deletion test, the child who correctly responds /e/ to [pe] or [le], may erroneously respond /e/ to [ple]. As far as literacy skills are concerned, the major and more persistent problems should occur in spelling rather than in reading. The starting point in spelling is either a perceptual representation (in the case of dictation) or some form of output lexical representation that may be consciously accessed. In this case, unless an orthographic or a phonemic-based representation is already consolidated, the speller must 'hear' in his or her head the sound of the intended word, i.e. form an auditory image of the word, and he or she thus encounters the same kind of difficulty as in the deletion task. In reading, however, the sight of each letter of the cluster should evoke the corresponding phonemic categories, and blending them is probably easy to do at this stage. The prediction is, therefore, that consonant clusters should yield more errors in spelling than in reading, during the initial stages of literacy acquisition. As far as I know, no direct comparison of such errors in reading and spelling has been attempted.

Werker, Bryson and Wassemberg (1989) have observed that disabled readers consistently make intrasyllabic additions, especially of liquids, when trying to read monosyllabic pseudo-words. This kind of error may be due to insufficient phonemic awareness. If the child is able to separate the two phonemes of a CV but unable to separate adjacent consonants such as /p/ and the liquid /l/ in /pl-vowel/ or /vowel-lp/, then when he or she encounters the letter 'p', this may stand for /p/, /pl/ and /lp/. When he tries to spell /pl/ and /lp/, the child may write 'p' (compare Stuart and Coltheart, 1988). This many-to-one mapping may affect reading the other way round. When presented with 'p' followed or preceded by a vowel, the child has no way of deciding between /p/, /pl/ and /lp/, and sometimes will read /pl-vowel/ or /vowel-lp/. The reverse mistake, i.e. reading 'pl' or /lp/ as /p/, should probably be less frequent, if the child already processes the phonemic category /l/ for the letter 'l'; thus, when 'l' is encountered, he or she would be unlikely not to read it. We need studies that would both make a fine analysis of reading and writing errors, and seek possible correspondence between these errors and levels of phonemic segmentation.

Having acquired simple, i.e. one-to-one, grapheme–phoneme correspondence, the child still has to learn that the phonemic values of letters may change in systematic ways as a function of the graphemic context; in other words, he or she has to learn complex grapheme–phoneme correspondences. Until the fourth grade, words which involve complex correspondences are usually read at a much lower accuracy level than words involving simple correspondences (A. Content, personal communication). It is reasonable to suggest that phonemic awareness plays a role in the acquisition of the complex correspondences. The fact that different letters may represent the same phoneme may contribute to the consolidation of the phoneme concept by ridding it of the ties with a visually coded representation. However, it is only after the phonemic analysis of the word's phonology has been made that it should be possible to notice that two or more phonemes are, in different contexts, coded by the same letter. Phonemic awareness thus probably helps the child to establish the rules of deviation from simple correspondence.

All the preceding remarks suggest that the acquisition of phonemic awareness and the acquisition of grapheme–phoneme correspondence knowledge are intimately related, although much work remains to be done in order to unravel these relationships. One interesting hypothesis to be tested is that, at the very beginning of reading acquisition, the major causal influence is from knowledge of simple correspondence rules to conscious phonemic ability rather than the reverse; and that, later on, there is the opposite asymmetrical relationship between the conscious phonemic ability and knowledge of complex correspondence rules. Reading of words characterised by simple correspondence rules might thus predict phonemic ability better than by using the latter to predict the former. On the contrary, phonemic ability might predict reading of words characterised by complex rules better than the reverse combination.

To what extent do phonemic awareness and grapheme–phoneme correspondence knowledge become separate capacities in the skilled reader? Our intuitive feeling is that we can think about, or even 'hear', the phonemes of words regardless of their mapping into letters. Furthermore, we seem to use the correspondence rules in an automatic way, without taking the time to think about phonemes. However, this apparent separation of the two capacities does not imply that the processing structures of the two capacities are separate. It would probably be difficult to design task interference situations that could provide useful information on this issue. It seems easier to examine a related neuropsychological issue: Are the two capacities represented in separate cerebral regions, or not?

With my colleague Phillipe Mousty, I have considered this question by testing two patients who display a selective impairment of phonological assembly and one who shows a selective impairment of orthographic reading. The performance of these acquired dyslexics in metaphonological tasks suggests that conscious phonemic abilities are selectively and severely affected by a lesion that affects phonological assembly. By contrast, the phonemic abilities of the 'surface' dyslexic, although not perfect, were relatively good. More evidence is needed, of course. In the meantime, the available data are consistent with the idea that phonemic awareness and phonological transcoding in reading and writing may be two functionally different aspects of the same capacity to represent the segmental constituents of language. If so, it would make sense that they depend on the same cerebral sites.

Acknowledgements

Preparation of this paper was supported by the Belgian Fonds de la Recherche Fondamentale Collective (Convention 2.4562.86) and the National Incentive Program for Fundamental Research in Artificial Intelligence. I thank Régine Kolinsky for helpful comments on a former version.

References

BACKMAN, J., BRUCK, M., HÉBERT, M. and SEIDENBERG, M.S. (1984). Acquisition and use of spelling–sound correspondences in reading. *Journal of Experimental Child Psychology* **38**, 114–133.

BERTELSON, P., DE GELDER, B., TFOUNI, L.V. and MORAIS, J. (1989). Metaphonological abilities of adult illiterates: New evidence of heterogeneity. *European Journal of Cognitive Psychology* **1**, 239–250.

BRYANT, P.E. and GOSWAMI, U. (1987). Beyond grapheme-phoneme correspondence. *Cahiers de Psychologie Cognitive* **7**, 439–443.

BRYANT, P.E., BRADLEY, L., MacLEAN, M. and CROSSLAND, J. (1989). Nursery rhymes, phonological skills and reading. *Journal of Child Language* **16**, 407–428.

BYRNE, B. (1988). Knowledge necessary for discovery of the alphabet principle. *Abstracts of the XXIV International Congress of Psychology*, S318.

CONTENT, A., MORAIS, J. and BERTELSON, P. (1987). *Phonetic segmentation in prereaders: A transfer of learning approach.* Paper presented at the Second Meeting of the European Society for Cognitive Psychology, Madrid.

CONTENT, A., KOLINSKY, R., MORAIS, J. and BERTELSON, P. (1986). Phonetic segmentation in prereaders: Effect of corrective information. *Journal of Experimental Child Psychology* **42**, 49–72.

DOCTOR, E.A. and COLTHEART, M. (1980). Children's use of phonological encoding when reading for meaning. *Memory and Cognition* **8**, 195–209.

FRITH, U. (1985). Beneath the surface of developmental dyslexia. In: K.E. Patterson, J.C. Marshall and M. Coltheart (Eds), *Surface Dyslexia: Neuropsychological and Cognitive Studies of Phonological Reading*, pp. 301–330. Hillsdale, NJ: Lawrence Erlbaum.

JORM, A.F. and SHARE, D.L. (1983). Phonological recoding and reading acquisition. *Applied Psycholinguistics* **4**, 103–147.

JUEL, C. (1988). Learning to read and write: A longitudinal study of 54 children from first through fourth grades. *Journal of Educational Psychology* **80**, 437–447.

KOLINSKY, R., CARY, L. and MORAIS, J. (1987). Awareness of words as phonological entities: The role of literacy. *Applied Psycholinguistics* **8**, 223–232.

LEROY-BOUSSION, A. (1975). Une habileté auditivo-phonétique nécessaire pour apprendre à lire: La fusion syllabique. *Enfance* **2**, 165–190.

LESGOLD, A.M., RESNICK, L.B. and HAMMOND, K. (1985). Learning to read: A longitudinal study of word skill development in two curricula. In: T.G. Waller and G.E. McKinnon (Eds), *Reading Research: Advances in Theory and Practice,* Vol. 4, pp. 107–137. New York: Academic Press.

LIBERMAN, I.Y., SHANKWEILER, D., FISHER, M.F. and CARTER, B. (1974). Explicit syllable and phoneme segmentation in the young child. *Journal of Experimental Child Psychology* **18**, 201–212.

MORAIS, J. (1990). Phonological awareness: A bridge between language and literacy. In: D. Sawyer and B. Fox (Eds), *Phonological Awareness in Reading: Evolution of Current Perspectives*, in press. New York: Springer Verlag.

MORAIS, J., CARY, L., ALEGRIA, J. and BERTELSON, P. (1979). Does awareness of speech as a sequence of phones arise spontaneously? *Cognition* **7**, 323–331.

MORAIS, J., BERTELSON, P., CARY, L. and ALEGRIA, J. (1986). Literacy training and speech segmentation. *Cognition* **24**, 45–64.

READ, C., ZHANG, Y., NIE, H. and DING, B. (1986). The ability to manipulate speech sounds depends on knowing alphabetic writing. *Cognition* **24**, 31–44.

SEYMOUR, P.H.K. (1987). How might phonemic segmentation help reading development? *Cahiers de Psychologie Cognitive* **7**, 504–508.

SEYMOUR, P.H.K. and MacGREGOR, C.J. (1984). Developmental dyslexia: A cognitive experimental analysis of phonological, morphemic and visual impairments. *Cognitive Neuropsychology* **1**, 43–82.

STUART, M. and COLTHEART, M. (1988). Does reading develop in a sequence of stages? *Cognition* **30**, 139–181.

WERKER, J.F., BRYSON, S.E. and WASSEMBERG, K. (1989). Toward understanding the problem in severely disabled readers. Part II: Consonant errors. *Applied Psycholinguistics* **10**, 13–30.

Chapter 8
Recent Work on Reading and Spelling Development

USHA GOSWAMI

Recently, an important advance has been made in work on the normal development of reading and spelling. This is the recognition that children's knowledge about the linguistic structure of the syllable plays an important part in what they learn about spelling patterns when they come to be taught to read and to spell. The kind of linguistic knowledge that is important is knowledge about the ways in which syllables can be subdivided into sounds. Perhaps most strikingly, this 'intrasyllabic' knowledge is usually developed *prior* to learning about print. It is purely phonological or sound based.

What is 'intrasyllabic' knowledge? Linguists hold differing views about the structure of syllables. According to the *linear* view, syllables are simply sequences of phonemes. A phoneme is the smallest unit of sound that can change the meaning of a word: 'pat' and 'bat' differ by a single phoneme. According to the linear view, a single-syllable word, such as 'trip', consists of the four phonemes /t/, /r/, /ɪ/ and /p/. An alternative view of syllabic structure, the *hierarchical* view, is that single syllables can be segmented into subunits that are larger than single phonemes. The two main subunits are called the *onset* and the *rime*. For a single-syllable word like 'trip', the onset would be /tr-/ and the rime would be /-ɪp/. The onset corresponds to the initial consonant(s) in words. The rime corresponds to the vowel and the final consonant(s). In our examples, both of these units contain two phonemes (i.e. /t/ and /r/ for the onset; /ɪ/ and /p/ for the rime). Onsets may be single phonemes, as in 'tip', where the onset is /t/. Rimes may also be single phonemes, as in 'tree', where the rime is /i/. In many words, however, the onset and rime units are larger than single phonemes.

The psychologist who has done most to draw attention to the possible importance of onsets and rimes for children's awareness of sounds within words is Rebecca Treiman. Phonological awareness (the ability to divide words up into their constituent sounds) has been recognised as an important component of reading and spelling development for some time (see review by Bryant and Goswami, 1987). However, early work concentrated on two levels of phonological awareness: the awareness of syllables (e.g. the recognition that a word like 'toybox' contained two syllables, 'toy' and 'box') and the awareness of phonemes (e.g. the recognition that 'box' contained three sounds, /b/, /ɒ/ and /x/).

Treiman pointed out that an intermediate level of phonological awareness might also be important – the awareness of onsets and rimes. She performed a series of experiments which showed that older children (8 year olds) found it easier to learn word games that required substitution of onsets and rimes (e.g. 'slu' for 'fru', requiring onset substitution) than games that required other substitutions (e.g. 'lug' for 'fog', which requires breaking up the rime) (Treiman, 1985). She also showed that 5 year olds had more trouble in making judgements about the beginning sounds in words (e.g. 's') when these judgements required segmenting the onset (e.g. 'sna') than when they did not (e.g. 'san'). So here at least is some evidence that onsets and rimes may be important to children.

What about reading? Both Treiman (1987) and Bryant and Goswami (1987) have suggested that these different levels of phonological awareness – syllabic, intrasyllabic and phonemic – may be important for the development of reading in different ways. It has been known for a long time that children are sensitive to rhyme long before they begin to learn to read (Lenel and Cantor, 1981; Maclean, Bryant and Bradley, 1987), and that sensitivity to rhyme is an important predictor of later reading development (Bradley and Bryant, 1985; Ellis and Large, 1987) as well as being linked to handicap (backwardness) in reading (Bradley and Bryant, 1978). Words that rhyme share common rimes. So the important phonological units prior to learning to read may be at the level of the syllable, the onset and the rime. Once a child has begun to read and so to learn about the alphabetic system, awareness of phonemes may develop, and may in turn help further in the development of reading and spelling.

In a recent review, we showed that there is a lot of evidence that this view of reading and spelling development may be correct (Goswami and Bryant, 1990). In this chapter, the focus will be on onsets and rimes. I will present recent evidence that onsets and rimes are important phonological units for children prior to learning to read and to spell. I will also discuss recent experiments which suggest that early reading partly depends on onset and rime units, and finally I will consider some evidence that early spelling also involves analysis at the onset–rime level.

Evidence for Early Awareness of Onsets and Rimes

One way of examining children's awareness of onsets and rimes is to give them a judgement task, in which they must decide whether different words begin or end in the same way. Bradley and Bryant (1978) developed just such a task for measuring children's awareness of rhyme: in their study, children had to spot the odd word out of sets of four words, such as 'weed', 'peel', 'need', 'deed', or 'red', 'fed', 'nod', 'bed'. These rhyme judgements involved rimes, as the odd word out had a different rime from the other words. However, the odd word also differed from the other words by only a single phoneme, rather than by an entire rime. Recently, Kirtley et al. (1989) adapted this method to study children's awareness of onsets and rimes in more detail.

Kirtley et al. wanted to find out whether oddity judgements were easier when onsets and rime units were involved in the judgement instead of single phonemes. They gave 5, 6 and 7 year olds an oddity task which either required them to make judgements on the basis of onsets and rimes, or on the basis of single phonemes. For example, in their *beginning* task, children had to select the odd word out of triples, such as 'doll', 'deaf' and 'can' (same initial consonant), or 'cap', 'doll' and 'dog' (same initial consonant and vowel (CV)). Both of these triples can be solved on the basis of the onset, although the former share one phoneme and the latter share two. In their *end* task, children had to select the odd word out of triples, such as 'mop', 'lead' and 'whip' (same final consonant), or 'top', 'rail' and 'hop' (same final VC). The former share only a single phoneme, whereas the latter share two phonemes and also a common rime.

If onsets and rimes are easier phonological units than phonemes for young children, the pattern of performance in the beginning and end tasks should differ. When judging beginning sounds, children should find the two beginning tasks equally easy, as both can be solved on the basis of the onset. The number of shared phonemes should not matter. However, for the two end tasks, one should be easier than the other. The shared VC task should be easy, as this is the one that can be solved on the basis of the rime. The task in which only the final consonant is shared should be difficult.

Kirtley et al. found exactly this pattern of results. Both beginning tasks were relatively easy, whether the matching words shared a vowel (cap, doll, dog) or not (doll, deaf, can). The end task requiring judgement on the basis of a single phoneme ('mop', 'lead', 'whip') was much more difficult than the end task requiring a rime judgement (top, rail, hop). These results held across all the three age groups tested. So children find it much simpler to break words up into onsets and rimes than into phonemic units. They only find phonemic judgements easy when single phonemes coincide with the onset.

Kirtley et al.'s result suggests that the natural phonological units for beginning readers are onsets and rimes. Support for this idea comes from a series of recent studies by Treiman and Zukowski (1990). They also tried to distinguish between judgements based on phonemes and judgements based on onsets and rimes, using a matching task in which children were introduced to a puppet who only liked certain sounds. If a pair of words shared a sound the puppet was happy, and if they did not he was sad. The children had to judge whether the puppet would like pairs of words that either shared common onsets, common rimes or common phonemes. For example, the pair 'plank' and 'plea' share a common onset, whilst 'spit' and 'wit' share a common rime. The pair 'plea' and 'pray' share a common initial phoneme, whilst 'rat' and 'wit' share a common final phoneme.

Treiman and Zukowski predicted that children would find the onset and rime judgements much easier than the phoneme judgements. They tested groups of 5-, 6- and 7-year-old children, and they found that all the age groups found the phoneme task (plea, pray; rat, wit) more difficult than the onset–rime task. However, within the onset–rime distinction, they found some evidence that judgements about rimes were easier than judgements about onsets. The children found it easier to judge whether the puppet would like pairs such as 'spit' and 'wit' than pairs such as 'plank' and 'plea'. This finding was difficult to interpret, because the onsets were all consonant clusters, whereas the rimes tended to involve single consonants. So the difference could have been to do with the number of consonants rather than with the units themselves. The study by Kirtley et al. (1989) suggests that, when both the onset and the rime contain a single consonant, then children's ability to make judgements about onsets and rimes does not differ significantly.

Evidence that Onsets and Rimes are Important in Reading

Recent investigations of children's phonological judgements have thus produced evidence that onsets and rimes are important phonological units for young children, units that are easier to deal with than phonemes. However, neither of the two studies described above directly examined reading. How important might onset and rime units be once written language is involved? My own recent research suggests that they are very important indeed.

When a child analyses a written word and tries to learn its sound, there are a number of different levels at which the analysis may take place. It may be at a global visual level, in which the shape of the word is matched to a sound pattern. An extreme example of this kind of global analysis occurs when a child learns to read a distinctive logo such as 'Pepsi', but such visual pattern recognition might underlie classroom word learning too. This is the level of analysis on which 'look-and-say' reading programmes are based.

A second possibility is that the analysis may be at the level of the individual letters in the word. This is the level of 'grapheme–phoneme correspondence', in which words are broken down into their constituent sounds on a letter-by-letter basis, and then these sounds are blended together into the spoken word. So the word 'cat' is built up from the sounds corresponding to the letters 'c', 'a' and 't'. This is the level of analysis at which traditional 'phonics' programmes of reading operate.

However, a third level of analysis is suggested by the recent research on children's recognition of onsets and rimes. At this level of analysis, children may break words down into the letter sequences corresponding to intrasyllabic units. The word 'cat' might initially be analysed into two units: 'c' (corresponding to the onset) and '-at' (corresponding to the rime). The spoken word 'cat' may be built up from these units. This third level of analysis may be easier for beginning readers than analysis at the phonemic level.

Do we have any evidence that young readers do analyse written words in this third way, extracting information about the sequences of letters that correspond to onsets and rimes? One way of studying this question is to ask how children transfer information about the relationship between spelling and sound between different words. When a child learns to read a new word, such as 'beak', we can measure how much he or she knows about the spelling–sound relationships in 'beak' by seeing whether learning this word helps him or her to read other words.

Given the three different levels of analysis distinguished above, there are three different levels at which we might expect any such transfer of knowledge to occur. At the first level, if 'beak' is learned as an unanalysed whole, then learning to read 'beak' should not help the child in reading any other words. At the second level, if 'beak' is analysed into the sequence of phonemes /b/, /i/, /k/, then learning 'beak' might help in reading other words that share these phonemes, such as 'bark'. Finally, if 'beak' is analysed into onset and rime units (the third level), then learning to read 'beak' should help in reading other words with common rimes, such as 'peak'.

Experimental evidence suggests that children quickly become able to analyse written words at the third of these three levels when they begin learning to read. Children aged from 5 to 7 years who are taught to read a 'clue' word such as 'beak' can use this word as a basis for reading new (test) words such as 'peak', 'weak' and 'speak' – words that share a rime with 'beak'. Children do not seem to use 'beak' to help them to read words that share common phonemes, such as 'bark' and 'bank' (Goswami, 1986, 1988a). Notice that the number of phonemes shared between the clue and test words is the same for both types of test word. 'Peak' and 'weak' share two common phonemes with 'beak' (/i/ and /k/), and so do 'bark' and 'bank' (/b/ and /k/). The important difference seems to be that the phonemes shared between 'beak' and 'peak' constitute the rime, whereas those shared between 'beak' and 'bank' do not. So it is the phonological status of the shared phonemes that is important (their status as onset and rime units), rather than the number of shared phonemes. Children's ability to use shared spelling sequences to make predictions about the pronunciations of new words has been described as reading by analogy.

However, 'beak' and 'peak' have something else in common as well as a shared spelling pattern. This is the fact that they rhyme. Obviously, these two things are intimately connected: the fact that the words share common spelling patterns for the rime allows children to predict that their pronunciations will rhyme. But it could also be the case that the presence of rhyme is helping children to read the 'analogous' test words by some kind of phonological priming, and that they are ignoring the common spelling patterns. This alternative explanation would mean that children may not be analysing the spelling patterns of the clue and test words at the onset–rime level at all.

If children are not paying attention to spelling patterns when they make analogies in reading, then they should be as likely to make analogies between rhyming words such as 'head' and 'said', which do not share spelling patterns for the rime, as between 'head' and 'bread', which do. The same clue word–test word technique can be used to examine what children do when asked to read these kinds of words. Goswami (1990a) taught children to read clue words such as 'head' and 'most', and tested transfer to new words such as 'said' and 'toast' (phonological priming words), as well as to words such as 'bread' and 'post' (analogous words). The analogous words shared the same spelling pattern for the rime and also rhymed with the clue words, whereas the phonological priming words had different spelling patterns for the rime even though they rhymed with the clue words. In this experiment, children showed significantly more transfer (i.e. made significantly more analogies) to the analogous test words than to the phonological priming words. So rime units do seem to play a genuine role when children are analysing the spelling patterns of written words.

Is there any evidence that onset units also play a role in childrens' analyses of the spelling patterns in written words? To test this idea, Goswami (1990b) examined analogies between consonant blends. A consonant blend at the beginning of a word constitutes the onset, e.g. the consonant blend 'tr' in the words 'trim', 'trap' and 'trot'. According to our argument, a child who learns to read 'trim' should analyse its spelling pattern into the units 'tr-' and '-im'. A consonant blend at the end of a word is part of the rime, for example the consonant blend 'sk' in 'desk', 'risk' and 'mask'. A child who learns to read 'desk' and then analyses its spelling pattern into onset and rime units should come up with the units 'd-' and 'esk'. So in the first case, the consonant blend might be transferred as a unit. In the second case, it might not.

This hypothesis about transfer was again tested with the clue word technique. If the onset is an important unit in analysing written words, then children who are taught to read a clue word such as 'trim' should make reading analogies to words such as 'trap' and 'trot'. Considerably less transfer would be expected to words such as 'tint' and 'torn', which share only the first sound of the onset (/t/). In contrast, when the shared consonant blend occurs at the end of a word, analogies between consonant clusters would not be predicted. A clue word such as 'desk' should not help in reading 'risk', because the shared consonant cluster is part of the rime.

This was exactly the effect found in a study with 6- to 7-year-old children. Those who were taught to read clue words such as 'trim' and 'flan' were helped in reading test words that shared common onsets, such as 'trap' and 'flop'. Those who were taught to read clue words such as 'desk' and 'wink' did not show transfer to test words such as 'risk' and 'tank'. So analogies were only made between consonant clusters when these corresponded to the onset. Analogies between consonant clusters were not made when they were part of the rime. So both onset and rime units seem to be important when children come to analyse written words.

The Relationship between Phonological Awareness of Onsets and Rimes and Analogies in Reading

At this point, an obvious question arises. Are children who are better at making phonological judgements about onsets and rimes the *same* children who make analogies between spelling patterns reflecting onset and rime units in reading? So far there is only a small amount of evidence on this question.

The evidence that we have comes from a study that measured the relationship between children's performance on a task measuring judgements about rime, and the same children's ability to make analogies between rimes in words (Goswami, 1990c). The rime judgement task was the Bradley and Bryant rhyme oddity task mentioned earlier. In this task, the children were asked to select the odd word out of sets of four words such as 'cat', 'hat', 'rat' and 'fan' (end sound different), or 'mop', 'hop', 'tap' and 'lop' (middle sound different). Both were judgements about rime. Children's use of analogies between the spelling patterns of the rimes in words was measured by the clue word task. Children were taught to read a clue word such as 'beak', and transfer to analogous words such as 'peak' and 'weak' was then examined. These analogies involved the spelling unit reflecting the rime.

First, it was found that performance in the two tasks was highly related. The Pearson Correlation Coefficients between the phonological tasks and the analogy measure were highly significant, being 0.61 (end sound) and 0.51 (middle sound) respectively (P values <0.01). However, these correlations on their own do not tell us very much. They could arise from a third variable common to both phonological judgements and reading analogies, such as general verbal skill.

To try and control for this possibility, children were also given a measure of general verbal ability – the British Picture Vocabulary Scales (Dunn et al., 1982). Performance on this task also correlated significantly with analogies between the rimes in words ($r = 0.55$, $P<0.01$)). This verbal measure was then entered as the first independent variable (the first step) in a fixed-order multiple regression, in which the dependent variable was the percentage of rime analogies that children made. The second step in the regression (the second independent variable) was performance in one of the oddity tasks. Fixed-order multiple regressions provide a way of examining the relationship between two variables after controlling for the effect of other extraneous variables which might create a spurious relationship between the two measures of interest. The extraneous variables are entered into the regression equation first, so that the amount of variance in the dependent variable that is due to these extraneous factors can be computed. The independent variable of interest is entered as the final step. By this stage all the variance in the dependent variable due to the extraneous variables has been accounted for and so, if the final step accounts for a significant amount of the remaining variance, then a genuine relationship can be said to exist between the independent variable of interest and the dependent variable.

In our case, we might expect that a significant relationship between rime analogies and rhyming judgements would still be found even after we have controlled for the effect of verbal skills. Two fixed-order multiple regressions were run to test this prediction, one for each oddity task (i.e. end sound different at step 2, and middle sound different at step 2, respectively). The results were the same in each regression: recognition of rime, as measured by the oddity tasks, was significantly related to rime analogies (P values <0.01), even after controlling for general verbal ability. This relationship was especially strong for rime analogies and the end sound different task, where it still accounted for 28% of the variance after controlling for verbal skill (for the middle sound different task, it was 15%). So judgements about rhyme and analogies about rimes in reading do seem to be connected.

However, it is still possible to argue that the relationship that we have found may not be a specific one between rime analogies and phonological judgements about rime. Instead, it may simply reflect the fact that there is a relationship between rime analogies and phonological ability as measured by the oddity task. To try and control for this second possibility, the children were also given a different phonological task: phoneme deletion. This task has been used as a phonological measure by Content et al. (1982). In the task, children heard words, such as 'peak' and 'bean', and were required to delete the initial phoneme in the words (the correct responses here would be '-eak' and '-ean'). This task can be described as an onset deletion task, but as the onset is also a single phoneme we will follow Content et al. and call it a phonemic task. Our question was whether the relationship that we had found between rime judgements and analogies between the spelling patterns representing the rimes in words would still be significant once phoneme deletion (another phonological task) was controlled.

This question was examined in a pair of three-step, fixed-order, multiple regressions, in which the percentage of rime analogies was again taken as the dependent variable. The three steps were: (1) performance on the British Picture Vocabulary Scales, (2) performance on the phoneme deletion task and (3) performance on one of the two oddity tasks. This second pair of multiple regressions showed that the relationship between rime analogies and rime judgements remained significant even after phonological skill, as measured by phoneme deletion, was controlled. Both the middle sound different and the end sound different tasks still accounted for a significant amount of the variance in rime analogies in these regressions (8.9% and 20.2% respectively). In contrast, if the equations were changed so that the phoneme deletion task was entered at step 3 and an oddity measure (end sound different) was entered at step 2, then no significant relationship between phoneme deletion and rime analogies was found.

This last set of results suggests that there is a strong and specific relationship between making phonological judgements about rimes and making analogies between spelling patterns that reflect the rime in reading. The relationship is independent of general verbal ability, at least as measured by the British Picture Vocabulary Scales. It is also specific to rime judgements, because performance on another phonological task (phoneme deletion) did not show the same pattern of results. However, at the moment we do not have any evidence about onsets. It would also be desirable to repeat the rime analogies study with a larger variety of phonological tasks. If phonological tasks at a number of levels (syllabic, onset–rime and phonemic) had been included in the Goswami (1990c) study, a stronger test of the specificity hypothesis would have been possible.

Evidence that Onsets and Rimes play a Role in Spelling

Finally we turn to the role of the intrasyllabic units of onset and rime in the development of spelling. Here too, recent research suggests that onsets and rimes have an important part to play in how children learn about written language.

When children learn to spell, they must analyse the sounds in the words that they wish to write, and then decide how to represent these sounds in print. As mentioned earlier, the smallest possible unit of analysis is the phoneme, and in most English spellings phonemes correspond to either one or two letters (for example, /t/ corresponds to 't', whereas /i/ corresponds to 'ee', 'ea' or 'ie'). However, onsets and rimes frequently correspond to sequences of letters, and this is particularly true of rimes. The rimes of simple words such as 'car', 'bell' and 'hen' contain the sequences of letters '-ar', '-ell' and '-en'.

There is also another point to notice about the rimes of these simple words: each rime also corresponds to the *name* of an alphabet letter, the letters R, L and N. So if we found that children's early spellings tended to omit vowels and to represent a whole rime by a single letter, this would be consistent with the possibility that the children were analysing the sounds of the words that they wanted to spell into onset–rime units and not into phonemes.

This elegant argument was first proposed by Rebecca Treiman. She collected an extensive corpus of children's early spelling errors, and analysed them for evidence of such a strategy (which we can call 'letter name spelling'). She found that children frequently spelled 'car' as 'CR', and hen as 'HN'. Her argument was that because the children were unaware that the rimes '-ar' and '-en' actually consisted of two sounds (phonemes) and not one (the rime), they used a single letter to represent these spellings.

Treiman also found that the children had difficulty in analysing onsets into their constituent sounds. This difficulty emerged when the onsets were consonant blends, such as 'bl-' in 'blow', 'st-' in 'haystack', or 'str-' in 'street'. Children's strategy with difficult onsets was simply to represent them by one letter in the blend, usually the first. This resulted in such misspellings as 'hasak' and 'set'. These misspellings are consistent with the idea that children initially hear the onset as a single unit, and find it difficult to analyse it into separate phonemes.

Treiman's evidence thus suggests that when children are trying to spell spoken words, they may begin by analysing them into onsets and rimes. Children may initially find it difficult to analyse spoken words into phonemes in spelling tasks. If these explanations of children's early attempts at spelling are correct, it would demonstrate that onsets and rimes play a role in early spelling as well as in early reading. Is there any direct evidence that children can learn spelling patterns for onsets and rimes in words when they begin to learn to spell?

One way of examining this question is to look at whether children use analogies in spelling in the way that they do in reading. If children are taught to spell a word such as 'beak', we can ask whether they will improve in spelling analogous words such as 'peak' and 'weak'. Notice that the analogy in spelling is between the sounds of the words. The child must notice that 'beak' and 'peak' sound the same at the end, and must reason that therefore they may be spelled with the same letters at the end.

Goswami (1988b) studied a group of 6-year-old children who were just beginning to learn how to spell. They could all spell simple words such as 'leg' and 'cut', but they were not very good at spelling words with vowel blends such as 'peak' and 'sail'. In the experiment, the children were taught to spell 'clue' words such as 'beak' and 'rail', and were then given analogous test words (e.g. 'peak' and 'sail'), or non-analogous test words (e.g. 'bask' and 'lain'), to try and spell. The results were very clear. Children improved significantly in spelling the analogous words that shared a rime with the clue words, words such as 'peak' and 'sail', compared to their ability to spell these words in a pre-test. But no improvement was found in spelling non-analogous words such as 'bask' and 'lain', even though these words shared grapheme–phoneme correspondences (e.g. /b/, /eɪ/) with the clue words.

Is this evidence for the importance of rimes in spelling? One possible objection is that, in spelling analogies, the clue word could be said to provide a better cue for the analogous test words than for the non-analogous test words, because the child's goal in spelling is to produce the correct letters to spell the (test) word. Although the analogous and non-analogous test words both shared grapheme–phoneme correspondences with the clue word, for the analogous words three of the letters in sequence were provided by the clue word. This in itself may have led to better spelling of the analogous test words, irrespective of the phonological status of the unit represented by these shared letters. We can test this idea by asking whether children will also transfer letter sequences at the beginnings of words. Children who are taught clue words such as 'beak' and 'rail' can also be asked to spell test words such as 'bean' and 'rain'. These words also share a sequence of three letters with the clue words, but the shared letters do not represent an intrasyllabic unit.

Children's ability to make analogies between the spelling sequences at the beginnings of words was actually tested in the same experiment (Goswami, 1988b). The results showed that the children were better at spelling end-analogous words such as 'peak' and 'sail' after they had learned to spell a clue word such as 'beak' and 'rail', than they were at spelling beginning-analogous words such as 'bean' and 'rain'. Although the shared spelling sequence at the beginnings of the words was helpful, the children used the spelling pattern of the clue word significantly less often to help with these beginning sequences than they did when the shared spelling sequences reflected the rime. So, children who were taught the spelling pattern of a word such as 'beak' did not make equal use of the spelling information about the beginning and end of the word. The extent to which they used the spelling patterns of the clue words in spelling the test words depended on whether the letter sequences coincided with intrasyllabic units (rimes) or not.

Conclusion

Whilst experimental work on the role of intrasyllabic units in the development of reading and spelling is still at an early stage, recent research suggests that their role is an important one. A number of exciting findings have already been made.

First, it is becoming clear that children's ability to make judgements about onset and rime units in spoken syllables is an important precursor of reading development. Kirtley et al. (1989) and Treiman and Zukowski (1990) have both shown that children aged between 5 and 7 years are much better at making phonological judgements about onsets and rimes than they are at making judgements about phonemes. So intrasyllabic units seem to be salient ones for young children prior to reading.

Secondly, we have evidence that when children begin to learn to read, and so have to analyse written words, the level of analysis seems to be at the onset–rime level rather than at the phonemic level. My own work (Goswami, 1986, 1988a, 1990b) has shown that children learn more about the letter sequences in single-syllable words that represent onsets and rimes than they do about letters representing single phonemes. Furthermore, they seem to be genuinely transferring information about spelling sequences in these experiments, as they do not make connections to the same extent about words that share rime sounds but that are spelled differently (Goswami, 1990a).

Thirdly, it seems to be that the same children who are skilled at making phonological judgements about rimes are the ones who are good at making analogies between the spelling patterns of rimes when they are reading. Children who do well in rhyme judgement tasks (such as the oddity task) make more rime analogies when they read new words (Goswami, 1990c). This relationship seems to be a specific one: it holds in spite of controls for verbal ability and phoneme deletion.

Finally, we have evidence that onset and rime units are also important in early spelling. The spelling strategies of beginning spellers are consistent with the idea that they are analysing words at the onset–rime level, as they frequently choose to represent a whole onset or a whole rime with a single letter (Treiman, 1990). Furthermore, when children are taught the spelling pattern of one word, they are better at transferring spelling information about the rime than about a spelling unit of equal letter length that is longer than the onset (Goswami, 1988b). So onset–rime knowledge is playing a role in analogies in spelling as well as in reading.

However, there is a lot that we still need to find out about how intrasyllabic knowledge effects reading and spelling development in normal children. For example, we need to know more about the role of onsets, and about exactly *how* intrasyllabic knowledge at the phonological level is related to the strategies that children adopt when they learn about written language. There are also interesting implications of this work for children with dyslexia, and these have hardly begun to be explored. For example, if dyslexic children find it more difficult to make judgements about onset and rime units in phonological tasks, then this difficulty may be related to their difficulties in learning about spelling patterns. There is some evidence that rhyming, which involves rime judgements, is impaired in dyslexic children (see Goswami and Bryant, 1990), and there is even some evidence that dyslexic children do not make connections between the spelling patterns representing shared rimes in words (Lovett et al., 1990). But the implications of intrasyllabic knowledge for handicap (backwardness) in reading are currently only beginning to be explored.

References

BRADLEY, L. and BRYANT, P.E. (1978). Difficulties in auditory organisation as a possible cause of reading backwardness. *Nature* **271**, 746–747.

BRADLEY, L. and BRYANT, P.E. (1985). *Rhyme and Reason in Reading and Spelling.* I.A.R.L.D. Monographs No. 1, Ann Arbor: University of Michigan Press.

BRYANT, P.E. and BRADLEY, L. (1985). *Children's Reading Problems.* Oxford: Basil Blackwell.

BRYANT, P.E. and GOSWAMI, U. (1987). Beyond grapheme-phoneme correspondence. *Cahiers de Psychologie Cognitive* **7**, 439–443.

CONTENT, A., MORAIS, J., ALEGRIA, J. and BERTELSON, P. (1982). Accelerating the development of phonetic segmentation skills in kindergarteners. *Cahiers de Psychologie Cognitive* **2**, 259–269.

DUNN, L.M., DUNN, L.M., WHETTON, C. and PINTILIE, D. (1982). *British Picture Vocabulary Scales.* Windsor: NFER-Nelson.

ELLIS, N.C. and LARGE, B. (1987). The development of reading: As you seek, so shall you find. *British Journal of Psychology* **78**, 1–28.

GOSWAMI, U. (1986). Children's use of analogy in learning to read: A developmental study. *Journal of Experimental Child Psychology* **42**, 73–83.

GOSWAMI, U. (1988a). Orthographic analogies and reading development. *Quarterly Journal of Experimental Psychology* **40A**, 239–268.

GOSWAMI, U. (1988b). Children's use of analogy in learning to spell. *British Journal of Developmental Psychology* **6**, 21–33.

GOSWAMI, U. (1990a). Phonological priming and orthographic analogies. *Journal of Experimental Child Psychology* **49**, 323–340.

GOSWAMI, U. (1990b). *Onset and rime units and transfer in reading.* Paper presented as part of a symposium on The Role of Orthographic and Phonological Knowledge in Beginning Reading at the Annual Conference of American Educational Research, Boston, USA, April 1990.

GOSWAMI, U. (1990c). A special link between rhyming skills and the use of orthographic analogies by beginning readers. *Journal of Child Psychology and Psychiatry* **31**, 301–311.

GOSWAMI, U. and BRYANT, P.E. (1990). *Phonological Skills and Learning to Read.* Hillsdale, NJ: Lawrence Erlbaum.

KIRTLEY, C., BRYANT, P., MacLEAN, M. and BRADLEY, L. (1989). Rhyme, rime and the onset of reading. *Journal of Experimental Child Psychology* **48**, 224–245.

LENEL, J.C. and CANTOR, J.H. (1981). Rhyme recognition and phonemic perception in young children. *Journal of Psycholinguistic Research* **10**, 57–68.

LOVETT, M.W., WARREN-CHAPLIN, P.M., RANSBY, M.J. and BORDEN, S.L. (1990). Training word recognition skills of reading disabled children: Treatment and transfer effects. *Journal of Educational Psychology* in press.

MACLEAN, M., BRYANT, P.E. and BRADLEY, L. (1987). Rhymes, nursery rhymes and reading in early childhood. *Merrill–Palmer Quarterly* **33**, 255–282.

TREIMAN, R. (1985). Onsets and rimes as units of spoken syllables: evidence from children. *Journal of Experimental Child Psychology* **39**, 161–181.

TREIMAN, R. (1987). On the relationship between phonological awareness and literacy. *Cahiers de Psychologie Cognitive* **7**, 524–529.

TREIMAN, R. (1990). *The Value of Independent Writing and Spelling.* Paper presented at the International Reading Association conference, Miami, USA, May 1990.

TREIMAN, R. and ZUKOWSKI, A. (1990). Children's awareness of rhymes, syllables and phonemes. In: S. Brady and D. Shankweiler (Eds), *Phonological Processes in Literacy*, in press. Hillsdale, NJ: Lawrence Erlbaum.

Part III
The Definition, Nature and Prevalence of Dyslexia

Chapter 9
The Theoretical and Practical Consequences of Discrepancy Definitions of Dyslexia*

KEITH E. STANOVICH

Introduction

Most professional and legal definitions of reading disability emphasize the existence of discrepancies between actual school achievement and assumed intellectual capacity. During the 1960s and 1970s, several proposed definitions of reading disability had considerable influence on both research and service delivery debates. The definition of the World Federation of Neurology had many features that became canonical for many researchers and practitioners. Specific developmental dyslexia was characterized as 'A disorder manifested by difficulty in learning to read despite conventional instruction, adequate intelligence, and socio-cultural opportunity. It is dependent upon fundamental cognitive disabilities which are frequently of constitutional origin' (Critchley, 1970, p. 11).

This particular definition highlighted the well-known 'exclusionary criteria' that subsequently caused much dispute in discussions of dyslexia (e.g. Applebee, 1971; Doehring, 1978; Eisenberg, 1978; Rutter, 1978; Ceci, 1986) – in particular it requires 'adequate' intelligence to qualify for the dyslexia label. The use of exclusionary criteria were carried over into the definition of learning disability employed in the landmark Legislation in the United States of America, such as the Education for All Handicapped Children Act (PL 94-142) passed in 1975. The National Joint Committee for Learning Disabilities (Hammill et al., 1981) responded to criticisms of the exclusionary criteria by proposing that learning disability may co-occur with mental handicap or other handicapping conditions, but that the learning disability is not the direct result of those conditions (see also Kavanagh and Truss, 1988).

*Portions of this chapter are adapted from material that has appeared in *Reading Research Quarterly* and *Learning Disability Quarterly*. Requests for reprints should be sent to Keith E. Stanovich, Department of Psychology, Oakland University, Rochester, Michigan 48309-4401,USA.

Regardless of how they deal with the issue of co-occurring disabilities, all of these professional and legal definitions highlight the same salient feature: the fact that a dyslexic child has an 'unexpected' disability in the domain of reading, one not predicted by his or her general intellectual competence and socioeducational opportunities. Practically, this has meant a statistical assessment of the difference between objectively measured reading ability and general intelligence (Shepard, 1980; Kavale and Nye, 1981; Reynolds, 1985; Frankenberger and Harper, 1987; Kavale, 1987). Typically, very little effort is expended in ascertaining whether adequate instruction has been provided or whether the child suffers from sociocultural disadvantage – in short, in ascertaining whether the disability is 'intrinsic to the individual'. So much conceptual confusion has surrounded the more operational discrepancy criterion that researchers and theoreticians have been reluctant to take on the potential additional complications of the other criteria. Briefly, despite repeated admonitions that the diagnosis of reading disability should be multidimensional (Tindal and Marston, 1986; McKinney, 1987; Johnson, 1988), in actual educational practice it is the assessment of a discrepancy between aptitude as measured by an individually administered intelligence test and reading achievement that is the key defining feature (Frankenberger and Harper, 1987). The choice of IQ test performance as the baseline from which to measure achievement discrepancies was accepted by teachers, schools, professional organizations and government agencies in the absence of much critical discussion or research evidence. Until quite recently, the field seems never to have grappled very seriously with the question of why the benchmark should have been IQ. It is thus not surprising that the concept of intelligence is the genesis of so many of the conceptual paradoxes that plague the concept of dyslexia (Stanovich, 1986a, 1986b, 1988b).

Why was professional assent to the use of IQ test scores in the discrepancy definition given so readily? Undoubtedly there were many reasons, but probably one factor was the belief that IQ scores were valid measures of intellectual potential. Certainly, an extreme form of this belief can be seen in the promotional activities of many advocacy groups and in media portrayals. The typical 'media dyslexic' is almost always a very bright child who is deeply troubled in school because of a 'glitch' (assumed to be biologically based, see Coles, 1978, 1987; McGill-Franzen, 1987) that prevents him or her from reading. This popular belief in the idea of 'unlocked potential' undoubtedly helped to fuel the rapid expansion of the learning disabilities field.

One major problem, however, was that most psychometricians, developmental psychologists and educational psychologists long ago gave up the belief that IQ test scores measured potential in any valid sense. Indeed, standard texts in educational measurement and assessment routinely warn against interpreting IQ scores as measures of intellectual potential (Thorndike, 1963; Cronbach, 1984; Anastasi, 1988). At their best, IQ test scores are gross measures of current cognitive functioning (Humphreys, 1979; Detterman, 1982). Therefore, we have been basing systems of educational classification in the area of reading disabilities on special claims of unique potential that are not psychometrically justifiable.

However, advocates of current practices might counter some of these criticisms by arguing that, despite conceptual difficulties, a strictly empirical orientation would support current procedures, i.e. an advocate of the status quo might argue that all of the philosophical and conceptual criticisms are beside the point, because measuring discrepancy from IQ in the current manner distinguishes a group of children who, cognitively and behaviorally, are sufficiently distinct so that the use of current procedures is justified on empirical grounds. Here we are getting to the heart of many recent research disputes.

The Construct Validity of Definitions of Reading Disability

The vast majority of poor readers in schools are, of course, not characterized by severe discrepancies between their reading ability and assessed intelligence (Eisenberg, 1979). Their below-average reading performance is predictable from their general cognitive abilities. They are what Gough and Tunmer (1986) term 'garden-variety' poor readers, and they tend to be more numerous than discrepancy-defined poor readers. The critical assumption that has fuelled theoretical interest in the dyslexia concept from the beginning – and that has justified differential educational classification and treatment – has been that the degree of discrepancy from IQ is meaningful: that the reading difficulties of the dyslexic stem from problems different from those characterizing the poor reader without IQ discrepancy; or, alternatively, if they stem from the same factors, that the degree of severity is so extreme for the dyslexic that it constitutes, in effect, a qualitative difference.

The operationalization of this assumption for purposes of empirical testing has been dominated by two different research designs. One is the reading-level match design (Bryant and Goswami, 1986), where an older group of dyslexic children is matched on reading level with a younger group of non-dyslexic children. The logic here is fairly straightforward. If the reading subskills and cognitive characteristics of the two groups do not match, then it would seem that they are arriving at their similar reading levels via different routes. In contrast, if the reading subskill profiles of the two groups are identical, this would seem to undermine the rationale for the differential educational treatment of dyslexic children and for their theoretical differentiation.

The second major design – one pertinent not only to theoretical issues but also to the educational politics of reading disability – is to compare dyslexic children with children of the same age who are reading at the same level, but who are not labelled dyslexic because they have lower IQs. Adapting the terminology of Gough and Tunmer (1986), I have termed this design the 'garden-variety control' design (Stanovich, 1988a). Again, the inferences drawn are relatively straightforward. If the reading subskill profiles of the two groups do not match, then this is at least consistent with the assumption that they are arriving at their similar reading levels via different routes. In contrast, if the reading subskill profiles of the two groups are identical, this would certainly undermine the rationale for the differential educational treatment of dyslexic children and would again make dyslexic children considerably less interesting theoretically.

Unfortunately, well-controlled studies employing the garden-variety control and reading-level match designs have begun to appear in sufficient numbers only recently. For a considerable period, the dyslexia literature was dominated by studies employing only chronological-age controls, a design of low diagnostic ability (Bryant and Goswami, 1986). It was not until the mid-1970s that we had the data from the ground-breaking epidemiological comparison of dyslexic and garden-variety poor readers conducted by Rutter and Yule (1975), and only in the last 5 years or so have their data been supplemented by other garden-variety control investigations. Additionally, only recently have enough studies employing reading-level matches been accumulated so that patterns are discernible.

Turning first to the latter, the data from investigations employing reading-level match designs were once a confusing mass of contradictions (see Stanovich, Nathan and Vala-Rossi, 1986), but have recently become considerably clarified. Olson and colleagues (Olson et al., 1990; J.P. Rack, M.J. Snowling and R.K. Olson, 1990, unpublished data) have recently completed a meta-analysis of these studies that explains some of the discrepancies in the literature. It appears that the cognitive profiles of discrepancy-defined dyslexic readers will not match those of younger reading-level controls. The dyslexics are actually inferior in the phonological processing domain (Bradley and Bryant, 1978; Snowling, 1980, 1981; Baddeley et al., 1982; Kochnower, Richardson and DiBenedetto, 1983; Olson et al., 1985, 1989; Snowling, Stackhouse and Rack, 1986; Holligan and Johnston, 1988; Siegel and Ryan, 1988; Aaron, 1989b; Lundberg and Hoien, 1989; Siegel and Faux, 1989; Bruck, 1990). Although there are some exceptions to this pattern in the literature (Beech and Harding, 1984; Treiman and Hirsh-Pasek, 1985; Vellutino and Scanlon, 1987; Baddeley, Logie and Ellis, 1988; Bruck, 1988), most of these can be explained by a variety of factors that Olson and colleagues (Olson et al., 1990; J.P. Rack, M.J. Snowling and R.K. Olson, 1990, unpublished data) discuss in their meta-analysis. The data from reading-level designs thus provide at least some modest support for the construct validity of the concept of dyslexia.

It has been considerably more difficult empirically to differentiate dyslexic subjects in garden-variety designs. Whilst some garden-variety comparisons have supported the idea of qualitative difference (Rutter and Yule, 1975; Horn and O'Donnell, 1984; Silva, McGee and Williams, 1985; Jorm et al., 1986; Aaron, 1987, 1989b; Ellis and Large, 1987), other investigations have demonstrated that it can often be surprisingly difficult to differentiate discrepancy-defined dyslexic readers from garden-variety poor readers (Taylor, Satz and Friel, 1979; Fredman and Stevenson, 1988; Siegel, 1988, 1989). Even Olson et al. (1989) have failed to find a correlation between degree of discrepancy within their sample of dyslexic twins and the degree of phonological deficit, a statistical test not quite equivalent to a garden-variety control design but troublesome nonetheless.

Regardless of how the muddled research evidence from the garden-variety designs is viewed, there is one conclusion that is forced by the very fact that the literature is so full of contradictions: namely, that this research has shown how surprisingly difficult it is to demonstrate cognitive differences among poor readers of differing IQs. I say surprising because it is *intelligence* that is supposed to be the more encompassing construct. Consider, for example, some data recently published by Siegel (1988). It is *reading skill* and *not* IQ that separates subject groups more strongly on such variables as visual processing, phonological processing, Illinois Test of Psycholinguistic Abilities (ITPA; Kirk, McCarthy and Kirk, 1968), performance, 'cloze' performance, sentence correction tasks, short-term memory tasks, working memory tasks, of course spelling, but also arithmetic performance, which tracks reading more closely than IQ. As a general cognitive probe, reading ability seems to be a more sensitive indicator than IQ test performance. Such findings prompt a rethinking of the very assumptions behind discrepancy measurement.

There are, indeed, further gaps in the empirical literature relevant to the issue of construct validity. For example, outside of the pioneering work of Lyon (1985) there are very few data on differential response to treatment. There are, for example, no good data indicating that discrepancy-defined dyslexics respond differently to various educational treatments than do garden-variety readers of the same age or than younger non-dyslexic children reading at the same level (Pressley and Levin, 1987; van der Wissel, 1987). This is not a trivial gap in our knowledge. Differential treatment effects are, in large part, the raison d'être of special education.

We are equally unenlightened on several other crucial issues. The data on differential prognosis for reading are contradictory. Rutter and Yule (1975) found differential growth curves for specifically disabled and garden-variety poor readers. The garden-variety poor readers displayed greater growth in reading but less growth in arithmetic ability than the specifically disabled children. However, this finding of differential reading growth rates has not been replicated in some other studies (van der Wissel and Zegers, 1985; McKinney, 1987; Share et al., 1987; Bruck, 1988; Labuda and DeFries, 1989). It now seems that a conclusion opposite to that of Rutter and Yule is justified. There seems to be no strong evidence indicating differential growth rates in reading for dyslexics and garden-variety poor readers.

Until convincing data on such issues as differential response to treatment are provided, the utility of the concept of dyslexia will continue to be challenged because the reading disabilities field will have no rebuttal to assertions that it is more educationally and clinically relevant to define reading disability without reference to IQ discrepancy (Seidenberg et al., 1986; Siegel, 1988, 1989; Share, McGee and Silva, 1989).

Problems Caused by Using IQ in Discrepancy Definitions

We are thus right back to the issue of why IQ scores should have been the benchmark from which to measure discrepancy in the first place. Indeed, it is surprising that for so long the concept of intelligence received so little discussion in the learning disabilities literature. Researchers and practitioners in the field do not seem to have realized that it is a foundation concept for the very idea of dyslexia. As currently defined, IQ is a superordinate construct for the classification of a child as reading disabled. Without a clear conception of the construct of intelligence, the notion of a reading disability, as currently defined, dissolves into incoherence.

But problems with the IQ concept are endemic. We should consider the fact that researchers, let alone practitioners, cannot agree on the type of IQ score that should be used in the measurement of discrepancy. For example, it has often been pointed out that changes in the characteristics of the IQ test being used will result in somewhat different subgroups of children being identified as discrepant and will also alter the types of processing deficits that they will display in comparison studies (Reed, 1970; Vellutino, 1978; Stanley, Smith and Powys, 1982; Lindgren, DeRenzi and Richman, 1985; Torgesen, 1985; Siegel and Heaven, 1986; Bowers, Steffy and Tate, 1988; Fletcher et al., 1989; Shankweiler et al., 1990). Yet it is not hard to look in the research literature and find recommendations that are all over the map. For example, a very common recommendation that is found in the literature is that performance and/or non-verbal IQ tests be used to assess discrepancy (e.g. Thomson, 1982; Beech and Harding, 1984; Perfetti, 1985, p. 180; 1986; Siegel and Heaven, 1986; Stanovich, 1986a) because verbally loaded measures are allegedly unfair to dyslexic children. In complete contrast, in a recent issue of *Learning Disabilities Research* devoted to the issue of measuring severe discrepancy, Hessler (1987) argues for the use of *verbally loaded* tests because

'Using a nonverbal test of intelligence because an individual has better nonverbal cognitive abilities than verbal cognitive abilities does not, of course, remove the importance of verbal processing and knowledge structures in academic achievement; it only obscures their importance and perhaps provides unrealistic expectations for an individual's academic achievement' (p. 46).

Of course, the use of full-scale IQ scores results in some unprincipled amalgamation of the above two diametrically opposed philosophies, but is still sometimes recommended precisely *because* the field is so confused and so far from consensus on this issue (Harris and Sipay, 1985, p. 145). Finally, there is a sort of 'either' strategy that is invoked by investigators who require only that performance *or* verbal IQ exceed 90 in dyslexic samples (e.g. Olson et al., 1985). As Torgesen (1986) has pointed out, the naturally occurring multidimensional continuum of abilities guarantees that such a criterion ends up creating more discrepancies with performance IQ.

The choice of different aptitude measures relates strongly to the possibility of isolating a modular cognitive dysfunction (see Stanovich, 1988b), perhaps in the phonological domain (Stanovich, 1988a), that differentiates dyslexic poor readers. The point is this: do we really want to look for a group of poor readers who are qualitatively differentiable in terms of etiology and neurophysiology? Officials at the National Institutes of Health, who are funding several program projects on the neurological, genetic and behavioral underpinnings of dyslexia, certainly want to look for such a group (Gray and Kavanagh, 1985). Many in the learning disabilities field share their enthusiasm for the quest to isolate – behaviorally, genetically and physiologically – a select group of 'different' poor readers.

Let us, for purposes of argument, accept this as a goal whether we believe in it or not. I want to argue that if we do, a somewhat startling conclusion results. The conclusion is that we must move away from measures of abstract intelligence as benchmarks for discrepancy analysis and towards more educationally relevant indices. In short, to get NIH's neurologically differentiable groups we need an aptitude benchmark of more educational relevance than IQ – than of non-verbal IQ in particular, contrary to some common recommendations.

However, it must be emphasized that the context for any such discussion must be the voluminous body of prior research on the cognitive correlates of individual differences in reading achievement. Our knowledge of the structure of human abilities in this domain puts severe constraints on the ability patterns that can be observed in studies of dyslexia. For example, an extremely large body of research has demonstrated that reading skill is linked to an incredibly wide range of verbal abilities. Vocabulary, syntactic knowledge, metalinguistic awareness, verbal short-term memory, phonological awareness, speech production, inferential comprehension, semantic memory and verbal fluency form only a partial list (Jackson and McClelland, 1979; Vellutino, 1979; Curtis, 1980; Frederiksen, 1980; Byrne, 1981; Carr, 1981; Chall, 1983; Stanovich, Cunningham and Feeman, 1984; Baddeley et al., 1985; Evans and Carr, 1985; Harris and Sipay, 1985; Palmer et al., 1985; Perfetti, 1985; Stanovich, 1985, 1986a; Just and Carpenter, 1987; Vellutino and Scanlon, 1987; Siegel and Ryan, 1988; Stanovich, Nathan and Zolman, 1988; Kamhi and Catts, 1989; Rayner and Pollatsek, 1989; Cunningham, Stanovich and Wilson, 1990; Rapala and Brady, 1990).

In contrast, the non-verbal abilities linked to reading are much more circumscribed (Vellutino, 1979; Carr, 1981; Aman and Singh, 1983; Stanovich, 1986a; Daneman and Tardiff, 1987; Hulme, 1988; Lovegrove and Slaghuis, 1989; but see Carver, 1990, for an opposing view). Here, the abilities associated with reading are more likely to be distinct and domain specific (e.g. orthographic storage, processing of certain spatial frequencies). In the verbal domain, however, there are many more abilities that are related to reading and that are more likely to have more global influences (e.g. inferential comprehension, verbal STM, vocabulary), thereby affecting general verbal IQ. Therefore matching dyslexics and non-dyslexics on performance IQ will necessarily lead to broad-based deficits on the verbal side. But even if there are visual/orthographic deficits linked to reading disability, the converse is not true. Because there are not as many reading-related non-verbal processes and because those that do exist will certainly be more circumscribed than something like vocabulary or verbal memory, verbal IQ matching will not necessarily result in dyslexic subjects with severely depressed performance IQs.

We will now travel across the continuum of potential aptitude candidates for discrepancy measurement with this research context and the goal of differentiating dyslexic children in mind. It immediately becomes apparent that the use of reading achievement discrepancies from performance IQ will make it extremely difficult cognitively to differentiate dyslexic children from other poor readers. Such performance-discrepancy dyslexics – because they are allowed to have depressed verbal components – will have a host of verbal deficits, some at levels higher than phonology, and they will not display the cognitive specificity required of the dyslexia concept. Torgesen (1986) has discussed how definitional practices which require only that verbal *or* performance scales be over some criterion value will have the same effect. The verbal scale is allowed to be considerably under that of the non-disabled control group, and it is not surprising that, subsequently, a broad range of verbal deficits is observed (see Vellutino, 1979). A behaviorally and neurologically differentiable core deficit will be virtually impossible to find, given such a classification.

In contrast, discrepancies based on verbal aptitude measures would be likely to isolate a more circumscribed disability that may be more readily identifiable by neurophysiological and/or genetic methods. Such a procedure would preclude the possibility of deficits in broad-based verbal processes. It could potentially confine deficits exclusively to the phonological module. For example, Bowers, Steffy and Tate (1988) demonstrated that if only performance IQ was controlled, dyslexic subjects were differentiated from non-dyslexics on the basis of rapid naming performance and on digit span and sentence memory. However, controlling for verbal IQ removed the association between reading disability and memory abilities. Importantly, an association with rapid naming remained. In short, verbal IQ control resulted in the isolation of a more circumscribed processing deficit.

Similarly, verbal IQ-based discrepancy measurement would be much more likely to demarcate a visual/orthographic deficit, if one exists (see Hulme, 1988; Lovegrove and Slaghuis, 1989; Solman and May, 1990; Willows, 1990). Verbal IQ matching in a comparison study would, of course, allow the performance IQs of the dyslexic group to fall below those of the control group. But since the number of non-verbal abilities linked to reading is much more circumscribed in the non-verbal than in the verbal domain, the groups would not become unmatched on a commensurately large number of abilities. Additionally, subtle, visually based deficits would not be 'adjusted away' by a procedure of performance IQ matching. Thus, verbal IQ control provides a greater opportunity for these visual/orthographic deficits — much harder to track than those in the phonological domain — a better chance to emerge in comparison studies. In summary, by adopting verbal IQ as an aptitude measure, we would be more likely to isolate a circumscribed deficit that would at least be more amenable to cognitive and neurological differentiation than are the samples of children defined by other methods.

Can we do without IQ? An Alternative Proposal

If we have come this far down the road of altering our treatment of IQ, why not go all the way? The learning disability field's seeming fixation on intelligence has driven a wedge between groups of investigators in the reading research community (McGill-Franzen, 1987). We have, for example, two organizations concerned with reading — the Orton Society and the International Reading Association (IRA) — who hold conventions with almost totally non-overlapping attendees; a strange state of affairs indeed and one directly attributable to how different subgroups within the reading community view the concept of dyslexia.

There is, however, a proposal for conceptualizing reading disability that could well result in a rapprochement between groups such as the IRA and the Orton Society. It is in fact a proposal that has been around for quite some time, but has never received a proper hearing because studies and definitions of dyslexia have so strongly emphasized the measurement of intelligence. In fact, many educationally oriented reading researchers have long suggested that measuring the discrepancy between reading ability and *listening comprehension* would be more educationally relevant and would seem to have been a more logical choice in the first place (see Durrell, 1969; Carroll, 1977; Carver, 1981; Hood and Dubert, 1983; Sticht and James, 1984; Gillet and Temple, 1986; Gough and Tunmer, 1986; Royer et al., 1986; Aaron, 1989a; Spring and French, 1990). Certainly, a discrepancy calculated in this way seems to have more face validity and educational relevance than the traditional procedure (Durrell and Hayes, 1969; Spache, 1981; Aaron, 1989a; Hoover and Gough, 1990). Children who understand written material less well than they would understand the same material if it were read to them appear to be in need of educational intervention. Presumably, their listening comprehension exceeds their reading comprehension because word recognition processes are inefficient and are a 'bottleneck' that impedes comprehension (Perfetti and Lesgold, 1977; Perfetti, 1985; Gough and Tunmer, 1986). Listening comprehension correlates with reading comprehension much more highly than full-scale or even verbal IQ. Children simultaneously low in reading and listening do not have an 'unexplained' reading problem (Carroll, 1977; Hoover and Gough, 1990), and we must always remember that the idea of 'unexplained' reading failure is the puzzle that enticed us into the idea of dyslexia in the first place.

As with verbal IQ, but only more so, listening comprehension isolates a modular deficit (Stanovich, 1988b), because in a comparison study dyslexic subjects would not become unmatched from non-dyslexics on a host of reading-related verbal abilities. In short, a large reading discrepancy from listening comprehension has probably isolated – as well as we are ever going to get it – a modular decoding problem that then may or may not be amenable to genetic and neurological analysis in the manner of the ongoing NIH program projects. It is indeed ironic that measuring discrepancies from listening comprehension – a procedure often suggested by those hostile to the dyslexia concept – may be just the procedure that allows those working from a neurological perspective to succeed in their quest.

There are, of course, several obstacles to implementing procedures of measuring reading disability with reference to discrepancies from listening comprehension. For example, whilst several individual measures of listening comprehension ability have been published (Durrell and Hayes, 1969; Carroll, 1972, 1977; Spache, 1981; CTB/McGraw-Hill, 1985) it may be the case that none has been standardized across the range of ages, nor attained the psychometric properties, to serve as an adequate measure from which to assess discrepancy (Johnson, 1988). Other complications may also arise, such as hearing problems or unfamiliarity with standard

English. However, many of these problems are no more severe for listening comprehension measures than they are for certain IQ tests. It is encouraging that work on listening comprehension as a diagnostic benchmark has recently been increasing in quantity, and some important progress is being made (see Horowitz and Samuels, 1985; Aaron, 1989a; Carlisle, 1989; Hoover and Gough, 1990; Royer, Sinatra and Schumer, 1990; Spring and French, 1990).

In light of the above arguments, it is important to state that educational practitioners may well want to demarcate children high in non-verbal abilities and simultaneously low in both listening and reading ability, and to give them special attention (this is a policy/political issue). But such children should not be considered dyslexic. They do not have a domain-specific difficulty in the area of reading if their general listening skills are also depressed. They may well present an important educational problem worth identifying and dealing with, but it is simply perverse to call them *reading* disabled. In a contentious field, one of the few areas of agreement is that 'The current sine qua non of learning disabilities is unexpectedly low achievement' (McLeskey, 1989, p. 435). We surely do not expect a child who does not comprehend spoken language to *read* well. Their poor reading is not unexpected; therefore they are not reading disabled. If the children would not understand the material were it spoken to them, then it would be highly unlikely that they would understand it when reading it (Carroll, 1977; Hoover and Gough, 1990). It cannot be sufficiently emphasized that to say this is not to deny that the child has an educational problem. It is simply to call for more logical consistency in our application of educational terminology and hence in our classification.

There remains, however, a further obstacle to measuring reading disability by reference to aptitude/achievement discrepancy – irrespective of the indicator used for the aptitude benchmark. Much evidence has now accumulated to indicate that reading itself is a moderately powerful determinant of vocabulary growth, verbal intelligence and general comprehension ability (Stanovich, 1986b; Share and Silva, 1987; Hayes, 1988; Hayes and Ahrens, 1988; Juel, 1988; Share, McGee and Silva, 1989; Stanovich and West, 1989; van den Bos, 1989; Cunningham and Stanovich, 1990). These reciprocal causation effects involving reading and other cognitive skills (Stanovich, 1986b) cause further problems for discrepancy-based classification. Such phenomena perniciously undermine the whole notion of discrepancy by weakening the distinction between aptitude and achievement. These effects indicate that the logic of the learning disabilities field has incorrectly assigned all of the causal power to IQ, i.e. it is reading that is considered to be discrepant from IQ rather than IQ that is discrepant from reading. However, such an assumption is unjustified given that there are potent effects running in both directions.

It appears, then, that any discrepancy-based conceptualization is going to require considerable refinement based on how the act of reading alters the course of development, bringing education-related cognitive skills more into congruence with age. Thus, conceptually justified discrepancy-based classification – even from listening comprehension – will be maddeningly tricky to carry out in a principled fashion.

Discrepancy Measurement: Where do we go from here?

The history of the concept of dyslexia has followed a confused 'cart before the horse' path in part because too many practitioners and researchers accepted at face value claims that IQ tests were measures of special 'unlocked potential' in particular groups of children with low reading achievement. We have seen that in the area of reading disability the notion of unlocked potential was misconceived, and that the use of certain types of IQ tests, particularly non-verbal or performance measures, will make it difficult empirically to differentiate dyslexic children from other poor readers.

An alternative proposal for measuring aptitude/achievement discrepancies with reference to listening comprehension ability was explored and found to be superior to that of IQ assessment. Nevertheless, it was argued that complications stemming from the increasing difficulty of differentiating aptitude from achievement as a child gets older will plague all efforts at definition based on the discrepancy notion. Problems such as these have led to Siegel's (1988, 1989) suggestion that reading disability be defined solely on the basis of decoding deficits, without reference to discrepancies from aptitude measures. Whether or not her proposal is adopted, the learning disabilities field is simply going to have to face up to the implications of current research findings, namely that:

1. Defining dyslexia by reference to discrepancies from IQ is problematic.
2. Much more basic psychometric work needs to be done in order to develop a principled method of discrepancy measurement from listening comprehension or some other verbal aptitude indicator.
3. If the field is unwilling to do the spade work necessary to carry out (2), or deems the potential benefit not worth the effort, then the only logical alternative is to adopt Siegel's proposal to define reading disability solely in terms of decoding deficiencies, without reference to aptitude discrepancy.

In summary, we are still in need of data indicating that the cognitive processing of dyslexic and garden-variety poor readers reading at the same level is reliably different, the data indicating that these two groups of poor readers have a differential educational prognosis, and the data indicating that they respond differently to certain educational treatments. These are, of course, the data that should have been presented in the first place, i.e. prior to the rapid expansion of discrepancy-based learning disabilities as a diagnostic and educational category.

References

AARON, P.G. (1987). Developmental dyslexia: Is it different from other forms of reading disability? *Annals of Dyslexia* **37**, 109–125.

AARON, P.G. (1989a). *Dyslexia and Hyperlexia*. Dordrecht, The Netherlands: Kluwer Academic.

AARON, P.G. (1989b). Qualitative and quantitative differences among dyslexic, normal, and nondyslexic poor readers. *Reading and Writing: An Interdisciplinary Journal* **1**, 291–308.

ADELMAN, K.A. and ADELMAN, H.S. (1987). Rodin, Patton, Edison, Wilson, Einstein: Were they really learning disabled? *Journal of Learning Disabilities* **20**, 270–279.

AMAN, M. and SINGH, N. (1983). Specific reading disorders: Concepts of etiology reconsidered. In: K. Gadow and I. Bialer (Eds), *Advances in Learning and Behavioral Disabilities*, Vol. 2, pp. 1–47. Greenwich, CT: JAI Press.

ANASTASI, A. (1988). *Psychological testing*, 6th Edn. New York: Macmillan.

APPLEBEE, A.N. (1971). Research in reading retardation: Two critical problems. *Journal of Child Psychology and Psychiatry* **12**, 91–113.

BADDELEY, A.D., LOGIE, R.H. and ELLIS, N.C. (1988). Characteristics of developmental dyslexia. *Cognition* **30**, 198–227.

BADDELEY, A.D., ELLIS, N.C., MILES, T.R. and LEWIS, V.J. (1982). Developmental and acquired dyslexia: A comparison. *Cognition* **11**, 185–199.

BADDELEY, A., LOGIE, R., NIMMO-SMITH, I. and BRERETON, N. (1985). Components of fluent reading. *Journal of Memory and Language* **24**, 119–131.

BEECH, J. and HARDING, L. (1984). Phonemic processing and the poor reader from a developmental lag viewpoint. *Reading Research Quarterly* **19**, 357–366.

BOWERS, P., STEFFY, R. and TATE, E. (1988). Comparison of the effects of IQ control methods on memory and naming speed predictors of reading disability. *Reading Research Quarterly* **23**, 304–319.

BRADLEY, L. and BRYANT, P.E. (1978). Difficulties in auditory organization as a possible cause of reading backwardness. *Nature* **271**, 746–747.

BRADLEY, L. and BRYANT, P.E. (1985). *Rhyme and Reason in Reading and Spelling*. Ann Arbor: University of Michigan Press.

BRUCK, M. (1988). The word recognition and spelling of dyslexic children. *Reading Research Quarterly* **23**, 51–69.

BRUCK, M. (1990). Word-recognition skills of adults with childhood diagnoses of dyslexia. *Developmental Psychology* **26**, 439–454.

BRYANT, P.E. and GOSWAMI, U. (1986). Strengths and weaknesses of the reading level design: A comment on Backman, Mamen, and Ferguson. *Psychological Bulletin* **100**, 101–103.

BYRNE, B. (1981). Deficient syntactic control in poor readers: Is a weak phonetic memory code responsible? *Applied Psycholinguistics* **2**, 201–212.

CARLISLE, J.F. (1989). The use of the sentence verification technique in diagnostic assessment of listening and reading comprehension. *Learning Disabilities Research* **5**, 33–44.

CARR, T.H. (1981). Building theories of reading ability: On the relation between individual differences in cognitive skills and reading comprehension. *Cognition* **9**, 73–114.

CARROLL, J.B. (1972). Defining language comprehension: Some speculations. In: J.B.T. Carroll and R. Freedle (Eds), *Language, Comprehension and the Acquisition of Knowledge*, pp. 1–29. Washington DC: W.H. Winston & Sons.

CARROLL, J.B. (1977). Developmental parameters of reading comprehension. In: J.T. Guthrie (Ed.), *Cognition, Curriculum and Comprehension*, pp. 1–15. Newark, DE: IRA.

CARVER, R.P. (1981). *Reading Comprehension and Rauding Theory*. Springfield, IL: Charles C. Thomas.

CARVER, R.P. (1990). Intelligence and reading ability in grades 2–12. *Intelligence* **14**, in press.

CECI, S.J. (1986). *Handbook of Cognitive, Social, and Neuropsychological Aspects of Learning Disabilities*, Vol. 1, Hillsdale, NJ: Lawrence Erlbaum Associates.

CHALL, J.S. (1983). *Stages of Reading Development*. New York: McGraw-Hill.

COLES, G.S. (1978). The learning-disabilities test battery: Empirical and social issues. *Harvard Educational Review* **48**, 313–340.

COLES, G.S. (1987). *The Learning Mystique*. New York: Pantheon.

CRITCHLEY, M. (1970). *The Dyslexic Child*. London: William Heinemann Medical Books.

CRONBACH, L.J. (1984). *Essentials of Psychological Testing*, 4th edn. New York: Harper & Row.

CTB/McGRAW-HILL (1981). *Listening Test*. Monterey, CA: Publisher.

CUNNINGHAM, A.E. and STANOVICH, K.E. (1990). Tracking the unique effects of print exposure in children: Associations with vocabulary, general knowledge, and spelling. *Journal of Educational Psychology* in press.

CUNNINGHAM, A.E., STANOVICH, K.E. and WILSON, M.R. (1990). Cognitive variation in adult students differing in reading ability. In: T. Carr and B.A. Levy (Eds), *Reading and Development: Component Skills Approaches*. New York: Academic Press.

CURTIS, M. (1980). Development of components of reading skill. *Journal of Educational Psychology* **72**, 656–669.

DANEMAN, M. and TARDIFF, T. (1987). Working memory and reading skill re-examined. In: M. Coltheart (Ed.), *Attention and performance*, Vol. 12, pp. 491–508. London: Lawrence Erlbaum Associates.

DETTERMAN, D. (1982). Does 'g' exist? *Intelligence* **6**, 99–108.

DOEHRING, D.G. (1978). The tangled web of behavioral research on developmental dyslexia. In: A.L. Benton and D. Pearl (Eds), *Dyslexia*, pp. 123–135. New York: Oxford University Press.

DURRELL, D.D. (1969). Listening comprehension versus reading comprehension. *Journal of Reading* **12**, 455–460.

DURRELL, D.D. and HAYES, M. (1969). *Durrell Listening–Reading Series*. New York: Psychological Corporation.

EISENBERG, L. (1978). Definitions of dyslexia: Their consequences for research and policy. In: A.L. Benton and D. Pearl (Eds), *Dyslexia*, pp. 29–42. New York: Oxford University Press.

EISENBERG, L. (1979). Reading disorders: Strategies for recognition and management. *Bulletin of the Orton Society* **29**, 39–55.

ELLIS, N. and LARGE, B. (1987). The development of reading: As you seek so shall you find. *British Journal of Psychology* **78**, 1–28.

EVANS, M.A. and CARR, T.H. (1985). Cognitive abilities, conditions of learning, and the early development of reading skill. *Reading Research Quarterly* **20**, 327–350.

FLETCHER, J.M., ESPY, K., FRANCIS, D., DAVIDSON, K., ROURKE, B. and SHAYWITZ, S. (1989). Comparisons of cutoff and regression-based definitions of reading disabilities. *Journal of Learning Disabilities* 22, 334–338.

FRANKENBERGER, W. and HARPER, J. (1987). States' criteria and procedures for identifying learning disabled children: A comparison of 1981/82 and 1985/86 guidelines. *Journal of Learning Disabilities* 20, 118–121.

FREDERIKSEN, J.R. (1980). Component skills in reading: Measurement of individual differences through chronometric analysis. In: R. Snow, P. Federico and W. Montague (Eds), *Aptitude, Learning, and Instruction*, Vol. 1, pp. 105–138. Hillsdale, NJ: Lawrence Erlbaum Associates.

FREDMAN, G. and STEVENSON, J. (1988). Reading processes in specific reading retarded and reading backward 13-year-olds. *British Journal of Developmental Psychology* 6, 97–108.

GILLET, J.W. and TEMPLE, C. (1986). *Understanding Reading Problems: Assessment and Instruction*, 2nd edn. Boston: Little, Brown.

GOUGH, P.B. and TUNMER, W.E. (1986). Decoding, reading, and reading disability. *Remedial and Special Education* 7, 6–10.

GRAY, D.B. and KAVANAGH, J.K. (1985). *Biobehavioral Measures of Dyslexia*. Parkton, MD: York Press.

HAMMILL, D., LEIGH, J., McNUTT, G. and LARSEN, S. (1981). A new definition of learning disabilities. *Learning Disability Quarterly* 4, 336–342.

HARRIS, A.J. and SIPAY, E.R. (1985). *How to Increase Reading Ability*, 8th edn. White Plains, NY: Longman.

HAYES, D.P. (1988). Speaking and writing: Distinct patterns of word choice. *Journal of Memory and Language* 27, 572–585.

HAYES, D.P. and AHRENS, M. (1988). Vocabulary simplification for children: A special case of 'motherese'? *Journal of Child Language* 15, 395–410.

HESSLER, G.L. (1987). Educational issues surrounding severe discrepancy. *Learning Disabilities Research* 3, 43–49.

HOLLIGAN, C. and JOHNSTON, R.S. (1988). The use of phonological information by good and poor readers in memory and reading tasks. *Memory and Cognition* 16, 522–532.

HOOD, J. and DUBERT, L.A. (1983). Decoding as a component of reading comprehension among secondary students. *Journal of Reading Behavior* 15, 51–61.

HOOVER, W.A. and GOUGH, P.B. (1990). The simple view of reading. *Reading and Writing: An Interdisciplinary Journal* 2, 127–160.

HORN, W.F. and O'DONNELL, J. (1984). Early identification of learning disabilities: A comparison of two methods. *Journal of Educational Psychology* 76, 1106–1118.

HOROWITZ, R. and SAMUELS, S.J. (1985). Reading and listening to expository text. *Journal of Reading Behavior* 17, 185–198.

HULME, C. (1988). The implausibility of low-level visual deficits as a cause of children's reading difficulties. *Cognitive Neuropsychology* 5, 369–374.

HUMPHREYS, L.G. (1979). The construct of general intelligence. *Intelligence* 3, 105–120.

JACKSON, M.D. and McCLELLAND, J.L. (1979). Processing determinants of reading speed. *Journal of Experimental Psychology: General* 108, 151–181.

JOHNSON, D.J. (1988). Review of research on specific reading, writing, and mathematics disorders. In: J.F. Kavanagh and T.J. Truss (Eds.), *Learning Disabilities: Proceedings of the National Conference*, pp. 79–163. Parkston, MD: York Press.

JORM, A., SHARE, D., MACLEAN, R. and MATTHEWS, R. (1986). Cognitive factors at school entry predictive of specific reading retardation and general reading backwardness: A research note. *Journal of Child Psychology and Psychiatry* 27, 45–54.

JUEL, C. (1988). Learning to read and write: A longitudinal study of 54 children from first through fourth grades. *Journal of Educational Psychology* **80**, 437–447.

JUST, M. and CARPENTER, P.A. (1987). *The Psychology of Reading and Language Comprehension*. Boston: Allyn and Bacon.

KAMHI, A. and CATTS, H. (1989). *Reading Disabilities: A Developmental Language Perspective*. Boston: College-Hill.

KAVALE, K.A. (1987). Theoretical issues surrounding severe discrepancy. *Learning Disabilities Research* **3**, 12–20.

KAVALE, K.A. and NYE, C. (1981). Identification criteria for learning disabilities: A survey of the research literature. *Learning Disability Quarterly* **4**, 363–388.

KAVANAGH, J.F. and TRUSS, T.J. (Eds) (1988). *Learning Disabilities: Proceedings of the National Conference*. Parkston, MD: York Press.

KIRK, S.A., McCARTHY, J.J. and KIRK, W.D. (1968). *The Illinois Test of Psycholinguistic Abilities*. Urbana, IL: University of Illinois Press.

KOCHNOWER, J., RICHARDSON, E. and DiBENEDETTO, B. (1983). A comparison of the phonic decoding ability of normal and learning disabled children. *Journal of Learning Disabilities* **16**, 348–351.

LABUDA, M. and DeFRIES, J.C. (1989). Differential prognosis of reading-disabled children as a function of gender, socioeconomic status, IQ, and severity: A longitudinal study. *Reading and Writing: An Interdisciplinary Journal* **1**, 25–36.

LINDGREN, S.D., DE RENZI, E. and RICHMAN, L.C. (1985). Cross-national comparisons of developmental dyslexia in Italy and the United States. *Child Development* **56**, 1404–1417.

LOVEGROVE, W. and SLAGHUIS, W. (1989). How reliable are visual differences found in dyslexics? *Irish Journal of Psychology* **10**, 542–550.

LUNDBERG, I. and HOIEN, T. (1989). Phonemic deficits: A core symptom of developmental dyslexia? *Irish Journal of Psychology* **10**, 579–592.

LYON, G.R. (1985). Educational validation studies of learning disability subtypes. In: B.P. Rourke (Ed.), *Neuropsychology of Learning Disabilities*, pp. 228–253. New York: The Guilford Press.

McGILL-FRANZEN, A. (1987). Failure to learn to read: Formulating a policy problem. *Reading Research Quarterly* **22**, 475–490.

McKINNEY, J.D. (1987). Research on the identification of learning-disabled children: Perspectives on changes in educational policy. In: S. Vaughn and C. Bos (Eds), *Research in Learning Disabilities*, pp. 215–233. Boston: College-Hill.

McLESKEY, J. (1989). The influence of level of discrepancy on the identification of students with learning disabilities. *Journal of Learning Disabilities* **22**, 435–438.

OLSON, R., KLIEGL, R., DAVIDSON, B. and FOLTZ. G. (1985). Individual and developmental differences in reading disability. In: T. Waller (Ed.), *Reading Research: Advances in Theory and Practice*, Vol. 4, pp. 1–64. London: Academic Press.

OLSON, R., WISE, B., CONNERS, F. and RACK, J. (1990). Organization, heritability, and remediation of component word recognition and language skills in disabled readers. In: T. Carr and B.A. Levy (Eds), *Reading and its Development: Component Skills Approaches*. New York: Academic Press.

OLSON, R., WISE, B., CONNERS, F., RACK, J. and FULKER, D. (1989). Specific deficits in component reading and language skills: Genetic and environmental influences. *Journal of Learning Disabilities* **22**, 339–348.

PALMER, J., MacLEOD, C.M., HUNT, E. and DAVIDSON, J.E. (1985). Information processing correlates of reading. *Journal of Memory and Language* **24**, 59–88.

PERFETTI, C.A. (1985). *Reading Ability*. New York: Oxford University Press.

PERFETTI, C.A. (1986). Continuities in reading acquisition, reading skill, and reading disability. *Remedial and Special Education* 7, 11–21.

PERFETTI, C.A. and LESGOLD, A.M. (1977). Discourse comprehension and sources of individual differences. In: M. Just and P. Carpenter (Eds), *Cognitive processes in comprehension*, pp. 141–183. Hillsdale, NJ: Lawrence Erlbaum Associates.

PRESSLEY, M. and LEVIN, J.R. (1987). Elaborative learning strategies for the inefficient learner. In: S.J. Ceci (Ed.), *Handbook of Cognitive, Social, and Neuropsychological Aspects of Learning Disabilities*, Vol. 2, pp. 175–212. Hillsdale, NJ: Lawrence Erlbaum Associates.

RAPALA, M.M. and BRADY, S. (1990). Reading ability and short-term memory: The role of phonological processing. *Reading and Writing: An Interdisciplinary Journal* 2, 1–25.

RAYNER, K. and POLLATSEK, A. (1989). *The Psychology of Reading*. Englewood Cliffs, NJ: Prentice Hall.

REED, J.C. (1970). The deficits of retarded readers—Fact or artifact? *The Reading Teacher* 23, 347–357.

REYNOLDS, C.R. (1985). Measuring the aptitude-achievement discrepancy in learning disability diagnosis. *Remedial and Special Education* 6, 37–55.

ROYER, J.M., KULHAVY, R., LEE, S. and PETERSON, S. (1986). The relationship between reading and listening comprehension. *Educational and Psychological Research* 6, 299–314.

ROYER, J.M., SINATRA, G.M. and SCHUMER, H. (1990). Patterns of individual differences in the development of listening and reading comprehension. *Contemporary Educational Psychology* 15, 183–196.

RUTTER, M. (1978). Prevalence and types of dyslexia. In: A. Benton and D. Pearl (Eds), *Dyslexia: An Appraisal of Current Knowledge*, pp. 5–28. New York: Oxford University Press.

RUTTER, M. and YULE, W. (1975). The concept of specific reading retardation. *Journal of Child Psychology and Psychiatry* 16, 181–197.

SEIDENBERG, M.S., BRUCK, M., FORNAROLO, G. and BACKMAN, J. (1986). Who is dyslexic? Reply to Wolf. *Applied Psycholinguistics* 7, 77–84.

SHANKWEILER, D., CRAIN, S., BRADY, S. and MACARUSO, P. (1990). Identifying the causes of reading disability. In: P. Gough, L. Ehri and R. Treiman (Eds), *Reading Acquisition*, in press. Hillsdale, NJ: Lawrence Erlbaum Associates

SHARE, D.L., McGEE, R. and SILVA, P. (1989). IQ and reading progress: A test of the capacity notion of IQ. *Journal of the American Academy of Child and Adolescent Psychiatry* 28, 97–100.

SHARE, D.L., McGEE, R., McKENZIE, D., WILLIAMS, S. and SILVA, P.A. (1987). Further evidence relating to the distinction between specific reading retardation and general reading backwardness. *British Journal of Developmental Psychology* 5, 35–44.

SHARE, D.L. and SILVA, P.A. (1987). Language deficits and specific reading retardation: Cause or effect? *British Journal of Disorders of Communication* 22, 219–226.

SHEPARD, L. (1980). An evaluation of the regression discrepancy method for identifying children with learning disabilities. *Journal of Special Education* 14, 79–91.

SIEGEL, L.S. (1988). Evidence that IQ scores are irrelevant to the definition and analysis of reading disability. *Canadian Journal of Psychology* 42, 201–215.

SIEGEL, L.S. (1989). IQ is irrelevant to the definition of learning disabilities. *Journal of Learning Disabilities* 22, 469–478.

SIEGEL, L.S. and FAUX, D. (1989). Acquisition of certain grapheme-phoneme correspondences in normally achieving and disabled readers. *Reading and Writing: An Interdisciplinary Journal* 1, 37–52.

SIEGEL, L.S. and HEAVEN, R.K. (1986). Categorization of learning disabilities. In: S.J. Ceci (Ed.), *Handbook of Cognitive, Social, and Neuropsychological Aspects of Learning Disabilities*, Vol. 1, pp. 95–121. Hillsdale, NJ: Lawrence Erlbaum Associates.

SIEGEL, L.S. and RYAN, E.B. (1988). Development of grammatical-sensitivity, phonological, and short-term memory skills in normally achieving and learning disabled children. *Developmental Psychology* 24, 28–37.

SILVA, P.A., McGEE, R. and WILLIAMS, S. (1985). Some characteristics of 9-year-old boys with general reading backwardness or specific reading retardation. *Journal of Child Psychology and Psychiatry* 26, 407–421.

SNOWLING, M. (1980). The development of grapheme–phoneme correspondence in normal and dyslexic readers. *Journal of Experimental Child Psychology* 29, 294–305.

SNOWLING, M. (1981). Phonemic deficits in developmental dyslexia. *Psychological Research* 43, 219–234.

SNOWLING, M., STACKHOUSE, J. and RACK, J. (1986). Phonological dyslexia and dysgraphia—a developmental analysis. *Cognitive Neuropsychology* 3, 309–339.

SOLMAN, R.T. and MAY, J.G. (1990). Spatial localization discrepancies: A visual deficiency in poor readers. *American Journal of Psychology* 103, 243–263.

SPACHE, G.D. (1981). *Diagnostic Reading Scales*. Monterey, CA: CTB/McGraw-Hill.

SPRING, C. and FRENCH, L. (1990). Identifying children with specific reading disabilities from listening and reading discrepancy scores. *Journal of Learning Disabilities* 23, 53–58.

STANLEY, G., SMITH, G. and POWYS, A. (1982). Selecting intelligence tests for studies of dyslexic children. *Psychological Reports* 50, 787–792.

STANOVICH, K.E. (1985). Explaining the variance in reading ability in terms of psychological processes: What have we learned? *Annals of Dyslexia* 35, 67–96.

STANOVICH, K.E. (1986a). Cognitive processes and the reading problems of learning disabled children: Evaluating the assumption of specificity. In: J. Torgesen and B. Wong (Eds), *Psychological and Educational Perspectives on Learning Disabilities*, pp. 87–131. New York: Academic Press.

STANOVICH, K.E. (1986b). Matthew effects in reading: Some consequences of individual differences in the acquisition of literacy. *Reading Research Quarterly* 21, 360–407.

STANOVICH, K.E. (1988a). Explaining the differences between the dyslexic and the garden-variety poor reader: The phonological-core variable-difference model. *Journal of Learning Disabilities* 21, 590–612.

STANOVICH, K.E. (1988b). The right and wrong places to look for the cognitive locus of reading disability. *Annals of Dyslexia* 38, 154–177.

STANOVICH, K.E. and WEST, R.F. (1989). Exposure to print and orthographic processing. *Reading Research Quarterly* 24, 402–433.

STANOVICH, K.E., CUNNINGHAM, A.E. and FEEMAN, D.J. (1984). Intelligence, cognitive skills, and early reading progress. *Reading Research Quarterly* 19, 278–303.

STANOVICH, K.E., NATHAN, R. and VALA-ROSSI, M. (1986). Developmental changes in the cognitive correlates of reading ability and the developmental lag hypothesis. *Reading Research Quarterly* 21, 267–283.

STANOVICH, K.E., NATHAN, R.G. and ZOLMAN, J.E. (1988). The developmental lag hypothesis in reading: Longitudinal and matched reading-level comparisons. *Child Development* 59, 71–86.

STICHT, T.G. and JAMES, J.H. (1984). Listening and reading. In: P.D. Pearson (Ed.), *Handbook of Reading Research*, pp. 293–317. New York: Longman.

TAYLOR, H.G., SATZ, P. and FRIEL, J. (1979). Developmental dyslexia in relation to other childhood reading disorders: Significance and clinical utility. *Reading Research Quarterly* **15**, 84–101.

THOMSON, M. (1982). Assessing the intelligence of dyslexic children. *Bulletin of the British Psychological Society* **35**, 94–96.

THORNDIKE, R.L. (1963). *The Concepts of Over- and Under-achievement*. New York: Teachers College, Columbia University.

TINDAL, G. and MARSTON, D. (1986). Approaches to assessment. In: J.K. Torgeson and B.Y.L. Wong (Eds), *Psychological and Educational Perspectives on Learning Disabilities*, pp. 55–84. New York: Academic Press.

TORGESEN, J. (1985). Memory processes in reading disabled children. *Journal of Learning Disabilities* **18**, 350–357.

TORGESEN, J.K. (1986). Controlling for IQ. *Journal of Learning Disabilities* **19**, 452.

TREIMAN, R. and HIRSH-PASEK, K. (1985). Are there qualitative differences in reading behavior between dyslexics and normal readers? *Memory and Cognition* **13**, 357–364.

VAN DEN BOS, K.P. (1989). Relationship between cognitive development, decoding skill, and reading comprehension in learning disabled Dutch children. In P. Aaron and M. Joshi (Eds), *Reading and Writing Disorders in Different Orthographic Systems*, pp. 75–86. Dordrecht, The Netherlands: Kluwer Academic.

VAN DER WISSEL, A. (1987). IQ profiles of learning disabled and mildly mentally retarded children: A psychometric selection effect. *British Journal of Developmental Psychology* **5**, 45–51.

VAN DER WISSEL, A. and ZEGERS, F.E. (1985). Reading retardation revisited. *British Journal of Developmental Psychology* **3**, 3–9.

VELLUTINO, F.R. (1978). Toward an understanding of dyslexia: Psychological factors in specific reading disability. In: A.L. Benton and D. Pearl (Eds), *Dyslexia*, pp. 59–111. New York: Oxford University Press.

VELLUTINO, F.R. (1979). *Dyslexia: Theory and Research*. Cambridge, MA: MIT Press.

VELLUTINO, F.R. and SCANLON, D.M. (1987). Phonological coding, phonological awareness, and reading ability: Evidence from a longitudinal and experimental study. *Merrill–Palmer Quarterly* **33**, 321–363.

WILLOWS, D.M. (1990). Visual processes in learning disabilities. In: B. Wong (Ed.), *Learning about Learning Disabilities*. New York: Academic Press.

Chapter 10
On Determining the Prevalence of Dyslexia

T.R. MILES

Introduction

It may perhaps seem curious at first glance that, although developmental dyslexia has been recognised for nearly 100 years and although a massive amount of research has been carried out, particularly in the last two decades, we still do not know with any degree of precision how many people in the general population are dyslexic. Many attempts have been made to summarise the evidence, for instance those by Hallgren (1950), Critchley (1970), Tansley and Panckhurst (1981) and Thomson (1989). What emerges, however, is a wide range of apparently conflicting percentages: some are as low as 0.05% and some as high as 30%.

It is obvious, of course, that different investigators were using different criteria. In particular, many of them were concerned to assess reading standards and may not therefore have wished to distinguish poor reading from what should strictly be called 'specific developmental dyslexia'. The limitations of such studies have been trenchantly criticised by Critchley (1970), who writes: 'To what extent these groupings represent a *melange* of the educationally inadequate, the intellectually deficient, the emotionally disturbed, the infirm of purpose, and the genuine dyslexics, has never been determined' (p.95).

Unfortunately, however, although there have been a number of *estimates* of the prevalence of dyslexia, there are not, as far as I know, any systematic population studies – none, at any rate, in which the distinctive characteristics of the dyslexic have been properly recognised. There have, of course, been studies of underachievement in reading, for instance those carried out in the Isle of Wight and elsewhere (for details see Yule et al., 1974), but it is impossible to say from the data provided how many of these underachievers were dyslexic. It seems, therefore, that we are forced to choose between questionable estimates of the prevalence of dyslexia and carefully conducted population studies into the prevalence of something else. What has so far been lacking is any population study explicitly aimed at discovering the prevalence of dyslexia.

It was in this context of uncertainty that Mary Haslum and I first tried to pick out dyslexics in the 1980 follow-up of the National Cohort Study. Our initial report (Miles and Haslum, 1986) was not concerned with prevalence as such, but rather with trying to convince doubters that the dyslexia concept was of value. We suggested that there was no point in using the word 'dyslexia' unless it stood for some kind of anomaly of development, and we contrasted 'anomaly' with 'normal variation'. The data were treated in a number of different ways and the combined effect was to show that the hypothesis of normal variation was untenable.

In the present chapter, I shall be using data derived from the Cohort Study to try to arrive at some kind of value for the prevalence of dyslexia. The task turned out to be no easy one as I attempt to indicate in the next section.

Some of the Difficulties

Investigation in large-scale surveys of children's medical or educational characteristics is liable to run into problems over the drawing of boundaries. In particular it is not always easy to distinguish the clear-cut cases from those that are marginal or doubtful. Dyslexia is no exception and, in attempting to determine its prevalence, there were a number of awkward issues which did not allow of easy solutions.

In the first place it may well be the case in this area, as in others, that nature is untidy, i.e. clear-cut boundaries do not exist. Many of those who work in schools for dyslexic pupils speak of 'grey areas' and of children with 'dyslexic tendencies', and this could be taken to imply not that a firm classification would be possible if more evidence were available but that some people are genuinely 'marginal'. Even if 'biological markers' for dyslexia were eventually to become available, for instance on the basis of neuroanatomical research, there might still be cases where it was impossible to assert decisively that such markers were or were not present.

Secondly, there is good reason to suspect that there are what Critchley and Critchley (1978) have called formes frustes of dyslexia, i.e. cases in which the condition, though present – and often occurring in a more severe form in other members of the person's family – does not constitute a major handicap. It is even possible, if Geschwind (1982) is right, that there can be 'dyslexia-related' conditions – in particular disorders of the autoimmune system – when literacy skills are largely unaffected. Clearly, however, there is no way in which the educational testing carried out in the present survey could have picked out children of this kind. Indeed, from a pragmatic educational point of view, it is arguable that no one can usefully be described as 'dyslexic' unless there is some degree of educational underachievement. In this respect, the situation is comparable to that of 'poor eyesight' or 'speech defect', where if an individual is only very mildly affected there is little point in saying that the condition is present. From a genetic point of view, of course, the position is different, because dyslexia in the genotype may not always show itself in the phenotype or may do so in only a very mild form. This, however, is a complication which could not be taken into account in the present study.

Thirdly, there is the factor of development (Frith, 1985; Snowling, 1987). Dyslexic children can learn and it is a somewhat fortuitous matter how much they happen to have learned at the time of a given survey. A child may be reading fairly adequately at the age of 10 years in spite of having been hopelessly behind at age 7, and even spelling may have improved if there has been appropriate tuition. If, however, as in the present investigation, no evidence is available as to how any of the children were performing at an earlier age, an important part of the picture is missing; as a result it becomes very much more difficult to distinguish a 'compensated dyslexic' from a normal reader or speller.

Fourthly, the amount of information available in respect of each child was limited. The precise tests which were used will be described in the next section. All that need be said here is that a diagnosis of dyslexia could have been made much more confidently had more been known about each child. The obtaining of additional data, however, would have been possible only at a prohibitive cost in terms of time and money.

Fifthly, since the tests were administered by many different teachers we cannot be fully sure that the instructions were always followed meticulously. This may or may not be a source of error, but it at least requires mention.

Finally, since the available data were in the form of test scores, there was the problem of how to choose the most appropriate cut-off points. Even if the decision is made to treat 'educational underachievement' as a necessary condition for dyslexia, there is still the problem of determining the point which most appropriately separates underachievers from normal achievers.

For all these reasons Dr Haslum and I decided that to attempt a 'head count' of the number of dyslexics would be unsatisfactory. In particular there was the risk that this would imply a degree of precision that was spurious and unjustified by our procedures. Instead, we thought it would be safer to offer alternative cut-off points both in respect of who was to count as an underachiever and who was to count as dyslexic. The resultant end-product would in that case not be a precise figure but an indication of possible upper and lower limits. The reader is thus offered a choice of criteria rather than being given fixed criteria.

Subjects and Procedure

The subjects of the study were all those children born in England, Wales and Scotland during the week April 5–11 1970. Data were collected at birth and, in 1975, when they were aged 5. In 1980, there was a follow-up in which the children were given a range of educational and cognitive tests. These included a word recognition test, a spelling test in the form of a dictation, three items from the British Ability Scales (Elliott, Murray and Pearson, 1983), namely Similarities, Matrices and Recall of Digits, and three items from the Bangor Dyslexia Test (Miles, 1982), namely 'Left–Right', 'Months Forwards' and 'Months Reversed'. The first requirement was to specify criteria for distinguishing those children who showed 'educational underachievement' from those who did not.

Now the commonly accepted criterion for underachievement is a discrepancy in the score on a reading or spelling test and the score on a test of intelligence. In the case of dyslexics, however, not every intelligence test is suitable, because, as Thomson (1982) has shown, there are certain subtests in the British Ability Scales at which dyslexics regularly perform badly; this is not, it seems, due to any lack of intelligence but is due to certain limitations imposed on them by their dyslexia. The Similarities and Matrices items, however, are not open to this objection. We therefore used the combined score on these two tests as a measure of general intelligence. To facilitate comparison, this score and the scores on the reading and spelling tests were standardised so as to give a mean of 100 and a standard deviation of 15. Then if either the reading or the spelling score fell below the intelligence score by more than a specified amount the child could be classed as an 'underachiever'.

Various methods of comparison would have been possible. For purposes of the present chapter, I decided simply to use the method of subtraction. The reading score was subtracted from the intelligence score, and similarly with the spelling score; whichever difference was the greater was treated as a measure of the child's underachievement. A further paper is planned (T.R. Miles and M.N. Haslum, unpublished data) in which linear regression will be used in place of subtraction.

The next requirement was to distinguish dyslexic underachievers from other underachievers. For this purpose the three items from the Bangor Dyslexia Test were used, along with the Recall of Digits item from the British Ability Scales. In the latter case, a result which was 1.5 standard deviations below the mean was scored as 'positive'. The other three items were scored in accordance with the instructions given in the manual: if the child showed distinctive difficulty the response was scored as 'plus' (or 'dyslexia positive'); if he or she showed no difficulty the response was scored as 'minus' (or 'dyslexia negative'), whilst those responses which could not be scored unambiguously as 'plus' or as 'minus' were scored as 'zero'. Our intention was to define a child as dyslexic if he or she came out as an underachiever and also showed a sufficient number of dyslexia positive indicators.

It should be noted that this procedure avoids any suggestion of 'definition by exclusion' and provides criteria by which dyslexic and non-dyslexic underachievers can be distinguished.

Results and Discussion

Scores were available in respect of 12 384 children.* What was needed, therefore, was to specify cut-off points in respect of both dyslexia and underachievement.

With regard to dyslexia, the evidence in Miles and Haslum (1986) had suggested that those with two or more 'positive indicators' on the 'dyslexia' items could reasonably be classed as dyslexic. In the present study, those who satisfied this criterion were said to be showing 'stronger evidence of dyslexia'. As has been indicated, however, we wished to give the reader alternative cut-off points and, in accordance with this policy, it was decided to create an intermediate group who were neither clearly dyslexic nor clearly non-dyslexic. These could be described as showing 'weaker evidence of dyslexia'. In this group were included all those who came out with one 'plus' and one 'zero' or with one 'plus' and two 'zeros'. All others were described as showing 'no evidence of dyslexia'.

With regard to underachievement, there were clearly many possible values for a discrepancy figure between reading or spelling score and Similarities plus Matrices score.

We also thought it would be helpful to check for what might seem to be indicators of dyslexia among normal achievers.

With these aims in mind we divided the cohort into six groups, as follows:

Group 1:   normal achievers; no evidence of dyslexia.
Group 2:   normal achievers; weaker evidence of dyslexia.
Group 3:   normal achievers; stronger evidence of dyslexia.
Group 4:   underachievers; no evidence of dyslexia.
Group 5:   underachievers; weaker evidence of dyslexia.
Group 6:   underachievers; stronger evidence of dyslexia.

Now if this subdivision had any validity, then despite any uncertainty about individual cases there would at least be a trend, namely that group

*The figure of 12 384 subjects in the present paper is larger than that (10 992) reported in Miles and Haslum (1986). When we wrote the 1986 paper we in fact warned (p.105) that it was an interim report only and that different uses of the data might be made in future publications. This is what we have now done, the result being a significant reduction in the number of 'missing data' entries; these will obviously vary according to which parts of the available information are used.

6 would contain the largest proportion of dyslexics and group 1 the smallest. There would be fewer dyslexics in group 5 than in group 6 and fewer still in group 4. Also, even if many of those in groups 3 and 2 came out as positive on the 'dyslexia' items for reasons not connected with dyslexia, we could not rule out the possibility that there might be a number of dyslexics in group 3 and, to a lesser extent, in group 2, who had learned to compensate for their handicap. The rank order of the groups in respect of the number of dyslexics that they contained would therefore be 6, 5, 3, 2, 4, 1.

At this point we came on a remarkable finding: we realised that there was an interesting way in which the validity of our procedure could be checked. This was because it is known independently that there are more dyslexic males than females (Hinshelwood, 1917; Orton, 1937; Mac-Meeken, 1939; Hallgren, 1950; Critchley, 1970; Goldberg and Schiffman, 1972; Hier, 1979; Finucci and Childs, 1981; Miles, 1983). Our classification would therefore be prima facie justified if the male:female ratio in the different groups was *also* in the rank order 6, 5, 3, 2, 4, 1. In addition, we decided that it would be helpful to examine how far this ratio varied in the different groups according to the cut-off point used for determining underachievement. We therefore examined the data with these two considerations in mind. The outcome is shown in Figure 10.1.

The differences between the groups are striking whatever cut-off point is chosen, and descending values of the male:female ratio turned out to be exactly as predicted. Also the fact that the boy:girl ratio is higher in group 3 and group 2 than in group 4 is support for the idea that in these two groups, particularly group 3, there were a number of genuine dyslexics who, because they had learned to compensate, were not sufficiently behind at reading or spelling to be picked out as underachievers. The slight preponderance of boys in group 4 is not unexpected in view of the many developmental anomalies to which they are prone (Hier, 1979). For present purposes, however, the most telling feature in the table is the way in which differences begin to occur in the boy:girl ratio in groups 5 and 6 when the discrepancy value reaches about 12 and become even more marked when it is 18 and over.

In the circumstances, it seemed to us to be appropriate to allow our choice of cut-off point to be influenced by these ratios. Indeed, it is hard to see what explanation of the changes in ratio there could be other than an increased number of dyslexics in the two groups.

In addition, given that we wanted to give the reader a choice of two cut-off points, the values of 12 and 18 seemed to make intuitive sense. If a value of over 18 had been specified, we would almost certainly have picked out only those dyslexics whose underachievement was extremely severe, whilst if a value of less than 12 had been chosen there could well have been a disturbing number of false positives.

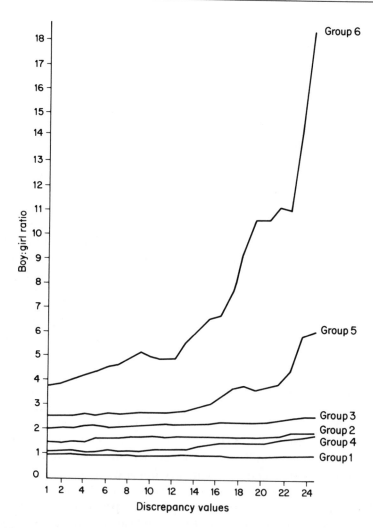

Figure 10.1 Discrepancy values and boy:girl ratios.

Table 10.1 shows the number of children in each of the six groups, first
if the discrepancy value between intelligence and reading or spelling is set
at 12 and secondly if it is set at 18. Now although, as was suggested above,
there may be some 'compensated dyslexics' in groups 3 and 2, there is no
way of knowing how many and, because the children in question do not
meet the criteria for underachievement, the reader may prefer not to count
them in any estimate of prevalence. It is also possible that there are some
'false negatives' in group 4 – underachievers who showed only minimal
signs of dyslexia on the four tests given but who might have shown further
signs had they been tested more fully. It is impossible to tell the exact

Table 10.1   Figures showing the numbers of children in the different groups (1) with a cut-off point of 12 and (2) with a cut-off point of 18*

Group	Cut-off point 12	Cut-off point 18
1	8091 (65.33)	9235 (74.57)
2	431 (3.48)	496 (4.01)
3	614 (4.96)	744 (6.01)
4	2725 (22.0)	1581 (12.77)
5	166 (1.34)	101 (0.82)
6	357 (2.88)	227 (1.83)
Total	12 384	12 384

*Percentages given in parentheses.

number, however, and it is also impossible to give the number of 'false positives' in groups 5 and 6. If we make the cut-off point 18 and assume that only those in group 6 are dyslexic, the prevalence figure comes out as 227 (1.83%), whilst if we also include group 5 the combined figure is 328 (2.65%). If the cut-off point is taken to be 12 the two figures are 357 (2.88%) and 523 (4.22%). Tentatively, therefore, a prevalence figure of between 2% and 4% could be suggested.

Concluding Remarks

The attempt to pick out dyslexics in a large-scale survey has both theoretical and practical implications.

On the practical side, it would perhaps be wise from the point of view of local educational authority planning to act on the assumption that a figure of 2% is an underestimate, because otherwise there is the risk that children who are significantly handicapped by dyslexia may not receive the help that they need. The evidence is now overwhelming that dyslexics are not just a heterogeneous group of underachievers and that, because of their distinctive weakness at certain kinds of task involving language and symbolism, distinctive teaching methods are needed (see, for instance, Miles and Miles, 1990). Moreover, in view of what can be achieved – at relatively modest cost – it would seem to be good policy to invest resources both in the training of teachers able to specialise in these methods and in the provision of awareness courses for non-specialists. In this connection, an overestimate of the number of dyslexics would do little harm, because there is no reason why the methods that have been found to be essential in the teaching of dyslexics should not also benefit other children; in contrast, an underestimate would be far more dangerous.

For research purposes the situation is different. For most types of research it is pointless, providing sufficient subjects are available, to run the risk of cluttering up the data with false positives, and there is therefore a very strong case for adopting more stringent criteria. The only exception to this is genetic research, where the formes frustes (Critchley and Critchley, 1978) and the compensated cases are of course very important.

The aim of the investigation, however, was not purely practical. Wittgenstein (1953, section 220) has said: 'In mathematics we sometimes say, Let the proof teach you what is being proved.' In the present paper one could perhaps substitute 'methods used' in place of 'proof'. The dictum would then be, 'Let the methods used for determining the prevalence of dyslexia teach you what "prevalence of dyslexia" might mean'. What has been offered here is a set of criteria, capable, if further research monies were available, of being considerably refined and enlarged, for distinguishing dyslexics both from normal achievers and from other underachievers. The fact that there is uncertainty about where precisely to draw boundaries does not mean that no boundary is possible. Indeed, however inadequate the tools in the present study, the attempt to specify adequate criteria for the drawing of a boundary is likely to be of more significance in the long run than a statement of precisely how many 10-year-old children in a particular survey were found to fall on one side of the boundary or the other. Basically, in exploring dyslexia we are exploring a proposed *taxonomy*, or method of classification and, as with any other proposed taxonomy, its advocates are logically committed to showing what can be done *with* it that cannot also be done *without* it. Mary Haslum and I plan in future studies to show how dyslexics differ not only from normal achievers but from other underachievers who are not dyslexic.

References

CRITCHLEY, M. (1970). *The Dyslexic Child*. London: Heinemann.

CRITCHLEY, M. and CRITCHLEY, E.A. (1978). *Dyslexia Defined*. London: Heinemann.

ELLIOTT, C.D., MURRAY, D.J. and PEARSON, L.S. (1983). *The British Ability Scales*. Windsor: NFER-Nelson.

FINUCCI, J.M. and CHILDS, B. (1981). Are there really more dyslexic boys than girls? In: A. Ansara, N. Geschwind, A.M. Galaburda, M. Albert and N. Gartrell (Eds), *Sex Differences in Dyslexia*. Towson, Maryland: Orton Dyslexia Society.

FRITH, U. (1985). Beneath the surface of developmental dyslexia. In: K.E. Patterson, J.C. Marshall and M. Coltheart (Eds), *Surface Dyslexia. Neuropsychological and Cognitive Studies of Phonological Reading*. London: Lawrence Erlbaum.

GESCHWIND, N. (1982). Why Orton was right. *Annals of Dyslexia* 32, 13–30.

GOLDBERG, H.K. and SCHIFFMAN, G. (1972). *Dyslexia: Problems of Reading Disabilities*. New York: Grune & Stratton.

HALLGREN, B. (1950). Specific dyslexia (congenital word blindness). A clinical and genetic study. *Acta Psychiatrica et Neurologica Supplementum* 65, i–xi, 1–287.

HIER, D.B. (1979). Sex differences in hemispheric specialisation: hypothesis for the excess of dyslexia in boys. *Bulletin of the Orton Society* 29, 74–83.

HINSHELWOOD, J. (1917). *Congenital Word-Blindness*. London: H.K. Lewis.

MacMEEKEN, M. (1939). *Ocular Dominance in Relation to Developmental Aphasia.* London: University of London Press.

MILES, T.R. (1982). *The Bangor Dyslexia Test.* Cambridge: Learning Development Aids.

MILES, T.R. (1983). *Dyslexia: The Pattern of Difficulties.* Oxford: Blackwell.

MILES, T.R. and HASLUM, M.N. (1986). Dyslexia: anomaly or normal variation? *Annals of Dyslexia* **36**, 103–117.

MILES, T.R. and MILES E. (1990). *Dyslexia: A Hundred Years On.* Milton Keynes: Open University Press.

ORTON, S.T. (1937). *Reading, Writing, and Speech Problems in Children.* New York: W.W. Norton.

SNOWLING, M.E. (1987). *Dyslexia: A Cognitive Developmental Perspective.* Oxford: Blackwell.

TANSLEY, P. and PANCKHURST, J. (1981). *Children with Specific Learning Difficulties: a Critical Review of Research.* Windsor: NFER-Nelson.

THOMSON, M.E. (1982). The assessment of children with specific reading difficulties (dyslexia) using the British Ability Scales. *British Journal of Psychology* **73**, 461–478.

THOMSON, M.E. (1989). *Developmental Dyslexia.* London: Whurr.

WITTGENSTEIN, L. (1953). *Philosophical Investigations*, translated by G.E.M. Anscombe. Oxford: Blackwell.

YULE, W., RUTTER, M., BERGER, M. and THOMPSON, J. (1974). Over and under achievement in reading: distribution in the general population. *British Journal of Educational Psychology* **44**, 1–12.

Chapter 11
Phonological and Visual Segmentation Problems in Poor Readers

RHONA JOHNSTON, MARJORIE ANDERSON and LYNNE DUNCAN

Introduction

In recent years, a great deal of research has emphasised the fact that many poor readers suffer from a phonological disorder. Some studies show poor auditory categorisation skills (Bradley and Bryant, 1978) and poor non-word naming (Snowling, 1980, 1981) for reading age. However, other studies show poor readers to have normal phonological skills for their reading age (Beech and Harding, 1984; Johnston, Rugg and Scott, 1987). The probable explanation of these disparate findings is that there are subgroups of reading disorders, and that group studies vary according to the proportions of poor readers suffering from the various types of disorders. Individual case studies do indeed support the idea of distinctive subgroups. One study has described an individual who relied on phonological information in word reading (Coltheart et al., 1983), and other studies have described individuals with phonological problems (e.g. Johnston, 1983; Temple and Marshall, 1983).

There is, however, a large literature showing visual disorders in poor readers. Since Vellutino's (1979) devastating attack on the visual deficit hypothesis, this literature has tended to be overlooked. One approach that Vellutino criticised was the attempt to show that poor readers have difficulty in detecting shapes embedded within more complex configurations. Several studies have shown this (Goetzinger, Dirks and Baer, 1960; Lovell, Gray and Oliver, 1964; Stuart, 1967), but Vellutino argues that as the poor readers performed normally on other visual analysis tasks they could not have had a deficiency in this area. However, it should not be assumed that all aspects of visual analysis will be found to be impaired in poor readers, in the same way that it is not argued that all aspects of phonological processing are impaired in these chileren.

Johnston et al. (1990) replicated the earlier finding that poor readers can have difficulty with visual segmentation tasks, and showed that this was in fact due to 40% of the sample performing more than two standard deviations below the mean of the chronological age controls, the rest performing in the low–normal range. However, they also showed that 35% of the sample performed poorly on a version of Bradley and Bryant's odd-word-out task, a quarter of the sample being very impaired on both tasks.

The aim of the current study was to examine whether patterns of strengths and weaknesses on visual and phonological segmentation tasks are associated with distinctive patterns of reading performance. Visual segmentation ability was again measured using the Children's Embedded Figures Test (Witkin et al., 1971), but phonological segmentation was now measured using a phoneme deletion task, where the child was read a word, e.g. 'flat', and asked what sound was left if the 'f' was removed.

Method – Subjects

Ten-year-old poor readers ($n=25$) with a mean reading age of 8 were compared with reading age ($n=26$) and chronological age ($n=22$) controls on a range of reading tasks. The children's reading was assessed by the British Ability Scales Word Recognition Test (Elliott, Murray and Pearson, 1977) and IQ was assessed by the short form of the Wechsler Intelligence Scale for Children (WISC; Maxwell, 1959). (See Table 11.1 for mean reading age, chronological age and IQ.)

Three subgroups of poor readers were identified on the basis of their visual and phonological segmentation scores, using the performance of Duncan's (1991) large sample of 10-year-old normal readers as a baseline. Five poor readers had normal visual segmentation skills for their chronological age, but had phonological segmentation scores appropriate for their reading age (subgroup 1). Three poor readers performed as their reading age controls on the visual and phonological segmentation tasks, performance on the latter task being similar to that of the first group (subgroup 2). Finally, four poor readers were identified who performed appropriately for reading age on the visual segmentation task, but who were very impaired even for their reading age on the phonological segmentation task (subgroup 3). (See Table 11.1 for mean reading age, chronological age and IQ for the subgroups of poor readers and their matched reading age controls.)

Procedure and Group Results

Four measures of reading and spelling were carried out. These are determined more fully in Johnston, Anderson and Duncan (1991). Initially, a group analysis was carried out to compare the poor readers, reading age and chronological age controls on these tasks, in order to obtain an overall impression of patterns of performance.

Table 11.1 Mean chronological age (CA), reading age (RA), spelling age (SA), IQ, and visual and phonological segmentation scores, groups and subgroups

	CA	RA	SA	IQ	Segmentation	
					Visual	Phonological
Phonological						
Poor readers	10;7	7;9	7;9	108.4	56.8	64.1
	(0.8)	(0.9)	(0.8)	(12.5)	(20.4)	(21.0)
Reading age	8;0	8;1	8;1	107.0	36.8	68.3
controls	(0.7)	(0.7)	(1.0)	(10.1)	(17.3)	(17.3)
Chronological	10;4	10;5	10;5	110.8	63.6	88.5
age controls	(0.7)	(0.9)	(0.9)	(12.1)	(17.7)	(7.1)
Subgroup 1						
Poor (*n*=5)	10;9	8;5	8;5	110.4	72.0	69.7
	(0.8)	(0.9)	(0.8)	(8.2)	(11.3)	(4.8)
RA (*n*=5)	8;0	8;5	8;5	109.2	44.8	74.6
	(1.0)	(1.2)	(1.7)	(9.3)	(17.3)	(17.8)
Subgroup 2						
Poor (*n*=3)	10;8	8;0	7;9	94.0	37.3	71.8
	(0.2)	(0.4)	(0.5)	(3.5)	(4.6)	(8.2)
RA (*n*=3)	8;3	8;1	8;1	96.3	24.0	66.6
	(0.4)	(0.4)	(0.4)	(9.5)	(6.9)	(12.7)
Subgroup 3						
Poor (*n*=4)	10;4	7;1	7;0	105.6	31.9	28.9
	(0.6)	(0.4)	(0.6)	(12.0)	(10.8)	(20.3)
RA (*n*=4)	7;1	7;3	7;1	102.9	25.0	63.6
	(0.2)	(0.3)	(1.1)	(8.4)	(6.0)	(27.1)

Standard deviations are given in parentheses.

Alternating case

The children were asked to read words with and without risers and descenders, e.g. 'plate' and 'cane', to see whether their reading accuracy was enhanced by these salient graphic features of the former items. Each item also appeared in both normal and alternating case, e.g. 'cream' and 'cReAm' – the means and standard deviations are shown in Table 11.2. Analysis of variance showed an interaction between groups and stimulus type: $F[2,70]=5.18$, $P<0.008$. Newman–Keuls tests showed that the poor readers and their reading age controls read words with risers and descenders better than those without, suggesting a logographic approach to reading, whereas the 10-year-old chronological age controls were unaffected by this manipulation. However, all of the groups performed less accurately when the stimuli were presented in alternating case: $F[1,70]=38.89$, $P<0.0001$.

Table 11.2 Mean percentage correct on alternating case, groups and subgroups

	Normal case		Alternating case	
	r/d[a]	No r/d[b]	r/d	No r/d
Poor readers	67.1	57.8	64.0	52.4
	(19.3)	(17.8)	(20.1)	(14.5)
Reading age controls	78.4	68.8	71.4	61.5
	(19.0)	(18.3)	(20.2)	(18.5)
Chronological age controls	97.5	94.4	91.1	90.4
	(2.9)	(5.7)	(5.6)	(9.4)
Subgroup 1 – poor	77.8	68.9	81.1	57.8
	(14.2)	(16.0)	(11.5)	(11.5)
Reading age controls	82.2	76.6	76.7	62.2
	(16.4)	(14.9)	(16.4)	(17.3)
Subgroup 2 – poor	66.7	70.4	72.2	51.8
	(5.6)	(8.5)	(5.6)	(6.4)
Reading age controls	77.8	66.7	70.4	64.8
	(24.2)	(5.6)	(22.4)	(6.4)
Subgroup 3 – poor	37.5	37.5	37.5	40.3
	(9.5)	(12.3)	(7.0)	(7.0)
Reading age controls	70.8	56.9	61.1	51.4
	(22.4)	(22.8)	(21.8)	(18.3)

Standard deviations are given in parentheses.
[a]With risers and descenders.
[b]Without risers and descenders.

Regularity effect

The children were given regular and irregular words of high and low frequency to read – the means and standard deviations are shown in Table 11.3. Analysis of variance showed an interaction between groups and regularity: $F[2,70]=7.41$, $P<0.001$. Newman–Keuls tests showed that the reading age and chronological age controls showed an advantage for regular words, indicating that they were using a phonological approach to reading, but the poor readers read regular and irregular words equally well. There was also an interaction between groups and frequency: $F[2,70]=18.22$, $P<0.0001$. Scheffé tests showed that, although all of the groups read high frequency words better than low frequency ones, this effect was larger in the reading age controls, the other two groups showing effects of similar magnitude.

One- and two-syllable non-words

The children were given lists of one- and two-syllable non-words to read, as a further measure of phonological skill in reading – the means and

Table 11.3 Mean percentage correct on regularity task, groups and subgroups

	High frequency		Low frequency	
	Irreg.	Reg.	Irreg.	Reg.
Poor readers	73.3	69.4	57.1	58.8
	(21.1)	(19.9)	(21.3)	(20.6)
Reading age controls	86.0	91.2	53.4	73.6
	(13.2)	(14.0)	(18.0)	(20.7)
Chronological age controls	96.4	98.4	83.1	94.8
	(4.8)	(3.8)	(12.4)	(6.8)
Subgroup 1 – poor	77.8	68.9	78.9	57.8
	(14.2)	(16.0)	(12.0)	(11.5)
Reading age controls	85.7	84.3	48.6	72.9
	(11.3)	(23.4)	(29.6)	(25.5)
Subgroup 2 – poor	81.0	90.5	64.3	66.7
	(14.9)	(4.2)	(7.2)	(18.0)
Reading age controls	83.8	92.9	46.2	78.5
	(10.9)	(12.4)	(9.7)	(18.9)
Subgroup 3 – poor	58.9	67.3	32.2	48.2
	(29.9)	(14.7)	(14.9)	(16.9)
Reading age controls	80.4	89.3	41.1	57.1
	(22.1)	(17.0)	(21.3)	(31.4)

Standard deviations are given in parentheses.

standard deviations are shown in Table 11.4. Analysis of variance showed an interaction between groups and syllable length: $F[2,70]=12.91$, $P<0.0001$. Newman–Keuls tests showed that the chronological age controls read two-syllable non-words better than the other two groups, and that the reading age controls performed better than the poor readers. However, the poor readers read one-syllable non-words as well as their reading age controls, but performed significantly worse than their chronological age controls.

Spelling

The children were asked to spell words and non-words with either high or low numbers of orthographic neighbours, e.g. 'barn', 'gulp'. The spelling errors were analysed according to Morris and Perney's (1984) developmental scheme. This classifies errors as *pre-phonetic*, e.g. motor- 'bott', grown – 'gneing', gulp – 'golp'; *phonetic 1*, e.g. wake – 'wak'; or *phonetic 2* ('transitional' in their terminology), wake – 'wacke'. The phonetic 2 errors were distinguished by the fact that they showed an emerging awareness of how to represent sounds according to the conventions of

Table 11.4 Mean percentage correct on non-word naming task, groups and subgroups

	One syllable	Two syllable
Poor readers	65.9 (18.7)	28.3 (22.7)
Reading age controls	79.9 (14.2)	43.7 (27.2)
Chronological age controls	86.6 (13.2)	73.9 (20.3)
Subgroup 1 – poor	56.0 (15.2)	21.0 (22.2)
Reading age controls	84.0 (15.2)	52.3 (26.0)
Subgroup 2 – poor	69.5 (15.0)	58.9 (8.4)
Reading age controls	81.7 (10.4)	43.6 (33.0)
Subgroup 3 – poor	65.0 (28.0)	16.3 (29.3)
Reading age controls	78.3 (11.8)	33.8 (28.4)

Standard deviations are given in parentheses.

English orthography. For example, the misspelling 'wacke' shows knowledge of the silent 'e' rule, which lengthens the vowel sound. This category closely resembles the 'phonetic' spelling errors of previous researchers (e.g. Nelson and Warrington, 1974).

As over one-third of the chronological age controls made no errors on at least one section of the task, a comparison was made between the poor readers and their reading age controls alone – the means and standard deviations are shown in Table 11.5. Analysis of variance showed no differences between groups, but an interaction was found between words–non-words, high–low orthographic neighbours and spelling error type. Newman–Keuls tests showed that, in response to low orthographic neighbour non-words, there were more pre-phonetic errors than either phonetic 1 and 2 errors, showing immature spelling of these items. The misspellings of the high orthographic neighbour non-words were a little more mature, there being more of the phonetic 2 than the phonetic 1 type; however, there were similar numbers of the pre-phonetic and phonetic 2 error types. The errors to words having either high or low orthographic neighbours were more consistent, there being more errors of the phonetic 2 type than of the less mature pre-phonetic and phonetic 1 type.

Subgroup comparisons

Subgroup 1

These children performed normally for their chronological age on the visual segmentation task, and similarly to their reading age controls on the phonological segmentation task. On the alternating case task, these poor readers showed an advantage for words with risers and descenders, as did their reading age controls. However, alternating case only impaired their

Table 11.5 Mean percentage spelling errors, pre-phonetic, phonetic 1 and phonetic 2, groups and subgroups

	Non-words			Words		
	Pre-phon.	Phon. 1	Phon. 2	Pre-phon.	Phon. 1	Phon. 2
Poor	40.3	27.0	32.7	26.5	14.9	58.6
readers	(18.2)	(16.3)	(19.3)	(17.3)	(11.9)	(18.2)
Spelling	46.6	17.6	35.8	29.6	16.6	53.8
controls	(24.1)	(18.1)	(22.9)	(25.7)	(13.4)	(23.0)
Subgroup 1	31.4	33.6	35.0	23.7	9.0	67.3
– poor	(13.6)	(15.6)	(22.8)	(16.3)	(9.3)	(21.9)
Spelling	57.1	9.2	33.8	49.6	7.6	32.8
controls	(18.0)	(14.6)	(18.0)	(17.6)	(8.2)	(22.4)
Subgroup 2	56.1	11.3	32.7	24.9	10.1	65.1
– poor	(13.7)	(12.0)	(25.6)	(9.7)	(5.8)	(14.4)
Spelling	35.3	27.4	37.3	37.5	14.3	48.2
controls	(18.3)	(21.9)	(9.2)	(40.2)	(14.3)	(33.6)
Subgroup 3	61.1	27.3	11.6	39.6	21.9	38.5
– poor	(15.5)	(14.5)	(2.4)	(25.8)	(9.6)	(18.5)
Spelling	57.6	9.5	24.5	40.9	14.5	44.7
controls	(30.3)	(8.0)	(21.4)	(29.7)	(9.8)	(22.5)

Standard deviations are given in parentheses.

performance on words without risers and descenders (see Table 11.2). On the regularity task, they showed a clear advantage for the irregular words, in marked contrast to their reading age and chronological age controls who showed the opposite effect (see Table 11.3). They found non-word naming very difficult, and were much worse at this task than their reading age controls (see Table 11.4). On the spelling task they showed an overall maturity compared to their spelling age controls, making a higher number of phonetic 2 responses to words, and more phonetic 1 and fewer pre-phonetic errors to non-words (see Table 11.5). This showed that they were capable of making phonetically accurate misspellings, despite a very visual approach to word reading, and very poor non-word naming.

Subgroup 2

This group performed similarly to the reading age controls on the visual and phonological segmentation tasks. Their performance on the phonological segmentation task was also very similar to that of the subgroup 1 poor readers. On the alternating case task, they actually found words without risers and descenders a little easier to read than those with these features when presented in normal case (unlike the reading age controls and the subgroup 1 poor readers), and only these items were affected by alternating case. However, words with risers and descenders were read better than those without when case was alternated (see Table 11.2). On the regularity task, there was a slight advantage for regular words on the high frequency items, but no such difference on the low frequency items (see Table 11.3). Interestingly, these children read long non-words quite well even for their reading age, and considerably better than the subgroup 1 children (see Table 11.4), with whom they were closely matched on the phonological segmentation task. In terms of spelling errors, their pattern of performance on words was very similar to that of the subgroup 1 poor readers, there being a high proportion of phonetic 2 misspellings. They also produced a similar number of phonetic 2 misspellings to non-words as their controls and subgroup 1 poor readers, but tended to have more pre-phonetic misspellings (see Table 11.3).

Subgroup 3

These children had visual segmentation skills similar to their reading age controls (and the subgroup 2 poor readers), but their phonological segmentation skills were much worse than those of their reading age controls. These children did not find words with risers and descenders easier to read than those without these features, and alternating case did not impair their reading (see Table 11.2). They showed a regularity effect, however, and read short non-words as well as the subgroup 2 poor readers (see Table 11.3). They were very poor at naming long non-words, their level of performance being similar to that of the subgroup 1 children, whose phonological segmentation skills were so much better than theirs (see Table 11.4). These poor readers tended to be immature spellers, producing fewer phonetic 2 misspellings to both words and non-words than their controls (see Table 11.5).

Correlational analyses

An analysis was made of the extent to which a visual approach to reading correlated with visual segmentation skills and IQ. These visual measures were calculated in the following way: for the regularity task, performance on regular words was subtracted from performance on irregular words for both high and low frequency words; on the alternating case task, performance on words with no risers and descenders was subtracted from performance on words with these features (for the normal case conditions only). As far as the poor readers were concerned, the advantage for high frequency irregular words correlated significantly with the advantage for words with risers and descenders: $r(23)=0.49$, $P<0.02$. These measures in turn correlated significantly with visual segmentation ability: $r(23)=0.53$, $P<0.01$ for the irregular word advantage, and $r(23)=0.44$, $P<0.05$, for the risers and descenders word advantage. Full-scale IQ correlated significantly with all of these variables: advantage for irregular words, $r(23)=0.55$, $P<0.01$, advantage for risers and descenders, $r(23)=0.62$, $P<0.01$, and visual segmentation ability, $r(23)=0.41$, $P<0.05$. None of these correlations was significant for the reading age or chronological age controls.

Discussion

This study shows that visual segmentation skills need to be taken into account when examining patterns of reading performance in poor readers, and that phonological segmentation skills alone do not provide an adequate explanation of how such children read. The subgroup 1 children were of particular interest. They were impaired on the phonological segmentation task for their chronological age but their naming of two-syllable non-words was much worse than would be expected both for their reading age and for their level of phonological segmentation skill. In terms of reading performance, they performed in a similar manner to the 'classic' developmental dyslexics described by Frith (1985), showing a logographic approach to reading.

Rather than describing the pattern of performance of subgroup 1 children purely in terms of their impaired phonological segmentation skills, a better understanding of their performance can be gained by taking into account their normal visual segmentation skills. These children were good at focusing on the parts within wholes, and this may have aided the detection of salient graphic features, such as risers and descenders, within words. By contrast, the other two subgroups of poor readers, who were impaired on the visual segmentation task, did not show this advantage for words with risers and descenders. Similarly, the subgroup 1 children read irregular words better than regular, whereas the other two subgroups did not. Their particularly severe deficit in reading two-syllable non-words seems to be more readily accounted for in terms of the overwhelmingly visual approach that they had to reading, rather than a severe deficit in phonological segmentation skill. There is evidence, however, of these children being able to use their phonological skills in spelling, as shown by the high percentage of phonetically acceptable spelling errors. In many ways this group of children is similar to Temple and Marshall's (1983) case H.M., who showed a phonological disorder in reading, but who spelt phonetically.

The subgroup 1 poor readers are also in some ways very similar to Funnell and Davison's (1989) subject Louise. She read words well, but was very poor at reading and spelling non-words. She was also poor at carrying out a phonological segmentation task. However, it was discovered that she read and spelt non-words very much better when she used the International Phonetic Alphabet. It was concluded that Louise's approach to reading novel stimuli presented in English orthography was a lexical one, which they described as 'lexical capture', and which led to very impaired non-word naming. It is possible that Louise in fact had very good visual segmentation skills, that she had capitalised on this strength when learning to read, and had consequently failed to use the phonological skills available to her.

Overall, this study shows that there is a good case for taking into account poor readers' visual as well as phonological segmentation skills when accounting for their patterns of reading performance. The actual levels of performance may not be as important as the *relative* strengths and weaknesses, which seem to interact in the reading process. The fact that a visual approach to reading correlated with both visual segmentation ability and IQ suggests that bright poor readers may have good pattern recognition skills available to them which they are able to use if their phonological segmentation skills are deficient. These findings may have implications for remediation, in that children with a strongly visual approach to reading may benefit from a remedial programme which helps them capitalise on their visual strengths as well as developing their phonological skills. However, it would be inadvisable to assume that visual and phonological segmentation deficits *cause* reading disorders, and further work will need to be carried out to examine these issues.

References

BEECH, J.R. and HARDING, L.M. (1984). Phonemic processing and the poor reader from a developmental lag viewpoint. *Reading Research Quarterly* **19**, 357–366.

BRADLEY, L. and BRYANT, P.E. (1978). Difficulties in auditory organisation as a possible cause of reading backwardness. *Nature* **271**, 746–747.

COLTHEART, M., MASTERSON, J., BYNG, S., PRIOR, M. and RIDDOCH, J. (1983). Surface dyslexia. *Quarterly Journal of Experimental Psychology* **35A**, 469–495.

DUNCAN, L. (1991). *Cognitive and perceptual impairments in poor readers.* Unpublished PhD thesis, University of St Andrews.

ELLIOTT, C.D., MURRAY, D.J. and PEARSON, L.S. (1977). *The British Ability Scales.* Windsor: NFER-Nelson.

FRITH U. (1985). Beneath the surface of developmental dyslexia. In: K. Patterson, J. Marshall and M. Coltheart (Eds), *Surface Dyslexia*. London: Erlbaum.

FUNNELL, E. and DAVISON, M. (1989). Lexical capture: A developmental disorder of reading and spelling. *Quarterly Journal of Experimental Psychology* **41A**, 471–487.

GOETZINGER, C.P., DIRKS, D.D. and BAER, C.J. (1960). Auditory discrimination and visual perception in good and poor readers. *Annals of Otolaryngology, Rhinology and Laryngology* **67**, 121–136.

JOHNSTON, R.S. (1983). Developmental deep dyslexia? *Cortex* **19**, 133–139.

JOHNSTON, R.S., ANDERSON, M. and DUNCAN, L. (1991). Strengths and weaknesses in the visual and phonological segmentation skills of poor readers: are they associated with differing reading strategies? In: G. Humphreys and J. Riddoch (Eds), *Cognitive Neuropsychology and Cognitive Rehabilitation*, in press. London: Erlbaum.

JOHNSTON, R.S., RUGG, M.D. and SCOTT, T. (1987). The influence of phonology on good and poor readers when reading for meaning. *Journal of Memory and Language* **26**, 57–68.

JOHNSTON, R.S., ANDERSON, M., PERRETT, D.I. and HOLLIGAN, C. (1990). Perceptual dysfunction in poor readers: evidence for visual and auditory segmentation problems in a subgroup of poor readers. *British Journal of Educational Psychology* **60**, 212–219.

LOVELL, K., GRAY, E.A. and OLIVER, D.E. (1964). A further study of some cognitive and other disabilities in backward readers of average non-verbal reasoning scores. *British Journal of Educational Psychology* **34**, 275–279.

MAXWELL, A.E. (1959). A factor analysis of the Wechsler Intelligence Scale for Children. *British Journal of Educational Psychology* **29**, 237–241.

MORRIS, D. and PERNEY, J. (1984). Developmental spelling as a predictor of first grade reading achievement. *The Elementary School Journal* **84**, 441–457.

NELSON, H.E. and WARRINGTON, E.K. (1974). Developmental spelling retardation and its relation to other cognitive abilities. *British Journal of Psychology* **65**, 265–274.

SNOWLING, M.J. (1980). The development of grapheme-phoneme correspondence in normal and dyslexic readers. *Journal of Experimental Child Psychology* **29**, 294–305.

SNOWLING, M.J. (1981). Phonemic deficits in developmental dyslexia. *Psychological Research* **43**, 219–234.

STUART, I.R. (1967). Perceptual style and reading ability. *Perceptual and Motor Skills* **24**, 135–138.

TEMPLE, C.M. and MARSHALL, J.C. (1983). A case study of developmental phonological dyslexia. *British Journal of Psychology* **7**, 517–533.

VELLUTINO, F.R. (1979). *Dyslexia: Theory and Research*. Cambridge, MA: MIT Press.

WITKIN, H.A., OLTMAN, P.K., RASKIN, E. and KARP, S.A. (1971). *Children's Embedded Figures Test*. Palo Alto: Consulting Psychologists Press Inc.

Chapter 12
Reading Development in Dyslexia: A Connectionist Approach

GORDON D.A. BROWN and FRANCES L. WATSON

Introduction: Models of Reading Development

Stage models and the dual-route approach

'Stage' models of reading development (e.g. Marsh et al., 1981; Frith, 1985) generally refer to early *logographic* (i.e. non-alphabetic) whole-word recognition of a small vocabulary, followed by an increasing awareness of the orthographic and sound structure of the language and the development of *alphabetic* reading of some variety. This requires the acquisition of knowledge about the regular spelling-to-sound mapping characteristics of English, along with knowledge of those words whose pronunciation is not predictable from their spelling. This stage is followed by increasing expertise leading to *orthographic* reading, with its emphasis on visual rather than (or in addition to) spelling-to-sound characteristics.

Thus, these descriptive models of normal reading development, and many models of skilled adult reading, typically postulate two processes by which words may be recognised. It is widely assumed that earliest reading is achieved by learning the visual forms of a small vocabulary. The subsequent ability to read new and unfamiliar words develops during an alphabetic stage where the child begins to abstract and learn letter–sound relationships, and so has access to a spelling-to-sound translation routine. The ability to recognise words by 'sounding out' continues and develops further as the child moves into an orthographic stage of reading where lexical representations of familiar words become accessible on the basis of orthographic segments. The final picture that emerges is one in which skilled readers have alternative strategies for decoding words available to them, and this is the notion embodied in 'dual-route' models of skilled reading processes.

Such models assume that there are both lexical and spelling-to-sound translation procedures operating in parallel when words are read aloud by skilled readers. Output phonology is either accessed directly from a stored lexical entry or (usually for less familiar or unknown words) constructed by means of an analysis of the spelling pattern.

Alternatives to the rule-based approach

The approaches to reading outlined above typically make reference to *rules* for translating written representations into phonological codes in reading. However, recent 'connectionist' models can associate different representations (such as orthographic and phonological strings) without reference to explicit rules of any kind. Instead, these models associate written word forms and their pronunciations by means of connections between simple representations of letters and sounds. The models can make use of learning procedures to adjust the strengths of connections between different representations in such a way that activation of a particular letter pattern can cause the corresponding pattern of sounds to become activated. Such models can exploit regularities and subregularities at many different levels in the mapping from spelling to sound without making use of spelling-to-sound rules (see Rumelhart and McClelland, 1986, for an introduction to connectionist models in general).

We shall be concerned with connectionist models of reading development in the present chapter. Most previous research which has adopted a developmental stage approach to describe reading development has been linked to the more traditional rule-based framework outlined earlier. In particular, it has often been assumed that developmental stages reflect reliance on one particular 'route' for spelling-to-sound translation.

It is therefore important to note that a connectionist approach does not preclude *describing* the development of reading in terms of progression through a series of stages. Descriptive accounts can be seen to stand or fall on their adequacy as descriptions, independently of whether the underlying mechanisms which give rise to different observed stages are best characterised as rule-based systems or connectionist systems. In the following survey of the relevant experimental evidence, we shall therefore attempt to remain neutral on the question of underlying mechanisms whilst assuming that it is possible to describe reading or spelling development in terms of a progression through identifiable stages.

The Development of Alphabetic Reading

The reading stage approach outlined above has been central to our current understanding of the nature of dyslexic reading difficulties. One major question is whether the development of reading in dyslexic children follows a normal pattern and is simply delayed, or whether the processes involved in dyslexics' word recognition differ from those used by normally achieving children. A predominant view is that dyslexic children have deficient phonological decoding skills and cannot rely on an adequate knowledge of letter–sound relationships to recognise single words. In terms of Frith's (1985) model, dyslexic reading development may be held back in the early logographic stage which precedes alphabetic reading, where a small vocabulary of words is learned and recognised on a purely visual basis. An alternative hypothesis is that dyslexic children are over-dependent on spelling-to-sound translation processes and continue to read alphabetically when normal readers have progressed towards an ability to recognise familiar words using direct visual access processes. These hypotheses predict opposite results in studies of non-word reading ability and the effects of phonological regularity on reading performance.

It has generally been assumed that greater use of phonological knowledge will be reflected in larger effects of phonological variables on a range of psychological tasks (see Barron, 1986, for a review). We focus here on single word reading, where the main evidence for the use of phonological knowledge has been the presence or absence of spelling-to-sound regularity effects on word naming. The logic is as follows: if words with pronunciations that are unpredictable from their written forms, such as HAVE (compare CAVE, RAVE, GAVE, SAVE etc.), are read less well by a child than predictable words such as HILL (compare MILL, KILL, FILL etc.), then this must reflect the use of spelling-to-sound translation by that child. Thus reading of regular and irregular words has frequently been used to assess the relative levels of spelling-to-sound translation ability in different groups of subjects. Whilst non-word reading ability can give a global assessment of phonological decoding skill, only comparisons between the different word types can indicate the degree to which spelling-to-sound skills are being used relative to purely visual decoding.

We now review previous research that has adopted the single word reading methodology. In one study comparing older and younger good readers, Backman et al. (1984) provided evidence for the use of different processes at different levels of ability. They suggested that the younger or less able groups were using alphabetic strategies (as evidenced by a spelling-to-sound regularity effect on their errors) whilst the older readers, whose error rate did not vary across word types, were using direct visual access processes in their reading. Backman et al. conclude that the ability to read irregular words clearly distinguishes skilled (orthographic) reading from less skilled (mainly alphabetic) reading. Consequently, the assessment of spelling-to-sound regularity effects in groups of readers with varying levels of ability and with specific reading disabilities provides a window onto the developmental stages and processes involved in normal and dyslexic reading.

Other studies have also examined developmental trends in normal readers (e.g. Szeszulski and Manis, 1987; Siegel and Ryan, 1988). These studies have looked primarily at error rates, and generally find larger spelling-to-sound regularity effects for younger children. There is, however, a difficulty in interpreting the decrease in regularity effects with age, because older subjects make far fewer errors overall. The possibility that ceiling effects could account for the reported interactions between regularity and subject age in normal readers is evident from the results described in the papers cited above. This makes it desirable to examine naming latency data as well as error rates, because ceiling effects are less likely to arise in reaction time studies. There are, however, methodological difficulties in obtaining reliable latency data from young children and research that has adopted this methodology has produced mixed results (Barron, 1980; Backman et al, 1984; Schlapp and Underwood, 1988).

Regularity effects and alphabetic reading in dyslexia

Because the spelling-to-sound regularity effects can be used as a measure for the presence or absence of alphabetic reading, several studies have used this methodology to examine the nature of the deficit in developmental dyslexia.

The absence of a spelling–sound regularity effect in dyslexia would be consistent with Frith's (1985) suggestion that dyslexic children may have difficulty in 'breaking through' to an alphabetic strategy in decoding, because whole-word lexical access (the assumed alternative) should lead to there being no effects of spelling–sound characteristics. (Here we ignore the possibility of individual differences and subgroups within reading-disabled populations – compare Seymour, 1986.) We should note that reduced effects of spelling-to-sound regularity could emerge either as a result of arrest at the logographic stage, or as a result of subjects having passed through the alphabetic stage and proceeded to the orthographic stage. Thus, good beginning readers may show enhanced regularity effects as they grasp the alphabetic principle (Frith, 1985), whilst a later reduction in spelling–sound effects on both error rate and naming latency is observed in highly skilled readers (Seidenberg et al., 1984). Thus there is a possibility of an 'inverted U' pattern of regularity effects, in which very young children show no phonological effects because they are not using spelling-to-sound information, and much older children show absent or reduced spelling-to-sound effects for the quite different reason that they have progressed to orthographic reading and are processing at a much faster level overall. The 'time-course model' of word recognition (Waters and Seidenberg, 1985) predicts that spelling-to-sound effects will generally be larger when processing is slow and phonological information has more time to become activated relative to visual information. This will be the case for lower-frequency words and less skilled readers, and such interactions have indeed been observed (Seidenberg et al., 1984). It is possible that this decrease in the magnitude of spelling–sound effects with increasing speed of processing will tend to cancel out any effects of spelling-to-sound characteristics that would be found in older children as they make increasing use of spelling–sound constraints.

Although spelling–sound effects can be found in highly skilled adult readers (e.g. Jared, MacRae and Seidenberg, 1990), these effects of overall processing speed make it difficult to interpret changes in effect sizes with age. These problems of interpretation do not alter the fact that observed regularity effects can be taken as a reliable indicator of alphabetic reading. The *absence* of a regularity effect can be taken as evidence that alphabetic reading has not been attained, whereas a merely *reduced* regularity effect could indicate either ineffective alphabetic reading or a progression beyond it.

Several studies provide evidence for a reduced sensitivity to spelling-to-sound regularity in dyslexics that is accompanied by non-word reading difficulty and a range of other phonological deficits relative to reading age matched control subjects. Frith and Snowling (1983) obtained these results with dyslexics aged 10–12 years (reading age 8–10 years), and Snowling, Stackhouse and Rack (1986) report a similar pattern for dyslexic subjects with a wide chronological and reading age range (compare also Szeszulski and Manis, 1987; Siegel and Ryan, 1988).

Several other studies have, however, failed to obtain the reduced effects of spelling-to-sound factors in reading-disabled populations which would be expected on the basis of deficient phonological decoding skills (Backman et al., 1984; Treiman and Hirsh-Pasek, 1985; Seidenberg et al., 1985; Stanovich, Nathan and Vala-Rossi, 1986; Snowling, 1987; Baddeley, Logie and Ellis, 1988). Unfortunately, these studies adopt different subject selection criteria. Whilst some examine the reading of formally diagnosed dyslexic subjects, others assess the performance of (non-dyslexic) subjects whose reading falls behind other measured skills. It is therefore difficult to draw any systematic conclusion about the nature of dyslexic, poor and normal word decoding skill.

In general, then, there is mixed evidence on the question of whether dyslexic readers are delayed or deviant in their phonological skills as assessed by spelling-to-sound regularity effects and non-word decoding skill. Although it is possible to point to methodological problems in many of the studies cited above, one possible conclusion is that drawn by Stanovich, Nathan and Zolman (1988; see also Stanovich, Nathan and Vala-Rossi, 1986), namely that the nature of the poor-reading population tested will determine whether or not a delay or deviance model is supported. It may be that, when highly conservative criteria for designating a population as 'dyslexic' or 'reading-disabled' are used, a qualitatively different performance profile relative to reading-age controls is more likely to emerge. Lower-level tasks and the use of younger subjects are also more likely to produce real differences, for compensatory strategies will be relatively less available for use under such circumstances. An alternative possibility is that only relatively complex phonological tasks will give rise to a deficit in poor or dyslexic readers relative to reading age controls (Holligan and Johnston, 1988).

In the absence of unambiguous evidence regarding the presence or absence of alphabetic reading in reading-disabled populations, as assessed by spelling-to-sound regularity effects, we now turn to a reconsideration of the theoretical framework which has motivated the experimental approach.

Theoretical models of underlying processes

Many of the experiments cited above have been interpreted in terms of dual-route models of reading. These models generally assume that there are lexical and rule-based procedures operating in parallel during word naming. A pronunciation is either accessed from a stored lexical entry, or it is constructed by means of spelling-to-sound correspondence rules. The rule-based pronunciation may not be utilised when access to a high frequency word can produce the required information faster and more reliably. However, phonology produced using spelling-to-sound rules may become available before pronunciation begins, when lexical access takes longer as it will for lower frequency items or slower subjects. If the word has an exceptional pronunciation, the rule-derived phonology will be incorrect and the resulting competition between assembled and accessed phonologies will slow the word's production (Norris and Brown, 1985). It is because of the assumed existence of spelling-to-sound rules that it has been natural to describe words as 'regular' or 'irregular', as we have done in the discussion above.

An alternative procedure by which word pronunciations may be synthesised involves a single system for words and non-words alike. Here, a letter string is pronounced by 'analogy' (Glushko, 1979) to the stored pronunciations of lexical items with similar spelling patterns. All possible orthographic segments of the presented letter string activate corresponding lexical-level phonology in this kind of model. Within this 'analysis-by-synthesis' framework, it becomes natural to describe a word's spelling-to-sound characteristics in terms of its 'friends' (defined as the number of the word's orthographic neighbours, i.e. words with the same vowel and final consonant cluster, that are pronounced in the same way as, i.e. rhyme with, the word in question) and 'enemies' (defined as the number of the word's orthographic neighbours that do not rhyme with the word in question). Words such as PINT have many enemies (MINT, HINT, TINT etc.) but no friends (there are no other -INT words that rhyme with PINT).* Regular consistent words, such as PILL, however, have only friends (HILL, MILL, TILL etc.). There are no -ILL words that do not rhyme with PILL. Finally, in terms of the spelling-to-sound classification suggested by Brown (1987a), there are words such as SOAP, which have neither friends nor enemies as they have no immediate orthographic neighbours. Brown termed these items 'unique'. Throughout the remainder of this chapter we will adopt this 'friends and enemies' terminology.

Connectionist models of reading

Connectionist models can serve many different roles. Here we are concerned with their use in providing psychologically plausible models. Within cognitive psychology and psycholinguistics, the attempt to build models that are sufficiently explicit to be implemented as computer programs has led to better-specified cognitive models in a range of domains. Another benefit is that connectionist modelling can force a reconsideration of how the global statistical properties of a set of input data can lead to 'friends' and 'enemies' effects for individual members of the input. This can be seen very clearly in the word naming literature discussed below. Finally, connectionist models may be able to underpin developmental stage models in psychology by specifying the causal mechanisms underlying transitions between developmental stages.

Brown (1987a) developed a computational model of word naming, within a connectionist framework, which attempted to specify the mechanisms underlying spelling-to-sound translation in word naming. The model was loosely based on Glushko's (1979) analogy approach. Our early connectionist model of reading, although it had no learning capability and operated only with a very small vocabulary, nevertheless made novel predictions concerning word naming time which could be tested experimentally. These arose largely as a result of the ability of connection-ist models to highlight the statistical properties of mapping systems (here, the mapping between English orthography and English phonology). We now describe these predictions.

Earlier accounts of word naming had assumed that number of *enemies* was the main spelling-to-sound influence on word naming time. In these accounts, pronunciation discrepancies associated with spelling-to-sound enemies were assumed to cause interference in processing and therefore slow word production. Brown's (1987a, 1987b) model, however, predicted that the relevant dimension of difficulty in word naming (at least

---

*There is considerable evidence that the vowel and terminal consonant cluster of a word is the relevant psychological unit (e.g. Treiman and Chafetz, 1987; Treiman and Zukowski, 1988). We follow standard practice in classifying words in terms of the pronunciation of this unit.

for skilled adults) is the number of spelling-to-sound *friends* that a word possesses. It was claimed that effects previously assumed to be due to enemies (exception effects) are in fact due to friends; exception words differ from regular consistent words in that they have fewer friends as well as more enemies. A word naming experiment reported by Brown (1987a) provided some evidence for the operation of friend-based facilitation rather than enemy-based interference processes. An effect of friends that was independent of number of enemies was obtained. Furthermore, no enemies effect emerged when friends were controlled for. To illustrate: high-friend no-enemy words such as PILL were named faster than the no-friend no-enemy words such as SOAP (i.e. there was an effect of friends independent of number of enemies), but words such as PINT (no friends, many enemies) were named as fast as SOAP type words with no friends or enemies (i.e. there was no effect of number of enemies when number of friends was held constant). It has also been claimed that number of spelling-to-sound friends rather than enemies predicts the errors made by patients suffering from various forms of severe brain injury (Brown, 1987c).

Seidenberg and McClelland (1989a) have recently described a much larger developmental model of word naming and lexical decision which predicts independent effects of both spelling-to-sound friends and spelling-to-sound enemies on word naming time, and they report an experiment which does find an effect of enemies when number of friends is controlled for. This finding has now been replicated by Jared, MacRae and Seidenberg (1990) and G.D.A. Brown and F.L. Watson (1990, unpublished data). The Seidenberg and McClelland (1989a) model of word reading development arguably does not yet permit detailed predictions concerning the nature of spelling-to-sound effects in early alphabetic reading. This is because the model does not start with the same knowledge about phonology that is already available to the child who is beginning alphabetic reading – children bring a large spoken vocabulary to the reading acquisition process. It is also clear that the acquisition of spelling is crucial to the development of reading (Frith, 1985; Ellis and Cataldo, 1990) and this insight has not yet been incorporated into connectionist models.

Despite some limitations in its current form, the Seidenberg/McClelland model can provide one possible characterisation of the nature of dyslexic reading. Seidenberg (1989; see also Seidenberg and McClelland, 1989b) has examined the performance of the connectionist model of reading when it is given fewer 'hidden units' over which to learn the relevant associations. This can simply be thought of as providing fewer computational resources to achieve the mapping. The basic finding was that the reduced-capacity model showed worse performance for all words, along with increased spelling-to-sound effects. This is similar to the pattern evident in children (Backman et al., 1984).

For present purposes, the key conclusion from connectionist models of word reading is that *independent* effects of spelling-to-sound friends and enemies are predicted, and that these predictions have been confirmed experimentally. These effects reflect the connection strengths between orthographic and phonological units within a single mechanism. Competing pronunciations of orthographic segments have opposite effects on the connection strengths in the system during the learning process and this leads to independent friends and enemies effects.

The development of alphabetic reading revisited

In terms of theories of the development of spelling-to-sound knowledge, these different effects allow us to specify developmental possibilities more precisely than simply asking whether and when spelling-to-sound knowledge is used by children of different ages. Previously, as we have seen, the presence or absence of a simple regularity effect was taken as evidence for the presence or absence of spelling-to-sound knowledge use. However, in the light of the subdivision of spelling-to-sound effects into independent friends and enemies effects, more sophisticated methodology is available. This methodology allows us to distinguish between different developmental possibilities, as friends and enemies effects can be taken as indices of different developmental processes.

For example, knowledge of exceptional spelling-to-sound correspondences (as occur in words with enemies) could develop independently of sensitivity to the *frequency* of spelling-to-sound correspondences (the latter being evident as friends effects in skilled adult reading). In other words, the fact that children show higher error rates for words with irregular or exceptional pronunciations does indeed show that children are using spelling-to-sound knowledge in their single word reading. However, exception effects do not necessarily mean that a fully adult-like reading system is present. Beginning readers could simply know some spelling-to-sound correspondences but not others without being sensitive to the frequency structure of the English spelling-to-sound system. We may summarise alternative developmental possibilities in terms of two characterisations of the developmental process.

Alphabetic reading type 1

On the first possible account, even children at an early stage of alphabetic reading are able to use spelling-to-sound knowledge in an adult-like way, even though there are many exception words whose pronunciations they have not yet learned. This would mean that they have implicit knowledge about the frequency of particular spelling-to-sound correspondences in English, and will have relatively little difficulty with high-friend words in comparison to words with no or few friends. During subsequent development of alphabetic reading, children continue to be sensitive to spelling-to-sound friends (as are adults), but also acquire knowledge about the correct pronunciations of an increasing number of exception words. The main prediction of this model of development is that children should be sensitive to number of friends from the beginning of alphabetic reading.

Alphabetic reading type 2

We now consider an alternative characterisation of the developmental process. In this model, young children begin alphabetic reading with a basic knowledge of spelling-to-sound correspondence and an understanding that this knowledge can be used in reading. However, this knowledge is not yet incorporated into an adult-like processing system, and may be applied only in a relatively unautomated manner. They know some exception words but not others, and the processing system is not yet sensitive to the relative frequencies of different spelling-to-sound correspondences. Two main processes occur during subsequent development of reading. First, children learn the pronunciations of more exception words. Secondly, the use of spelling-to-sound constraints becomes more fluent, automatic and adult like (i.e. frequency sensitive). Two basic predictions follow from this characterisation of the development of alphabetic reading: (1) higher error rates for exception words would be expected on this model, simply as a consequence of lack of knowledge about exceptional pronunciations early on; (2) more crucially, only older children should show effects of spelling-to-sound friends on error rate and naming latency.

Thus, the development of more fine-grained classifications of word naming phenomena, prompted by recent connectionist models, makes it possible to formulate new and more precise characterisations of early alphabetic reading. In particular, it can be seen that higher error rates for exception than for regular words do not thereby indicate that children are using spelling-to-sound knowledge in an adult-like way.

Development of early alphabetic reading: experimental evidence

G.D.A. Brown and F.L. Watson (1990, unpublished data) describe an experiment designed to test the idea, outlined above, that normal children begin alphabetic reading in a relatively unautomated manner. If this is so, then they will only show effects of spelling-to-sound friends in the relatively late stages of alphabetic reading. In the early stages of alphabetic reading, they may show only enemies effects.

In an experiment conducted with Kathryn Taylor, children from four different reading age ranges (mean reading ages for the groups ranged from 7;9 years to 12;11 years) were given words of three different types to name, and reading time and error rate for each word type were measured. The words were the same as those used by Brown (1987a) and were selected so that independent effects of spelling-to-sound friends and enemies could be assessed. Thus one set of words had neither friends nor enemies (e.g. SOAP). A second set of words (e.g. HILL) had several friends (compare KILL, PILL, FILL etc.) but no enemies. The third set of words had enemies but no friends (e.g. HAVE, compare RAVE, GAVE, SAVE etc.). Thus any effect of friends independent of enemies would emerge as a difference between SOAP-type words and HILL-type words, and any effect of enemies independent of friends could be assessed by comparing SOAP-type words with HAVE-type words. Our three sets of words were controlled for other relevant factors such as frequency, initial phoneme, length and purely orthographic regularity (positional bigram frequency: Solso and Juel, 1980).

Before describing the results of this experiment, an important method-ological point must be noted. In this experiment, as in all the others we describe in the rest of this chapter, we analysed only error rates to words that were known to the individual subjects. Most of the studies described did not take account of whether or not the children *knew* the meanings of the words they were required to read aloud, although in most cases there was an attempt to ensure that the selected words would be within the subjects' vocabularies. This strategy may not always be adequate for a number of reasons (see Brown and Watson, 1990b, for more details). An additional reason for indicating a comprehension test is that it allows us to perform both 'comprehension-level matching' and 'decoding-level matching' (compare Stanovich, Nathan and Zolman, 1988), although we do not discuss this further here. The importance of controlling for com-prehension was confirmed in this experiment by the results of our com-prehension tests, which found a clear tendency for subjects to know fewer of the words that possessed spelling-to-sound enemies, and even fewer of the words with neither friends nor enemies. This occurred even though the words were matched for frequency of occurrence.

In this study of the development of spelling-to-sound knowledge in normal children, we found strong effects of spelling-to-sound friends, and weaker effects of spelling-to-sound enemies, present throughout the age range (although there was some tendency for enemies rather than friends effects to be stronger in the youngest age group).

When naming latencies to known words were examined, there was a clear effect of number of friends, but, as in other experiments using the same materials but different subject populations, there was no reliable effect of number of enemies. Unfortunately, it was only possible to collect naming latency data for the more able subjects, and so it was not possible to identify any developmental trend on reaction time.

The fact that normal children are generally sensitive to spelling-to-sound friends effects throughout development suggests that they do not have a problem with automating their use of spelling-to-sound knowledge. As soon as spelling-to-sound knowledge is used, it is used fluently and automatically. Our next experiment was designed to test the idea that the same might not be true for developmental dyslexics.

Developmental dyslexia: a revised hypothesis

Frith (1985) suggested that classic developmental dyslexia might be best characterised as an inability to move on from early logographic to alphabetic reading. This interpretation is somewhat difficult to reconcile with the many findings, described in the earlier part of this chapter, that dyslexic subjects do sometimes appear to show equivalent spelling-to-sound regularity effects to appropriately matched normal readers. However, we have argued above that the presence of regularity (enemy) effects in reading does not necessarily entail a fully functioning, automated adult system. It is therefore possible that limited alphabetic reading might be present in developmental dyslexics, who would then be sensitive to spelling-to-sound enemy effects, but would fail to go on to automate this process fully and show additional spelling-to-sound friends effects.

Frith herself raised the possibility that limited alphabetic reading might be possible for dyslexics: 'With drill in "phonics" certainly a resemblance of alphabetic skills can be achieved. These skills, however, would never becomed automatic enough to be applied effortlessly' (Frith, 1985, p. 316). This would be consistent with recent suggestions that dyslexics have a deficit in 'automaticity' across a wide range of tasks (e.g. Nicholson and Fawcett, 1990). Thus, it is possible that developmental dyslexics do achieve a measure of alphabetic reading, but never automate the process to the point where they will, as skilled adults do, show effects of spelling-to-sound friends as well as enemies. In the following section we report an experiment designed to test this hypothesis.

Alphabetic reading in developmental dyslexia: experimental evidence

The experiment was designed to test the suggestion that developmental dyslexia is best characterised as an arrest at a stage of early alphabetic reading. If this is so, we would expect dyslexic readers with high and low reading ages to show similar spelling-to-sound *enemies* effects to normal readers of the same reading age, but reduced spelling-to-sound *friends* effects.

The experiment was run using the same methodology and stimulus materials as in the experiment described above. As before, only error rates to words that were known to the individual subjects were analysed. There were two groups of 10 subjects: dyslexics and matched controls. Control subjects were taken from the 80 subjects run in the experiment described above.

Dyslexic and control reading performance was assessed in the following way. A regression equation that predicted the reading age (RA) of each of the 80 non-dyslexic subjects on the basis of their chronological age (CA) and performance IQ (Standard Progressive Matrices: Raven, 1958) was derived. The equation was then used to obtain a predicted normal RA for each of the dyslexic and control subjects in our present sample, and reading performance was assessed by the discrepancy (residual) between each subject's predicted and observed reading age scores. RA was measured using both the Schonell (1942) and British Ability Scales (BAS; Elliott, Murray and Pearson, 1978) tests, although only BAS RA was used as the measure in the regression equation.

The dyslexics and controls were matched as closely as possible both on reading age and the total number of errors made in the word naming experiment. The dyslexics (mean CA=11;3 years) had an actual BAS RA 28.8 months below the predicted RA. Thus the dyslexics were, on average, reading about two and a half years behind the level that would be expected on the basis of their chronological age and IQ.

Some of the control group subjects were below-average readers for their chronological age, but their reading level was on average a month ahead of the level predicted on the basis of their chronological age and IQ. The controls (mean CA=8;9 years) had an actual BAS RA 1.1 months above predicted RA.

The spelling-to-sound 'friends' and 'enemies' effects of the two subject groups are shown in Figure 12.1.

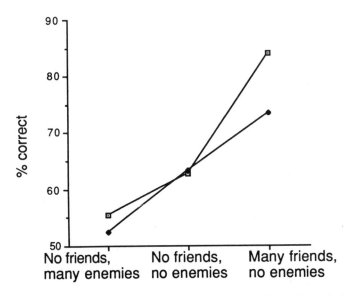

Figure 12.1 Percentage correct responses for three different word types for dyslexics (▣) and controls (◆).

As can be seen from the figure, the dyslexic and matched control subjects showed clear friends effects. The friends effects were clearly significant, and enemies effects marginally so, for both groups. The results therefore did not support the hypothesis that developmental dyslexics are arrested at an early stage of alphabetic reading. Even the dyslexics, who were making errors in reading to over 32% of the words they knew the meanings of, showed the independent effects of spelling-to-sound friends that are characteristic of skilled adult reading. They do not suffer from a deficit in automating their alphabetic knowledge, for this would have been evidenced by a failure to demonstrate effects of spelling-to-sound friends on error rate.

In the face of these results, in combination with those described earlier in this chapter, it appears difficult to preserve the hypothesis that developmental dyslexics differ qualitatively from appropriate controls in their reading strategy. The picture that emerges is one of delay rather than deviance.

In the following section we report an alternative test of the hypothesis under consideration.

Reading in skilled adult dyslexics

A more stringent test of the hypothesis that developmental dyslexics make use of qualitatively different reading strategies was made by examining a group of highly compensated dyslexic subjects (this experiment is reported in full in Watson and Brown, 1990). We examined the performance of a group of high-achieving dyslexics – those who were actively pursuing courses in further or higher education. It seemed probable that these relatively unusual subjects would have developed efficient and possibly idiosyncratic strategies for reading. If these subjects have developed visually based compensatory strategies, then we would expect them to show no effect of spelling-to-sound characteristics on word naming latency. If, however, they are using the same word decoding strategies as normal readers, we would expect them to show effects of spelling-to-sound friends but not enemies. If they are making use of spelling–sound mapping constraints, but in an idiosyncratic manner, they may show larger enemy effects than are evident for normal subjects. In particular, this experiment provided a test of the idea (discussed above) that dyslexics will be less able to automate their alphabetic reading and that this will be evident in reduced effects of spelling-to-sound friends. By using an adult population, it was possible to collect naming latencies for each word for each subject. Only these data are reported here as error rates were negligible.

Ten dyslexic students from the Bangor area took part in this word naming experiment. All were actively pursuing further or higher education courses at the time of testing. All subjects had been independently assessed as dyslexic, and additionally they all had a highly dyslexic profile across a wide range of background tests that we administered. Despite their high degree of educational achievement, the subjects showed a mean spelling age of only 12;0 years. They nevertheless had a mean score on Raven's Advanced Matrices of 25.1 (maximum 36). Six of the subjects fell in the top 5% range on this measure of performance IQ.

The results of the word naming experiment on these subjects were straightforward. The adult dyslexics showed clear effects of spelling-to-sound friends on word naming latency. There was a statistically significant friends effect of 141 milliseconds (ms), and a non-significant 24-ms enemies effect.

The results of this experiment demonstrated that our student dyslexics, despite their highly deviant profile across a range of background tests, clearly exhibited a qualitatively similar profile to a range of other groups on a single word reading task, i.e. they showed a clear facilitative effect of number of spelling-to-sound friends, and no clear effect of spelling-to-sound enemies when number of friends was held constant. Their overall word naming times were, however, considerably slower than those of any other group we have tested. A number of different factors could be responsible for this baseline increase, and we do not wish to attach any great theoretical significance to these elevated naming latencies per se. It is possible, however, that the actual effects of spelling-to-sound factors on word naming time are greater for our dyslexics than for other groups, even when the effects are expressed as a proportion of overall mean naming latency. This would be consistent with their generally lower reading speed overall.

Conclusions

We have shown how connectionist modelling techniques, by permitting us to distinguish between two different types of spelling-to-sound effect, have allowed us to formulate and test a revised hypothesis of developmental dyslexia. This hypothesis was that dyslexics might attain a limited degree of alphabetic reading, but never fully automate their alphabetic reading to the extent of showing spelling-to-sound friends effects. This hypothesis was not supported by our experiments. Our conclusion is that developmental dyslexics do achieve alphabetic reading, and this alphabetic reading is qualitatively similar to that of same reading age control subjects. In terms of the delay vs deviance debate, our results clearly support the delay hypothesis. Even with the more fine-grained methodology that the connectionist modelling has allowed us to develop, dyslexics show the same pattern of effects as control subjects matched for reading age.

We believe that our approach also illustrates some of the advantages of developing computational models of reading development. Verbally specified cognitive approaches to the deficits in developmental dyslexia have proved useful and influential. However, we believe there remains an urgent need for a more explicit (e.g. computational) specification of the low-level causal mechanisms that underly the development of strategic changes and of phonemic awareness. We are attempting to meet this need using connectionist modelling techniques. Thus, we do not view our approach as being incompatible with existing methods. Rather, we aim to make use of existing cognitive-level insights whilst also providing more explicit models of the relevant mechanisms at a subcognitive causal level. Some success has already been achieved with this approach.

In conclusion, connectionist modelling can inform research into developmental dyslexia by providing well-specified models and by focusing attention on the nature of the mapping system that must be learned by children. The learning process is, we claim, well characterised as a statistical one, involving the mastery of mappings between spelling and sound.

Acknowledgements

The research reported in this paper was supported by grants to the first author from the Medical Research Council (UK), the Economic and Social Research Council (UK) and the Leverhulme Trust. We are grateful to the many schools which allowed us to collect the data reported here, and to Joanna Romney and Kathryn Taylor for collecting the control data.

References

BACKMAN, J., BRUCK, M., HEBERT, M. and SEIDENBERG, M.S. (1984). Acquisition and use of spelling-sound correspondences. *Journal of Experimental Child Psychology* **38**, 114–133.

BADDELEY, A.D., LOGIE, R.H. and ELLIS, N.C. (1988). Characteristics of developmental dyslexia. *Cognition* **29**, 197–228.

BARRON, R.W. (1980). Visual and phonological strategies in reading and spelling. In: U. Frith (Ed.), *Cognitive Processes in Spelling.* London: Academic Press.

BARRON, R.W. (1986). Word recognition in early reading: A review of the direct and indirect access hypotheses. *Cognition* **24**, 39–119.

BROWN, G.D.A. (1987a). Resolving inconsistency: A computational model of word naming. *Journal of Memory and Language* **23**, 1–23.

BROWN, G.D.A. (1987b). On the difference between the regularity and the frequency of spelling-to-sound correspondences. *The Behavioral and Brain Sciences* **10**, 332–333.

BROWN, G.D.A. (1987c). Constraining interactivity: Evidence from acquired dyslexia. *Proceedings of the Ninth Annual Conference of the Cognitive Science Society*, pp. 779–793. Hillsdale, NJ: LEA.

ELLIOTT, C.D., MURRAY, D.J. and PEARSON, L.S. (1978). *The British Ability Scales.* Windsor: NFER-Nelson.

ELLIS, N.C. and CATALDO, S. (1990). The role of spelling in learning to read. *Language and Education* in press.

FRITH, U. (1985). Beneath the surface of developmental dyslexia. In: K.E. Patterson, J.C. Marshall and M. Coltheart (Eds), *Surface Dyslexia* Hillsdale, NJ: LEA.

FRITH U. and SNOWLING, M. (1983). Reading for meaning and reading for sound in autistic and dyslexic children. *British Journal of Developmental Psychology* **1**, 329–342.

GLUSHKO, R.J. (1979). The organization and activation of orthographic knowledge in reading aloud. *Journal of Experimental Psychology: Human Perception and Performance* **5**, 674–691.

HOLLIGAN, C. and JOHNSTON, R.S. (1988). The use of phonological information by good and poor readers in memory and reading tasks. *Memory and Cognition* **16**, 522–532.

JARED, D., MACRAE, K. and SEIDENBERG, M.S. (1990). The basis of consistency effects in word naming. *Journal of Memory and Language* in press.

MARSH, G., FRIEDMAN, M.P., WELCH, V. and DESBERG, P. (1981). A cognitive–developmental approach to reading acquisition. In: T.G. Waller and G.E. MacKinnon (Eds), *Reading Research. Advances in Theory and Practice, Vol. 3.* New York: Academic Press.

NICHOLSON, R.I. and FAWCETT, A.J. (1990). Automaticity: A new framework for dyslexia research. *Cognition* **35**, 159–182.

NORRIS, D. and BROWN, G.D.A. (1985). Race models and analogy theories: A dead heat? Reply to Seidenberg. *Cognition* **20**, 155–168.

RAVEN, R.C. (1958). *Standard Progessive Matrices.* London: H.K. Lewis.

RUMELHART, D.E. and McCLELLAND, J.L. (1986). *Parallel Distributed Processing: Explorations in the Microstructure of Cognition.* Volume 1 Cambridge, MA: Bradford Books/ MIT Press.

SCHLAPP, U. and UNDERWOOD, G. (1988). Reading, spelling and two types of irregularity in word recognition. *Journal of Research in Reading* **11**, 120–132.

SCHONELL, F. (1942). *Blackwardness in the Basic Subjects.* London: Oliver & Boyd.

SEIDENBERG, M.S. (1989). Visual word recognition and pronunciation: A computational model and its implications. In: W. Marslen-Wilson (Ed.). *Lexical Representation and Process.* Cambridge, MA: MIT Press/Bradford Books.

SEIDENBERG, M.S. and McCLELLAND, J.L. (1989a). A distributed, developmental model of word recognition and naming. *Psychological Review* **96**, 523–568.

SEIDENBERG, M.S. and McCLELLAND, J.L. (1989b). Visual word recognition and pronunciation: A computational model of acquired skilled performance and dyslexia. In: A. Galaburda (Ed.), *From Reading to Neurons.* Cambridge, MA: MIT Press/Bradford Books.

SEIDENBERG, M.S., WATERS, G.S., BARNES, M.A. and TANENHAUS, M.K. (1984). When does irregular spelling or pronunciation influence word recognition? *Journal of Verbal Learning and Verbal Behavior* **23**, 383–404.

SEIDENBERG, M.S., BRUCK, M., FORNAROLO, G. and BACKMAN, J. (1985). Word recognition processes of poor and disabled readers: Do they necessarily differ? *Applied Psycholinguistics* **6**, 161–180.

SEYMOUR, P.H.K. (1986). *Cognitive Analysis of Dyslexia.* London: Routledge & Kegan Paul.

SIEGEL, L.S. and RYAN, E.B. (1988). Development of grammatical-sensitivity, phonological, and short-term memory skills in normally achieving and learning disabled children. *Developmental Psychology* **24**, 28–37.

SNOWLING, M.J. (1987). *Dyslexia: A Cognitive Developmental Perspective.* Oxford: Blackwell.

SNOWLING, M.J., STACKHOUSE, J. and RACK, J.P. (1986). Phonological dyslexia and dysgraphia: A developmental analysis. *Cognitive Neuropsychology* **3**, 309–339.

SOLSO, R.L. and JUEL, C.L. (1980). Positional frequency and versatility of bigrams for two- through nine-letter English words. *Behaviour Research Methods and Instrumentation* **12**, 297–343.

STANOVICH, K.E., NATHAN, R.G. and VALA-ROSSI, M. (1986). Developmental changes in the cognitive correlates of reading ability and the developmental lag hypothesis. *Reading Research Quarterly* **21**, 267–283.

STANOVICH, K.E., NATHAN, R.G. and ZOLMAN, J.E. (1988). The developmental lag hypothesis in reading: Longitudinal and matched reading-level comparisons. *Child Development* **59**, 71–86.

SZESZULSKI, P.A. and MANIS, F.R. (1987). A comparison of word recognition processes in dyslexic and normal readers at two reading-age levels. *Journal of Experimental Child Psychology* **44**, 364–376.

TREIMAN, R. and CHAFETZ, J. (1987). Are there onset-and-rime-like units in written words? In: M. Coltheart (Ed.), *Attention and Performance XII*. London: LEA.

TREIMAN, R. and HIRSH-PASEK, K. (1985). Are there qualitative differences in reading behaviour between dyslexic and normal readers? *Memory and Cognition* **13**, 357–364.

TREIMAN, R. and ZUKOWSKI, A. (1988). Units in reading and spelling. *Journal of Memory and Language* **27**, 466–477.

WATERS, G.S. and SEIDENBERG, M.S. (1985). Spelling-to-sound effects in reading: Time course and decision criteria. *Memory and Cognition* **13**, 557–572.

WATSON, F.L. and BROWN, G.D.A. (1990). Single word reading in college dyslexics. *Applied Cognitive Psychology* in press.

Part IV
Intervention: Theoretical and Practical Issues

Chapter 13
Dyslexia: The Obvious and Hidden Speech and Language Disorder

JOY STACKHOUSE and BILL WELLS

Introduction

For many years, practitioners in the field of special education have been aware that children who have speech disorders are at risk for reading and spelling problems, and that children with specific learning disabilities often have subtle speech problems. An important question of theoretical and practical significance is the extent to which the speech-disordered and the reading-disordered population are one and the same.

In pursuing this issue, it is illuminating to examine the literature reporting the deficits found in dyslexic children. There is often a history of late or troublesome speech and language development, with persisting deficits involving speech perception, segmentation and blending, articulation, memory and sequencing, syntax and lexical development (Snowling, 1987).

These verbal deficits occur in varying degrees in children with reading and spelling difficulties. This paper discusses the cases of two children of similar age and of normal intelligence. Both had reading and spelling difficulties but the extent and severity of their underlying speech and language problems varied.

Michael, a boy aged 11;9 years, had been educated in a language unit attached to a normal school because of his persisting speech and language problems. Richard, at 11;8 years, was struggling in mainstream school because of his reading and spelling problems although he was receiving help from a private teacher.

Michael (Chronological Age: 11;9 years)

Michael had been referred for speech therapy at the age of 3 years and he had attended a language unit since he was 6 years of age. He had a specific speech and language disorder known as developmental verbal dyspraxia –

a motor speech programming difficulty which results in inconsistent and distorted speech output. When he was seen at 11 years, his speech errors included omissions, perseverations and sequencing problems as well as articulatory imprecision and groping as in: BUTTERCUP – ['kʌkə,kʌʔ]; SPAGHETTI – [bɪs'kɛki]; SCARECROW – ['skʊɛə'skwɛə,ʊɛʊz sk'skɛə,kgəʊ]. At this age he was reading at the level of a 7 year old with a spelling age of 6;8 years. By 15 years of age, Michael's speech was more intelligible, but there were still persisting articulatory difficulties, particularly in longer complex words and in continuous speech. Errors included: omitted segments and syllables (FIRE ENGINE – ['faɪ,ʒɪn]), repeated and distorted segments (CARAVAN – ['kævə,ʊæn]), reduced clusters (SCARE-CROW – ['kɛə,kəʊ]), and transposed segments and syllables (BISCUITS – ['bɪs,tɪʔ]).

In addition to these articulatory difficulties, there were obvious language deficits in comprehension and expressive skills. Syntax was simplified and vocabulary limited as can be seen in the piece of free writing produced by Michael at the age of 11, just before the Christmas holidays (Figure 13.1).

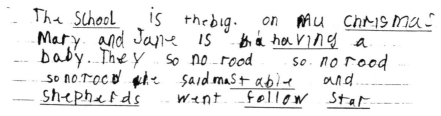

Figure 13.1 Michael's free writing: words underlined were copied following Michael's request for the correct spelling.

He read back the passage as:

> The school is big. On my Christmas Mary and Joseph is having a baby. They sorry no room, sorry no room, so, sorry no room, said stable, stable man and the shepherds went follow star.

Michael's approach to written language tasks indicated that he relied on visual strengths in order to overcome auditory processing weaknesses. When reading single words, over 50% of his errors were words with a similar orthographic form to the targets, for example 'paint' for PINT, 'varnish' for VASE. The next highest proportion of his errors were unsuccessful sound attempts where he tried to apply phonics (which he had been taught) but was unable to do so, for example, 'to-we, tuk, tuk-we, tuf, tka, tup-char' ['tuːwəʰ 'tʌkʰ 'tʌk³ wə 'tʌfː 'tka 'tʌp'tʃaː] for TUTOR. His difficulty with phonological strategies was even more obvious when spelling, where there was a predominance of bizarre or non-phonetic errors. For example, he spelt UMBRELLA as rberherrelrarlsrllies, and CIGARETTE as satesatashaelerari.

According to Frith's (1985) model of literacy development, Michael's reading and spelling could be said to be arrested at the logographic phase. This phase is characterised by reliance on visual memory for reading and spelling. The logographic reader cannot read unfamiliar material and cannot apply phonetic rules to spelling, so his attempts are non-phonetic. Michael clearly had not broken through to the next phase of literacy development – the alphabetic. He could neither read nor spell non-words. We presumed that his difficulties were a consequence of his marked phonological processing difficulties: his auditory discrimination, rhyme, syllable and consonant segmentation skills were all poor. His inconsistent speech output compounded his difficulties with reading and spelling and at follow-up 4 years later, there was still little evidence of breakthrough to the alphabetic phase (Stackhouse, 1989).

There was never any danger of Michael's problems being missed; he had unintelligible speech, obvious language problems and severe literacy difficulties. However, there are other children whose speech, language and learning problems are more subtle, and so much more easily overlooked. These children may have had speech therapy in the past and been discharged following improved intelligibility. It is not uncommon for these children to be referred back to a speech therapist at around 8 years of age with a query as to whether their 'past' speech problem could have affected their reading and spelling development. This may indeed be the case: the reading and spelling difficulties may well be the earlier speech problem in a different guise.

The speech- and language-disordered child most at risk of remaining undetected is the one whose speech is intelligible and who has no documented history of speech and language difficulties. For whatever reason, be it lack of opportunity or lack of obvious difficulty, he or she has never been seen by a speech therapist. If this child presents with a literacy problem, help may be available for reading and spelling, but a comprehensive speech and language investigation will seldom be carried out.

Richard's case illustrates the subtle speech and language problems which were uncovered in an 11-year-old boy, referred by his parents for an investigation of his spoken and written language development. Richard had never been seen by a speech therapist before, but his parents were concerned about his poor progress at school and his 'unclear' speech. They reported a family history of dyslexic difficulties, word-finding problems and poor memory.

Richard (Chronological Age 11;8 years)

Richard was a boy of above average intelligence. However, at 11 years, he had a reading age of 8;9 years and a spelling age of 7;2 years – he was behind by at least 3 years in his literacy skills.

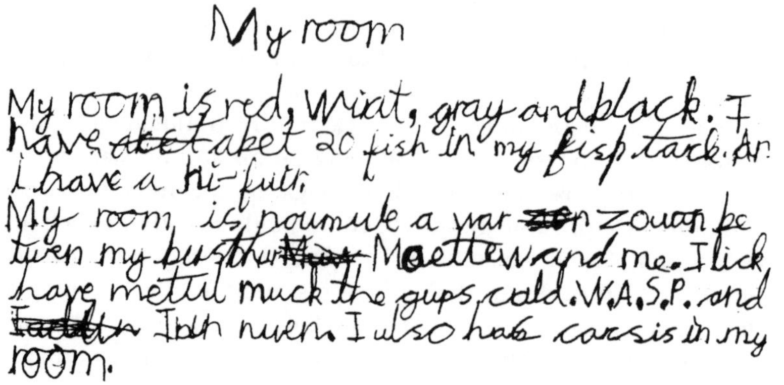

My room

My room is red, wriat, gray and black. I
have atet aket 20 fish in my fish tark. An
i have a hi-futh.
My room is noumule a war zon zouan be
tuen my busthur Maettew and me. I lick
have mettul muck the gups cald. W.A.S.P. and
Iath Ith nuen. I ulso has carsis in my
room.

Figure 13.2 Richard's free writing.

Richard's spoken language was informative but his written language was limited and laboured. He had been working very hard to improve his handwriting and produced the piece of free writing shown in Figure 13.2 when seen. This was read back as:

> My room is red, white, grey and black. I have about twenty fish in my fish tank. And I have a hi-fi in my room.
>
> My room is normally a war zone between my brother Matthew and me. I like heavy metal (don't know) the groups called WASP and Iron Maiden. I also have cactus in my room.

Richard's free writing reveals a wide range of problems, not just language difficulties. Consequently, we carried out a comprehensive analysis of his speech and language skills. First, linguistic analysis of tape-recorded conversation together with the results of standardised tests confirmed that Richard had at least age-appropriate verbal comprehension and use of syntax in spoken language. His speech was intelligible most of the time and, even though he lacked confidence in verbal situations, he gave the impression of having adequate speech and language skills.

Nevertheless, investigations of his lexical development revealed some difficulties. Although his receptive vocabulary was age appropriate, he had specific difficulties on expressive naming tests. This indicated a word finding difficulty: although the words were within his vocabulary, he was unable to produce them spontaneously.

Richard also had difficulty providing definitions for spoken words which can have more than one meaning, e.g. homophones such as FARE/FAIR. He was always able to come up with the meaning for one of the pairs but only produced phrases illustrating two meanings for half of the items. Moreover, he never came up with more than two meanings. Similarly, when asked to name as many different items as he could from a particular category in 20 seconds, e.g. different parts of the body or different types of sports, Richard produced an average of 8 items per category. This is well below the expected average of 12 (Thorum, 1986). Finally, Richard also had difficulty explaining the meaning of well-known idioms such as 'to pull the wool over your eyes', scoring at the lower end of average on a test containing such items.

It can be concluded that Richard had particular difficulty retrieving words from his mental dictionary that were related either by sound (MAIL/ MALE), or by sense (different things found in a grocer's shop). His 'low average for age' recognition and retrieval of words was in contrast to his above-average grammatical skills, and therefore constituted a specific lexical difficulty for him.

Next, we presented him with a number of tasks tapping auditory processing. Richard had no difficulty on tests of auditory discrimination even when complex non-word stimuli were included. Thus, his speech input was normal. In contrast, his performance on segmentation tests requiring the manipulation of auditory–verbal information was impaired. We focused on the tests given below.

Syllable segmentation

Awareness of the number of syllables (or 'beats') in a word is particularly important when spelling. Richard was able to count the number of 'beats' in his name and some common words. However, on the Fullerton subtest of syllabification of words and sentences, his score of 10/20 was significantly lower than expected for his age (Thorum, 1986). He had difficulties with words of four syllables and was only accurate on sentences containing up to five syllables.

Rhyme

Richard had no difficulties matching two rhyming pictures from a choice of three, e.g. BALL/WALL/bell. He scored 16/16 correct on this test (Stackhouse, 1989). Rhyme production, however, was more problematic for him. Although he could produce a rhyming word for each of ten target words, he could not produce a fluent rhyming string for these targets (mean number of responses per item was two, with a range of one to four). On the seven occasions when he did produce more than one rhyming word for the target, he only did so by repeating the target each time. His initial response to the first six items was to produce a word beginning with /m/, suggesting the use of a rigid strategy: HAT/mat, KEY/me, COMB/moan, BIN/min, SHELL/mell, DRAW/more.

Phonological awareness

Although, Richard could play I-Spy perfectly well, formal tests of phonological segmentation were more tricky for him. On the Bradley Test of Auditory Organisation (Bradley, 1980), he performed at chance level when required to spot the odd one out in a series of four items in which three shared the same initial consonant (pip, pin, HILL, pig). He found it much easier to identify the odd one out in a series of words where three shared the same final consonant and therefore rhymed (sun, gun, RUB, fun), scoring 7/8 correct. He could not, however, explain on what basis he was making these judgements.

Spoonerisms

To see how Richard tackled more difficult phonological processing tasks, he was introduced to spoonerisms. This is where the task is to interchange the initial consonants of two spoken words, e.g. Dolores Perin gives 'Polores Derin' (after Perin, 1983). He enjoyed this game and appeared to understand the principle when the written form was used as a cue. He could not, however, spoonerise on any test items. His responses were as follows:

Chuck Berry → Bruck Kerry
John Lennon → Glon Lennon
Bob Dylan   → No response
Bob Marley   → Barley for his last name
                        Marley Barley
                        Bob Marey

Richard's performance on consonant segmentation tasks was poor given his reading age. In addition, it was clear that Richard's reduced auditory memory hindered his performance on these tasks. For example, on the 'middle sound' subtest of the Bradley test, Richard could identify the odd one out in a series of three words, two of which had the same vowel, but not when four words were presented. Taken together, the results suggested that, as with Michael, he may have been relying on visual memory in order to increase his reading skills and to compensate for poor auditory–verbal skills.

Indeed, Richard's ability to apply alphabetic skills was limited. On a non-word reading test, he read 5/12 one-syllable non-words correctly (TIB, ZOG) and only 2/12 two-syllable items (AGWOP, LUMSEG). His errors indicated possible articulatory incoordination (SHUP – ['ʃʌmp], FID – [flɪd]), as well as syllabic and sequencing errors (STIPNOCK – [slɪ'po͵nɪk] [slɪ'to͵nɪk], ILDPOS – ['ɪdlɪ͵ops]). To investigate his use of alphabetic skills in spelling, words of increasing syllable length were presented (Snowling,

Stackhouse and Rack, 1986). He was able to spell 7/10 one-syllable words (PET, LIP), 1/10 two-syllable words (TULIP), but no three-syllable words. Unlike Michael, however, the majority of his errors on two-syllable words were phonetic in nature (APPLE/appul, KITTEN/kitun) and, on three-syllable words, his errors were semi-phonetic with some resemblance to the target (UMBRELLA/umbualar, REFRESHMENT/refashmnt).

Lastly, we investigated Richard's supposed 'unclear' speech. We began by asking him to repeat real words and nonsense words. He had no difficulty with simple non-words (DAKS, BIKUT) but he produced a number of errors on multisyllabic real words and non-words. The following examples summarise the main features of Richard's high level articulatory difficulty:

1. Perseveration of consonants when it is difficult to change articulation quickly – hence the two [d] consonants in the following:
   HAZARDOUS – hadardous ['hædədəs]
2. Problems programming longer words that contain consonant clusters, e.g. /sp st sk spl skr/:
   STATISTICS – sa sasis sasistiks
   [sə sə'sıs sə'sıs,tıks]
3. Consonant replacement, as with [g] in the following:
   SWIBBERY – swigery ['swıgə,ri]
4. Transposition of consonants or metathesis, for example /t/ and /k/ are reversed in:
   SPAPISTICS – spapiskits [spə'pıs,kıts]

Further difficulties arose in spontaneous speech where Richard wanted to use complex words in complex sentences. For example, he had to practise the pronunciation of new vocabulary before he could use it in his speech. An example he gave of this was his rehearsal of 'the greater spotted dog fish' – this interest in fish and sharks provided plenty of complex vocabulary to work on!

Problems with multisyllabic words and complicated phrases would explain why Richard's speech could be difficult to understand. He had gone beyond the more obvious level of having difficulty with articulating individual consonants. Instead, his problem was of sequencing consonants and producing them at speed in continuous speech. A phonetic analysis of Richard's speech confirmed these impressions. There were frequent examples of weak articulations in certain contexts, particularly at the ends of words and in phrases. He also omitted vowels and syllables on occasions particularly in longer phrases. For example, the following items in parenthesis were omitted:

whe(n) I we(nt) dow(n) f(or) my hol(i)day in Poole

they('ve) got a(n a)quarium

they('ve) got (to) turn over on th(eir) stoma(ch).

Richard's speech errors were similar in nature to those produced by Michael. Compared to Michael, however, Richard had a more 'hidden' speech disorder. The omissions, together with the imprecise articulation, would account for his parents' impression that sometimes Richard 'mumbled' and had unclear speech.

In summary, Richard had high level, and not very obvious, expressive speech and language difficulties. He did not have problems with speech input tasks and was functioning around the age-appropriate level on comprehension and production of grammatical structures. He did, however, have problems with speech output tasks. He had lexical difficulties, speech processing problems and specific articulatory difficulties.

At 11 years of age, both Michael and Richard presented with specific reading and spelling difficulties, and also speech and language difficulties. However, the different ways in which their difficulties manifested themselves led to them being labelled in different ways: Michael as a child with a speech and language disorder, and Richard as a child with reading and spelling problems.

Certainly, Michael's difficulties were much more severe. He had problems at the level of speech input, representation and output, and his reading and spelling development was seriously affected. In contrast, Richard's difficulties were specific to the speech output stage and this was reflected in his slightly more advanced reading and spelling development. However, although Richard's problems were not as *severe* as Michael's, they were no less *serious.* He was underachieving at school and in danger of being overlooked because he did not have an obvious speech and language disorder. His teachers saw him as being well behaved in class and in some respects to be coping better than others in his peer group. This had never been the case with Michael, because he had such an obvious speech and language disorder from the very beginning. When his reading and spelling problems emerged during the school years, the appropriate specialists were already at hand and ready to carry out a joint spoken and written language programme for him. Paradoxically, then, Michael was in a better position than Richard to receive early specialist help and to realise his potential in his literacy development.

Implications for Management

The view of 'dyslexia' as a special kind of language disorder (Snowling, 1987) has major implications for the management of children like Richard in particular. If reading and spelling problems are a later manifestation of a developmental speech and language disorder, it is important that speech and language therapists collaborate with teachers and educational psychologists in assessment and remediation. It is essential that psycholinguistic tests appropriate for investigating older children with subtle speech and language difficulties are used. The assessment needs to differentiate the child's strengths and weaknesses in different modalities at the input, representational and output levels of spoken and written language.

The view of 'dyslexia' as a speech and language disorder also has implications for remediation programmes. In addition to the teaching methods employed by specialist teachers, specific help with articulatory precision and associated metalinguistic awareness may strengthen the child's reading and spelling skills. To ensure that this work carries over, the speech therapist and teacher need to plan a programme based on their pooled knowledge of phonetics, linguistics, psychology and educational methods.

Conclusion

To return to the initial question: are the speech-, language- and reading-disordered populations the same or different? We would argue that both children presented in this chapter have a speech and language disorder, a manifestation of which is their reading and spelling difficulty. In this sense, they are from the same broad population. Within this group of speech- and language-disordered children, however, there is a range of patterns of deficits which will determine the precise nature of the reading and spelling problems shown (Snowling, Stackhouse and Rack, 1986).

It would be wrong to suggest that *all* children with reading and spelling problems have a speech and language disorder, and it would be equally wrong to give the impression that all children with speech and language problems will also have specific learning difficulties (Bishop and Adams, 1990). Further, when children with speech and language problems do have reading and spelling problems, this may be for a variety of reasons. For example, children with speech problems arising from poor health, or physical problems such as cleft lip and palate or cerebral palsy, may have prolonged absences from school and so miss out on essential teaching. Fluctuating hearing and attention problems are also correlates of delayed spoken and written language development. Such children, however, are no more at risk than the normal population for *specific* reading and spelling problems (Stackhouse, 1982; Bishop, 1985).

The speech-disordered children who do seem to be at risk for dyslexic difficulties are those described as having a phonological disorder – a problem with contrasting sounds meaningfully in speech (Robinson, Beresford and Dodd, 1981) – or those who have developmental verbal dyspraxia – a problem with programming and coordinating the vocal tract for speech (Stackhouse, 1982). Unlike the cases of cleft palate or cerebral palsy, there is no obvious cause of these children's speech problems but they have persisting speech, language and learning difficulties. Both Michael and Richard had speech problems of unknown aetiology, although at very different degrees of severity, and both had specific reading and spelling difficulties.

There is increasing evidence that children with specific speech and language disorders have associated reading and spelling problems (Stackhouse, 1990). We now need to turn our attention to the more subtle speech and language deficits to be found in children with reading and spelling difficulties. We need to develop more sensitive and probing assessments of higher level speech and language deficits in the older child and to work together on planning appropriate remediation programmes.

References

BISHOP, D.V.M. (1985). Spelling ability in congenital dysarthria: evidence against articulatory coding in translating between phonemes and graphemes. *Cognitive Neuropsychology* **2**, 229–251.

BISHOP, D.V.M. and ADAMS, C. (1990). A prospective study of the relationship between specific language impairment, physiological disorders and reading retardation. *Journal of Child Psychology* **31**, 1027–1050.

BRADLEY, L. (1980). *Assessing Reading Difficulties.* London: Macmillan Educational.

FRITH, U. (1985). Beneath the surface of developmental dyslexia. In: K.E. Patterson, J.C. Marshall and M. Coltheart (Eds), *Surface Dyslexia.* London: Routledge & Kegan Paul.

PERIN, D. (1983). Phonemic segmentation and spelling. *British Journal of Psychology* **74**, 129–144.

ROBINSON, P., BERESFORD, R. and DODD, B. (1982). Spelling errors made by speech disordered children. *Spelling Progress Bulletin* **22**, 19–20.

SNOWLING, M. (1987). *Dyslexia: A Cognitive Developmental Perspective.* Basil Blackwell.

SNOWLING, M., STACKHOUSE, J. and RACK, J. (1986). Phonological dyslexia and dysgraphia: a developmental analysis. *Cognitive Neuropsychology* **3**, 309–339.

STACKHOUSE, J. (1982). An investigation of reading and spelling performance in speech disordered children. *British Journal of Disorders of Communication* **17**, 53–60.

STACKHOUSE, R.J. (1989). *Phonological Dyslexia in Children with Developmental Verbal Dyspraxia.* Unpublished PhD Thesis, Psychology Department, University College, London.

STACKHOUSE, J. (1990). Phonological deficits in developmental reading and spelling disorders. In: P. Grunwell (Ed), *Developmental Speech Disorders.* Edinburgh: Churchill Livingstone.

THORUM, A.R. (1986). *The Fullerton Language Test for Adolescents.* Palo Alto, CA: Consulting Psychologists Press.

Chapter 14
Visual Dyslexia/Auditory Dyslexia: Is this a Valuable Distinction to Make?

ELAINE MILES

In their book *Learning Disabilities: Educational Principles and Practices*, Johnson and Myklebust (1967) came to the subject of dyslexia after a lengthy discussion of disorders of auditory language. In relation to disorders of reading, it was the visual aspect that struck them most. Reading, they say, is 'primarily a visual symbol system', although later they acknowledge that 'many auditory integrities are essential for its acquisition' (Johnson and Myklebust, 1967, p.173). Hinshelwood and Orton were similarly impressed with the visual appearance of the written work of dyslexics (see Miles and Miles, 1990). But, what is meant by visual dyslexia?

Visual Dyslexia

Johnson and Myklebust are clear that not all visual learning disabilities affect reading: 'Some affect non-verbal functions more than reading, others interfere with several forms of symbolic behavior including arithmetic and music' (1967, p.152).

They thus see a clear distinction between verbal and non-verbal behaviour. Nowadays, we would want to make this distinction even more pronounced, perhaps because we have abundant evidence that dyslexics perform no worse than anyone else in visual, non-verbal tasks. For a discussion of this evidence I would refer you to Hulme (1981) who cites a number of research experiments in which dyslexics performed as well as normal readers, e.g. when asked to pick the odd one out from several visual patterns. He also quotes evidence that they do not perform worse than normal readers on the Block Design subtest of the Wechsler Intelligence Scale for Children (WISC; Wechsler, 1977), and may even do better (see Thomson, 1990, for a review). Further evidence that visual processing is intact in dyslexia comes from an experiment carried out in Bangor by Ellis and Miles described in Chapter 6.

It therefore seems legitimate to exercise caution when reviewing the characteristics that Johnson and Myklebust list as prevailing among visual dyslexics, e.g. their tendency to produce inferior drawings, lacking in detail. By contrast we have evidence from group studies of dyslexic weaknesses in the WISC subtests of Digit Span, Coding and Arithmetic, involving verbal labelling skills.

The first example which Johnson and Myklebust give in their list of characteristics of visual dyslexics is failure to notice internal detail, the result being that there is confusion between words such as 'beg' and 'bog', or 'ship' and 'snip'. In fact the visual distinctions between 'beg' and 'bog' and between 'ship' and 'snip' are very tiny — one very small line in each case. Are the rest of us always so observant of visual detail? No. When faced with the well-known example of 'Paris in the the Spring' written inside a triangle in a particular formation, most of us fail to see the extra 'the'. The reason is that the force of context is so compelling. Similarly, we would notice the difference between 'beg' and 'bog' in most circumstances because the context would argue strongly for one rather than the other, 'beg' being a verb and 'bog' a noun and a much less common word at that. After all, those reading Hebrew manage to make a similar distinction without the vowels being there at all! We are influenced to pay attention to that small visual difference because we automatically see it as representing a difference in vowel sound. Dyslexics are not, of course, acutely aware of sound–symbol correspondences, and may be unable, in a difficult text, to hold semantic and phonological considerations in mind simultaneously.

The second characteristic of visual dyslexics, according to Johnson and Myklebust, is that their rate of perception is slow. They illustrate this by pointing to slow performance on a 'Visual Discrimination' exercise. The example that they give (1967, p.154) is one of those exercises in which there is a letter at the beginning of the line which has to be matched to a letter or letters further along the line, and these must be circled. An extra feature in Johnson and Myklebust's example is that the letter at the beginning of each line follows the order of the first ten letters of the alphabet, starting with 'a' for the first line. Thus, although such tests are *labelled* 'Visual Discrimination' tests, there is much more to them than visual discrimination: the letter has to be 'carried' in the mind as the subject scans along the line – this involves short-term memory; since short-term memory is phonologi- cally coded (Baddeley, 1986), it is obviously a great help if the letter to be matched is named. It is also an advantage if the person knows his or her alphabet, and can anticipate the next letter to be matched. Furthermore, efficient tracking is required and the eye or hand must not slip from one line to the next in doing the circling. It is entirely possible that the subject could discriminate between the letters if each were placed next to the letter at the beginning, and yet be slow in completing the task with all these complications. In short, test-labels can be very misleading, and may suggest an over-simplification of the factors involved.

A third characteristic of visual dyslexics mentioned by Johnson and Myklebust is 'reversal tendencies both in reading and writing'. The example given is the reading of 'dig' and 'big'. The term 'reversals' has often been used to cover both what Orton (1937) called 'kinetic' reversals – the transposition of letters – and what he called 'static' reversals such as these, which consist of the wrong orientation of a single letter. It is worth noting that these are not always found to be related in any way. For instance, in their study of a group of handicapped readers, Liberman and her colleagues (1971) found no correlation between these two types of errors. They also found that neither type of reversal accounted for a large proportion of errors in their sample (only about 25% altogether). Tordrup (1966), who studied reversals in reading, in spelling in written work and in dictation, found no significantly greater proportion in handicapped/retarded readers than in normal readers of similar levels in reading and spelling. In any case, it seems doubtful if these errors are all purely visual, because 'static' reversals seem to be bound up with letter production. Starting in the wrong place when writing the letter readily leads to reversals of orientation. Much the same can be said about the fourth characteristic mentioned by Johnson and Myklebust – the inversions of letters of which they show an example produced by a 6 year old. These seem, on inspection, to be an attempt to draw the way the letters move, zig-zag or curly respectively (from a starting place at the bottom, as children often do), rather than a *copy* of the finished product, and the fact that they end up exactly the wrong way up seems relatively accidental.

The fifth characteristic is the type of 'kinetic' reversal mentioned above – a transposition of the letters in a word. What Johnson and Myklebust quote is a case where the child has to copy a pattern of letters from memory after they have been withdrawn. However, spelling is not just copying a visual pattern; letters are put down to correspond to the sounds in a word. If the significance of each letter is not perceived, the order can easily be jumbled, as I myself often do on a word processor when I am already thinking of the next word as I type the previous one.

What we have come to realise, to a great extent because of the work of Liberman and her colleagues, is that it is not enough to consider letters purely from an optical point of view; we have to remember their linguistic function. Consequently, what Johnson and Myklebust took for granted as visual errors can be interpreted as being due to general insecurity in the use of the alphabetic code and in the reproduction of the symbols.

Auditory Dyslexia

The characteristics of the auditory dyslexic are also described by Johnson and Myklebust (1967). These include problems with auditory discrimination and phonetic analysis. Auditory dyslexics, they say, cannot 'hear' similarities in initial or final sounds of words or double consonant sounds, which they tend to write as one consonant; they find it difficult to discriminate short vowel sounds or recognise rhymes; they cannot break words up into syllables or into their constituent sounds; they cannot remember the sound of a letter, cannot say a word even knowing its meaning, cannot remember a rhythmic pattern. They are inferior in tasks that involve auditory memory, sequence and discrimination.

The immediate impression given by this list is that the children suffer from much more serious disadvantages than the ones with 'visual dyslexia'. Many of them are the weakness that Bryant and Bradley (1985), in their longitudinal study, found to be associated with least progress in learning to read and spell in the first 3 years of schooling. They seem to be fundamental and of an earlier stage by comparison with the characteristics of visual dyslexics, and this impression is reinforced by the ways of teaching recommended for each group. Whilst Johnson and Myklebust claimed that the visual dyslexic could start to learn the sounds of the letters, auditory dyslexics often have to start with more basic concepts.

> Often it is necessary for the teacher to begin instruction by explaining to the children that things have names that we can *hear* or *see* and what we *see* can also be written. Some auditory dyslexics, in particular, are unaware of the relationship between the spoken word and the printed symbol. (p.176)

This is a fundamental basis for learning to read that all infant teachers need to establish, if it is not already understood by their pupils. They do so by putting labels on pictures and by reading to children out of books while pointing to the pages and making clear that they get the story from the book in some way. However, there is nothing particularly related to any *auditory* weakness here. It is the 'symbolic' stage, later refined into a 'logographic' stage, of Frith (1985). It is only when the alphabet element comes in that the difficulties described above as characteristic of auditory dyslexics come into play. The 'visual dyslexics' do not seem to be failing at such a fundamental stage. They therefore seem to be milder cases. They have made progress *so far.* The 'auditory dyslexics' are the really severe cases.

Thus, the division into 'visual' and 'auditory' weaknesses is over-simplistic, although it is true that the weaknesses of the 'auditory dyslexic' (as described by Johnson and Myklebust) can be spotted before vision comes into the story (e.g. Bradley and Bryant, 1983). Also rather simplistic perhaps is the idea that we must start teaching them with completely contrasting methods. In the case of the 'auditory dyslexic', according to Johnson and Myklebust, a start must be made with whole words, and in the case of the 'visual dyslexic' with parts. However, Bryant and Bradley went straight into training in analysis with children who showed the weaknesses that Johnson and Myklebust call 'auditory', and made successful progress. In defence of Johnson and Myklebust, they never pursue their different teaching approaches to extremes; they claim that the two approaches converge. Both visual dyslexics and auditory dyslexics are said to need to acquire a systematic means of attacking words and this is described in much the same terms (compare Johnson and Myklebust, 1967, p.156 and p.176). It is more a question of the point at which a start is made.

I now want to turn from the pioneer work of Johnson and Myklebust themselves to examples of more recent judgements that a child is an 'auditory dyslexic' or a 'visual dyslexic'.

Visual and Auditory Tests

I have already mentioned that test labels are misleading, in that they list only some of the factors involved in the test. This is particularly important to bear in mind in connection with the use of apparently parallel tests, one auditory, one visual, to try to show children to be visual or auditory dyslexics. In the Illinois Test of Psycholinguistic Abilities (ITPA; Kirk, McCarthy and Kirk, 1968), there are a whole series of tests in pairs, one in the auditory modality, one in the visual modality, which superficially appear to be parallel to each other, e.g. Auditory Sequential Memory and Visual Sequential Memory. Liberman (1983), picking out the auditory and visual receptive language subtests of this battery, listed six differences between the so-called parallel tests other than the modality in which they were presented:

> A question to be answered 'yes' or 'no' is the test format in one, a multiple choice procedure in the other. One includes a time limit, the other does not. A memory factor is built into one and not in the other. Vocabulary level increases in difficulty in one and not in the other. In one, the subjects must know the words in order to perform the task, while in the other they receive credit simply by recognising objects and their functions or their relationship to other items, without knowing the names of any of the items.

As Liberman points out, the presence of all these other differences makes it quite unreasonable to suppose that such tests can determine modality preference. It is sometimes forgotten that these auditory tests and visual tests are really *auditory–vocal* tests and *visual–motor* tests. The full titles make it clear that there are *four* factors involved, not two: not just input, but also output. There are also other differences; in the Auditory Sequential Memory Test, a series of digits is presented one at a time, whereas in the Visual Sequential Memory Test, a sequence of nonsense patterns is presented at one time and then taken away. It then has to be reproduced by the manipulation, deft or otherwise, of tiles (in the case of the ITPA) or cards. It would be possible to present digits visually over time, but not easily within the confines of a test kit. However, McCarthy and Kirk did not design their test to determine modality preferences; their object, they tell us, was to cover three main psycholinguistic processes, two levels of organisation and two (out of a possible four) channels of communication. For the channels of communication, 'auditory–vocal' and 'visual–motor' were chosen simply 'as being most relevant for the developmental level of subjects in the test's age range'.

With these points in mind, we need also to approach the Aston Index with caution (Newton and Thomson, 1982). Here there are two visual sequential memory tests (one pictorial and one symbolic) and one auditory sequential memory test. On each of these tests, during the validation trials, dyslexic children had significantly lower scores than the control group of good readers and spellers. However, this does not seem to warrant sorting children into groups with auditory problems and groups with visual problems and allotting them teaching methods on that basis, as is suggested in the Aston Portfolio (Aubrey et al., 1982). The reason is once again that the tests are not similar in every respect other than modality. Although the Aston Index is a useful tool for teachers, in that it picks out areas in which low performance is likely to be a mark of dyslexia, there is the danger of taking the visual–auditory distinctions too seriously, rather than concentrating on linguistic teaching.

Boder's Classification

A classification into three subtypes was proposed by Boder (1973). She called them 'dysphonetic', 'dyseidetic' and 'mixed'. A child is 'dyseidetic', by her criterion, if he or she is better at attempting to spell unknown words phonetically than at spelling words already in his or her reading-sight vocabulary, and also if he or she cannot read words on a flash card within 10 seconds (supposedly only possible by 'whole word' methods). However, van den Bos (1984) classified a group of children of 9 and 10 years old according to Boder's instructions – but in Dutch, of course – and tested them afterwards on memory of single letters presented auditorily and visually respectively. Although all the dyslexics did poorly compared with controls on these tests, he found no difference between the groups according to whether the letters were presented auditorily or visually. If the classification does not have implications of this kind, then we must doubt whether the terms 'auditory' and 'visual' mean much as regards the nature of the children's disabilities. Yet certainly it is this sort of implication that teachers are likely to assume in choosing their teaching methods. Another study of 50 neurologically impaired children between 11 and 19 years of age by Casey Dorman (1987) found Boder's dyseidetic spelling patterns equally in the good readers and the poor readers among the group.

Furthermore, Boder gives as her typical examples of 'dysphonetic' and 'dyseidetic' pupils, two boys of widely different ages (15 and 8;6 years), intelligence level (IQ 92 and IQ 145) and past school experience (the older boy had been in a remedial reading class for 3 years, where, in view of his age, the emphasis might well have been on acquiring sight words). The differences in reading/spelling 'style' may therefore reflect stages in learning the different subskills rather than permanent characteristics of the individuals. It seems unreasonable to assume that the emphasis in school teaching and the length of time for compensatory strategies to have developed would have *no* influence at all on a child's approach; the compensatory strategies that Frith (1985) talks about are developed both by the child him- or herself and by the efforts of his or her teachers.

Thus, before we start assigning type distinctions we must surely pick cases of similar age and life experience. I would suggest that the comparisons which do not have this similarity (e.g. in Snowling, Hulme and Goulandris, 1990, between JM and JAS), do not start off very strongly in this respect. The compensatory strategies resorted to independently over the years by an intelligent, context-conscious college student who is only mildly dyslexic, cannot easily be compared with the struggles of a very severely dyslexic child; there is too much overlay of different experience. There have been other attempts to classify dyslexia into subtypes (see Thomson, 1990, for a review), but the above have been used to support teaching approaches.

Conclusions

To return to the initial question: Is visual dyslexia/auditory dyslexia a valuable distinction? It would seem not.

First of all it seems that we are on very shaky ground in talking about visual dyslexia at all, since many so-called 'visual' errors can be viewed as due to linguistic deficiencies which prevent mastery of the alphabetic code, its symbols and its relationship to the oral language on which it is based. It seems that weaknesses shown up by tests are not necessarily modality-related; we deceive ourselves if we assume that any weakness on a visually presented test is necessarily connected with that modality. Even when a stimulus is presented visually, it may be represented in short-term memory in a phonological form. This was demonstrated, e.g. by Conrad (1964), who showed that when his subjects (normal readers) attempted to recall sequences of capital letters presented visually, letters chosen in error *sounded* like the correct ones. For instance 'B' might be remembered as 'C', 'P', 'T' or 'V'.

The main difference that can be noted between Johnson and Myklebust's 'visual dyslexics' and their 'auditory dyslexics' is that the former are much milder cases. They may be children who have *strengths* that have enabled them to cope to some extent and adopt compensatory strategies to add to the diversity of the pattern of behaviour that they show. The children certainly need teaching which will make them more secure about grapheme–phoneme relationships and more able to combine context and phonic information in the right ways, and that should be the main concern of their teachers rather than preoccupation with stressing one particular modality. Reading and writing *are* multisensory activities and the senses can and do support each other and interact with each other.

As regards the other group, if group it is, who by comparison seem to be non-starters, perhaps we should shift the emphasis just a little from *hearing* towards *speech*; the two are closely related when it comes to acquiring phonological skills. Campbell, Wright and Burden (1990), in an interesting study of school leavers who were born deaf, found that *some* deaf people achieve phonological awareness and that this seems to be related *more to the extent to which they have acquired speech than to a degree of deafness.* Some of these deaf people showed some of the same characteristics of phonological coding of visual stimuli as normal hearers, when the Conrad experiment mentioned earlier was tried with them as subjects. We therefore should remember that so-called auditory tests are auditory–*vocal.* It is interesting to note the difference of emphasis if a digit span test is called a 'repetition test' rather than an 'auditory test' – this is perfectly legitimate. I remember a child who was given pairs of words, as in an auditory discrimination test, and asked whether they were the same or different. He found it very hard, and finally he cried out 'But I can't *say* those words!'. To hear the differences he seemed to need to be able to say them himself, not just hear them from others. Then again phonemes are in fact not just *heard* separately; they tend to be articulated together and are therefore simultaneously transmitted. A child has to learn to analyse words, to separate the phonemes by 'toying' perhaps with the articulation as we do when rhyming. A severe dyslexic in a specialist lesson may notice for himself his chin dropping each time as he reads aloud a list of words all with a (short) 'a' in them, and then he is able to abstract that chin-dropping sound, better than if he were just told to listen. This articulatory factor makes it important that we encourage dyslexic children to talk things through, to try out words aloud and to say for themselves in their own words what they have to do, for instance in adding suffixes or following other linguistic rules.

Finally, dividing dyslexics into groups by such artificial distinctions as we have found visual/auditory dyslexia to be leads to equally contrived artificial distinctions in teaching, instead of efforts being concentrated on those aspects of the written language which this particular child lacks, at the level that he or she has reached.

References

AUBREY, C., EAVES, J., HICKS, C. and NEWTON, M. (1982). *The Aston Portfolio.* Wisbech: Learning Development Aids.

BADDELEY, A.D. (1986). *Working Memory.* Oxford: Clarendon Press.

BODER, E. (1973). Developmental dyslexia: a diagnostic approach based on three atypical reading-spelling patterns. *Developmental Medicine and Child Neurology* **15**, 663–687.

BRADLEY, L. and BRYANT, P. (1983). Categorising sounds and learning to read: a causal connection. *Nature* **301**, 419.

BRYANT, P.E. and BRADLEY, L. (1985). *Children's Reading Problems.* Oxford: Blackwell.

CAMPBELL, R., WRIGHT, H. and BURDEN, V. (1990). Spelling and speaking in prelingual deafness; old wine in new bottles or new wine in old bottles? *Proceedings of Conference on Psychology, Spelling and Education*, Newcastle 1990, in press.

CONRAD, R. (1964). Acoustic confusion in immediate memory. *British Journal of Psychology* **55**, 75–84.

DORMAN, C. (1987). Reading disability sub-types in neurologically-impaired students. *Annals of Dyslexia* **XXXVII**, 166–168.

ELLIS, N.C. and MILES, T.R. (1978). Visual information processing in dyslexic children. In: M.M. Gruneberg, P.E. Morris and R.N. Sykes (Eds), *Practical Aspects of Memory.* New York: Academic Press.

FRITH, U. (1985). Beneath the surface of developmental dyslexia. In: K.E. Patterson, J.C. Marshall and M. Coltheart (Eds), *Surface Dyslexia.* London: Lawrence Erlbaum.

HULME, C. (1981). *Reading Retardation and Multisensory Teaching.* London: Routledge & Kegan Paul.

JOHNSON, D.J. and MYKLEBUST, H.R. (1967). *Learning Disabilities: Education Principles and Practices.* New York: Grune & Stratton.

KIRK, S.A., MCCARTHY, J.J. and KIRK, W.D. (1968). *The Illinois Test of Psycholinguistic Abilities.* University of Illinois.

LIBERMAN, I.Y. (1983). Should so-called modality preferences determine the nature of instruction for children with reading disabilities? Paper given at the International Consortium on Dyslexia, Halkidiki, Greece.

LIBERMAN, I.Y., SHANKWEILER, D., ORLANDO, C., HARRIS, K. and BELL-BERTI, F. (1971). Letter confusions and reversals of sequence in the beginning reader: implications for Orton's theory of developmental dyslexia. *Cortex* **7**, 127–142.

MILES, T.R. and MILES, E. (1990). *Dyslexia: A Hundred Years On.* Milton Keynes: Open University Press.

NEWTON, M. and THOMSON, M. (1982). *The Aston Index.* Wisbech: Learning Development Aids.

ORTON, S.T. (1937). *Reading, Writing and Speech Problems in Children.* New York: Norton.

SNOWLING, M., HULME, C. and GOULANDRIS, N. (1990). Phonological coding deficits in dyslexia. *Proceedings of the BDA First International Conference.*

THOMSON, M.E. (1990). *Developmental Dyslexia: Its Nature, Assessment and Remediation*, 3rd edn. London: Whurr.

TORDRUP, S.A. (1966). Reversals in reading and spelling. *The Slow Learning Child* **12**, 173–183.

VAN DEN BOS, K.P. (1984). Letter processing in dyslexic subgroups. *Annals of Dyslexia* **34**, 179–193.

WECHSLER, D. (1977). *Wechsler Intelligence Scale for Children – Revised.* New York: The Psychological Corporation.

Chapter 15
Is Medicinal Treatment of Dyslexia Advisable?

C.R. WILSHER

I have argued elsewhere (Wilsher, 1978) that the learning disability sometimes called dyslexia should not be viewed as a 'disease', but as a handicap. This handicap might be ameliorated by providing 'environmental' help, e.g. word processing or by attempts to influence the child by, for example, teaching. Attempts at 'medical' intervention have varied widely and the purpose of this chapter is briefly to review a number of different approaches, but the main focus will be the evidence and issues surrounding the use of 'nootropic' drugs.

Megavitamins

It has been popularly proposed that taking extremely large doses of vitamins will help children with learning disabilities to function better. There appears to be no medical basis for the idea that taking several times the recommended daily dose will help learning; in fact some vitamins are toxic and must not be taken in excess. Rimland (1981), at a conference of the Association for Children with Learning Disabilities (Atlanta, 1981), described a study in which interested doctors could enroll learning-disabled children and prescribe large doses of the exact combination of vitamins thought necessary. Following this, each doctor was telephoned some months later and asked for his or her reactions. According to this survey, large numbers of learning-disabled children began to perform better at school, and only a few encountered toxic side effects. Rimland concluded that 'solid, incontestable research, as well as an enormous amount of clinical evidence, shows megavitamin therapy ... to be the treatment of choice for learning and behavior disorders'.

This study is too easy to criticise for its lack of controls, objective measures or double-blind procedures. The only data presented were a 'head-count' of the number of children 'said' to have improved by a doctor over the telephone. This is a very 'low' level of measurement, and of an extremely subjective nature. The study would have more credibility if it had employed more objective measures (i.e. performance tests), which would yield a more sophisticated form of measurement (i.e. reading ages), which in turn would allow us to see the amount of improvement.

However, there has been a recent study that has looked, in a scientific manner, at the effect of the daily recommended dose of multivitamins on intellectual performance. Benton and Roberts (1988) conducted a double-blind, placebo-controlled study of 30 children treated for 8 months. They found no improvement in verbal IQ, but a significant increase in non-verbal IQ. Although this is a properly controlled study, it is of limited relevance to dyslexia: normal children were studied, not dyslexics; reading performance was not studied; and improvements in non-verbal IQ are of little use to a group who perform well on this measure. An attempt to replicate this result by Naismith et al. (1988) with a much larger sample ($n = 154$) failed to find the same result. This again highlights the problem of small group studies in which a positive (or for that matter negative) result may appear by chance. Further replication studies have disagreed about the size of effect and whether the results are chance effects.

Antihistamines

The use of antihistamines to treat dyslexia was pioneered by Levinson (1980) in the USA. His theory is that dyslexics suffer from a cerebellar–vestibular disorder which results in their feeling motion-sick. This, according to Levinson, causes difficulty in processing text which seems to move. Reviews of this work (e.g. Masland, 1984) show that there is no substance to this theory. In fact, there are patients with such severe vestibular disorders that they find it extremely difficult to maintain balance but yet suffer no problem with their reading. In addition, a study of developmental dyslexics (Brown et al., 1983) shows that dyslexics have no greater incidence of vestibular problems than controls.

Unfortunately, these methodological shortcomings do not seem to diminish the enthusiasm of Levinson and his followers. Levinson's treatment is by drug – 'Each individual was treated with one or more of a series of such antimotion sickness drugs as cyclizine (Marezine), meclizine (Antivert), dimenhydrinate (Dramimine), diphenhydramine (Benadryl), methylphenidate (Ritalin), etc.' (Levinson, 1980, p.236). Levinson evaluates the efficacy of the treatment by soliciting reports from the children treated and their parents. He also assesses them on a device designed to test the speed of fusion of moving pictures of elephants. He does not use control groups because he argues it is unethical to withhold treatment. However, Levinson's own measures failed to be affected by the treatment, 'the expected ability to objectively record and quantitatively measure these responses via … blurring speeds did not materialize' (p.252). In these studies only the subjective impression of the child or the parents supports the claim that 88% of dyslexics 'were found to demonstrate some clinical measure or degree of favourable therapeutic response' (p.237). It is not known whether the same degree of improvement could be found in placebo groups.

Applied Kinesiology

Chiropractors in the USA have recently advertised that they can cure dyslexia and learning disabilities. The basis for the theory and treatment is a book by Ferreri and Wainwright (1984) *'Breakthrough for Dyslexia and Learning Disabilities'*. The authors theorise that learning disabilities are caused by damage to two specific cranial bones, the sphenoid and the temporal, by what they call 'cloacal reflexes', and by an ocular muscle imbalance they term 'ocular lock'. Silver (1986) in his review of 'magic cures' for dyslexia concluded that their treatment was 'not based on any known research; that some of it was based on anatomical concepts that are not held by the majority of anatomists; that there was no research done by others that replicates the proposed cures; and, that there were no follow-up research studies to document the claimed results'.

Psychostimulants

Psychostimulants such as methylphenidate and dexamphetamine have been shown to improve attention in hyperactive learning-disabled children (Cohen, Douglas and Morganstern, 1971; Barkley, 1977; Barkley and Jackson, 1977). However, studies of educational performance of treated children compared to unmedicated hyperactive children reveal no gain due to the drugs (Quinn and Rappoport, 1975; Weis et al., 1975). Furthermore, when non-hyperactive learning-disabled children are studied (in double-blind controlled trials), no benefit to reading is documented (Gittelman-Klein and Klein, 1976; Aman and Werry, 1982; Gittelman et al., 1983). Stimulants do not appear to address themselves specifically to the central problem area of the reading-disabled child, i.e. reading performance.

Nootropics

Since 1979 there have been several reports that piracetam (2-oxopyrrolidin-1-ylacetamide, trade names Nootropil, Nootropyl, Nootrop, Noostan) may be of use in treating children with reading disability. It was first used clinically some 25 years ago and is now on sale in 85 countries, mainly for memory problems in the elderly. Piracetam is structurally related to the naturally occurring neurotransmitter, γ-aminobutyric acid (GABA), and is purported selectively to improve the efficiency of higher cognitive functions, and to belong to a class of psychoactive drugs known as 'nootropics' (Giurgea and Salama, 1977).

The exact mechanism of the action of piracetam is unknown. Whilst its similarity to GABA seems to be only structural, there is some evidence that piracetam increases the turnover of ATP (adenosine triphosphate), which would increase the energy of cells (Gobert and Temmerman, 1974). The neuropsychological effect of piracetam has not been sufficiently studied, but work so far suggests that the drug seems to improve left hemisphere functioning (Dimond, 1975). In the last two decades over 20 centres, involving over 900 children, have reported studies on learning disabilities and piracetam. To save space only a few of the larger studies will be reviewed.

A large-scale, multicentred, long-term study of piracetam in dyslexia was undertaken at five universities in the USA (Wilsher et al., 1987): 225 dyslexic children were recruited in a 36-week, double-blind, placebo-controlled trial of 3.3 grams of piracetam per day. Children of below average intelligence, or with abnormal findings on audiological, ophthalmological, neurological, psychiatric and physical examinations, were excluded from the trial. The children were of average IQ (full-scale IQ, WISC-R = 104.3) and an average of 3.4 school grades (years) behind expected reading age on the Gray Oral Reading Test. In this study all centres were closely and regularly monitored (by independent monitors) to ensure comparability of diagnosis and veracity of data recording. Two hundred children completed the 36-week study, conducted during the 1983–84 school year. Primary efficacy measures were:

1. The Gray Oral Reading Test (Gray, 1963) – this is a prose reading test with a total passage score which combines speed and accuracy, and a comprehension checklist.
2. Both forms C and D (at baseline and 36 weeks) of the Gilmore Oral Reading Test (Gilmore and Gilmore, 1968) – a prose reading test similar to the Neale Analysis of Reading, yielding rate, accuracy and a standardised comprehension score. However, unlike the Neale test, children are not supplied with words they cannot read (or read incorrectly) and they are given credit for comprehension questions within their ability but to which they have not gained access because of their accuracy. These two provisions mean that the Gilmore test is a more rigorous test and not given to sudden changes in comprehension score when accuracy improves slightly.
3. The Wide Range Achievement Test – Revised (WRAT-R) Reading subtest (Jastak and Wilkinson, 1984) – a single-word reading test which yields a score of the number of words correctly read.

Both groups of children had the same amount of remediation at baseline. However, during the course of this very long controlled trial, 12 children on placebo had extra help given to them (compared to 5 in the piracetam group), and 4 had their help reduced (compared to 6 on piracetam). This means that there was an educational influence against finding a drug effect (i.e. in favour of placebo). Analysis of baseline scores revealed that, although the demographic profile of the piracetam treatment group was similar to that of the placebo group, some reading test scores were slightly lower ($P<0.05$). Only one of the five centres was found to have significant differences between treatment groups of baseline, and the removal of that site's data eliminated the significant baseline differences for the whole group. Consequently, the results of the study were reported both with and without these data. In addition, co-variance analysis was performed, co-varying change by baseline score to eliminate any baseline effects. Significant effects common to both analyses were found on the Gray Oral Total Passage score ($P<0.05$) and the Gilmore Oral Comprehension score ($P<0.01$). There were also significant effects found in the more homo-geneous sample (the sample with equal baselines) on the Gray Oral Comprehension score ($P<0.05$) and the WRAT-R Reading score ($P<0.05$) (details of these results are reported in Wilsher et al., 1987). This study does contain some 'internal replication' because three of the five study centres produced significant drug-related findings within their own patient samples.

Conners and Reader (1987) found that dyslexic children treated with piracetam made significantly more progress than those taking placebo on the Gray Oral Reading Test Passage score, the Gilmore Oral Reading Test Accuracy (form D only) and Comprehension Scores. They concluded that their results suggest that 'the gain made by children who received piracetam is greater than the academic gain made by learning-disabled children who participated in other controlled treatment outcome studies'. The second team (Chase and Tallal, 1987) found significant drug-related improvements in the Gray Oral Reading Test Passage score, the improve-ment in the piracetam group being 58% compared to 33% in the placebo group. There were also significant improvements in reading comprehen-sion at 36 weeks (Gilmore Oral test), the piracetam group making 22% gain compared with 7% in the placebo group. The single word reading test (WRAT-R) showed significant results favouring piracetam at 24 and 36 weeks, culminating in a 12% improvement in the treated group and a 6% change on placebo. Finally, Helfgott et al. (1987) report the clinical results of their part of the 36-week study.

Their results showed a significant improvement in single word reading (WRAT-R) at 12 weeks, but by 24 weeks this diminished to only a trend. On the Gray Oral Reading Test Passage Score the piracetam group improved significantly more than the placebo group at 12 and 24 weeks; however, by 36 weeks, although the piracetam group had made more progress than the placebo group, this was no longer statistically significant.

In contrast, the effect of piracetam on reading comprehension appeared to be very durable: there were significant drug-induced improvements in both the Gray Oral and the Gilmore Oral Reading Comprehension Scores.

The results of the individual centres of this multicentre study show the advantage of pooling results from many centres. Although there are many results that replicate between centres and are significant in the overall analysis (Gray Oral Reading Test and Gilmore Oral Reading Test comprehension), there is one result that does not. The significant piracetam group improvements in single word reading (WRAT-R), seen by several sites, was not significant in the total analysis. Therefore we may conclude that piracetam may have a significant effect on reading and understanding paragraphs (similar to reading a book), but the effects seen on single word reading may possibly be chance occurrences.

Levi and Sechi (1987) conducted a double-blind study of 127 Italian learning-disabled children, aged 7;6–12;6 years, treated with 3.2 grams of piracetam per day for 20 weeks. All the children were of average IQ, had no psychiatric or medical problems and were at least 2 years behind in one of the following tests: silent reading comprehension, oral reading accuracy, oral reading speed and writing accuracy. Most of the children were behind in all of these. The results of the study showed a complete lack of action of piracetam on tests of spatial ability or tests of concentration (attention). However, piracetam did significantly improve the recall of an oral story, the ability to solve anagrams and prose reading accuracy on a standardised reading test. A co-variance analysis of the standardised reading test (co-varying change by baseline), for all children having baseline and end-point data, showed a 35% improvement in the piracetam-treated group, compared to a 7.8% improvement in the placebo group. This result independently replicates the result on the Gray Oral Reading Test found by Wilsher et al. (1987). Although silent reading comprehension was more significantly improved in the piracetam group, in the Levi study there was no significant difference between treatment groups (no measure of *oral* reading comprehension was taken). In a special subgroup ($n=38$) of children with extremely poor written language ability, piracetam significantly improved reading accuracy and writing accuracy (however, subgroup analysis should always be regarded with caution).

A large open study by Castello et al. (1985) in Spain studied 80 learning-disabled children aged 5–15 years. These children were given piracetam for 6 months. The researchers rated 48.5% as progressing very well, 32.2% as progressing well and 19.1% did not improve. There were also significant improvements from baseline in verbal, performance and full-scale IQ and the Boder Test. There was no control group so all of these improvements could be natural changes or just test–retest changes. Studies such as this do not advance our knowledge much except to demonstrate the long-term use of piracetam with what the authors say is excellent acceptance of the medication.

In an attempt to understand the neurophysiological mechanisms underlying the clinical findings, Conners et al. (1984, 1987) conducted two electrophysiological studies into the effect of piracetam on dyslexia. The first was a pilot study using visual event-related potentials of dyslexic boys after a 12-week double-blind trial of piracetam. The paradigm was one in which the subjects carried out a continuous performance task that involved identifying letter pairs or shape pairs. The results of this pilot study were not conclusive (probably due to the small number of subjects), but they did demonstrate that piracetam had an effect on late potentials to letter hits (correctly detecting letters) in the left hemisphere. A second, much larger study ($n=29$) used dyslexic children who had been treated (double-blind) for 32 weeks. Using the same paradigm, the investigators reported significant drug effects on performance (enhancing letter detection), and on event-related potentials associated with letter hits. This led them to conclude that 'piracetam enhances feature analysis and increases attentional resources among dyslexics when the stimuli are recognised as having linguistic significance'.

Discussion

The results from 'medical' methods of treatment of dyslexia have been mixed to say the least. Most of these methods rely upon the replacement of deficits that have *not* been proved to be aetiologically significant in dyslexia (such as vitamin deficiency). Others have been shown to have little theoretical or practical formulation.

However, a recent increase in neuropsychological investigations of dyslexia has revealed problems with verbal short-term memory, phonological encoding, sequencing and naming. These findings coincide with the neuroanatomical findings which implicate left hemisphere language and adjacent areas in the brains of dyslexics (Galaburda and Kemper, 1979; Galaburda et al., 1985). The possibility of treating the neuropsychological deficits in dyslexic children by the use of nootropics opens up interesting and intriguing possibilities. However, it must be remembered that no treatment offers a 'cure' and perhaps the notion that large improvements can be gained from any intervention may be misguided.

References

AMAN, M.G. and WERRY, J.S. (1982). Methylphenidate and diazepam in severe reading retardation. *Journal of the American Academy of Child Psychiatry.*
BARKLEY, R.A. (1977). The effects of methylphenidate on various types of activity level and attention in hyperkinetic children. *Journal of Abnormal Child Psychology* **5**, 351–369.

BARKLEY R.A. and JACKSON, T.L. (1977). Hyperkinesis, autonomic nervous system activity and stimulant drug effects. *Journal of Child Psychology and Psychiatry* **18**, 347–357.

BENTON, D. and ROBERTS, G. (1988). Effect of vitamin and mineral supplementation on intelligence of a sample of schoolchildren. *The Lancet* 140–143.

BROWN, B., HAEGERSTROM-PORTNOY, G., YINGLING, C.D., HERRON, J., GALIN, D. and MARCUS, M. (1983). Dyslexic children have normal vestibular responses to rotation. *Archives of Neurology* **40**, 370–373.

CHASE, C.H., SCHMITT, R.L., RUSSELL, G. and TALLAL, P. (1984). A new chemotherapeutic investigation: piracetam effects on dyslexia. *Annals of Dyslexia* **34**, 29–48.

CHASE, C.H. and TALLAL, P. (1987). Piracetam and dyslexia: A thirty-six week double-blind clinical trial. In: D. Bakker, C. Wilsher, H. Debruyne and N. Bertin (Eds), *Child Health and Development*, Vol. 5: *Dyslexia and Learning Disorders*. Basel: Karger.

COHEN, N.J., DOUGLAS, V.I. and MORGANSTERN, G. (1971). The effect of methylphenidate on attentive behavior and autonomic activity in hyperactive children. *Psychopharmacology* **22**, 282–294.

CONNERS, C.K., BLOUIN, A.G., WINGLEE, M., LOUGE, L., O'DONNELL, D. and SMITH, A. (1984). Piracetam and event-related potentials in dyslexic children. *Psychopharmacology Bulletin* **20**, 667–673.

CONNERS, C.K. and READER, M. (1987). The effects of piracetam on reading achievement and visual event-related potentials in dyslexic children. In: D. Bakker, C. Wilsher, H. Debruyne and N. Bertin (Eds), *Child Health and Development*, Vol. 5: *Dyslexia and Learning Disorders*. Basel: Karger.

CONNERS, C.K., READER, M., REISS, A., CALDWELL, L., CALDWELL, A., ADESMAN, A. et al. (1987). The effects of piracetam upon visual event-related potentials in dyslexic children. *Psychophysiology* **24**, 513–521.

DIMOND, S.J. (1975). Drugs to improve learning in man: implications and neuropsychological analysis. *NATO Conference*, Denmark.

DIMOND, S.J. and BROUWERS, E.Y.M. (1976). Increase in the power of human memory in normal man through the use of drugs. *Psychopharmacology* **49**, 307–309.

FEINGOLD, B.F. (1975). Hyperkinesis and learning disabilities linked to artificial food flavors and colors. *American Journal of Nursing* **75**, 797–803.

FERRERI, C.A. and WAINWRIGHT, R.B. (1984) *Breakthrough for Dyslexia and Learning Disabilities*, p.504. Pompano Beach: Exposition Press of Florida.

GALABURDA, A.M. and KEMPER, T.L. (1979). Cytoarchitectonic abnormalities in developmental dyslexia: A case study. *Annals of Neurology* **6**, 94–100.

GALABURDA, A.M., SHERMAN, G.F., ROSEN, G.D., ABOITIZ, F. and GESCHWIND, N. (1985). Developmental Dyslexia: four patients with cortical anomalies. *Annals of Neurology* **18**, 222–233.

GILMORE, V.J. and GILMORE, C.E. (1968). *Gilmore Oral Reading Test*. New York: Harcourt Brace Jovanovich.

GITTELMAN-KLEIN, R. and KLEIN, D.F. (1976). Methylphenidate effects in learning disabilities. Psychometric changes. *Archives of General Psychiatry* **33**, 655–664.

GITTELMAN, R., KLEIN, D. and FEINGOLD, I. (1983). Children with reading disorders: II Effects of methylphenidate in combination with reading remediation. *Child Psychology and Psychiatry* **24**, 193–212.

GITTELMAN, R. (1983). Treatment of Reading Disorders. In: M. Rutter (Ed.), *Developmental Neuropsychiatry*. New York: Guilford Press.

GIURGEA, C. and SALAMA, M. (1977). Nootropic drugs. *Progressive Neuropsychopharmacology* **1**, 235–247.

GOBERT, J.G. and TEMMERMAN, J.J. (1974). Piracetam induced modifications of the brain polyribosome content in ageing rat. In: D. Platt (Ed.) *Altern*, pp. 143–147. Stuttgart: Schattauer Verlag.

GRAY, W.S. (1963). *Gray Oral Reading Test.* Austin, Texas: ProEd.

HELFGOTT, E., RUDEL, R.G., KOPLEWICZ, H. and KRIEGER, J. (1987). The effect of piracetam on reading test performance of dyslexic children. In: D. Bakker, C. Wilsher, H. Debruyne and N. Bertin (Eds), *Child Health and Development*, Vol. 5, *Dyslexia and Learning Disorders*. Basel: Karger.

JASTAK, J. and WILKINSON, S. (1984). *Wide Range Achievement Test – Revised.* Wilmington, Delaware: Jastak Associates.

LEVI, G. and SECHI, E. (1987). A study of piracetam in the pharmacological treatment of learning disabilities. In: D. Bakker, C. Wilsher, H. Debruyn and N. Bertin (Eds), *Child Health and Development*, Vol. 5: *Dyslexia and Learning Disorders*, pp. 129–139. Basel: Karger.

LEVINSON, H.N. (1980). *A Solution to the Riddle Dyslexia.* New York: Springer-Verlag.

MASLAND, R.L. (1984). Book Review, *Newsletter of New York Branch of the Orton Dyslexia Society*, November.

NAISMITH, D.J., NELSON, M., BURLEY, V.J. and GATENBY, S.J. (1988). Can children's intelligence be increased by vitamin and mineral supplements? *The Lancet* **ii**, 335.

QUINN, P.O. and RAPPOPORT, J.L. (1975). One year follow-up of hyperactive boys treated with imipramine or methylphenidate. *American Journal of Psychiatry* **132**, 241–245.

RIMLAND, B. (1981). *Megavitamin therapy and other nutritional approaches to correcting learning and behaviour disorders.* Paper presented at the International Conference of Association for Children and Adults with Learning Disabilities, Atlanta, Georgia, USA, February 18–21, 1981. Abstracts, p.52.

SILVER, L.B. (1987). The 'Magic Cure': A review of the current controversial approaches for treating learning disabilities. *Journal of Learning Disabilities* **20**(8), 498.

WEISS, G., KRUGER, E., DANIELSON, U, and ELMAN, M. (1975). Effect of long-term treatment of hyperactive children with methylphenidate. *Canadian Medical Association Journal* **11**, 159–165.

WILSHER, C.R. (1978). Is dyslexia a disease? *QMM Journal of Birmingham Medical and Dental Schools* **65**, 13–15.

WILSHER, C.R., BENNETT, D., CHASE, C.H., CONNERS, C.K., DIIANNI, M., FEAGANS, L. et al. (1987). Piracetam and dyslexia: Effects on reading tests. *Journal of Clinical Psychopharmacology* **7**, 4.

Part V
Intervention: Empirical
Studies of Teaching

Chapter 16
The Remediation of Reading Comprehension Difficulties

JANE OAKHILL and NICOLA YUILL

This chapter is in two main sections. In the first, we will provide a brief overview of some of the experimental work on ways of improving children's reading comprehension. In the second, we will describe two experiments of our own which have explored different methods of remediation for children who have a specific comprehension problem.

Review of Research into Improving Reading Comprehension

In this section, we will consider ways in which comprehension of, and learning from, text might be improved. In many cases, normal readers can also benefit from the aids and strategies we will discuss, but our focus will be on ways to improve the comprehension of poor readers. We will consider studies comparing good and poor readers, and some dealing just with normal readers. Any method for improving comprehension generally is likely to be of help to children with particular comprehension difficulties, although specific proof that a particular method helps such children may not be available.

Since the process of remediation always takes time, some measure should be obtained of how children given no specific remediation progress over the same time period. If improvements are to be attributed to the remediation instruction, it must be shown that these improvements occur *over and above* any improvement that would have occurred anyway. The scores of the control groups can be used as a baseline, against which the effectiveness of the remediation treatment can be measured.

There are three main ways in which comprehension and learning from text can be improved, only one of which will be considered in any detail here. First, there are various additions or changes that can be made to a text to improve its comprehensibility and memorability. Such additions and changes are made *for* readers, and require no active effort on their part. Additions might include pictures, titles and summary statements; other changes are usually aimed at improving the organisation and coherence of the text. Secondly, readers can engage in various activities either during or after reading the text, e.g. underlining, note-taking and summary writing. Such activities are usually referred to as 'study aids'. Although such aids are generally thought of as a means by which students *learn from* text, research has also shown that they can be used to improve comprehension (for a summary, see Oakhill and Garnham, 1988). The third set of aids to comprehension are processing strategies that children can be taught to apply as they are reading – ways to think about the text, about whether it relates to what they know and about whether their understanding is adequate. Such strategies are designed primarily to improve comprehension rather than to aid learning. They differ from the first two types of aid in that they rely entirely on what goes on in the reader's head, rather than on 'external' aids to understanding and learning. Most remediation studies have trained children in the use of this third type of aid because poor comprehenders can most usefully be helped by giving them procedures that they can apply to any text.

If a skill which poor comprehenders lack is *causally* related to their comprehension problems, training in that skill may improve their comprehension. The outcome from a training study comparing good and poor comprehenders which most strongly suggests a causal role for the trained skill is when training brings poor comprehenders up to the level of good comprehenders, but the good comprehenders do not benefit from the training programme (presumably because they already possess the skills being trained). Below some research efforts are considered that have attempted to improve comprehension skill.

Training in rapid decoding

Many people regard decoding speed and automaticity as a crucial factor in reading comprehension (see Perfetti, 1985, for a review). However, attempts to improve comprehension by training in rapid decoding have generally failed (e.g. Fleisher, Jenkins and Pany, 1979). Such results suggest that rapid decoding, although necessary for efficient comprehension, may be only one of a number of skills required, and that training may have no *direct* effect on comprehension. Alternatively, rapid decoding may develop from practice and skill at reading, rather than vice versa.

Background knowledge, inferences and question generation

Less skilled comprehenders *can* make inferences and use their background knowledge to interpret a text (Oakhill, 1982, 1983), so it seems reasonable to suppose that they might make more use of such skills if they were more aware of their value. Such children might not fully appreciate that they ought to use relevant knowledge and experience to interpret a text. One way of encouraging poorer comprehenders to make information explicit would be to train them in the selection of pictures or summary statements which integrate the information in the text. Another way might be for teachers to discuss stories with children, and to encourage them to make predictions and inferences by asking appropriate questions.

Such methods have been shown to be successful in improving comprehension. Au (1977: cited by Wittrock, 1981) found that children's reading comprehension was improved considerably by a 1-year training programme which emphasised the construction of meaning from text. The children verbalised their experiences as they read stories, and were encouraged to relate what was happening in the stories to their background knowledge, and to make inferences from the text.

Hansen (1981) attempted to train children in awareness of how their prior knowledge could be used in story comprehension. All of her subjects (7 year olds) were average or above-average readers. There were three groups: the first (control) group read a series of texts which was followed by a mixture of about one inferential to five literal questions; the second group received *only* questions requiring an inference; the third ('strategy') group was encouraged to integrate information in a text with prior knowledge. With this third group, a weaving metaphor was used to suggest how prior knowledge and information from the text should be put together, and the children were encouraged to predict what might happen in the text, using their own relevant prior knowledge. Both of the latter two groups showed better performance than the control group, with strategy training tending to be more effective. However, the results held only for the passages used in training, and did not transfer to new stories, although there was some improvement on a standardised reading test. These results emphasise the need for children to be taught when to apply newly acquired skills.

Such training might prove to be particularly helpful to children with comprehension difficulties. Hansen and Pearson (1983) used a training programme, with 9-year-old good and poor comprehenders, which combined Hansen's strategy training with inferential question techniques. The training helped the poor comprehenders in understanding both the original passages and new ones, but there was no training effect for the good readers. These findings suggest that encouraging poor comprehenders to make inferences can be effective in improving their comprehension, but that better readers do so spontaneously.

Yuill and Joscelyne (1988, experiment 2) provided further support for this conclusion. They instructed 7- to 8-year-old good and poor comprehenders in how to make inferences from specific words in texts. In the stories they used, the settings and main consequences were not explicitly stated, and had to be inferred. The children were trained to use 'cue words' in the story to infer the missing information. The trained poor comprehenders, but not the good comprehenders, were better at answering comprehension questions than control subjects who were given no training.

Other studies have explored the efficacy of asking children to generate their own questions about texts as a means of improving comprehension. Some studies of self-generated questions have failed to show effects (see Tierney and Cunningham, 1984, for a review). However, as Tierney and Cunningham point out, few such studies have given the children training or practice in question generation and, in other cases, the training procedures have often severely limited the types of question that can be asked. As Weaver and Shonkoff (1978) argue, if only factual questions are generated, children may need to think very little about what they are reading, and may miss the major points of a text. What is needed, they suggest, is a mixture of questions, requiring responses at various levels — literal, inferential, interpretive or evaluative. Cohen (1983) showed that training in question generation, combined with instruction in how to apply such skills to reading short stories, improved the comprehension of third grade children (8 year olds).

The results of the studies reviewed above show that relatively simple procedures can increase constructive processing of text, and enhance reading comprehension. Obviously, to benefit from the use of such procedures, children must possess the relevant prior knowledge to draw inferences and to elaborate on what is explicit in a text. However, readers may possess the relevant background knowledge but fail to access and use it in comprehension. Strategies for organising and retrieving information might also need to be taught.

Training in metacognitive skills

Our own interviews with poor comprehenders suggest that, when they are not specifically instructed about what they should get out of a text, they are not usually aware of their comprehension problems. For example, they are less likely than skilled comprehenders to notice anomalies in a text (Yuill, Oakhill and Parkin, 1989). The ability to decide whether or not a text has been adequately understood is a crucial step towards becoming an independent reader. Young children are often not aware that their understanding is inadequate and they are poor at detecting omissions and inconsistencies (Markman, 1977).

In the previous section, we saw that question generation can be used to improve comprehension. Although the ability to generate and answer questions is not, in itself, a metacognitive skill, question generation can be used as part of a metacognitive training programme if children are taught to make up questions that help them assess whether they have understood the text.

Reis and Spekman (1983) showed that 11- and 12-year-old poor comprehenders were considerably better at detecting 'reader-based' inconsistencies (i.e. those that violate what the reader knows about the world) than they were at detecting 'text-based' inconsistencies (conflicting information in the text). Although even those children who were very poor at detecting inconsistencies could be trained to do so, such training only improved their ability to detect reader-based, and not text-based, inconsistencies. Reis and Spekman suggest that even poor comprehenders evaluate their comprehension to some extent, but tend to use different standards from those used by better readers — they are able to monitor how a text relates to their own knowledge about the world, but not whether it is internally consistent.

Brown, Palincsar and Armbruster (1984) combined training in question generation, summarisation, clarification and prediction in a programme specifically designed to enhance the comprehension skills of 12 year olds with comprehension difficulties. The children were also informed about why and how the activities were important. Their ability to ask effective questions and to produce good summaries improved dramatically during the training period, but it again emerged that fairly extensive training may be necessary before children can incorporate such skills into their repertoire, and can use them effectively. The children also showed reliable and lasting improvements on various measures of comprehension, including standardised reading tests. Similar studies by Paris and his associates have also shown that training in metacognitive awareness can improve both reading strategies and comprehension. For instance, Paris, Cross and Lipson (1984) gave third and fifth graders training in a rich variety of comprehension strategies, including understanding the purpose of the text, attending to main ideas, monitoring comprehension and drawing inferences. They found that the children given such training performed better on 'close' comprehension and error-detection tasks, although not on standardised comprehension tests.

Collins and Smith (1982) have suggested a three-stage programme of training in comprehension monitoring and predictive skills. In the first, 'modelling', stage the teacher takes the lead, reading stories and commenting on what is entailed in understanding them. For example, the teacher generates hypotheses about the text, points out sources of difficulty and how to overcome them, and comments on ways of gaining insight into the text. During this stage, the teacher gradually encourages the children to take an active part in these activities, in preparation for the next, 'student participation', stage. During this stage, the teacher shifts the responsibility for generating hypotheses, and for detecting and remedying comprehension failures, to the children. In the final, 'reading silently', stage, the children are expected to use the skills they have learned in independent reading. Collins and Smith suggest that children can be encouraged to use these skills by giving them texts with problems to spot, or texts with questions that encourage them to predict what will happen next.

Imagery

There is some evidence that imagery can be used to improve comprehension monitoring, but imagery might also improve comprehension more generally – it may have its effects by maintaining attention, or by promoting deeper semantic processing of the text.

Imagery instruction has proved successful with children. For instance, Pressley (1976) taught 8 year olds to generate images for sections of stories as they read them. Compared to children who only read the stories, those who produced images were better able to answer questions about them. However, the ability to use imagery instructions improves with age, and it is not until about 8 that children can learn to use self-generated images to improve their comprehension of stories. Guttman, Levin and Pressley (1977) found that the reading comprehension of third graders, but not kindergarteners, could be improved by imagery instructions, or by 'partial pictures'. Those children given partial pictures were told to use them to help to construct an image of what they could not see. By contrast, the same study showed that children from kindergarten, first and third grades all recalled more information when the stories were accompanied by complete pictures – the amount of improvement was similar at all three ages. However, as with many of the other comprehension aids we have discussed, imagery instructions do not automatically enhance comprehension, even for children older than 9 (see Levin, 1981, for a review). Levin argues that one reason for the discrepant findings is that not all types of image are equally helpful, and that different types of material may call for different types of image.

Although we have by no means provided an exhaustive survey of the many different learning aids and strategies, we hope that the above review will provide some idea of ways in which children's comprehension might be improved. There is obviously no 'best' aid or strategy that can be recommended, and the effects of training are often crucially dependent on the type and length of the training given. An important consideration in educational settings is that some methods may be more practicable than others. The above review includes studies of poor readers generally, as well as average readers, but very few studies have explored the effects of remediation techniques on poor comprehenders, such as those we have studied, who have a *specific* comprehension (not a word recognition) problem. We will now turn to some of our own work which has addressed this issue.

Two Experimental Studies

In a series of experiments, we have identified a group of children who have a specific comprehension problem. They can identify words adequately, but have difficulty in remembering and understanding connected text (see e.g. Oakhill, 1982, 1984). A salient feature of these poor comprehenders is that they do not make inferences from text and do not integrate the ideas from different parts of a text to form a coherent representation to the same extent as do skilled comprehenders. Given the necessity of adequate comprehension for many aspects of school learning, it is important to identify effective remediation procedures for poor comprehenders.

First training study: use of imagery

In the present experiment, we explored whether giving children training in imagery strategies would improve their comprehension. As discussed in the first section, such techniques have been shown to be effective with children, although between about 8 and 10 years they cannot benefit from simply being told to use imagery – they need to be instructed in its use.

We addressed the issue of whether imagery is particularly suitable for aiding memory for some sorts of information by asking the children three different types of question. The first type, which we term 'factual', tapped memory for facts that were explicit in the text. The second main type of question, 'inferential', asked about information that could only be inferred from the story, and the third type, 'descriptive', asked about details that would be particularly likely to come to the reader's attention if an effective image had been formed.

Peters et al. (1985) suggest that different forms of imagery instruction might be suitable for different passages, and identified two distinct types of imagery which they termed 'representational' and 'transformational'. Representational imagery is the fairly direct translation of the text into an image. In transformational imagery, however, as the name suggests, some aspects of the text are transformed so that the image does not correspond directly to the text, but is used as a sort of mnemonic. Peters et al. argued that this form of imagery might be useful for recalling difficult-to-remember things, such as names and numerical data, which are more prevalent in non-narrative passages, and which do not necessarily lend themselves to representation in an imageable form. An example from Peters et al.'s study provides an illustration of how transformational imagery might be used. Their subjects (8 year olds) had to remember what each person was famous for, given sentences such as:

Larry Taylor was famous for inventing a house on a turntable.

They were instructed to transform the names into more imageable forms (in this case, a tailor), and to integrate this image with one of the rest of the sentence. The results confirmed the authors' prediction: transformational imagery substantially improved subjects' recall of difficult-to-remember factual information (e.g. names), but was not critical for information that could be more directly coded into an image. Representational imagery, by contrast, did not significantly facilitate memory for the difficult information. In our experiment, we incorporated training in *both* sorts of imagery technique, in order to optimise the effectiveness of imagery training.

Some work has investigated the effects of imagery training on poor comprehenders specifically, and has shown that they seem to derive special benefit from visual imagery instructions. Levin (1973) tested two groups of fourth-grade poor comprehenders – those with decoding and vocabulary problems, and those with adequate decoding and vocabulary skills. The subjects given imagery instructions were told to try to 'think of a picture in their mind' as they read each sentence. Such instructions improved comprehension (compared with simply reading the story) for the second, but not for the first, group of poor readers. Indeed, the second group (those with adequate decoding skills) performed as well as good comprehenders when they were given imagery instructions.

In the present experiment, we also investigated the effects of imagery instructions on good and poor comprehenders, but explored in more detail whether imagery might facilitate recall of different types of information, by asking the subjects different types of question about the passages, as outlined above.

Subjects

The children were selected using a test of sight vocabulary (Gates–MacGinitie Primary Two; Gates and MacGinitie, 1965) and one of word recognition and comprehension (Neale Analysis of Reading Ability; Neale, 1966). The Neale test provides age-related measures both of children's ability to read words aloud in context (accuracy score) and of their ability to answer open-ended questions about what they have read (comprehension score). In order to provide a rapid assessment of their comprehension, the Neale test was adapted as a group test of listening comprehension. (Previous work by Oakhill (e.g. 1982, 1983) has shown that children who have a reading comprehension problem also have difficulty with listening comprehension.) The children were tested in groups of six and, instead of their reading the passages aloud, the passages were read to them. They were given booklets containing the questions for each passage, with one set of questions on each page. When the experimenter had finished reading the passage, the children turned to the appropriate page in their booklet, and the questions were read aloud to them, one at a time. After each

Table 16.1 The mean reading test scores of the four groups of children

	Comprehension score (max. = 36)	Vocabulary score (max. = 50)
Less-skilled comprehenders		
Trained ($n=11$)	14.9	31.3
Control ($n=11$)	14.8	31.4
Skilled comprehenders		
Trained ($n=11$)	24.2	31.4
Control ($n=11$)	24.5	31.4

question, the children were given time to write a response under the written version of the question.

From the 90 children who showed average, or above average, performance on the Gates–MacGinitie test, and who then went on to do the Neale test, 22 good and 22 poor comprehenders were selected, on the basis of their ability to answer the questions about the Neale passages. Since we did not use the test in the prescribed way, the raw scores cannot be converted to age equivalents. The mean score for the poor comprehenders was 14.26 and, for the good group, 24.3 (max. = 36), and these scores were significantly different: $t(42)=9.70$, $P<0.001$. The good and poor comprehenders were matched on chronological age (9;7 years for both groups), and on Gates–MacGinitie Vocabulary scores (31.4 and 31.3 respectively out of a maximum of 50). The good and poor comprehenders were subdivided into two matched groups, one of which was given training in imagery. The reading test scores of the four groups of children are shown in Table 16.1.

Materials

Nine stories were written using suitable vocabulary, so that all participants would be able to read them without difficulty. Four of the stories were allocated for use in the training sessions, and the remaining five were used in the test session. For each passage, three types of question (inferential, descriptive and factual) were asked. An example passage, and its accompanying questions is shown in Table 16.2. The inferential questions tapped information that was not explicit in the text. For example, in the illustrative passage, the information that the ladder was kept in the kitchen is not explicit, but is implied because there is mention of a cooker. The descriptive questions asked about details that would be more likely to be available to subjects using an imagery strategy, so we expected that performance on these questions might be particularly aided by imagery instructions. The stories also incorporated factual statements, so that straightforward factual questions could also be asked. For each passage, we

Table 16.2   An example story and questions

The step ladder was put away safely behind the door which was just to the right of the cooker. The three shelves were up at last and, even with a sore thumb, Terry Butcher was happy. The hammer which had caused the pain was put away in the tool box with the other tools.

Linda, Terry's wife, came into the room with a box of crockery. 'The shelves are for my little model aeroplanes', said Terry with a stern voice. 'We'll see', was the reply from Linda.

A little while later, when Terry was putting away the tool box, he heard a loud scream and the sound of breaking glass and china. Terry walked back into the room and was angry. 'I warned you about those shelves', he said to Linda and sadly went to get the tool box out again.

Questions
(F = factual, I = inferential, D = descriptive)
1. Exactly where was the step ladder put away? (D)
2. In which room was the step ladder put away? (I)
3. How many shelves had been put up? (F)
4. Why did Terry have a sore thumb? (I)
5. Who was carrying the crockery? (F)
6. Why did Linda scream? (I)
7. Describe the scene in the room when Linda screamed. (D)
8. Describe Terry's face when he saw the state of the room. (D)
9. What was the full name of the person who had put up the shelves? (F)

derived three questions of each type (inferential, descriptive, factual). The stories and questions were typed on separate sheets of paper and made into booklets. Appropriate representational and transformational pictures were also produced for the training sessions.

Procedure

In both the imagery training, control training and final test sessions the children were seen in small groups of four or five. The good and poor comprehenders were trained and tested in separate groups. They read the stories themselves, and were allowed one-and-a-half minutes for each. The children then turned to the next page of the booklet which contained the appropriate questions. They answered the questions one at a time: the experimenter read out each question, and the children were allowed enough time between questions to write in an answer under the appropriate question in their booklet.

Imagery training
The imagery training took place over three sessions of 20–30 minutes, on different days. The children were told that they would be learning to 'think in pictures' as they read stories, to help them to answer questions about the stories. In the first training session the children read one of the stories,

and the experimenter then produced two drawings: one was a cartoon-like sequence of four pictures which represented the sequence of events in the story. The other was a single picture, depicting the main event in the story. (For example, the main event of the story illustrated in Table 16.2 would be the crockery crashing to the floor as the shelves collapse.) The children were shown how each of the pictures related to the story. They were then told to imagine that the pictures were in their minds, and that they were to use them to help them to answer some questions about the story. The stories and pictures were taken away before the questions were presented. The children were then given a second story to read, and were told to try to form mental pictures as they read it, and to formulate a picture of what they thought was the main event of the story. After the children had attempted to answer the questions with the aid of their 'mental pictures', the experimenter asked each child to describe the images they had used, and gave feedback and suggestions for improving their images. Many questions, of a general and specific nature, were also asked, such as 'Did you see colour?', 'Could you describe what X looked like?'

In the second training session, both representational and transformational drawings were used. The children were told that the transformational drawings were specifically designed to help them to remember details from the stories, and the way in which this could be achieved was explained. The children were then told that they should try to form three different types of image as they read through a new story: a cartoon sequence with four frames to represent the sequence of events in the story, an image of the main event and a transformational image to help them remember specific details. When they had completed the task and answered the questions, their images were discussed with them, as in the first session.

In the third session the children were not shown any drawings. The imagery procedure was reiterated, and the children read and answered questions about a new story and a final discussion of their 'mental pictures' took place, as in the first two sessions.

Control condition
The children who did not receive imagery training saw the same stories, also in three sessions. They read the stories and answered the questions, and their answers were then discussed with them. The children in this condition spent as long with the experimenter as those in the imagery training groups.

Test phase
The children were tested in groups of 6–10. Those who had received imagery thinking were tested separately from the children in the control group. The stories and questions were presented in a booklet (again with

stories and questions on separate pages), and the questions were read aloud to the children as before. The groups who had received the imagery training were reminded to form mental images as they read the stories, and to use their pictures to help them to answer the questions. The children in the control condition were told to read the stories very carefully, and to answer the questions in as much detail as possible.

Results

The mean number of correct responses is shown in Table 16.3. An analysis of variance showed an effect of comprehension skill, with good comprehenders answering more questions correctly than poor ones: $F[1,40] = 10.64$, $P<0.01$. There was also a main effect of training condition, the children given imagery training performing better than those in the control group: $F[1,40] = 12.32$, $P<0.01$. The main effect of question type, although significant ($F[2,80] = 12.41$, $P<0.01$) is uninteresting because the questions in the different conditions were not matched in any systematic way.

Table 16.3 Mean post-training scores as a function of comprehension skill, training group and question type (max. = 15)

Question type	Inferential	Descriptive	Factual	X
Less skilled				
Imagery training	8.55	9.82	10.46	9.61
Control	7.46	6.05	8.32	7.27
Skilled				
Imagery training	10.27	9.50	10.73	10.17
Control	8.96	8.46	11.09	9.50

The interaction between comprehension skill and training condition approached significance: $F[1,40] = 3.80$, $P=0.058$. The prediction that the poor, but not the good, comprehenders would benefit from imagery training was tested by comparing the effects of training for the two groups. As predicted, the poor comprehenders given imagery training showed a marked improvement in memory for the passages; they performed significantly better on the test questions than did the control group of poor comprehenders [$t(22) = 3.98$, $P<0.001$] but there was no such difference in the case of the good comprehenders: $t(22) = 1.07$.

No other interactions reached significance. In particular, the interaction between training condition and type of question was not significant ($F = 2.51$, $P<0.09$), although imagery training tended to have a particularly large effect on the descriptive questions.

Discussion

The results show that imagery training was especially effective for those children who do not possess adequate comprehensive skills, but that it had a general effect on their performance, and did not differentially affect the retention of information of different types.

Poor comprehenders may show a particular benefit from imagery training because it enables them, or forces them, to integrate information in the text in a way that they would not normally do. Our earlier work (see, for example, Oakhill, 1982; Oakhill, Yuill and Parkin, 1986) has led to the suggestion that poor comprehenders do not engage in constructive and integrative processing to the same extent as do good ones. Training in the production of images to represent the information in the stories may have encouraged the poor comprehenders to integrate the information in a way that they did not normally do, particularly the training in deriving an image for the main point of the story.

The finding that the comprehension of the good group did not improve with imagery training does not *necessarily* mean that they already use imagery and, hence, do not benefit from training in its use. It may be that they have some other equally efficient strategy for remembering information from text, and that training in imagery provides them with no *additional* advantage.

One way in which training in imagery strategies may help poor comprehenders is by giving them a strategy to help them overcome some of the limiting factors on their comprehension skills. For instance, recent work of our own has shown that good comprehenders have better working memories than poor ones (Yuill, Oakhill and Parkin, 1989). Working memory skill has been shown to be highly correlated with several indices of text understanding in adults (e.g. Daneman and Carpenter, 1980, 1983) and is obviously important in comprehension skills such as inference-making and integration. The ability to use imagery strategies may give poor comprehenders a way of helping to circumvent their memory limitations by enabling them to use a different, and perhaps more economical, means of representing information in the text.

As we pointed out earlier, our results do not enable us to conclude *which sort of* imagery training was more effective, or whether the two sorts (representational and transformational) affected memory for different sorts of information from the stories.

Second training study: inference skills

In this study, we explored another way in which children's comprehension might be improved, by giving them a series of short training sessions in inference making. A full account of the experiment can be found in Yuill and Oakhill (1988).

As we saw in the above review, several studies have found that encouraging children to make inferences can be effective in improving comprehension (although most of these studies have looked at the effects of training on poor readers generally, rather than children who have a specific comprehension deficit). However, inference training in itself may not be enough. We have some evidence that poor comprehenders do not always understand when it is appropriate to use their everyday knowledge in interpreting a text and, thus, may make unwarranted and inappropriate inferences. In the present study, training in question generation was combined with instruction in making inferences, to sensitise the children to the *types* of inference they should make, as well as helping them in the *techniques* for drawing inferences. We also aim to encourage and guide the children in going beyond the information given in the passages, by including a type of 'macrocloze' task, in which they read stories with sentences omitted, and tried to guess what information was missing. In general, the aim of the procedure was to encourage the children to take a more active part in their comprehension – to encourage both appropriate inferential processing and comprehension monitoring.

The inference training procedure included fairly explicit training in activities to help comprehension. However, it may be possible for children to develop appropriate inference skills without such explicit instruction. To assess this possibility, we included a control comparison condition in which the subjects were given intensive practice in standard comprehension exercises, i.e. simply answering comprehension question about the texts.

An alternative account of poor comprehension – discussed briefly at the beginning of this chapter – is in terms of decoding speed: the 'decoding bottleneck' hypothesis (e.g. Perfetti, 1977). This hypothesis proposes that, if readers do not recognise words sufficiently quickly and automatically, the processing required for word recognition will place an additional burden on short-term memory, and will consequently reduce the resources available for comprehension processes. In fact, several sources of evidence have indicated that inefficient decoding is not *causally* implicated in poor reading comprehension but, in order to rule out such an explanation of poor comprehension in the present subjects, a comparison training group given practice in rapid decoding was included in the study. This group also served as a control for various features of the two treatment conditions that could contribute indirectly to any improvements in performance, namely individual attention, familiarity with the experimenter and reading practice. The group trained in rapid decoding had practice reading the same texts as the other groups, and practice in rapid decoding of word lists from them.

Subjects

We assessed the effects of three types of training (inference skills, comprehension exercises and rapid decoding) on separate groups of good and poor comprehenders. The children were selected using the Gates–MacGinitie and Neale tests, as in the first study, except that the Neale test was administered on an individual basis, in the usual manner. Skilled and less-skilled comprehenders were matched on chronological age and Neale accuracy age, but had a significantly greater mean comprehension age (8.80 years) than the less skilled group (7.25 years). The children were also selected so that the scores on the Gates–MacGinitie vocabulary test did not differ between the skill groups. The children within each comprehension skill group were allocated to the three different conditions so that the subjects in each treatment group were adequately matched on the measures of interest. The characteristics of the six groups of subjects are shown in Table 16.4.

Table 16.4   Means of subject characteristics

	Chronological age (years)	Accuracy age (years)	Comprehension age (years)	Vocabulary score
Less skilled				
Decoding	7.6	8.3	7.3	37.9
Exercises	7.7	8.4	7.2	33.0
Inference trained	7.7	8.2	7.3	35.8
Skilled				
Decoding	7.7	8.3	8.9	40.7
Exercises	7.9	8.4	8.9	32.3
Inference trained	7.6	8.2	8.7	36.1

Materials

The same ten narrative texts were used in all three conditions for both skill groups. The texts were either adapted from children's reading materials, or were specially written for the purposes of this study, and all were judged appropriate to the children's reading level.

Procedure

The experimenter saw children in groups of three to five. In all, each group received seven training sessions of about 30 minutes each, over a period of 3.5 weeks.

Inference-trained groups
These groups engaged in three types of activity:

1. Lexical inference (all sessions): this activity was introduced with

sentences such as the following: 'Sleepy Tom was late for school again.' Each child had to pick one of the words, and to say what information it gave about the sentence. For example, we know that 'Tom' is a male person and, combined with the word 'school' that he is probably a pupil, since his first name is given. 'Sleepy' suggests that he overslept, perhaps because he stayed up late the previous night, and suggests why he was 'late'. 'Again' suggests that he has often been late before, perhaps because he habitually stays up late. The children then applied such analyses to short, abstract, stories such as the following:

> Billy was crying. His whole day was spoilt. All his work had been broken by the wave. His mother came to stop him crying. But she accidentally stepped on the only tower that was left. Billy cried even more. 'Never mind', said his mother, 'we can always build another one tomorrow.' Billy stopped crying and went home for his tea.

For example, the word 'wave' is a clue that the story setting is a beach. The children were then encouraged to link together single lexical inferences, for example by using the location inferred from 'wave' to guess that the 'tower' was a sandcastle.

2. Question generation (four occasions): after discussing 'question-words' (*who*, *where*, *why* etc.), and being given examples of how questions can be derived from a text, the children were invited to generate their own questions from single sentences, then from stories. For example, the children generated questions such as 'Who was crying?' and 'Where was Billy?' for the story given above. Each child took turns at being 'the teacher', and the other children answered the questions put to them.

3. Prediction (one occasion): the children read texts in which sentences had been obscured by adhesive tape, and tried to guess what each hidden sentence was, based on clues from surrounding sentences. The hidden sentence was then revealed, and the predictions checked.

Comprehension exercise groups

The children in these groups were told about the importance of reading for comprehension and, after sharing between them the reading of a given text, they were asked comprehension questions by the experimenter in strict rotation. The experimenter did not give detailed feedback about responses, but did correct obviously wrong answers. In addition, the children often discussed the answers, and corrected one another. The questions were designed to be similar to those in the sorts of comprehension exercises for slightly older children commonly found in school, and comprised a mix of inferential and literal questions. For example, the questions for the 'beach' story given above were as follows: (1) 'Where was Billy?' (2) 'Why was Billy crying?' (3) 'What had the wave broken?' (4) 'Why did his mother go to him?' (5) 'Why did Billy cry even more?'

Rapid decoding groups

The children in these groups were first told of the importance of rapid word recognition. Each session then followed a similar pattern. First, the children were shown a list of words taken from that session's text, and the experimenter read the list through. Each child practised reading the list as quickly and accurately as possible. Then the children took turns at reading the specified text. Finally, each child read the word list again, and the experimenter recorded the time taken, using a stopwatch. In the subsequent session, the children re-read the previous word list, and their time was recorded. The word lists comprised about 20% of the words of each text, and included those that were the most difficult to recognise.

Results

After the training had been completed, the children's comprehension was assessed again using a different (parallel) version of the Neale test from that used originally. The mean gains in comprehension age in the different conditions are shown in Table 16.5. An analysis of variance on these data showed a marginally significant interaction between comprehension skill and training group: $F[1,46]=2.65$, $P<0.08$. Planned comparisons showed that the less-skilled comprehenders benefited from inference training more than did the skilled group ($P<0.001$). Furthermore, the less-skilled comprehenders given inference training improved significantly more than those given decoding practice ($P<0.05$).

The results can also be considered in terms of the effect that training had on individual children. After training, each child was classified as 'poor' (comprehension age below accuracy and chronological ages), 'good' (comprehension age above accuracy and chronological ages) or 'mixed' (comprehension age above either accuracy or chronological age, but not both). The percentages of children who fell into each of these categories are shown in Table 16.6. Sixty-nine per cent of the poor comprehenders given inference training could be classified as 'good' by the end of the training period, compared with only 23% of those who received the decoding training or standard comprehension exercises.

Table 16.5 Mean improvement (months) in comprehension age as a function of comprehension skill and training group

Training group	Rapid decoding	Comprehension exercises	Inference training
Less skilled	6.00	13.71	17.38
Skilled	10.33	5.43	5.92
X	8.16	9.57	11.65
Difference between skill groups	−4.33	8.28	11.46

Table 16.6 Percentages of children falling into different comprehension categories after training

Training group	Percentage in comprehension category		
	Poor	Mixed	Good
Less skilled			
Decoding	67	33	00
Exercises	29	29	43
Inference trained	15	15	69
Skilled			
Decoding	00	00	100
Exercises	14	00	86
Inference trained	00	15	85

There were no differences between the groups in reading speed or accuracy at the end of the training period. It is also interesting to note that the skilled comprehenders were not, in general, superior to the less-skilled group in speed of decoding – in fact, they tended to be slower.

Discussion

These results show that, for less-skilled comprehenders, inference training was both more beneficial than was decoding practice, and more helpful to them than it was to the skilled comprehenders. The less-skilled comprehenders given inference training improved slightly, but not significantly, more than those given comprehension exercises. The effect of inference training was very marked for the less-skilled comprehenders, with an average increase in Neale comprehension age of over 17 months within a period of 2 months. This result is particularly impressive given that few training studies have demonstrated improvements on standardised tests – most have reassessed performance only on the particular skills trained.

The absence of a significant difference between inference training and comprehension exercises suggests that both contained some extra element that the decoding training lacked, such as the discussion of stories, and that both promoted comprehension processes normally lacking in less-skilled comprehenders. We had not expected the comprehension exercises to be so successful in improving comprehension, but the effects may have been due to the fact that children in the exercise group often corrected one another, and discussed their answers. These incidental activities may have increased their awareness of their own comprehension. In addition, as the passages used were rather obscure, and left a good deal of information to be inferred, they may have caused the children to do more inferential processing and reflecting on their comprehension processes than would the sorts of passages standardly used in such activities. Thus, the inference training might have been effective *not* because the children adopted wholesale the strategies they had been taught, but because they developed a greater degree of awareness of their own comprehension. Such awareness might be fostered either by training such as that given, or by intensive small-group practice in comprehension exercises.

Conclusions

We end this chapter with two notes of caution. First, most methods for improving comprehension assume that poor readers will benefit from being taught strategies that skilled ones use naturally. However, the fact that poor readers have failed to acquire these skills might indicate that, at least in some cases, they are unable to do so. A study by Brown and Smiley (1978) illustrates this problem. They showed that children who learned best from text were those who spontaneously took notes or underlined, but less proficient learners did not benefit from the suggestion that they should use these strategies. So, it cannot be assumed that poor comprehenders will automatically become good ones if they are taught the skills that good comprehenders possess.

Secondly, instruction in skills such as comprehension monitoring should be restricted to children who have reached the stage where they are reading to learn. The introduction of such training to children who have not yet mastered decoding may be counterproductive because they may not have enough processing capacity to do both aspects of reading together. It therefore seems sensible to wait until decoding is reasonably automatic before introducing training in comprehension strategies. This does *not* mean that children should not learn from the outset that comprehension is the purpose of reading. The claim is simply that training in conscious comprehension strategies should not be introduced too early.

Acknowledgements

The research reported in the second experiment here was supported by an ESRC project grant. We should also like to thank Sima Patel, who ran the first experiment as an undergraduate project.

References

BROWN, A.L., PALINCSAR, A.S. and ARMBRUSTER, B.B. (1984). Instructing comprehension-fostering activities interactive learning situations. In: H. Mandl, N.L. Stein and T. Trabasso (Eds), *Learning and Comprehension of Text*. Hillsdale, NJ: Lawrence Erlbaum Associates.

BROWN, A.L. and SMILEY, S.S. (1978). The development of strategies for studying prose passages. *Child Development* 49, 1076–1088.

COHEN, R. (1983). Self-generated questions as an aid to reading comprehension. *The Reading Teacher* **36**, 770–775.

COLLINS, A. and SMITH, E.E. (1982). Teaching the process of reading comprehension. In: D.K. Detterman and R.J. Sternberg (Eds), *How and How Much can Intelligence be Increased.* Norwood, NJ: Ablex.

DANEMAN, M. and CARPENTER, P.A. (1980). Individual differences in working memory and reading. *Journal of Verbal Learning and Verbal Behavior* **19**, 450–466.

DANEMAN, M. and CARPENTER, P.A. (1983). Individual differences in integrating information between and within sentences. *Journal of Experimental Psychology: Learning, Memory and Cognition* **9**, 561–583.

FLEISHER, L.S., JENKINS, J.R. and PANY, D. (1979). Effects on poor readers' comprehension of training in rapid decoding. *Reading Research Quarterly* **15**, 30–48.

GATES, A.I. and MACGINITIE, W.H. (1965). *Gates–MacGinitie Reading Tests.* New York: Columbia University Teachers' College Press.

GUTTMAN, J., LEVIN, J.R. and PRESSLEY, M. (1977). Pictures, partial pictures and young children's oral prose learning. *Journal of Educational Psychology* **69**, 473–480.

HANSEN, J. (1981). The effects of inference training and practice on young children's reading comprehension. *Reading Research Quarterly* **16**, 391–417.

HANSEN, J. and PEARSON, P.D. (1983). An instructional study: Improving the inferential comprehension of good and poor fourth-grade readers. *Journal of Educational Psychology* **75**, 821–829.

LEVIN, J.R. (1973). Inducing comprehension in poor readers. *Journal of Educational Psychology* **1**, 19–24.

LEVIN, J.R. (1981). On functions of pictures in prose. In: F.J. Pirozzolo and M.C. Wittrock (Eds), *Neuropsychological and Cognitive Processes in Reading.* London: Academic Press.

MARKMAN, E.M. (1977). Realizing that you don't understand: A preliminary investigation. *Child Development* **48**, 986–992.

NEALE, M.D. (1966). *The Neale Analysis of Reading Ability*, 2nd edn. London: Macmillan Education.

OAKHILL, J.V. (1982). Constructive processes in skilled and less-skilled comprehenders' memory for sentences. *British Journal of Psychology* **73**, 13–20.

OAKHILL, J.V. (1983). Instantiation in skilled and less-skilled comprehenders. *Quarterly Journal of Experimental Psychology* **35A**, 441–450.

OAKHILL, J.V. (1984). Inferential and memory skills in children's comprehension of stories. *British Journal of Educational Psychology* **54**, 31–39.

OAKHILL, J.V. and GARNHAM, A. (1988). *Becoming a Skilled Reader.* Oxford: Basil Blackwell.

OAKHILL, J.V., YUILL, N.M. and PARKIN, A.J. (1986). On the nature of the difference between skilled and less-skilled comprehenders. *Journal of Research in Reading* **9**, 80–91.

OAKHILL, J.V., YUILL, N.M. and PARKIN, A.J. (1988). Memory and inference in skilled and less-skilled comprehenders. In: M.M. Gruneberg, P.E. Morris and R.N. Sykes (Eds). *Practical Aspects of Memory: Current Research and Issues*, vol 2. Chichester: Wiley.

PARIS, S.G., CROSS, D.R. and LIPSON, M.Y. (1984). Informed strategies for learning: A program to improve children's reading awareness and comprehension. *Journal of Education Psychology* **76**, 1239–1252.

PERFETTI, C.A. (1977). Language comprehension and fast decoding: Some psycholinguistic prerequisites for skilled reading comprehension. In: J. Guthrie (Ed.), *Cognition, Curriculum and Comprehension.* Newark, Delaware: IRA.

PERFETTI, C.A. (1985). *Reading Ability.* Oxford: Oxford University Press.

PETERS, E.E., LEVIN, J.R., MCGIVERN, J.E. and PRESSLEY, M. (1985). Further comparison of representational and transformational prose-learning imagery. *Journal of Educational Psychology* **2**, 129–136.

PRESSLEY, G.M. (1976). Mental imagery helps eight-year-olds remember what they read. *Journal of Educational Psychology* **24**, 53–59.

REIS, R. and SPEKMAN, N. (1983). The detection of reader-based versus text-based inconsistencies and the effects of direct training of comprehension monitoring among upper-grade poor comprehenders. *Journal of Reading Behavior* **15**, 49–60.

TIERNEY, R.J. and CUNNINGHAM, J.W. (1984). Research on teaching reading comprehension. In: P.D. Pearson (Ed), *Handbook of Reading Research*. New York: Longman.

WEAVER, P. and SHONKOFF, F. (1978). *Research Within Reach: A Research-Guided Response to Concerns of Reading Educators*. St Louis: Cemrel Inc.

WITTROCK, M.C. (1981). Reading comprehension. In: F.J. Pirozzolo and M.C. Wittrock (Eds). *Neuropsychological and Cognitive Processes in Reading*. New York: Academic Press.

YUILL, N.M. and JOSCELYNE, P. (1988). Effects of organisational cues and strategies on good and poor comprehenders' story understanding. *Journal of Educational Psychology* **80**, 152–158.

YUILL, N.M. and OAKHILL, J.V. (1988). Effects of inference awareness training on poor reading comprehension. *Applied Cognitive Psychology* **2**, 33–45.

YUILL, N.M., OAKHILL, J.V. and PARKIN, A.J. (1989). Working memory, comprehension ability and the resolution of text anomaly. *British Journal of Psychology* **80**, 351–361.

Chapter 17
The Beneficial Effect of Accelerating Reading Rate on Dyslexic Readers' Reading Comprehension

ZVIA BREZNITZ

Previous Work on Reading Rate and Comprehension

Reading rate is often viewed as dependent upon the effectiveness of decoding and comprehension of the text (Gough and Tunmer, 1986). For this reason, reading rate can become a diagnostic measure of reading ability (Stanovich, 1981; Perfetti, 1986).

In an earlier study (Berznitz, 1980), I investigated the causal relationships between oral reading errors, comprehension and reading time among first grade novice readers. Novice readers were chosen as there can still be a great deal of variation in demonstrated reading skills which does not arise from reading difficulties. Path analysis indicated that reading time influences the level of comprehension, such that when reading time is decreased, comprehension increases. There is some prior evidence that when mature readers read faster, the level of comprehension improves (Miller, 1987), but no such data are available for beginners.

In a series of studies (Breznitz, 1987a,b; 1988; 1990a,b), the reading rate of subjects who were in their last quarter of the school year was controlled and manipulated. In all the experiments, subjects were required to read orally three parallel forms of a normative reading comprehension test for grades 1 and 2 (Ortar and Segeve, 1980). Each form of the test contained six items of increasing difficulty, in terms of the length (the number of words) and comprehension. The test was presented on an IBM PC computer screen under different reading rates. The subjects read the test orally. In the first set of studies, in condition 1, the subjects read one form of the test at their own self-paced reading rate. In condition 2, subjects read another form of the test at a fast pace. In order to avoid a possible warm-up effect, a third test was read by the subjects, again at their own self-paced reading rate. In a second set of studies in conditions 1 and 3, subjects read the test forms at their self-paced reading rate, but in condition

2 subjects read the test form at a slow-paced reading rate. In all the experiments, a special procedure was devised in order to determine the fast- and the slow-paced reading rate for each of the subjects. The fast- and the slow-paced reading conditions were calculated for each subject separately according to the reading time of his or her first self-paced condition.

The calculation for the reading rate manipulation was as follows: first, the reading time of each test item the subject read at the first self-paced condition was measured. Then, only the reading time of the test items answered correctly by the subjects was taken. Since the length of the items varied, the total time of each item was divided by the number of letters it contained. This produced a maximum of six different reading rates. For each subject the fastest rate out of the six became the target fast pace. This procedure eliminated the effect of length of the text and also ensured that the fast- and slow-paced reading remained within the demonstrated capacity of each subject. Items in either the fast- or slow-paced conditions were presented on the computer screen at those rates. In the three conditions, each item appeared on the screen separately, followed by four multiple choice questions. In the fast-paced condition, the whole item was presented on the screen. Immediately following this, words from the beginning of the item to the end were erased at a rate that forced the subject to read at the calculated fast pace. In the slow-paced condition, parts of the item appeared on the computer screen at the slow, calculated rate until the whole item was presented on the screen. Then it disappeared at once.

For all three conditions in all the studies, reading times, comprehension and oral reading errors were measured. The highest comprehension scores were under the fast-paced reading rate. The lowest comprehension score was under the slow-paced condition. The highest number of oral reading errors was under the self-paced reading rate; the lowest number of errors was under the slow pace. No differences in reading time, comprehension score or number of reading errors were found between the first and the second self-paced reading conditions. The self-paced reading rate was found to be the least effective for either comprehension or accuracy. Data are presented in Table 17.1. These data include the subjects in the previous studies reported above, with the inclusion of additional students.

Results of the studies supported the original finding that increased reading rate leads to improved comprehension and reduced oral reading errors. Our results also indicated that first grade novice readers can read faster than they normally do. In another study (Breznitz, 1990a), we found that bad habits prevent first graders from reading more effectively and from performing at a higher level. Of the 60 first-grade teachers who provided reports on how they teach reading, 59 claimed that in teaching reading they deliberately slow pupils down in an attempt to gain more accuracy.

Table 17.1 Means and standard deviations for reading time, oral reading errors and comprehension for first-grade novice readers, according to conditions ($n=235$)

Reading speed	Reading time (s) (max. 82)		Errors		Comprehension (max. 6)	
	Mean	s.d.	Mean	s.d.	Mean	s.d.
Self-paced	27	13.4	16.2	12.3	3.5	1.2
Slow-paced	41.8	11.1	5.3	2.5	1.2	2.9
Fast-paced	21.5	10.8	12.4	10.9	4.4	1.1

Difference significance at $P<0.001$ (between fast and slow paced, separately against self-paced baseline).

However, our data suggest that slowing the reading pace down more often impairs comprehension.

Three arguments were proposed to explain the increased comprehension in the fast-paced improvement to reading rate:

1. Constraints of the working memory: faster reading rate increases the units available in working memory, which thereby allows for a greater amount of contextual information.
2. Reduction of distractibility.
3. Fast pace may enhance the similarities between the vocal outputs of oral reading and the use of familiar words in speech, i.e. a slow pace may artificially distort words compared to a normally faster speech rate.

All three arguments were tested following the same research procedure as above. Subjects (first graders) read different reading materials at self- and fast-paced reading rates.

One series of studies tested the hypothesis that comprehension gains in fast-paced reading rates are attributable primarily to changes in working memory function (Breznitz and Share, 1990). Tasks such as word recall and recognition, forward and backward item order recall, recency as opposed to primacy effects, and probed recall were given with subjects reading the test material. These working memory-sensitive tasks showed large gains in the fast-paced manipulation. The magnitude of these gains in some cases was over 100%. Our findings suggested that the fast-paced manipulation operates specifically on a working memory component of the reading process.

In another series of studies, I tested the second hypothesis that accelerated reading rate reduced distractibility (Breznitz, 1988, 1990b). Both visual and auditory distractions were inserted into the reading material, and these distractions comprised meaningful and meaningless stimuli. In condition 1, the visual distractions were in the form of a continually flashing cursor in the corner of the computer screen. In condition 2, they were small, meaningful drawings positioned in the lined text. The auditory distractions included continuous white noise in the first condition and a common children's song in the second condition. Reading time, accuracy, comprehension and recall/recognition of the distractions were measured under all conditions.

The results indicated that only the meaningful distractions had any effect upon the reading performance, whether they were visual or auditory. Once again, accuracy and comprehension improved under the fast-paced reading rate. Subjects recall more visual distractions under self-paced conditions. Our results suggested that, at the initial stage of reading acquisition when there is not enough space capacity to process both central tasks (reading) and the incidental tasks (distractions), the distractions interfere with the reading performance under the self-paced reading rate. When in the fast-paced reading condition, the subjects were aware that the text would disappear, and they paid attention only to the central task and improved their reading performance.

The third experiment tested the hypothesis that fast-paced reading may enhance the similarities between the vocal production of the phonemes of the reading materials and familiar words from the lexicon (Breznitz, 1990b). Oral reading performance under self- and fast-paced conditions was analysed with a voice analyser. It was found that subjects significantly increased their vocalization (phoneme production in reading) and shortened their pause time within and between words under the fast-paced reading rate, in comparison with their own self-paced reading rate.

In all of our studies we found that, under the fast-paced reading rate, subjects significantly reduced their oral reading errors. By analysing the reading errors of the subjects under self- and fast-paced reading rates, I found that at the self-paced reading rate about 60% of the errors are phoneme substitution of grapheme. These kinds of errors decreased significantly under the fast-paced reading rate. Our findings suggested that grapheme–phoneme correspondence might benefit from the fast-paced manipulation. Our data also demonstrated that poor readers gain the most from the fast-paced manipulation.

Replication of Studies with Dyslexics

Based on the above findings, we wanted to determine whether the fast-paced reading manipulation could also increase the reading abilities of dyslexic readers. Several studies indicated that dyslexics are deficient in decoding skills (Snowling, 1980; Gough and Tunmer, 1985), in verbal working memory, and in the ability to concentrate and to avoid distractibility (Siegal, 1988).

Our data (Breznitz, 1987a, 1988, 1990a,b; Bretnitz and Share, 1990) suggested that, for the normal novice reader, fast-paced reading manipulation can help to overcome some of the above limitations in reading.

In the present study, it was hypothesized that accelerating the reading rate would increase reading comprehension and accuracy of dyslexic readers.

Subjects

Sixty-eight dyslexic subjects were participants in the study. They were all referred by their teachers to the Learning Disability Clinic of the Department of Education at the City of Haifa, Israel. All subjects came from middle-class families. Hebrew had to be their primary language. They were free from 'hard' neurological signs, primary or severe behavioral or psychiatric disturbances or lack of opportunity to learn. Table 17.2 shows the characteristics of the group.

Table 17.2   Age, grade levels and IQ of experimental group ($n=68$)

	Age (years)	Grade level	WISC IQ*
Mean	9;3	3.5	107.7
s.d.	2.9	1.1	12.2
Range			93–130

*WISC = Wechsler Intelligence Scale for Children (Wechsler, 1946).

Method

At the referral, the subjects' reading skills were assessed by a normative reading diagnostic battery (Kidron, 1984). The Kidron battery includes an assessment of decoding skills, phonemic awareness, word recognition, reading list of pseudo-words and oral reading of a paragraph. The assessment of comprehension included reading eight passages of increasing difficulty, in terms of length (number of words per passage) and level of comprehension. The subjects were required to read four of the passages orally and four in silent reading. After reading each passage, the subjects were required to answer inferential comprehension questions. Reading time was measured for each of the passages the subjects read orally. Based on this test battery, all of the 68 subjects who participated in the study fell under the category of dyslexic readers (Vellutino, 1979). Their general reading score was at least 2 years below their reading grade level. They read only about 25% of the pseudo-words correctly and they accomplished only 20% on the phonemic awareness test.

For the purposes of our study, all subjects were tested with our basic experimental manipulation (as described above). Subjects read orally the three parallel forms of the normative reading comprehension test (Ortar and Segeve, 1980). The items for each test form were presented on an IBM computer screen under self-, fast- and, again, self-paced reading rates. All the test items were followed by multiple-choice comprehension questions. For all three conditions, the reading time for each item (oral reading errors and comprehension) was measured. In addition, subjects were tested with a verbal working memory test (Hebrew version) and the d_{11} Continuous Performance Test (d_{11} CPT) (Tannenbaum, 1987). The d_{11} CPT tested for the distractibility level.

No significant statistical differences were found between reading time, comprehension and accuracy in the first and the second self-paced reading conditions. Therefore, only the first self-paced condition was used as the baseline.

In order to assess the research hypothesis, three planned comparisons were performed. Reading time, comprehension and accuracy were compared under self- and fast-paced reading conditions.

Results

Results indicate that, as predicted, dyslexic subjects gained from the experimental manipulation. Thus, they not only read about 20% faster, but, at the same time, significantly increased their comprehension score (by about 0.5 of a question). This gain took place even though the number of mistakes made did not alter. Results are shown in Table 17.3.

Table 17.3 Means and standard deviations for reading time, oral reading errors and comprehension for dyslexic readers, according to the conditions ($n=68$)

Conditions	Time (s)		Errors		Comprehension	
	Mean	s.d.	Mean	s.d.	Mean	s.d.
Self-paced	25.1*	15.1	27.5	16.4	2.7	0.85
Fast-paced	17.3*	10.8	26.8	22.3	3.2*	0.94

*Differences significant at $P<0.001$ between two conditions.

Typically, there is a negative relationship between errors and comprehension. Normal novice subjects have a correlation of $r=0.42$ in the self-paced condition. However, no such relationship appears to exist in the dyslexic group ($r=0.05$), suggesting that the independence of comprehension and decoding skills may be a characteristic feature of these subjects. This may also account for the fact that comprehension could gain from the experimental manipulation, despite no improvement in accuracy.

Data available in this study make it possible to have an initial evaluation of the role of verbal working memory and distractibility in the reading of dyslexics. Correlations between a total reading score (tested at the referral) and distractibility was $r=-0.52$; that between the reading score and the verbal working memory was $r=-0.53$.

With regard to individual differences among the dyslexic population, the question arises of who benefits most from the fast-paced manipulation – subjects who were more distracted, subjects with a lower verbal memory score or the converse.

Correlations between (residualized) gains in reading rate, comprehension, distractibility and verbal working memory scores were performed.

Distractibility correlated ($r=0.37$) with (residualized) gains in reading comprehension and $r=0.41$ with gains in reading rate produced by the fast-paced manipulation. Verbal working memory correlated ($r=0.36$) with (residualized) gains in reading comprehension and $r=0.42$ with the gain of reading rate. This suggests a tendency for subjects, who are more distracted or have lower verbal working memory spans, to benefit more from the experimental manipulation.

Our research demonstrates the usefulness of accelerating the reading rate on comprehension of dyslexic readers, suggesting that even among dyslexics there is a discrepancy between ability and actual performance.

The promising results obtained in this study warrant further explication of the various factors involved in the potentially beneficial effects of accelerated reading in dyslexics. Systematic replication of earlier studies which manipulate distraction and test for working memory in a more explicit fashion is now being carried out.

References

BREZNITZ, Z. (1980). *The relationships among comprehension, errors and reading rate in first grade.* Unpublished Masters thesis, University of Haifa, Israel.

BREZNITZ, Z. (1987a). Increasing first-graders' reading accuracy and comprehension by accelerating their reading rates. *Journal of Educational Psychology* 79, 236–242.

BREZNITZ, Z. (1987b). Reducing the gap in reading performance between Israeli lower and middle-class first-grade pupils. *Journal of Psychology* 121, 491–501.

BREZNITZ, Z. (1988). Reading performance of first graders: The effect of pictorial distractions. *Journal of Research in Education* 83, 47–53.

BREZNITZ, Z. (1990a). Teacher evaluation of pupil's reading performance: criteria for assessment. *Reading Improvement* 26(2), 174–181.

BREZNITZ, Z. (1990b). Vocalization and pauses in fast-paced reading. *Journal of General Psychology* 117(2), 153–161.

BREZNITZ, Z. and SHARE, D.L. (1990). The effect of accelerated reading rate on memory for text. *Journal of Educational Psychology* in press.

GOUGH, P. and TUNMER, W. (1986). Decoding reading and reading disability. *RASE* 7(1), 6–10.

KIDRON, R. (1984). *Reading Diagnostic Test.* Israel: Ministry of Education.

MILLER (1987). *Reading rate of variety of passages among university students.* Unpublished MA Thesis, University of Haifa, Israel.

ORTAR, G. and SEGAN, N. (1980). *Reading Comprehension Test for Grades 1–4.* Israel: Ministry of Education.

PERFETTI, C. (1986). Continuities in reading acquisition, reading skill, and reading disability. *RASE* 7(1), 11–21.

SIEGAL, L. (1988). Development of grammatical-sensitivity, phonological and short-term memory skills in normally achieving and learning disabled children. *Developmental Psychology* 24, 28–37.

SIEGAL, L. and LINDER, B. (1984). Short-term memory processes in children with reading and arithmetic learning disabilities. *Developmental Psychology* 20(2), 200–207.

SNOWLING, M. (1980). The development of grapheme–phoneme correspondence in normal and dyslexic readers. *Journal of Experimental Child Psychology* 29, 294–305.

STANOVICH, K. (1981). Relationships between word decoding speed, general name retrieval ability, and reading progress in first-grade children. *Journal of Educational Psychology* 73, 809–815.

TANNENBAUM, G. (1987). Attention and Concentration: Parameters in D_{11} Continuous Performance Test. Israel: Wingate Institute.

VELLUTINO, F. (1979). *Dyslexia: Theory and Research.* Cambridge, MA: MIT Press.

WECHSLER, D. (1946). *The Wechsler Intelligence Scale for Children.* Windsor: NFER.

Chapter 18
The Teaching of Spelling Using Techniques of Simultaneous Oral Spelling and Visual Inspection

MICHAEL THOMSON

Introduction

It has been an accepted principle of teaching the dyslexic that 'multisensory' techniques are required (see Thomson and Watkins, 1990), and yet there has been little systematic research to investigate or support this principle. Research has shown the effects of a general programme in helping dyslexics (Hornsby and Miles, 1980) and others have focused on the evaluation of specific techniques (Thomson, 1990a).

According to Frith (1985), dyslexics are arrested at the logographic stage of development, in which reading and spelling are visually based. Thus, they should benefit from learning phoneme–grapheme correspondence rules and phoneme analysis. Further if, as Bryant and Bradley (1985) suggest, phonological skills are particularly important in spelling, then the need for dyslexics to improve phonological skills would be particularly relevant in improving their spelling performance. Hence, it may be that encouraging dyslexics to be aware of the phoneme–grapheme correspondences in spelling is an effective way of teaching them to spell.

One method which may help dyslexics to be aware of the phoneme–grapheme correspondences in spelling is the multisensory method of learning spellings called 'simultaneous oral spelling'. Simultaneous oral spelling emphasises the relationship between auditory, visual and kinaesthetic modalities. In simultaneous oral spelling, the child must hear a word, say the word out loud, spell it out loud letter by letter, write the word saying each letter as it is written and then read what has been written. This method relates phonemes to graphemes explicitly as well as focusing awareness on individual sounds, and has been found to be effective with dyslexics (Thomson, 1990a,b) (see later under 'Teaching procedure' for details). An earlier paper (Thomson, 1988) did not include control children, making it difficult to ascertain whether dyslexics respond differently from non-dyslexics to specific teaching methods. If they do, this would imply that dyslexics require a different form of teaching, and not just 'extra remedial help' (see Tansley and Panckhurst, 1981). The question has important theoretical implications too, particularly in relation to whether 'dyslexia' is qualitatively different from other learning disorders.

Evidence regarding the effectiveness of simultaneous oral spelling with dyslexics does not, however, help us to understand which aspect of the simultaneous oral spelling procedure is vital. It may be that its effectiveness is due to some factor other than the emphasis on grapheme–phoneme correspondences. For example, Bryant and Bradley (1985) suggest that such multisensory methods may work due to the emphasis on movement and organisation. Bradley (1981) suggests that the vital element is the relating of a motor movement to a sound pattern. Hulme, Mark and Ives (1987) propose, on the basis of paired-associate learning, that tracing improves the learning of names by its effect on the ability to recognise visual forms. They found that tracing improves the learning of letter names paired with letter-like forms. However, their experiments did not focus on learning real word spelling, and did not enable the examination of different routes to the spelling process. Another possiblity is that simultaneous oral spelling encourages the acquisition of word-specific knowledge, an idea that I shall explore more fully later.

The study reported here examines two methods of teaching spelling: by simultaneous oral spelling and a 'visual inspection' method (VI) that is commonly used to teach spelling in schools. Dyslexics were matched with younger children of similar spelling age as controls. As a good deal of research suggests that dyslexics have phonological processing deficits within verbal short-term memory (Thomson, 1990b), the simultaneous oral spelling method should be relatively more effective for the dyslexics than for the control group who, it was assumed, have an operational phonological or 'alphabetic' route. The study also used regular and irregular words – the latter require more 'direct route' or 'visual to meaning' processing, whereas regular words allow a greater use of the grapheme–phoneme or alphabetic conversion route. Dyslexics would, therefore, if simultaneous oral spelling worked by improving grapheme–phoneme skills, do better with regular words in the simultaneous oral spelling condition compared with controls.

Teaching Procedures

The procedure for the simultaneous oral spelling conditions was as follows:

1. Children paired off to test each other.
2. Child A says (e.g.) 'confirm'.

3. Child B
   (a) listens and without sight of the word;
   (b) repeats 'confirm';
   (c) spells out orally using letter names, one by one;
   (d) writes down letter by letter, saying each letter out loud as it is written;
   (e) reads the word he has written out loud.
4. Child A marks right or wrong.

The process is seen to be multisensory because the child hears (auditory), says (follows speech/motor articulation), writes (kinaesthetic/motor), says as written (speech/auditory linked to motor) and reads out loud (visual/auditory feedback).

In the visual inspection conditions the children were given the same list of words and did the following:

1. Looked at the words.
2. Covered them up and said the letters out loud.
3. Checked the words by looking at them again.

This 'look, cover, check' is a commonly used procedure for teaching spelling. The children were given the same length of time to learn the words as in the simultaneous oral spelling condition.

Subjects

All the subjects were of at least average intelligence. The dyslexic group were taken from an independent school for dyslexic children, and the controls, matched on spelling age, from a local primary school. Relevant data are presented in Table 18.1. The subjects were allocated, randomly, to the simultaneous oral spelling (SOS) and visual inspection (VI) conditions.

Table 18.1 Age and attainments of subjects

	No.	Chronological age (years)	Spelling age (Vernon Graded Word Spelling) (years)	Range (years)	s.d.
Dyslexics	20	9;10	7;0	6;2–7;10	0.71
Controls	28	7;6	7;3	6;8–8;2	0.58

Materials

The dyslexics were given a spelling test of 20 regular and 20 irregular words. Regularity was defined as the ability to spell a word by applying common phoneme–grapheme conversion rules, and irregularity by words that could not be spelt by following speech sounds or applying common phoneme–grapheme conversion rules. From these, ten words consistently spelt incorrectly were chosen: five regular words (system, vandal, confirm, turban and nectar) and five irregular words (biscuit, enough, special, beauty and yachtsman). The ten words chosen were, therefore, all incorrectly spelt by both groups of children.

Method

Using the five regular and five irregular words, the children were given a daily teaching session for 2 weeks using simultaneous oral spelling or visual inspection techniques. At the beginning of the third week, the children were given a spelling test of the ten words used in the trials.

Table 18.2   Mean scores for post-teaching spelling test*

	Simultaneous oral spelling			Visual inspection		
	Regular	Irregular	Totals	Regular	Irregular	Totals
Dyslexics	2.61	1.23	3.84	0.51	0.43	0.94
Controls	2.32	2.12	4.44	1.96	1.23	3.19
Totals	4.93	3.35		2.47	1.66	

*Maximum score 5 (max. 10 for totals).
Range of scores: dyslexics 0.00–4.00; controls 1.00–5.00.

Results

The results are shown in Table 18.2 and the data presented there were subjected to an analysis of variance, for group × teaching method × regularity. The significant effects were as follows:

1. Although matched on spelling age, dyslexics scored less well than controls ($F = 6.1$, d.f. 1.43, $P < 0.02$ level).
2. The performance of both groups was better under the simultaneous oral spelling condition ($F = 6.9$, d.f. 1.43, $P < 0.02$). However, a significant interaction ($F = 4.5$, d.f. 1.43, $P < 0.02$) showed that:
   (a) simultaneous oral spelling produced better learning than visual inspection for dyslexics, but the two methods of learning were equally effective for controls;
   (b) the difference between dyslexics and controls was significant for the visual inspection condition but not for the simultaneous oral spelling condition.

3. Both groups learned regular words better than irregular words ($F = 61.4$, d.f. 1.43, $P<0.01$). However, a three-way interaction indicated a non-significant trend ($F = 3.7$, d.f. 1.43, $P<0.059$) that the effect of the simultaneous oral spelling method for dyslexics was particularly marked for regular words.

Discussion

The findings demonstrate that, although of equivalent spelling age, dyslexics learn less efficiently than normal spellers. Thus, they are not generally delayed in spelling, but have a specific weakness. Furthermore, whilst simultaneous oral spelling is more effective than visual inspection for dyslexics, it is not more effective than visual inspection for normal subjects. Theoretically, this implies that dyslexics are an atypical group and do not lie on a continuum from bad spellers to very good spellers. Bryant and Bradley (1985) suggest that, if the idea of a continuum is valid, then the same experiences will help all children. Using this logic, they deny the existence of 'dyslexia' as a syndrome. However, using this same logic, this study shows that dyslexics are an exceptional group; the experiences which helped the normal children in the visual inspection condition to spell did not help dyslexics. Indeed, the mean performance of the dyslexics in the visual inspection conditions was almost at basal level.

There are important educational implications to these findings. If dyslexics do not respond to the same teaching as normal children, any remedial teaching of 'more of the same' will be ineffective. A recent guide on specific learning difficulties produced by a local authority comments that (teaching methods are) '.... not necessarily different from the method used for children with general learning difficulties at the lower end of the continuum'. In contrast, this study shows that a teaching method which is theoretically based can help dyslexics to perform at the same level as a developmentally matched control group. Teaching needs to be appropriate to the children in question, dyslexics requiring a specialist approach rather than methods that might be used for children generally delayed in written language. This conclusion is not new (see Miles and Miles, 1983; Thomson and Watkins, 1990) but receives experimental support here.

As both groups of subjects learned regular words more easily than irregular words, it cannot be argued that the dyslexics are bereft of alphabetic or grapheme–phoneme skills. If the dyslexics were unable to apply any grapheme–phoneme rules, they would perform no differently on regular compared with irregular words. Thus, Frith's (1985) notion that dyslexics are arrested at the logographic stage of literacy development is not fully supported by these data, although it is likely that the ability to use a phoneme–grapheme conversion route in spelling has been fostered in these particular dyslexics by attendance at a specialist school.

As far as mechanisms are concerned, there are a number of possible reasons for the superiority of simultaneous oral spelling. It may be that simultaneous oral spelling focuses attention on the letter-by-letter sequence of words, thereby improving subsequent lexical retrieval (Ellis and Miles, 1981). Alternatively, the kinaesthetic code invoked during simultaneous oral spelling may enhance memory for the words (Hulme, 1981).

However, there was a trend for the efficacy of simultaneous oral spelling in dyslexics to be particularly marked for regular words. This suggests that simultaneous oral spelling may be acting to improve the dyslexic's use of phoneme–grapheme correspondence.

As irregular words are harder for both dyslexics and the control group, it may be that grapheme selection for each word is based on rules at a deep level of linguistic analysis, where rules are known only implicitly. The existence of implicit rules in subjects is given support by Frith's (1985) finding that subjects have preferred spellings for nonsense words. This suggestion fits in with theories of language acquisition which emphasise the role of implicitly known rules in language acquisition. It is possible, therefore, that the fact that the dyslexics performed less well in the visual inspection condition suggests that dyslexics may have a problem with selecting the appropriate graphemes for a word. This might be, as suggested by Seymour (1986), a 'double deficit' in that both the lexical and non-lexical (i.e. phonological) routes to spelling are impaired. Irregular words requiring this 'graphemic–lexical' choice would therefore be particularly difficult for dyslexics. The simultaneous oral spelling technique would not bolster relevant skills for irregular words, whereas it would aid the skills required for regular word spelling. Therefore simultaneous oral spelling seems to be a particularly useful technique for regular words. In respect of the visual inspection condition, it is apparent that either technique helps the control group, presumably because they have good phonological and lexical skills. The visual inspection condition gives very poor results in the dyslexics. This is of great pedagogic importance given that one of the most common forms of learning to spell in schools is visual, e.g. Look–Cover–Remember–Spell. This manifestly does not help dyslexics, either with regular or irregular words.

Acknowledgements

This paper was based on a project report following data collected and analysed by Ms J. Robertson with the additional supervision of Dr M. Forrester, both at the Social Psychology Department, University of Kent.

References

BRADLEY, L. (1981). A tactile approach to reading. *British Journal of Special Education Formal Trends* **8**(4), 32–36.

BRYANT, P. and BRADLEY, L. (1985). *Children's Reading Problems.* Oxford: Blackwell.

ELLIS, N. and MILES, T. (1981). A lexical coding deficiency. In: G. Pavlides and T. Miles (Eds), *Dyslexia Research*. Chichester: Wiley.

FRITH, U. (1985). Beneath the surface of developmental dyslexia. In: J.C. Marshall, K.E. Patterson and M. Coltheart (Eds), *Surface Dyslexia in Adults and Children*. London: Routledge & Kegan Paul.

HORNSBY, B. and MILES T. (1980). The effects of a dyslexia-centered teaching programme. *British Journal of Educational Psychology* **50**, 236–242.

HULME, C. (1981). *Reading Retardation and Multi-sensory Teaching*. London: Routledge & Kegan Paul.

HULME, C., MARK, A. and IVES, S. (1987). Some experimental studies of multi-sensory teaching. The effects of manual tracing on children's paired-associate learning. *British Journal of Developmental Psychology* **5**, 299–309.

MILES, T.R. and MILES, E. (1983). *Help for Dyslexic Children*. London: Routledge & Kegan Paul.

SEYMOUR, P. (1986). *Cognitive Analysis of Dyslexia*. London: Routledge & Kegan Paul.

TANSLEY, P. and PANCKHURST, J. (1981). *Children with Specific Learning Disabilities*. NFER Report. Slough: NFER/Nelson.

THOMSON, M. (1988). Preliminary findings concerning the effects of specialised teaching on dyslexic children. *Applied Cognitive Psychology* **2**, 19–33.

THOMSON, M. (1990a). Teaching programmes for children with specific learning difficulties: implications for teachers. In: C. Elliott and P. Pumphrey (Eds), *Primary School Pupils' Reading and Spelling Difficulties*. London: Palmer Press.

THOMSON, M. (1990b). *Developmental Dyslexia: Its Nature, Assessment and Remediation*. London: Whurr.

THOMSON, M. and WATKINS, E. (1990). *Dyslexia: A Teaching Handbook*. London: Whurr.

Part VI
Intervention: The Practical Skills of Dyslexic Teaching

Chapter 19
Factors to Consider when Designing a Test Protocol in Mathematics for Dyslexics

S.J. CHINN

Although many individual tests exist for examining a range of mathematics achievements, aptitudes and attitudes, there is no test protocol that brings together a battery of tests designed to diagnose the mathematical strengths and weaknesses of a dyslexic student.

Such a protocol must strike a balance between providing a clear and full picture of the child's abilities in mathematics and overwhelming him or her with lengthy tests. The protocol will need to use a range of tests and procedures to obtain this picture.

Learning Difficulties and Mathematics

Dyslexia can be considered as a syndrome (Miles and Miles, 1990) or as a 'pattern of difficulties' (Miles, 1983), with the pattern including difficulties with certain mathematical facts and operations. The National Conference in Maryland, USA (Kavanagh and Truss, 1988), which was convened to consider and review the definition of learning disabilities, included mathematical difficulties in its definition.

The experiences of the author in two secondary specialist schools in the UK for boys diagnosed as dyslexic and at a co-educational school in the USA were of a high percentage of students who had some problems in learning mathematics. Although some areas of difficulty were frequent (e.g. learning tables by rote), the overall range of problems and the different degrees of severity of each problem within each child created a wide range of difficulties.

Subskill Deficits

There are a range of subskill deficits which may affect aspects of performance in arithmetic (for discussion see Miles and Miles, 1991).

Some of these have more direct effects than others, but all must be considered as background factors that may influence the design of the test protocol. These same deficits may also create language difficulties and thus explain the two areas of difficulty occurring concurrently.

The difficulties which must be considered as possible contributors to learning problems in mathematics, and therefore as background factors in setting up a test protocol, are the following:

1. Visual perceptual difficulties can affect a child's ability to identify differences between similar shapes, e.g.
   $+$ and $\times$ 3 and 5   6 and 9.
   The child may misread symbols and copy work slowly and inaccurately. The problem may persist into secondary mathematics with $\times$ and x, θ, d and δ.
2. Directional confusion may lead to pupils writing numbers the wrong way round and create difficulties in arithmetic calculations that may start at the left and work right (long division), or start at the right and work left (addition) or go from top to bottom, or bottom to top.
3. Sequencing problems which may result in the child having to return to the beginning each time, e.g. if asked 7×2 he or she may have to start at 1×2 and work up to the required answer. It is often extraordinarily difficult for a child to count backwards. Some algorithms (especially long division) create great demands on sequencing abilities.
4. Spatial awareness is needed to appreciate place value, or to distinguish between $2x$ and x^2. Sums on the blackboard or in the textbook may merge and confuse the child who has spatial problems as he or she copies out the data.
5. Short-term memory can cause difficulties in several areas. It may cause the child to forget the teacher's instructions. The child may forget a carried number part way through a sum, especially if he or she has to break off to work out a basic fact needed to complete the calculation. The child's short-term memory may become overloaded and this may lead to a total loss of a calculation or a set of instructions. These problems may be visual, aural or both.
6. Deficiencies in long-term memory may limit the child's store of basic facts (e.g. learning times tables – Pritchard et al., 1989) and procedures. This, in turn, may handicap the development of concepts (see point (10) below).
7. Difficulties in naming. These may result in problems with the language of mathematics. The child must learn the names of the symbols used in mathematics (the names of $\times$ $+$ $-$ $=$ etc.), a task made more difficult by the range of names used for a particular symbol: share, divide; multiply, of, times; and so forth.

8. Word skills, reading: the child must be able to read accurately. Mathematics tends to be written in very precise language, so that one misread word can completely change the meaning of a question.

9. Learning style (and teaching style): not all people process numbers in the same way. Bath, Chinn and Knox (1986) identified 'grasshoppers' as intuitive, answer-oriented learners and, at the opposite end of a continuum of styles, 'inchworms' as formula, process-oriented learners. Sharma (1989) identifies the two styles as qualitative and quantitative. A mismatch between learner style and teacher style may cause learning problems. Learning style may be affected by any of the other factors listed here.

10. Conceptual ability: a child who has had difficulties in mathematics over a long period of time may not have had adequate experience to progress conceptually. Constant returning to the learning of the times tables, for example, may cause the child to miss out on developmental work carried out by the rest of the class.

Test Length and Subject Matter

The final consideration is the age of achievements of the child to be tested. Recent reports from the Assessment of Performance Unit focused on arithmetic skills. As this is a basic, fundamental and 'everyday' area of mathematics, and as the testing described here is aimed primarily at younger children whose experience of mathematics is limited to arithmetic, then a restriction to arithmetic seems reasonable.

Children who are experiencing problems in arithmetic are likely to be anxious. Indeed, many people admit to mathematics anxiety (see, for example, Cope, 1988). Some control can be obtained by minimising the length of the test, although a compromise has to be made between obtaining adequate information and reducing the time needed to complete the tests. A further reduction in anxiety or at least an increase in test tolerance may be achieved by using a varied format of question and presentation.

More information is obtainable if the test is diagnostic (Underhill, Uprichard and Heddens, 1980). To achieve this it should consider errors (Ashlock, 1982) as well as correct answers. This means the test is considering more than just a 'score'. Further valuable information can be obtained by allowing the child to contribute more than just answers. The key question (as used in the Test of Cognitive Style in Mathematics – Bath, Chinn and Knox, 1986) can be used again here, i.e. 'How did you do that?'

The type of mathematics question used in the test should be varied in presentation as well as content. In addition to increasing test tolerance (see above), the test is also ascertaining whether the child is set in his or her knowledge to a particular format – the Einstellung effect (Luchins,

1942). Does the child actually think through a question or is he automatically applying his knowledge without any understanding of the underlying numerical concepts and values?

Finally, the test protocol must be designed to obtain useful information. This begs the questions 'What is useful?' and 'For whom is it intended to be useful?'

The author considers that 'useful' information is most likely to come from arithmetic questions, rather than by extrapolation from other test material, such as the Raven's matrices.

Test Contents: What is Useful?

'What is useful?' is answered in part by that other question, 'Who is it for?'.

The Dyslexia Institute test protocol was designed to give a picture of the child's present status in arithmetic which a teacher/tutor could use for remedial instruction. It also serves to provide a basic explanation of the child's abilities, strengths and weaknesses for parents.

Thus the test protocol will include:

1. A 'standardised' mathematics age.
2. An assessment of the child's ability to recognise and use mathematics symbols.
3. An assessment of basic fact knowledge, compensatory strategies and understanding of numbers and their interrelationships.
4. The child's cognitive style.
5. The child's level of understanding of place value.
6. A measure of his or her accuracy in calculations.
7. A measure of his or her speed of working.
8. An analysis of the child's error patterns.
9. An assessment of the child's understanding and accuracy in using algorithms.
10. The child's knowledge and understanding of the special language of mathematics.
11. A test of his or her ability to solve basic word problems.

This mathematical information could be supported by measurements of IQ, memory and reading skills.

The Test Protocol

The tests in the protocol are most effective if administered one on one (Lankford, 1971). They are even more effective if the tester observes the child and makes incidental, clinical observations. Thus the teacher should sit in a position where he or she can see the child as he works. This, in turn, is helped by encouraging the child to think aloud.

The standardised age test could be the Basic Number Screening Test by Gillham and Hess (1976), or the Wide Range Achievement Test by Jastak and Jastak (1978). Both will give a mathematics 'age' and some initial clues as to how the child processes mathematics.

Basic fact testing requires the question 'How did you do that?' to discover the child's use of strategies. It also requires a variety of presentations to test the flexibility of the child's knowledge. So, for example, if testing knowledge of number bonds below 10, the tester gives the child a mixture of 1p, 2p and 5p coins and asks, 'How many different ways can you make 9p?'.

When testing addition facts the child is presented with cards, such as:

$$8+4 = [\quad]$$
$$[\quad]+7 = 15$$
$$9+[\quad] = 12$$

It is reasonable to simply ask the child, 'Which of the times tables do you know?'. It is also reasonable to check! For example, when the tester asks the child if she knows her two times table, he should then ask, 'What are seven twos, seven times two?' The tester is trying to find out if the child knows this information straight out or if she had to start at 1×2, 2×2 and work up, or if the child starts at a reference point such as 5×2.

Due to the fact that sequencing is a probable area of difficulty, and because the ability to sequence fowards and backwards is an important arithmetic skill, the tester should ask the child to sequence numbers forwards (3 6 9 12.....) and backwards (20 18 16 14........).

Test items should also cover the use of the four operations. These also allow the tester to examine error patterns. The examples chosen are designed to expose typical errors, such as failure to carry digits, inaccurate renaming and so forth. They are structured to be progressively harder. Again much may be learned from clinical observations.

The child's knowledge of the language of mathematics is tested with symbol cards. Each card (e.g. =) is shown to the child and he is asked to name the sign. Also the child is asked to explain what the word (e.g. equals) means.

The protocol has to include some carefully structured and graded word problems. These progress from 'Add 6 and 9' to 'Mike has 6 marbles, 3 are red, 3 are green. Bill has 9 marbles. Anita has eight marbles, six are red and two are green. How many more red marbles does Anita have than Mike?'. Finally the tester may ask some general questions such as, 'Do you like maths?', 'Do you think you are good at maths?', 'Which bits do you like best/least?'

Conclusion

The full test protocol, based on the considerations outlined above, was constructed by the Dyslexia Institute Mathematics Committee. Publication is expected in 1991. Although the protocol is set out in detail, a vital part of it remains beyond documentation. This is the tester's ability and experience to make all the required observations and still have the time and judgement to make perceptive clinical observations.

The final format of the protocol is based on the principle that testing requires a mixture of formal and informal procedures – a mixture of tests that provide a full and relevant picture of the child's status in mathematics.

Acknowledgement

The author wishes to think all the members of the Dyslexia Institute Mathematics Skills Committee for their stimulating ideas, work and assistance in setting up the Dyslexia Institute's Teaching and Testing Manual.

References

ASHLOCK, R.B. (1982). *Error Patterns in Computation.* Columbus, OH: Merrill.

BATH, J., CHINN, S. and KNOX, D. (1986). *The Test of Cognitive Style in Mathematics.* East Aurora, NY: Slosson.

COPE, C.L. (1988). Math anxiety and math avoidance in college freshmen. *Focus on Learning Problems in Mathematics* 10(1), 1–13.

GILLHAM, W.E.C. and HESSE, K.A. (1976). *Basic Number Screening Test.* Sevenoaks: Hodder and Stoughton Educational.

JASTAK, J.F. and JASTAK, S. (1978). *Wide Range Achievement Test,* revised edn. Wilmington, DE: Jastak Associates.

KAVANAGH, J.F. and TRUSS, T.J. (Eds) (1988). *Learning Disabilities: Proceedings of the National Conference.* Parkton, MA: York Press.

LARKFORD, F.G. (1971). What can a teacher learn about a pupil's thinking through oral interviews? *The Arithmetic Teacher* 22, 26–32.

LUCHINS, A.S. (1942). Mechanisation in problem solving: The effect of Einstellung. *Psychological Monographs* 54(6).

MILES, T.R. (1983). *Dyslexia: The Pattern of Difficulties.* Oxford: Blackwell.

MILES, T.R. and MILES, E. (1990). *Dyslexia. A Hundred Years On.* Milton Keynes: Open University Press.

MILES, T.R. and MILES, E. (Eds) (1991). *Dyslexia and Mathematics,* in press. London:

PRITCHARD, R.A., MILES, T.R., CHINN, S.J. and TAGGART, A.T. (1989). Dyslexia and knowledge of number facts. *Links* 14(3), 17–20.

SHARMA, M. (1986). Dyscalculia and other learning problems in mathematics: a historical perspective. *Focus on Learning Problems in Mathematics* 8, 7–45.

SHARMA, M. (1989). Mathematics learning personality. *Mathematics Notebook* 7, 1–10.

UNDERHILL, R.G., UPRICHARD, A.E. and HEDDENS, J.W. (1980). *Diagnosing Mathematical Difficulties.* Columbus, OH: Merrill.

Chapter 20
Mathematics and Dyslexics – After Basics what then?

ANNE HENDERSON

My experience as a teacher of dyslexics made me realise that I had to identify basics in mathematics as well as looking beyond basics to see where and how these skills could be transferred and used correctly. I was hopeful that children experiencing mathematical difficulties could be taught the basics and then be able to transfer those skills to more complex mathematical situations.

As my pupils had language difficulties, it seemed appropriate to start with a language approach to mathematics. This has forced me to be flexible in my teaching methods and now my experience in this field of mathematics and dyslexia has allowed me to work with pupils who approach mathematics in a very different way to my own.

The following 'basics' are the ones that I have worked with successfully with many pupils over the last 5 years.

Language

Obviously, if a student has difficulties in reading he or she would then have difficulty in reading words in mathematics. However, the additional problem in mathematics is connecting words to the correct symbols and then understanding the various mathematical processes the symbols are representing. By using the five basic symbols as a starting point and identifying them in words the student understands, the learning process is initiated. Pointing out that the (+) and the (×) are symbols which indicate a process that makes the original number increase and that (−) and (÷) make the original number decrease is a way of cutting down options from four to two when the student has to decide which symbol he or she is going to use. (*Note*: as in teaching spelling rules, there is always an exception to the rules because multiplying fractions makes them smaller and dividing makes the original answer bigger.)

Other symbols $<$, $>$ or : need to be looked at, talked about and used so that the pupil can gradually add them to the basic symbols he or she is now familiar with. As each new topic is met the new symbols need to be discussed along with the key words the pupil will be meeting while dealing with the topic. If possible, just as in language teaching, a special card can be prepared containing all the appropriate words and symbols connected to the new topic for the pupils' constant reference. Apart from the language, a topic needs to be analysed into very small teaching steps to aid the building-on process continually. Obviously, each teacher has an individual style of teaching, just as every pupil has a different style of learning, so that analysis of topics must be carried out to suit both. Some teachers prefer to show a pupil the whole topic to start with and then gradually allow the pupil to participate in the calculation, eventually allowing the pupil to demonstrate his expertise on his own. Others prefer to split a topic up into levels of achievement, then to check that the pupil is happy and competent with the work, and then move on to a more advanced level. Eventually once she is secure in the basic symbols and connecting language, the pupil will begin to develop her own attack strategies and enjoy using them to solve more advanced mathematical problems.

Direction

Knowing which direction to move is difficult for some dyslexics. Addition, subtraction and multiplication are all carried out from right to left, but division is usually carried out from left to right, especially if it is done on paper,

e.g. $48 \div 4$.

This can be interpreted in different ways:

1. It can be read as forty-eight divided by four which a pupil will probably rewrite like this: $4\overline{)48}$
2. It can be read as 'How many fours in forty-eight?'.

Quite often my pupils will read the problem as in (2) and, saying it aloud, will punch into their calculator $4 \div 48$ and, on getting the answer 0.0833, they will quickly switch off and try to do the calculation themselves without any aids. However, by this time they are getting anxious so they seem to start making error after error and so end up with yet another failure. This situation can be avoided some of the time if the teacher brings the pupil's attention to the problem or if the pupils get into the habit of estimating the rough size of the answer.

We usually read numbers from the left, but if we are presented with a large series of digits to read as a whole number

e.g. 1 6 8 5 4 3 5

we then have to begin from the right to count in threes to split up the number into thousands and millions. Identifying marks have to be put into the number

e.g. 1, 6 8 5, 4 3 5.

Now it is easy to read the number as one million, six hundred and eighty-five thousand, four hundred and thirty-five. I have found that several of my students have to have a little card which shows the following:

> To read a number start on the right and count in threes and put in commas to split the number up.
> The first comma is the thousand comma.
> The second comma is the million comma.
> To read this number:

> 2 4 5 7 4 8 8 0 START HERE

> million   thousand
> 2 4 ,5   7   4 ,8 8 0

The number is 24 million, 574 thousand, 880.

However, even with these guides some pupils will, when punching it into the calculator, press the decimal point for the thousand comma and so get a completely incorrect answer,

e.g. 1, 642 .4

will be entered as

1. 642 .4

As the first decimal point is the one that registers on the calculator, the number has an incorrect value. It seems to be important to encourage pupils to read the number aloud or to say it to him- or herself while he or she is punching it into the calculator. If this does not seem to be having the desired effect, then try putting a piece of card under the number to identify it clearly and perhaps read it onto a tape with instant playback. A combination of visual and auditory methods encourages correct use of the calculator. I have found using a combination of these methods initially promotes both accuracy and confidence and then the pupil can eventually abandon any aids he or she no longer needs.

Individual Style

In order to aid each pupil and give him or her confidence to achieve, a teacher needs to look out for error patterns and to offer help in a manner suited to the learning style of the pupil. Sharma (1986) identifies the quantitative learning personality (Quant P) and the qualitative learning personality (Qual P). Bath, Chinn and Knox (1986) identify the 'Inchworm and Grasshopper' types of mathematicians. Both of these identifications show quite clearly the need for varying approaches, strategies and apparatus when teaching pupils who have a specific learning difficulty in mathematics. With investigations at GCSE level now being a very important part of the assessment, it is essential that a pupil is encouraged at an early level to explore his own ideas thoroughly and to find answers. Working with dyslexic pupils with Qual P/Grasshopper tendencies, it is clear they have the ability to 'see' solutions but need a great deal of persuasion to actually write down a method. Pupils need to be encouraged to find their own particular way of recording their work as well as the solutions. Talking about various ways of recording and deciding which one is appropriate for that pupil allows for the best method to be identified and used so that it too becomes a basic skill on which to build. Organisational skills, so often lacking in dyslexic pupils, are vital here. Spacing work out, using rulers and colours to identify 'minor' answers within the calculation, or promoting the use of computers allows the pupil to produce an excellent piece of work. All these methods help to promote confidence and allow a pupil to begin to achieve.

Times Tables

Not knowing their times tables is an obvious way others within the peer group can spot someone who is 'thick'. Self-esteem is very soon eroded away by constant failure with tables, particularly if the pupil is nervous, self-conscious or reaching adolescence when life seems to become so full of other problems. I have tried various methods of teaching tables using the Gypsy Method, finger tables (9's), arrays and table patterns, table tapes and several variations incorporating the use of table square. Should a pupil specifically ask to be taught tables, I try to find a method out of the ones mentioned that perhaps will help this particular student. The ability to find quick answers to easy multiples does help with more advanced work, but I do try to emphasise the fact that it is just as beneficial to be able to estimate correctly.

Estimation

Dyslexic pupils find approximation and estimation very hard so they have to be encouraged to do it as often as possible, because it is an important skill. In adult life, estimation is the one aspect of mathematics that is used most. Very often pupils will agree with me that estimating is sensible but, in practice, many will not even attempt to try it. They tell me that they have enough trouble using exact numbers so what is the point of them trying to find an answer with numbers that are wrong to start off with. However, in spite of all these negative comments, I still continue to try to persuade all my pupils to try some estimation, regardless of how rough an estimate it is. For example, you can show that:

£27.60 × 22 = £607.20

can be estimated to £30 × £20 = £600

If this rough estimate of the answer is written down, an error on the calculator, like pressing the + for the × symbol, can be spotted immediately. Then this can quickly be re-checked.

There are several ways of teaching a pupil to estimate:

1. Depending on the size of the original number it can be rounded up to the nearest ten, hundred or thousand

	e.g.	27	nearest ten	30
		358	nearest hundred	400
		6146	nearest thousand	6000

2. Use a whole number that the pupil can handle easily,

   e.g. 7 × 18

        7 × 20

   Show that you can put the nought in the answer, then you only need to know 2 × 7.

3. If the original number incorporates a decimal point then forget anything to the right of the decimal point,

   e.g.   2.3   estimate 2

   Pupils need to be taught that the digit on the right has great power when we are rounding off numbers. If the digit we are about to drop from the original number is 5 or above, then it has the power to make the number on its left go one place higher when it is actually removed from the number,

   e.g. 6.5 becomes 7 when the 5 is dropped.

   Should pupils experience difficulties with this, it is possible to work with amounts of money,

   e.g. I owe you £7.62.

   If I am not paying you in anything less than whole pound coins would you prefer £7 or £8?

   Pupils very quickly recognise the power of the number on the right!

Number Patterns

Number patterns using a 1–100 square can be identified at an early stage:

    odd/square/rectangle/triangular/prime numbers

can all be identified and their individual shapes drawn and coloured. This directly leads to factors being clearly seen so that the word plus the meaning can be shown together. Making the numbers and patterns out of card that can be stuck onto paper to show the patterns clearly helps, as does tracing both the number and pattern shape with fingers, especially if the card has a surface texture. Spending time on this very important aspect of your number system pays dividends later when investigatory techniques are employed to find answers, so vital now at GCSE level:

e.g.

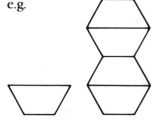

Containers are piled up in the manner shown. Investigate the connection between the 7th container and the 11th one.

State which way up the 59th container will be.

Pupils aware of odd, even and prime numbers quickly see the connection and give the correct answer.

Area and Volume

Although area is about visual patterns, not all my pupils are able to deal with this topic successfully. Teaching a child to recognise a centimetre square and then to count up the squares in a given shape seems easy but often pupils do not see the connection between the answer and the fact that the length × width = area because, as mentioned earlier, times tables are difficult for them so indeed they cannot make the link between 20 cm square and 4 cm × 5 cm.

Even after doing several of the calculations and getting correct answers, a newer slightly different shape needs to be talked about thoroughly to try to avoid error

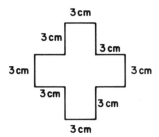

One of my pupils insisted that the area of this shape was:

$9 + 9 + 9 + 9 = 36\,cm^2$

He was unable to see the other square in the middle of the shape. We only solved this problem when we made the shape and cut out the individual squares.

Areas of triangles can be worked out using concrete examples, i.e. cutting out shapes and counting up squares until the pupil is able to deal with the concept easily.

Circles too have to be dealt with carefully especially as a new symbol π (pi – not to be confused with pie charts or indeed apple pie!) is being introduced. I have found it useful to point out that π has an approximate value of 3 as an aid to doing simple estimates. Language too is important, for example: perimeter/diameter/radius/circumference and their abbreviations p/d/r/c; all need careful discussion. Colour coding helps as do comparative relationships of sizes,

e.g.

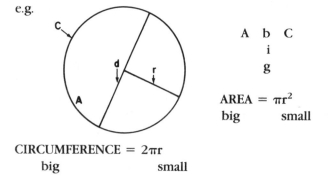

Area is always something squared so connect this to the formula πr^2.

The author has found that volume can be taught in many different ways but having lots of 'concrete' shapes that can be cut up into slices helps as do some of the following:

1. Sweets such as 'Polo' mints, 'Rolo' chocs or 'Toblerone' can demonstrate volume as the areas × the number of slices.
2. Talking of how a scanner machine takes X-ray slices of the body thus connecting surface area to volume.
3. Notelet pads – especially the newer thick telephone ones – demonstrate volume well.

Mathematical Questions

Here is an example of a 'typical mathematics question' relating to volume.

Find the volume of a can of soup which is 15 cm high and has a base diameter of 8 cm.

To tackle this I would suggest the following stages:

1. Draw the question out pictorially
2. Diameter = 8   radius = 4
              r   = 4
3. Height = 15   h   = 15
4. Area of circle   = πr^2 Estimate
                    = $\pi \times r \times r$ 3 × 4 × 4
                                              (dyslexics can usually deal with
                                              2's better than 3's
                                              5's better than 4's)
                    = $\pi \times 4 \times 4$ 2 × 5 × 5
                    = 50.3 cm²   10 × 5 = 50 cm²
5. Volume   = 50.3 × 15   50 × 15 = 50 × 10
                    = 754.5 cm³   = 500 ÷ 2
                                                 = 250 + 500
                                                 = 750 cm³

Once steps through the calculation are identified the pupils are able to work slowly through the problem at their own pace 'sticking' the 'bits' together to find a solution, just as they might with syllables to create a multisyllabic word.

In answering questions, it is useful to draw parallels between English and mathematics. This is shown in Table 20.1.

Trigonometry

After working with pupils who have difficulties in trigonometry for some 5 years, we have finally worked out a series of questions in the form of a flow chart that a pupil can ask him- or herself as an aid to solving the problem.

Table 20.1 Approaching a question: parallels between English and mathematics question

	English	Mathematics
1	(i) Read the passage	(a) Read through the question
2	(ii) Understand the meaning	(b) Understand it
3	(iii) Read the questions	(c) Draw a diagram to illustrate the facts given
4	(iv) Then return to the passage and highlight the relevant part of the prose in order to work out the answer systematically	(d) Decide which method to use, identifying the different mathematical processes and record the appropriate symbols in the order required

Language is sorted out first (colour-coded if necessary).

opposite side = O	adjacent side = A	hypotenuse = H
sine = Sin = S	cosine = Cos = C	tangent = Tan = T
SOH	CAH	TOA
S = O/H	C = A/H	T = O/A

Then a flow chart is used:

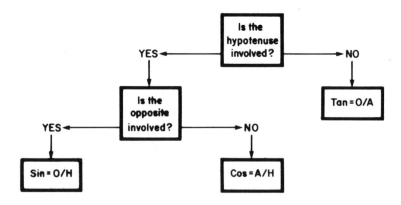

For example, consider the following question:

A gun is due south of its target. From an observation point 40 m due west of the gun, the target is on a bearing of 005.
Find the distance of the target from the gun.
Now this protocol can be suggested:
1. Read and understand the question.
   What does on a bearing of 005 mean? Highlight this.
   Highlight 40 m due west
2. Draw out the problem and identify different points.
3. Is the hypotenuse involved? NO. Use Tan = O/A.

4. Tan 85 = distance/40
   × each side by 40
   Tan 85 × 40 = distance of T from gun
5. In order to enter this correctly in the calculator, it must be *read from the right*, i.e.
   press 40/press ×/press 85/press Tan/press =
   The target is 457 m from the gun.

Pupils using a systematic approach with which they have previously experienced success find that they are able to work their own way through complex problems and reach a correct answer. By building on their positive strengths, I am finding that my pupils are beginning to achieve in a subject that they used to fear and dread. Many of my pupils have told me that now they feel confident in the methods they are using; they are able to proceed slowly to reach a solution. Particularly in trigonometry, they reported back to me that they were able to remember the flow chart easily and so, what was once a process that was avoided if possible, became one that was deliberately chosen.

References

BATH, J., CHINN, S.J. and KNOX, D. (1986). *Test of Cognitive Style in Mathematics.* New York: Slosson.

SHARMA, M. (1986). Dyscalculia and other learning problems in mathematics: a historical perspective. *Focus on Learning Problems in Mathematics* **8**, 7–45.

Chapter 21
Communication and Study Skills at Primary Level

PATIENCE THOMSON*

The focus of this chapter is on study skills for younger pupils, and the importance of introducing these at an early stage of the child's education.

Oral to Written Work

We concentrate in class almost entirely on oral discussion, with clarity of expression at a premium. There is virtually no written work involved, but pictorial or cartoon records are kept by the children of the stories or of other points at issue. It is to these cartoon 'notes' that the children refer when they are retelling a story or marshalling arguments in favour of or against the issue under discussion. The cartoon records are also excellent aide-memoires, enabling the child to remember a week later in considerable detail the content of the preceding lesson. The more stimulation and challenge you offer in verbal discussion to an intelligent dyslexic child, the more positively you reinforce his or her oral communication skills. These are the necessary precursors of the written skills which he or she will need later at secondary level.

With 10 and 11 year olds, the objective must be to bridge the gap between articulate speech and coherent writing. It must also be to teach a child to study independently and effectively, to monitor his or her own output and to develop strategies for information processing and memory skills which will enable him or her to survive at secondary school, particularly if he or she returns to a mainstream classroom.

Mapping Skills

At the beginning of the school year, the first lesson of the study skills course involves drawing a sketch map of the classroom. A vital ingredient of this lesson is the time-factor; the children have 30 minutes to complete the task. It is explained to them that it is essential that all the desks should be included with the name of the relevant children. They are given a typed class list to help them (names are particularly difficult for dyslexic children). They are also encouraged to discuss briefly the minimum points of reference necessary for the map to be clear – the door, window, teacher's desk etc. – the choice is theirs. The point of the exercise is that I, or any other teacher, should be able to enter the room, refer to the map and identify any child immediately.

This is a popular task and quickly highlights individual problems. Some become bogged down in petty detail, some draw pictures rather than scale drawings, some draw maps which are completely disoriented and others wear through their paper with frequent erasions and pitiful results. The whole diagram may be cramped into a small corner of a page. The aberrations of dyslexic children are often the same as those of the 'normal' younger child. But there are always a minority in my classes who, with no more effort but logical planning, produce an impressive and appropriate plan. The final results are discussed. What was the *minimum* which must be included to ensure success? Was it worth while (and quicker) to use a ruler? How did preliminary planning work towards a quicker end-result? How did certain individuals manage to complete the task on time?

At a later stage in the course, this idea is developed with a map of Britain. Only the ten most important towns are included, the major rivers and vital points of reference, such as the Irish Sea, Isle of Wight etc. All names again are copied from a list. The object of this exercise is to show how the use of colour, letter size and small or large case can determine both relative importance and logical connections. The choice is the child's. ENGLAND, SCOTLAND and WALES may all be written large in black, rivers lower case in blue, but there must be consistency and the overall effect must be coherent and immediately comprehensible. An important part of the exercise is that, before they start, the children are shown similar maps, of anonymous authorship, also done by dyslexics of the same age. The children rank them in order of effectiveness, pick from each the attractive features, and feel certain they themselves can improve on their predecessors' performance. Often they do.

Memory Skills

Throughout the first term, but not necessarily in consecutive lessons, memory skills are considered and developed. The dyslexic children are weighed down by the conviction that they are 'hopeless at remembering'. This problem is freely discussed, and I promise them that I can teach them to remember over 75 per cent of an entire list of twelve items without difficulty. I write up on the board as follows: 'Raspberries, oranges, plums, figs, lemons, strawberries, kiwi, peaches, mangoes, grapefruit, apricots, blackcurrants.' They copy out the list. I hint to them that they can regroup the fruit into subsections, and to tell me when they see how this could be done. One by one the hands shoot up. There are three citrus fruit, three stone fruit, three soft fruit, or berries, and three exotic fruit. Not all will have found these categories. Some may have grouped them in alphabetical order, or by colour, or size, or shape. We discuss this. They memorise, take a clean sheet of paper and rewrite the list (the spelling is quite immaterial). In the two top classes, every child but one remembered more than nine of the items.

The first experiment is quickly followed up by asking the children to create their own lists of twelve items, which can be categorised into groups of three. This could refer to items in different rooms in the house, items required for different sports, buildings or animals. The possibilities are endless. The children test each other.

In later lessons, we will study prose passages of increasing difficulty and about four paragraphs in length, selecting two, three or four of the most important points in each paragraph. This is best done by conferencing, either in pairs or as a class, with as little intervention from the teacher as possible. Highlighters can be used on the actual photocopied sheet, but only key words, not whole sentences, are identified. I may then test them, or they may test themselves or each other. Flexibility is good practice. It is easy to prove to the children that information which has been discussed, rationalised, categorised and rehearsed can be remembered.

Where new information can immediately be related to a previous fund of knowledge, it can be processed more efficiently and thus more easily retrieved. Passages which I use with the children may relate to history, geography, science or general knowledge, or they may be literary. Whatever the subject matter, the class will approach it by cross-referencing it with any already familiar facts or ideas which the children can identify as relevant. Many children without specific learning difficulties do this automatically. Dyslexics often do not; they compartmentalise. They need to be taught the techniques of cross-reference as a routine part of learning. General discussion in class after a first reading of a passage triggers related ideas and helps to set the text in a wider context. Reference may need to be made to maps, and to encyclopaedias. Historical material will have to be put in a timescale. For dyslexic children, who often feel lost in space and time, study skills should incorporate showing them how to use reference books to anchor facts, and how to share information among themselves so as to benefit from a corporate stock of knowledge.

Comprehension Skills

Comprehension, one of the most important ingredients of study skills, develops naturally in tandem with these exercises in note-taking and memorisation, because, unless a passage has been fully understood, it is impossible to pick out the essential facts. Additional lessons are spent studying passages, not directly for note-taking purposes, but with a view to formulating comprehension questions. Here there are great advantages in teaching study skills in the classroom and not on a one-to-one basis. Each child will formulate in turn a question relating to the passage. He must also identify in his own mind the expected answer he requires. He then puts his question to the class and evaluates the response.

Dyslexic children, snarled up in detail, are prone to miss the main point. An item entitled 'Fish Facts' had the sentence: 'Fish swim chiefly by moving their tails and tail fins from side to side.' The question a highly intelligent dyslexic once produced was, 'Fish swim chiefly, true or false?'. This sort of question recurs frequently in early sessions, but is gradually phased out as the children learn to formulate relevant and logical comprehension questions. Some of these will refer to vocabulary: 'What is a vertebrate?' Some relate directly to the text: 'What noises do fish make?' But some, as we advance, will extend beyond the text itself. 'Some fish spend part of their lives in fresh water and part in salt water', says the article. 'Can you give some examples?' is the question, calling for more general information, beyond the scope of the text. The role of the teacher in these lessons is that of judge or arbiter. It is the children who are the initiators.

Descriptive Writing

The first stage with younger children, which can begin with pictorial or cartoon records, could be substituted for written notes. With older children, I use their own pictures to develop their descriptive prose. To take an example, if we are discussing the devil: 'How is a devil recognisable as a devil?', I ask. 'Name me three or four features.' 'A long forked tail', 'Hooves' and 'A pitchfork' might be their replies. 'Right, draw me a devil', I say. Later I add, 'Now describe your picture in words'. Again it is the importance of stressing the essentials and consigning more minor details to a secondary place which must be brought home to these children, whose specific learning difficulties almost always seem to include a tendency to ramble on, to digress and to talk or write peripherally and non-specifically about the point at issue.

For more vivid, varied and precise descriptions, a Thesaurus is often much more helpful than the dictionary and more accessible to the dyslexic, whether it is in book form or offered as a built-in facility on the word processor. Once the children can read well enough to decode the options supplied, they have a great fund of possibilities to extend their vocabulary. Again, discussing and defining words in class, with examples supplied by different children, sharpens their minds to shades of meaning. Look up 'fat' in the Thesaurus and you have 'plump', 'gross', 'tubby', 'stout' and a host of other words to play with, which are not, incidentally, necessarily hard to spell. By the age of 10 or 11 years, dyslexics often appear unadventurous and timid in their choice of vocabulary, partly because they read less, but even more because they do not wish to make spelling mistakes. Pursuing a wider range as a group gives confidence and trying words out on each other to identify their exact meaning fosters experimentation. This leads to the more effective and accurate use of a wider vocabulary, both in oral communication and in written work.

Increased vocabulary skills are obviously useful for story telling, but considerable work has also to be done both on the content of creative writing and on style. At least one lesson will be spent in inventing 'attention-grabbers', first sentence introductions to any piece of writing. These should challenge and intrigue the listener or the reader and capture his or her attention. It is not difficult to convince a child that the statement 'I got up and had breakfast', or 'We set off along the M4', is not going to have the audience begging for more. By the end of one recent lesson, typical examples of improved 'attention-grabbers' ranged from the purely fantastic, 'A small green hand was poking its way through the letter box', to the interesting remark, 'My mother is a crazy person to go shopping with'. The effective opener not only wins over its audience, it gives inspiration to the writer to continue.

Initially, they will all individually (and it is most important that in all the exercises even the shyest and least confident member of the class should be included) produce an 'attention-grabber' suitable to be an initial phrase for their weekend diary. The quality of a child's choice of words can be instantly assessed by its effect on the other children.

Group Teaching

This is perhaps the moment to pause and to state what must by now be apparent, that teaching study skills in this way cannot be done on a one-to-one basis, but needs a classroom situation, an audience and response, not just from the teacher, but also from the peer group. It must also be said that, for the study skills course to be effective, all the children in the group need, to some degree, to have similar problems with information processing and with short-term memory. The pace would seem pedestrian to children without such difficulties. Dyslexics need to learn the unfamiliar skills slowly and systematically. New strategies will need much reinforcement and repetition. Above all, the children will need time to formulate and express ideas, first in their minds and then aloud. This is seldom possible in a normal mainstream classroom, where the cut and thrust of able children without learning difficulties leave the dyslexic tongue-tied and frustrated.

The National Curriculum lays great emphasis on communication skills and, indeed, a large part of study skills revolves round the organisation and memorisation of information so that it can be retrieved and intelligibly communicated to others. Experimentation and instant feedback, conferencing among a familiar group – these are the first steps in developing communication skills within the classroom. At the same time a wider audience may be necessary at times if the children are to appreciate the pleasure and the response which successful communication can provide.

Links outside the classroom can be forged in many ways and at many levels. When teaching skimming and scanning, I had imported a text written by a dyslexic unknown to my class, but of similar age and interests. This passage consisted of nine paragraphs. Its purpose was to reinforce the 'CK' spelling rules. There were 54 'CK' words included in the text, which the instructions required the readers to identify. The author was a passionate bike-rider as the following extract will reveal:

> When they got down to the track there was a great racket going on in the ticket office, where some boys had thrown a brick through the window. They wanted to nick the takings from the locked till. The officer was shouting, 'Hooligans make me sick. They lack all sense of responsibility'. 'Lucky they didn't hit Mack's new Kuwahara Laserlight', said Richard. 'It's worth £1000, a wicked price. He'd have been in for a shock.' 'More like a heart-attack!' chuckled Andy, another friend.

The children in the class identified immediately with the author, enjoyed the exercise and were eager to 'have a go' themselves at a similar task. This involved several skills, including selecting a rule, telling a story and imagining the reader's response. This awareness of the impact a story will make on others is a quality that needs to be fostered and developed. The children's stories were typed out (not necessarily by the children), tried out on others and their comments reported back. Honest compliments from peers are often more rewarding than praise from the teacher.

Study skills, communication skills and life skills are closely linked, and all are needed for the dyslexic whose problems extend far beyond difficulties with reading and writing. Well taught initially, and developed throughout a school career, these skills will carry the dyslexic child through into adult life. It is never too early to begin teaching them.

Chapter 22
Curriculum-based Study Skills

VIRGINIA KELLY

This chapter focuses on the progression towards GCSE in secondary schools. There are a number of broad themes in the context of school work. Due to space limitations only three can be presented here. These are:

1. *Study reading:* work-sheets, key texts, source material, stimulus material. All require selection of ideas or evidence preparatory to reformulation or response.
2. *Data handling and display:* diagrams, charts, graphs, tables and other visual methods of arranging information. Students must be able to interpret and eventually produce a range of these.
3. *Notes:* for a variety of uses from a wide variety of sources.

To make the discussion manageable, a selection of techniques we have found useful in each of the school task areas indicated above will now be looked at.

Study Reading

Students' work often begins with reading material and other work depends on dealing adequately with it. Even where help is available for decoding – teachers commonly read through material with a class before setting the students to work – our students commonly find themselves still 'at sea' when individual work begins. Frequently, this goes back to the student having little or no sense of the purpose of the reading at the time the help is given. The student is therefore trying to remember everything without focus – an impossible task.

The first aid we suggest, therefore, is that students say to themselves before beginning to read: *Why am I reading this?* There are likely, of course, to be several parts to a complete answer, and students should learn to be aware of this and look at different levels. For example:

- So I can answer the questions at the end.
- As part of the class study of Plains Indians.
- To practise using source material for the history examination.

This ability to define task and purpose is then the first step towards the mature reader's skill of matching reading style to reading purpose.

The second aid we offer to all our students is the *development of a general attack plan* for reading assignments. We always develop this with the student, even though we know where we are headed already. It does not work to tell them how to tackle reading, but several well-chosen examples and some leading questions always enable them to arrive at a variation of our five-point plan (Table 22.1).

Table 22.1   Five-point plan

---

1. Read the TITLE and HEADINGS and anything in **bold type**
   (What do you know about this topic?
   What do you predict the writing will be about?)

2. Study any PICTURES, DIAGRAMS or GRAPHS
   Read the captions
   (Think: what questions you would like to ask?)

3. Read the questions or what you have to do
   (What do you think the answers will be?)

4. Highlight the KEY words in the questions
   There are two sorts of KEY words:
   (i) content words – telling important facts or ideas
   (ii) activity words – telling you what to do, such as list, compare, describe, explain
   You can use different colours for the two sorts of words

5. SKIM and SCAN the text for the answers
   (Were you right in your predictions?)

The sheet, suitably annotated to show individual variations, can then be taken as a reminder. Notice the importance given to gaining an overall view of the reading material quickly, but then establishing purpose before proceeding. Virtually all of our students arrive with a sense that they must begin reading immediately at the top left corner and read through to the end before doing anything else. This is inefficient for any reader, and a disaster for those who need every possible context clue in order to succeed.

A common reaction from students is that reading the questions first is really a kind of cheating. It is important to help them work this through. Useful points to discuss are:

Why are the questions there?
Do the questions cover the main points of the text?

How closely do the questions 'fit' with your reasons for reading the text? Do you need to/want to know the other information in the text?

Photocopying (often including enlarging) and *highlighting* are together a powerful and flexible tool for extracting meaning related to a task at hand. Students usually take to highlighting immediately, with a rewarding improvement in focus, but they need to work many supported examples to be able to use it efficiently. Highlighting too much is common, and can be countered by a second go on the same sheet, using a colour which will overlay the first, and give the instruction, 'Now highlight as few words as possible'. Prompt the student to compare the two versions and explain when each might be most useful.

In a more subtle problem, new students commonly latch on to their introductory criteria for highlighting as a paradigm for all use. For example, a student who began by highlighting the most important issues in one article may not see how to make the change to highlighting all the consequences of an action in another. A good device is to choose a text with questions whose answers call for different types of evidence (perhaps finding causes, consequences, what changed over time – all in separate questions). A different colour highlighter should be provided for each question and the student helped to highlight the key words in question and text in matching colour. At the end, the student is prompted to explain what is different about the matched sets. Listen carefully to the wording used. Some students can see and express the needed distinctions easily; others grasp the idea but have trouble expressing the distinctions in words; still others will have difficulties at both levels. What you do in the next few exposures to this type of work will depend on where your student is now.

Defining purpose, using an overall plan of attack and highlighting for specific information are all ways of turning a potentially daunting global task (read and remember this) into a series of actions the student feels he or she can perform. All are easy to grasp in principle and immediately useful, and all will become more useful as the student's sophistication in using them increases.

Students readily see the relevance of the techniques to their school reading tasks, but may need considerable prompting and support in transferring them to active use as strategies in class. Working through examples together is only the first stage. Time devoted to regular discussion of how the techniques are being used in different subjects will demonstrate to the student that the teacher puts a high priority on developing them outside support lessons. At first the occasions will need to be precise: 'Let's go through an example where you used the Five Point Plan and you can tell me how it went.' 'This looks like a lot to read; what was the purpose in doing it?' Ideally, as the student becomes more confident, arrange for him or her to teach someone else how and when to use the technique. There is no learning as effective as being the teacher.

These three ideas alone will not settle all a student's problems with study reading! Whole books have been written on active things to do with text, and new articles come out monthly in reading journals. A file should be collected of the ideas most relevant to your own students, and a file of work done by students on different types of reading assignment is useful for discussion by students and tutors together.

The question arises of how to handle this type of work with a student whose decoding skills are so poor that they effectively prevent almost all reading for information. Our answer is that we have found it profitable to press on and deal with higher-order skills anyway, supporting the decoding as much as is necessary by paired reading, taped passages, parental or NTA help or whatever we can find. We call this 'supported study reading' and explain to students, parents and teachers that it is a way of tackling reading from the grown-up end. Any student whose reading is this poor by 12 years or over needs to be highly efficient at extracting meaning, and that is just what study skills aim to teach. This sort of student is expected to do the same sort of thinking as the others; only the decoding is different. Time spent this way has two potential pay-offs:

1. A diagnostic gain: we find out what the student can do that has been hidden by the decoding problem. Some turn out to be able to manage sophisticated information extraction and handling techniques; decoding was the only problem. Give them a tape recording and they are off. Others are all at sea, and need large amounts of supported experience with text before they can extract and formulate ideas. We can give them a start on this without waiting any longer for decoding skills.
2. A reading efficiency gain: almost every student can actually decode better after study-reading experience. Defining purpose, establishing tasks clearly, having general attack skills and focusing on selecting relevant information all contribute to a more confident and effective approach to decoding individual words.

Data Handling and Display

Presentation and interpretation of data in diagrammatic, tabular or graphical form is much stressed in GCSE courses. Indeed the criteria for marking projects in years 10 and 11 specifically give extra marks for variety of appropriate presentation.

This may be an area where students with special learning difficulties can shine. Some are highly efficient at coding information as long as large numbers or words are not involved. Others find some types of display difficult, perhaps because of orientation or coordination problems. Both types of student benefit from a controlled introduction to the often bewildering variety of possibilities.

The key is, once again, to make explicit the relationship between purpose and choice of technique. Most students have been exposed to a variety of diagrams and displays, but they rarely have experience of categorising them explicitly. Thus, a student may not connect the idea of a table used in mathematics with one used in history, because one listed numbers and the other listed events and causes. Diagrams may have been used in geography for the water cycle and in science for life cycles without the vital connection of a closed circle having been made. For our students, the closely monitored feedback of a tutorial approach is crucial to bringing out explicitly connections and generalisations which other students may make on their own.

Students also often fail to appreciate the different levels of complexity at which most diagrammatic display can be used. A simple flow chart may be manageable while a more sophisticated input–output diagram for business studies is rejected as impossible to understand, although it is only the same idea developed further.

We begin, then, with younger pupils building up a stock of known forms of display and, as each new elaboration is encountered, encourage the student to fit it into a developing pattern of categories useful for specific tasks. A useful reference at the early stages is the *I See What You Mean* books (Kilpatrick, McCall and Palmer, 1982) which contain short samples of text matched to suitable types of visual model: hierarchy, cycle and flow diagrams, annotated pictures, comic strips, cross-sections. The texts provide particularly clear examples to supplement the student's own work. The usual leading questions feature: What sort of thing does this show you? What could you use this for? So we have steps in a process – What are good ways to show that sort of thing? The aim is gradually to build a body of experience which can be used for reference later. Naming the different types of diagram is quite important as an aid to classification and discussion, and some students resist it, preferring 'that thing I used for my notes on the Saxons'. A bit of pressure plus encouragement will pay dividends in the long run.

Data display must be used by students at three levels:

1. Receptive: interpret charts, tables etc. you are given.
2. Active (1): make your own display from information you are given – for example, making notes from text by creating a table.
3. Active (2): collect your own data and present them in your own way – for example, in science or geography field studies.

These are in ascending order of difficulty, and it makes sense to encounter them in that order. However, some students find it very hard to appreciate the elements essential to the display – spacing, perhaps, or alignment – until they are actively involved in creating it. Hence, even in introductory work, we frequently find it worth while to work together on active creation and then compare our result with what 'the book' did.

Our major resource for display work is a large ring binder containing samples arranged by category – lots of different flow charts, for example. These can be explored to help define what they have in common, how they can vary and what they are good for. The examples come from books, magazines, student's work, brochures – indeed anywhere. Students are encouraged to bring examples in for the collection. The binder is also consulted when students have to create work: 'Could you do it like this? Collections of reference books serve this same purpose, as do well-designed exercise texts such as the *Head Work* series (Culshaw and Waters, 1984). (Students will be amazed that they do not have to do the exercise, only consider the format!)

Diagrams are efficient for many students as a way of making notes or presenting work with a minimum of writing. We actively encourage this, but have to spend quite a lot of time in reassurance that this is not 'cheating' if others are writing long-winded sentences.

A word of caution: the mechanics of creating neat display can be forbidding for some students with coordination problems. These difficulties must be identified and worked through or bypassed. Communication with subject teachers is absolutely vital here, as is reassurance to the student that difficulty in drawing neat lines is not a sign of stupidity. A short, clear plastic ruler and a computer programmer's template, which includes a variety of shapes to trace around, can be invaluable.

Notes

Secondary school students are called upon to make notes from a wide variety of sources: text, teacher talk, class discussion, video or film, for example. Students with fluent writing skills at this age often work by making a copious written record and then reorganising it later; gradually, the best students evolve a more efficient technique and learn to write less, but more to the point, initially. Our students, with limited writing speed and many demands on their time, must learn to plan their organisation first and then write efficiently from the beginning.

Once again, the key to effective help is to stress the importance of task analysis. Why do I need these notes? What form will be most useful? When will be the best time to record the information? This last question is not often spontaneously considered by students, but many of ours find it liberating to realise that it could be most efficient to listen intently to the teacher or watch the video and actually compile the notes after class, perhaps using a tape-recorder for speed.

Linking the notes to a future task can be greatly facilitated by class teachers. Unfortunately, far too many say something like, 'Take notes on the important points in this video', and then at the end announce that the homework task is to write an essay with a very specific focus, for example 'Explain the major differences between life in 1850 and life now'. How much easier it would have been to plan from the beginning for a table with two columns headed 'Then' and 'Now'! Students can, however, learn to anticipate the likely focus needed for their notes, even where teacher guidance is lacking or delayed. Two useful questions to ask themselves are:

1. How does this fit into the pattern of what we have been doing?
2. If I were the teacher, what task would I set about this information?

Students need to develop, through guided practice, a set of basic note-making structures which are likely to be widely applicable. Tables are usually a good beginning, and one of the easiest and most useful is points for and against anything. We use Edward De Bono's name tag: PMI for Plus, Minus and Interesting points about any idea (De Bono, 1981). ('Interesting' allows a space for things which should be considered but do not quite fit into the Plus and Minus categories: often questions which cannot be answered from the available data.) Thus a few quick pen(cil) strokes gives a structure like this:

Plus	Minus	Interesting

which can cope with a video on new housing to replace a shanty town in Brazil, a class discussion on enlarging the local airport, or the arguments for and against America entering World War II. The structure specifically discourages the writing of sentences, a common problem for new note-makers, and leaves the information in a compact form for later review.

We have found one of the great virtues of De Bono's work to be the catchy name tags he has developed for common structures. They give everyone a short-hand way to refer to the techniques and students respond to the implicit sense of fun. 'Shall we do a PMI on it?' can be the response to assessing anything, from the latest government policy to changing your boy-/girlfriend or skipping French. Using the tag in many different situations helps students to see the common process of weighing up and judging which links what they have to do.

The table idea is easily extended and it is a good sign when students say, 'I could make a chart like PMI but the headings could be ....'. If they do not make this leap themselves, it must be encouraged. TAN (Then and Now) and SAD (Similarities and Differences) have passed into our local folklore.

Another important extension of the table idea is numbering to show order of importance. De Bono calls this FIP (First Important Priority), and it becomes particularly important when a note table is to be used as the basis for later writing (see below).

Basic to the idea of note-making is deciding on categories of information, and students need to be taught to watch for this explicitly. Lunzer and Gardner's work on effective reading skills (Lunzer and Gardner, 1984) provides good background for teachers on analysing text types which can be extended by analogy to other sources of information. Our students need a very simple course in such analysis to help them decide quickly on what note-making structures will serve particular purposes. The categories which come up most commonly, and their associated techniques, are:

- Comparing two viewpoints → tables: PMI etc.
- Structure → map/diagram.
- Process → flow chart.
- Development → time line or chain diagram.
- Factors in a situation → headings and lists; matrices.

The last of these is probably the most difficult for students to grasp and to manage, but guiding them through a variety of examples will win through in the end. Again, De Bono is useful with the tag CAF: Consider All Factors. He uses this as a broadening technique for generating ideas: What factors do you need to consider when opening a new business in the High Street? Equally, however, it can be used to develop headings for classifying a mass of information which must be noted down. 'Make notes on the conflict between the Plains Indians and the Settlers', can be turned into a question: 'What (factors) caused the conflict between the Plains Indians and the Settlers?', which in turn suggests lists under headings such as 'lifestyle', 'views of nature', 'recognition of authority', and so on.

Students vary, by age, experience and personality, in the degree to which they can stand back and see noting devices as associated with types of information. Some find it helpful to be told the groups early on and to categorise examples as they come up. Others need more experience of each type before they can begin to separate them explicitly. Once again the key lies in adjusting the support to the individual while the learner develops independence.

Tape-recorders can be a useful aid to note-making, but their use needs to be thought about carefully. Use of tape-recorders is likely to be individualistic and to take some time and practice to develop, and a tape-recorder will not transform a badly organised student into a well-organised one; it only adapts the means of noting down information. Students using a tape-recorder should, therefore, be taught the same task analysis and organising skills as those who will write their notes. Thought also needs to be given to whether the tape is an interim stage, leading to written notes, or whether the information will stay on tape (LDC, 1990a,b).

Two techniques for producing notes, which are still common in some secondary classrooms, are copying from the board and writing from dictation. Both of these are employed by teachers who want to be sure students get the 'right' information quickly, and both fail to achieve that goal with most of our students who can neither finish in the time nor produce an accurate result which they can read later. The answer is generally to enlist teacher or an able pupil to provide a clearly written copy which our student can highlight for the main points and keep for reference. Any 'spare' time this releases can be spent extracting key words and practising them as individual spellings.

References

CULSHAW, C. and WATERS, D. (1984). *Headwork, Books 1–4*. Oxford: Oxford University Press.

DE BONO, E. (1981). *CoRT Thinking*, 2nd edn, vol. 1. Oxford: Pergamon Press.

KILPATRICK, A., MCCALL, P. and PALMER, S. (1982). *I See What You Mean, Books 1 & 2*. Edinburgh: Olivier & Boyd.

LDC (1990a). *Hints on Using Tape Recorders with Pupils with Specific Learning Difficulties* Southampton University: Learning Disabilities Clinic booklet.

LDC (1990b). *Supported Study Reading: Principles and Examples*. Southampton University: Learning Disabilities Clinic booklet.

LUNZER, E. and GARDNER, K. (1984). *Learning From The Written Word*. Edinburgh: Olivier & Boyd.

Chapter 23
The Road to Reading: Basic Skills to College Allowances

ARLENE W. SONDAY

Adults and adolescents with written language problems can be identified and placed in three instructional levels (Sonday, 1986). Level I includes students whose skills are second grade (age 7) or below and who frequently cannot recognise the symbols and sounds of the language. Sequencing sounds and blending them into words are not familiar routines for these students even when print is not involved. Their lack of skill, however, has not always prevented them from obtaining high school diplomas.

Level II students read contextually connected material at the third to seventh grade level (8–12 years) or above, but below the student's academic placement. Their spelling level and word attack skills for words in lists are considerably lower. Difficulty with word attack causes interruptions as the reader attends to the mechanical aspects of decoding words and loses the fluency needed to maintain comprehension. Some adolescents may have been diagnosed and are currently receiving special education services. Others may not have met the criteria for inclusion in a special programme but experience serious difficulty in their academic settings.

Level III students can read slowly, but comfortably, at the eighth grade level or above, yet not at the level of their academic placement. Word attack, spelling and writing are below the level of contextual reading. They are usually college and graduate students or professionals who are functionally literate but continue to need allowances in a demanding academic or job setting.

Stages of Written Language Development

There is a confusion between the process of learning to read and the process of reading to learn. Learning to read involves the skills prerequisite to fluent or automatic decoding (reading) and encoding (spelling). Reading to learn, however, focuses on the refinements of reading such as comprehension, skimming, scanning and summarising. Learning to read must precede reading to learn. The student must possess the basic abilities before these abilities can be refined; automatic decoding is a prerequisite to adequate comprehension (Chall, 1983; Clark, 1988; Kitz and Tarver, 1990; Levine, 1990; see also Chapter 16).

The curriculum for special education teachers at the secondary level often does not include how to teach decoding and encoding. Their instructional expertise is basically in three areas:

1. Teaching study skills and other refinements, such as summarising or reading critically.
2. Teaching bypass strategies to help students avoid the word attack and spelling deficits.
3. Providing allowances.

Bypass strategies, such as taped textbooks, oral testing and dictating reports to a transcriber, provide important short-term support. They are nevertheless a detour around basic reading and writing requirements. Allowances, which include extended time for tests or papers, foreign language requirement substitutions and reduced load permit the student to complete written language tasks under relaxed requirements. Bypass strategies and allowances should always be accompanied by remediation at levels I and II and often at level III to establish the foundation that will allow the learner the freedom to branch out into more sophisticated skills. When only bypass strategies and accommodations have been implemented, students can graduate from high school and even college with knowledge, but without the ability to communicate effectively in the workplace.

The Initial Contact

The first session must include some assessment of the current functioning level of the student. Space does not permit a full description of assessment procedures. Suffice it to say that these are an important part of the initial contact.

For undiagnosed students or for adults who do not plan to access formal programmes, test results may be unavailable. Adequate information to begin remediation, however, can be obtained in a short time by administering a word identification test for reading and a criterion-referenced spelling test. A criterion-referenced spelling test begins with easy words, and gradually incorporates more difficult words and increasingly complex patterns and rules following the development of language or the language continuum.

Beginning Instruction for Level I Students

Instruction begins where the students' skills become insecure. When starting the learner with very low skills, the instructor must first determine how well the student can isolate and read the consonant and vowel sounds, and then, by dictating the sounds, determine whether or not these sounds can be translated into the written symbol. When the teacher points out the rules that students are successfully using, the students are encouraged to know that they already have a solid body of knowledge, however modest, from which to build. For example, the student may remember and correctly spell 'tack', 'pick' and 'thick', using the -ck rule, but miss 'tackle', 'picket' or 'thicket' because the rule is not consciously known or applied.

Some students with low language skills have great difficulty with blending and segmenting words, indicating a weakness in phonological awareness. Practice should be provided to enable the student to take sounds and blend the sounds into words. For example, the student is asked to make a word from the sounds /f/ /ee/ /t/ or /m/ /a/ /t/. This is purely an auditory drill with no visual stimuli involved. Sounds are separated so the student has to blend the sounds together. If blending three sounds proves too difficult, words with two sounds, such as 'me', 'see', 'by' or 'my' can be used. Once the student can do this with simple combinations, the difficulty of the sound sequences should be increased to include three sounds as in 'feet' or 'mat' and then add beginning and ending blends. Next, the visual letters are used, including only letters where the sound is known by the student. The student sounds out the letters and sequences the sounds into a known word, beginning with very simple consonant–vowel–consonant words. This practice should take place over a series of lessons. For non-readers, this is a crucial prerequisite to reading and spelling words which can be taught as a separate activity concurrently with teaching sound–symbol associations and later incorporated with reading and spelling words.

Segmenting skills must also be taught to students with low phonological awareness as they begin to spell their first words. When a word is dictated, the student divides the word into its component sounds. Pit would be broken into three segments, /p/ /i/ /t/. Finger spelling, or having the students put up one finger for each sound, enables the student to use mechanical or motor strengths to manage this task. After successfully segmenting the dictated word, the student writes it on paper. Once instructional sessions are under way, blending and segmenting strategies would be used only in conjunction with reading and spelling words and not as isolated activity. The succeeding sessions involve reading and spelling words, phrases and sentences in a systematic structured routine.

Beginning Instruction for Level II and Level III Students

The phonological drill can be omitted for learners whose spelling ability is at the fourth grade or above. However, all students with spelling difficulty, even professionals with advanced degrees, will be insecure with short vowel sounds. After learning the short vowel sounds, poor spellers will need to work on syllable types and syllable division because segmenting does not come automatically and is a necessary skill when attacking new words or spelling words (Cox and Hutcheson, 1988). Next comes clarification of the endings rules, input concerning the 'ie–ei' dilemma, and a review of roots and affixes with emphasis on their interchangeability and the rules which govern their spelling. Serious multisensory reinforcement at each step, with endless spelling dictation, forces students to apply new skills and provide feedback to the teacher who uses that information to determine how to pace and structure the sessions. Useful instructional materials for this group include those listed above and *Megawords* (Johnson and Bayrd, 1985) and *Solving Language Difficulties* (Steere, Peck and Kahn, 1984).

Structuring a Lesson Plan

Lessons can be structured as follows:

1. Show the student flashcards and ask the student to recite the sound. At first, the cards will consist of letters and phonograms. Later, prefix, suffix and root cards will be added. Since this is a review, only elements which have been taught can be used.
2. Ask the student to write the symbol for the dictated sound, starting with phonograms and then move to affixes and roots as they are taught.
3. Ask the student to read a list of words reinforcing previously learned components.
4. Dictate review words in random order to reinforce previous learning. Ask eliciting questions about rules so that the student reinforces concepts and provides feedback for the teacher.
5. Dictate sentences involving known words.
6. Introduce new material.
7. Ask the student to read aloud from a book or an article. Some level III students may not need practice reading aloud (Sonday, 1986).

The lesson plan includes visual, auditory and kinaesthetic–tactile reinforcement of phonograms, isolated words and contextually connected material for both reading and spelling. The same basic plan can be used at all levels of instruction, but each section increases in difficulty and length as students progress.

Advanced Language Structure

Mature advanced level II students and most level III students learn by an analytical approach, seeing the whole concept and then analysing the structure and practising the specific elements using an intellectual and reasoning approach rather than purely visual memory. Children and level I adults, however, learn by a synthetic approach, through exposure to the specific components and then putting the pieces together with them to form the whole concept (Clark, 1988).

The analytical approach can be used when teaching concepts such as advanced language clusters. One example is assimilative prefixes, 'ad', 'ac', 'af', 'ag', 'an', 'ap', 'ar' and 'as', which are actually the same prefix but the final letter has changed to facilitate pronunciation. The consonant doubles in many words when the last letter of the prefix and the first letter of the root are the same. Furthermore, each variation has two pronunciations depending on whether it is the accented or the unaccented syllable. In an accented syllable, the vowel will make its regular short sound and in the unaccented syllable, the vowel will take the 'schwa' sound which is like a short 'u' or a slurred vowel.

	Accented	*Unaccented*
ad-	advent	addiction
ac-	accent	accord
ag-	aggravate	aggressive
an-	annex	announce
ap-	appetite	appear
ar-	arrogant	arrange
as-	asset	assert

An analytical approach can also be used when teaching suffix families. After basic suffixes such as -ous, -or, -al, -an and -ence are taught, the connective 'i' can be placed at the beginning of each to form another suffix.

Basic	*Connective 'i'*	
-or	-ior	junior
-ous	-ious	obvious
-al	-ial	remedial
-an	-ian	comedian
-ence	-ience	experience

By preceding the connective 'i' with 'c' or 't', another family of suffixes is formed.

Connective 'i'	*'c' or 't' plus connective 'i'*	
-ious	-cious	spacious
	-tious	cautious
-ial	-cial	social
	-tial	partial
-ian	-cian	musician
-ience	-cience	conscience

Some published materials to help with advanced language structure include *Tutor 2* and *Tutor 3* (Henry, 1990a,b), *Megawords* (Johnson and Bayrd, 1985) and *Solving Language Difficulties* (Steere, Peck and Kahn, 1984).

Correcting Errors

Once a concept has been taught, errors during practice are brought to the attention of the student by using an eliciting question to lead the student to the correct answer. Negative signals, such as 'No', 'Wrong', 'Try again', are avoided. The teacher can guide the student through an intellectual or critical thinking process which leads to the correct response and the accurate spelling, while building the student's self-esteem and enabling the student to rely on personal resources. For example, this dialogue resulted when <u>mess</u> was spelled as <u>mes</u>.

Teacher:	What do you hear at the end?
Student:	/s/
Teacher:	(Pause to see if the question and response trigger the correct answer.)
	What kind of a vowel do you have?
Student:	Short.
Teacher:	(Pause to give the student time to process.)
	How do you write /s/ after a short vowel?

If the questions do not enable the student to spell the word correctly, the teacher provides the answer and re-teaches the rule. If the student is able to spell the word correctly, dictating two or more words such as <u>pass</u> and <u>less</u> will reinforce the same rule.

Most learners are able to make the correction after one or two questions. If the teacher has asked eliciting questions, but has not provided the exact number or used a negative term to highlight the error, students feel they have made the correction themselves. Leading students to successful self-correction through a critical thinking process motivates the learner. Nothing succeeds like success!

College Allowances for Level III Students

Students with learning disabilities or dyslexia who plan to go on to college or post-secondary training need a complete educational and intellectual assessment in order to qualify for allowances for students with learning deficits. Some allowances may be available to students who are not certified, but who can provide documentation, such as earlier diagnostic reports or recent letters describing a deficit.

If testing reveals a sixth or seventh grade reading level and a spelling level below the sixth grade, there is little likelihood of a student successfully managing the college curriculum. With a tenth grade reading level and eighth or ninth grade spelling level, college will be very difficult, but can be managed by the very bright student with serious motivation, well-defined goals, determination, and through the use of accommodations. Bypass support, tutorials and study skills are generally available on campus to help the dyslexic student put together a programme and plan for success.

Students who are planning for post-secondary education should get a head start in high school. They should take one to four courses in study skills beginning in high school and continuing in college. Students must learn to study smarter, not harder. These classes include suggestions for effcient studying and writing, tips for test taking, organisation, time management and an orientation to available campus resources. Students who are uncomfortable with mathematics may have to re-take a mathematics course in high school or a review course in college. Often no credit is given for such a course and it may not transfer. However, the investment will prove invaluable for future science or mathematics requirements, especially statistics. Similarly, students who know they have trouble writing may choose to take an extra course in basic writing, which includes the art of thesis statement and development. Most importantly, for level II students, word attack and spelling must be remediated before entering college or by taking time off in college and substituting a quarter or semester of basic skills for college classes.

The most common allowances are a reduced course load, course substitutions or waivers, notetakers, taped textbooks and extended time on tests. Not all colleges provide all allowances, but there are many general aids available in areas of scheduling, note-taking and text handling, testing and writing papers. Support can be accessed appropriately once the students understand their needs. Students with deficits may require professional help to determine which allowances would be useful. In addition to an evaluation of basic skills in reading, writing, spelling and mathematics, a learning styles inventory is helpful. The student may learn best by using sketches, imagery, manipulatives, audio-tapes, studying with others or reading orally. Organising allowances and a support system is a coordinated effort and requires reflection and self-appraisal on the part of the student long before registration.

Note-taking and textbooks

Some colleges provide note-takers at lectures for certified learning-disabled students. Students who cannot write and listen at the same time should ask for them. If a note-taker is not available, a classmate might be willing to use a carbon notebook or share notes by regularly heading for the copying machine. Students who must take their own notes should briefly write ideas, concepts or examples using phonetic approximations for difficult words. Teacher gestures, verbal and non-verbal, may signal an important point or change of topic. Immediately after class, students should organise notes to isolate and highlight concepts, fill in blank spots and make corrections.

Students taking their own notes in class, especially those who learn best by listening, can request permission to use tape-recorders during lectures. Using a tape-recorder with a counter allows the student to note the number on the counter for quick access to a point of confusion during the lecture. Listening to an entire lecture more than once will reinforce learning, but it is time-consuming. Tapes are ideal for students who commute or spend time driving.

Tape-recorded text books are an important allowance for low level or slow readers. A four-track tape-recorder is useful to adjust listening speed. Tape-recorded texts should be ordered early because there are often delays when tapes are in short supply or new texts must be recorded.

Testing

The area that causes most anxiety is, of course, testing. The most common allowance requested and granted to learning-disabled students is extended time on tests. Many faculty members still oppose extended time on tests, believing that it gives the learning-disabled student an unfair advantage over other students. There is evidence that, on untimed tests, the learning disabled student's score increases significantly whilst the non-disabled student's does not increase with extra time. Students should be prepared to advocate for themselves and have the necessary arguments and suggestions to negotiate for the requested allowances. Time and a half on examinations, for example, would be a reasonable starting point. It can be renegotiated to double time in the future, if necessary. Instructors may feel overwhelmed and welcome help in finding a solution to the problem.

Studying for tests involves condensing and organising as an aid to learning the material. This process should be extended over several days to enhance long-term memory. Reviewing a copy of an old test also helps the learner become familiar with the instructor's style, expectations and priorities. For persistent test-taking difficulties, it may be possible to take oral examinations, an alternative test format or complete a special project as a substitute for a written examination. Sometimes a word processor can be used to take an essay test, making the writing and organisation easier and the copy more readable.

Writing

A word processor with a spell check is an absolute necessity and locating one is a top priority. Word processing facilitates not only writing, but also organising, rewriting, correcting, editing and refining, not one, but multiple drafts. Spell checks are essential but they have limitations. They locate mis-spelt words but do not correct grammar or homonyms and often generate malapropisms. A reliable human proofreader must be at hand. All drafts should be saved because pre-writing is often included for a grade.

Of course, it is most important to attend classes regularly, have complete notes, study for tests in advance and take all tests in time. Under these priorities, it is the course papers that can be postponed. A grade of incomplete, can be requested to extend the deadline for a paper, at which time the paper is turned in and a grade is received.

Conclusion

Dyslexic and learning-disabled adolescents and adults can learn to read and write at a higher than functional level of literacy. If traditional teaching approaches have failed, an alternative approach, usually code-emphasis, must be implemented. After phonological awareness deficits for level I students have been addressed, the language continuum can be taught using consistent and relentless multisensory reinforcement, asking eliciting questions to reinforce learning and requiring feedback concerning sounds, rules and generalisations. When a level of automatic word recognition and reading fluency develops, students learn how to read for new information, concepts, vocabulary and other refinements. Learners who are comfortable with spelling learn writing refinements. Level II and III students will need to advocate for themselves in post-secondary settings. These students must know their strengths, weaknesses and learning styles as well as the array of available allowances they may access to succeed in academic programmes and in the workplace.

References

CHALL, J. (1983). *Stages of Reading Development.* New York: McGraw-Hill.
CLARK, D.B. (1988). *Dyslexia: Theory and Practice of Remedial Instruction.* Parkton, MD: York Press.

COX, A.R. and HUTCHESON, L. (1988). Syllable division: a prerequisite to dyslexics' literacy. *Annals of Dyslexia* **38**, 226–242.

HENRY, M.K. (1990a). *Tutor 2*. Los Gatos, CA: Lex Press.

HENRY, M.K. (1990b). *Tutor 3*. Los Gatos, CA: Lex Press.

JOHNSON, K. and BAYRD, P. (1985). *Megawords: Multisyllabic Words for Reading, Spelling and Vocabulary*. Cambridge, MA: Educators Publishing Service, Inc.

KITZ, W.R. and TARVER, S.G. (1990). Comparison of dyslexic and nondyslexic adults on decoding and phonemic awareness tasks. *Annals of Dyslexia* **39**, 196–205.

LEVINE, M. (1990). *Keeping A Head in School*. Cambridge, MA: Educators Publishing Service, Inc.

SONDAY, A.W. (1986). Language Skills Seminars: adult dyslexics learn to learn. *Learning Disabilities Focus* **1**(2), 90–96.

STEERE, A., PECK, C.Z. and KAHN, L. (1984). *Solving Language Difficulties*. Cambridge, MA: Educators Publishing Service.

Chapter 24
Setting Up a Learning Programme for Adult Dyslexics

CYNTHIA KLEIN*

This chapter is a result of the specialist work developed in London with students in basic education classes as well as mainstream college, polytechnic and university courses, and is what I hope is a practical response to all those who, when faced with a dyslexic adult, continue to ask, 'What *do* I do to help this student?'

Basis of the Learning Programme

The students we most often work with have rarely been diagnosed at school and many come from working class or ethnic minority backgrounds. Almost all are confused about their abilities and have no model for understanding the reasons for their failure at school and their continuing failure to 'pick up' or master reading, writing or spelling. They range from complete non-readers to competent (if slow) readers who continue to have great difficulty expressing themselves on paper. Some have responsible jobs, others are on academic, vocational or craft courses; still others are in unskilled jobs or are unemployed.

For all these students, regardless of their background and situation, we find that there are three essential criteria for establishing a successful learning programme:

1. It must be completely relevant to students' individual needs and goals.
2. It should give them immediate (or almost immediate) experience of success.
3. It should enable them to participate in and eventually take charge of their own learning.

It is important to stress that these criteria are useful for the tutor as well as the student. It is easy to be overwhelmed when a student presents you

---

with a piece of writing that is almost or even mostly unreadable due to bizarre spelling, ill-formed letters, much crossing out, confused sentence structure, lack of punctuation and so on.

Therefore it is important for both tutor and student that the tutor begin immediately to clear away some of the muddle, identify realistic short-term and long-term goals and convey confidence in his or her methods and in the student's ability to learn.

Relevance to Individual Needs and Goals

Before plunging in, it is valuable to talk with students about past learning experiences, current work situation, and future aims and ambitions. It is also important to determine whether or not they can read, if they read for pleasure or work, or study only, what sorts of things they do read, what they need to or want to write, and what they find most difficult about reading and/or writing. The programme should then be geared to these needs and aims.

Adults are often very clear and definite about both their goals and their particular reading and writing needs. However, sometimes their self-esteem is poor and they require considerable support.

Immediate Experience of Success in Learning

Spelling nearly always plays a key role in setting up a learning programme for many reasons, not least because most dyslexic students identify spelling as their biggest problem. But another very important reason is that it is relatively easy to ensure success in learning spellings and achievement is also easily measured compared to more complex tasks.

Due to the urgency of giving students a successful learning experience to generate confidence and a positive approach to learning, and to counteract negative experiences of spelling, it is essential to take great care in the initial phases of setting up the programme. This means exploring and clarifying with the student the following issues: (1) unlearning, (2) learning how to learn, (3) selecting words to learn and linking spelling with writing, (4) finding strategies for remembering and (5) following the method.

Unlearning

It is astonishing how few students were ever taught *any method at all* for learning spellings. Most were just given lists of words 'to go away and memorise'. It is also interesting to discover the myths students have absorbed about spelling, e.g. 'If you read more, your spelling will improve', 'I can't spell because I don't pronounce words right'. These myths must be unlearned before learning can take place. Many other beliefs that students have acquired need to be explored and let go of before they can begin to learn. For example, one student told me she had enjoyed using long words when she was at school until a teacher had told her not to use long words until she could spell the short ones. That was the end of her writing career!

Other students come with the notion that they will learn to spell *first* and *then* they will start to write. They need to understand that spelling is a part of writing and that only when they begin to write can they learn to spell. This is true even for beginners where a language experience approach (Pratley, 1982), in which the student dictates to the tutor who operates as scribe, can be used in combination with a spelling programme. In fact, many beginner readers have such poor word recognition skills that they only learn to read through learning to spell.

Learning how to learn

Unlearning is only the beginning of learning how to learn. Students need to be confident that the new method will work for them and to acknowledge that the way they have tried to learn spellings (for instance, sounding out words) has not worked for them in the past and is not the way good spellers spell. Occasionally, this can take some time as students cling on to what seems safe to them, even if it has been unsuccessful. At this point, it may help to have a discussion of spelling as a visual–motor activity (such as learning to ride a bike or swim) and therefore the need to *practise*, and to practise *over time*.

For reluctant writers, those who want to be able to spell before they will write, it is useful to introduce the idea of inventing spellings rather than trying to look them up or asking for them. Many students feel that guessing is 'bad': witness the red corrections all over their writing at school, or friends or workmates laughing at their spelling attempts. These students need to learn that, when we make a guess we are 'forming a hypothesis or theory, about a spelling. This "having a theory" about something makes us more likely to remember an amendment or correction to our guess than to remember a spelling we have never attempted. Thus guessing helps learning' (Klein and Millar, 1990). In this way, students can also discover that there is often logic in their errors. An obvious example is the attempt 'pearants' for parents. This attempt shows the student knows one way the sound 'pear' is represented and also an appropriate option for 'ent/ant'. What she needs to do is to learn or make new links with other options, e.g. 'pare', the correct option in this case, and perhaps 'rent' (as in 'parents pay the rent').

A less obvious example is 'hapervensive' for apprehensive. However, even here, where the sounds are confused, the student knows the ending for 'sive' plus the 'en' bit. The 'h' at the beginning is due to her London accent, so she needs only to learn that it doesn't have an initial 'h' and to learn the 'preh(en)' in the middle. She already knows most of it in fact, in spite of its odd look. She could easily learn this word (and did) with practice and gain tremendous confidence from being able to spell it and use it in her writing.

Selecting words to learn and linking spelling with writing

One of the keys to a successful spelling programme is selecting and grouping appropriate words to learn. These words should *always* come from the student's own writing so that they are a part of the student's personal writing vocabulary. This is why it is very important that the student brings in a piece of writing each week from which to choose spellings to learn. Students need to understand that they must write regularly, both to generate spellings to learn and to reinforce those they have learned. Students will often write more and use a richer vocabulary when they realise they can learn any word they want to. If students are not in a situation where they have to do a lot of writing, we usually encourage them to enrol in a course where they will be expected to produce written work on a regular basis. This may mean a general literacy class, some sort of return to study course or a specialist subject class. This is very, very important because poor spellers usually avoid writing and it is only with writing practice that spelling really improves.

Words selected to learn should include those where the student's invented spelling is nearly correct, those that the student uses frequently, common words and words that the student particularly wants to learn. This last type is important because the student's motivation is high and he or she is therefore likely to be successful, even if the word is difficult. One student on an Access to Higher Education course had a great deal of trouble with the word 'psychology', which he wanted to learn but was sure he could not. I persuaded him to put it on his weekly list, along with its Greek root 'psyche' and 'psychologist'. He not only learned it but, as he wrote it with comparative ease the following week, he commented, 'If I can learn this I can learn *any* word!'. Even though dyslexic students may never become good spellers, this confidence in their own ability to learn transfers to other areas of learning and tends to generate further success.

The final point about selecting words is the importance of grouping them in ways which encourage students to develop an awareness of common letter patterns, word structure and meaning. Words should be linked with similar known words or words with similar patterns. Homonyms or words with easily confused patterns (e.g. 'hote*l*' and 'bott*le*') should never be given together. A sample of a GCSE student's list (taken from a piece of writing on her early schooling) follows:

beat	strict
seat	picture
treat	
	here
lesson	where
	there
punish	twenty
punishment	twentieth

Finally, it is important that the number of words to be learned each week is kept to 10 or 12, with no more than 15 when words are grouped together. Students may find that they can learn more, but they need to understand that the aim is to *retain* the words in their long-term memory and that trying to learn too many words will result in memory overload and consequently forgetting.

Developing strategies for remembering

Understanding how our short-term and long-term memory works is particularly helpful to dyslexic students who generally seem to have problems with short-term or 'working' memory. Students are often much more willing to practise their spellings over the week as prescribed, when they understand how this helps them learn. (Discussions of memory and learning can be found in Tony Buzan, 1974, and Klein and Millar, 1990.)

Students also need to discover learning strategies that will work for them individually; for this they need to destroy the myth that there is only one 'right' way to learn spellings and they also need to identify their own 'learning style'. This is why a diagnostic assessment is so beneficial to students; it helps them realise the nature and pattern of their difficulties and thus to understand why they need to explore alternative ways of learning. For instance, students with difficulties remembering the 'look' of the word find that inventing a spelling pronunciation helps, like pronouncing the 'k' in 'know'. Students with problems holding sounds remember best by finding words within words or by changing the look of the word. A painting and decorating student who was confused between gloss and glass learned the former as: gl̈o̊'ss.

Another student who got easily lost in a sound sequence found that visual patterns, such as acc*ommo*dation helped her with the confusing middle.

Most dyslexics seem to be holistic-type learners and find it difficult to see words as a precise sequence of letters or to 'chunk' them; consequently, they need to be shown how to break them up into bits that aid learning, with spaces between, and to highlight difficult bits. This helps them to see words more precisely and in manageable chunks. I use the word 'bits' here specifically to emphasise that breaking words into *syllables* is frequently *not* an effective strategy for many dyslexic students. If tutors want adult dyslexics to experience success in learning, they must help the student find strategies that work for *them*.

Following the method

Finally, the student must agree to follow the prescribed method and *understand why*. We use Margaret Peters' 'Look, Cover, Write, Check' method (Peters, 1975) because it is multisensory, structured, easily adapted to individual needs and strategies, and because it emphasises the visual–motor nature of spelling. Details of how we use it, including testing and review, can be found in Klein and Millar (1990). The points we stress include the importance of practising rather than testing, the need to visualise, and the importance of checking back letter for letter to see if the word is correct. This self-checking cannot be sufficiently emphasised. Many students who make mistakes as they practise discover that, if they find and correct their error (by writing the *whole* word correctly once after finding their mistake), they do in fact learn the word by the end of the week. It also seems to be true that much failure to learn can be traced back to hurried checking or not checking at all. It is difficult for dyslexic students to attend to words letter by letter, so they often tend to skip this step; in order to make the effort needed they may therefore require much repeated discussion about its importance for learning. The other significant aspect of self-checking as a strategy is that it is transferable to other areas and is an important factor in students taking charge of their own learning.

I have spent some time discussing these points about learning because it is my experience that much failure in the teaching of adult dyslexics is due to these issues not being thoroughly dealt with by the student *and* the tutor.

Enabling Students to Take Charge of Their Own Learning

Dyslexic adults often come to classes feeling overwhelmed by and at the mercy of their difficulties. Gaining understanding of their problems is the beginning of a control over them. Although they may need support of one kind or another all their lives, knowing how, when and where to ask for help and precisely what sort of help they need is very different from feeling generally needy or helpless. There are three things in particular which tutors can do to assist students in making the change from passive to active learners: (1) help them to identify their own learning style (including difficulties and strengths) and to explore their learning needs; (2) make the conventions of written language explicit; and (3) work with them to develop practical skills and self-monitoring tools.

Identifying their own learning style and needs

I have already commented on the importance of a diagnosis as part of the learning programme, in helping students to make sense of what has happened to them in the past and to understand their particular learning needs and learning style. To have this effect, however, the diagnosis and its implications must be thoroughly discussed with the student. For many students a diagnosis releases a great deal of emotion, most frequently relief, but also often anger at the education system for failing them. This is usually the beginning of a much more constructive approach to learning, however, because students no longer perceive their past failure as their own fault. Once they have identified their learning strengths, weaknesses and needs, they begin to know what they can and what they cannot do and so what *specific* help they need. Students with this awareness become confident enough to ask for and receive appropriate support, whenever and wherever they need it, from subject tutors, examiners, librarians, supervisors, friends; *and* they know what they can do themselves. They are also better able to develop strategies for coping with their difficulties, e.g. a dyslexic social worker keeps four diaries – in two places at work, in her car and at home – to make sure she keeps her appointments; a teacher learns all the words the children are likely to ask for before her class and reads stories silently to herself before reading them aloud to the children; a student dictates her essays to herself, sentence by sentence, as she writes. Students also find out about their strengths; for instance, many dyslexic students are good at holistic thinking. One student found that, although he needed help with structuring and organising essays, he could help other students see new and more creative relationships between ideas.

Making explicit the conventions of written language

Dyslexics do not seem to 'pick up' the conventions of written language; they often do not 'see' or omit the obvious. Some dyslexic non-readers are unaware of how a word is represented or completely fail to notice punctuation marks. More advanced students find it exceptionally difficult to grasp the conventions of formal discursive writing. One had never noticed either margins or paragraphs in writing, many have little idea of what to put in and what to leave out – for them everything is equally relevant; most find linking ideas linguistically particularly difficult.

Clarifying conventions means being very precise, checking the student's understanding both through their comments and questions, and through observation of their changing approaches and development as readers and writers. Most importantly, it means *taking nothing for granted* in the reading, writing and spelling processes. Most tutors make many implicit assumptions about learning which fail to take into account the dyslexic student's particular problems. For example, one student complained that she had tried to discuss her difficulties writing an essay with her tutor. The tutor had asked her several questions about the content which she had answered and he had then told her, 'You understand it all very well – now, just go away and write it all down'. As the student complained despairingly, he just couldn't grasp that the going away and writing it down was where the problem was.

Teachers often feel that talking about processes and conventions is wasting time, but it is my experience that it is never wasted if the points made in discussion are then applied practically by the student. For instance, a clear explanation, along with examples, of the purpose and need for linking words to show the connection between two points can result in less disjointed writing if students are then encouraged to identify where such words would help in their own writing. This is particularly likely to happen if there has also been discussion and illustration of the difference between written and spoken language, and the needs and expectations of the reader.

Working with students to develop practical skills and self-monitoring tools

Although I have placed much emphasis on discussing and exploring learning processes, it is extremely important that such discussion leads to the effective teaching of practical skills. When students attending several learning support classes in London were asked what they found most beneficial, nearly all of them said that being taught an effective method for learning spellings had helped them the most, above and beyond having a sympathetic tutor and being in a group with other dyslexics (although these were also felt to be helpful). Students reported gaining the most confidence from improving their spelling; this helped them develop their writing, and for some it helped with their reading as well. Many said that finding out they *could* learn to spell gave them the courage to pursue courses of study they might otherwise have felt unable to do.

Developing self-monitoring strategies is not only vital to mastering skills such as spelling, but also gives students control over their own learning and thus encourages autonomy as learners. Self-checking strategies mean anything and everything from making personal check-lists to learning to proofread and to becoming a critical reader of one's own work. An example of the use of a personal check-list was the case of a young woman who repeatedly punctuated 'which' clauses as if they were full sentences. She had a great deal of difficulty seeing that these were not sentences; a way round this was to have a rule of thumb never to start sentences beginning with 'which' (because in her case they rarely ever *were* sentences). When she proofread her writing, this was number one on her check-list. Proofreading her writing with this in mind actually did cut down considerably on the number of incomplete sentences in her work and she began to develop alternative forms of expression. She also tended to omit '-ed' endings; this too went on her check-list, and so forth. Some students will pin up a list of linking words and phrases both to remind themselves to use them and to decide which ones might be appropriate.

At the same time, students need to develop proofreading skills; this can be accomplished through tutors using error analysis marking, i.e. using a symbol such as Sp for spelling, SS for sentence structure etc. in the margin of the line where the error is. This helps guide the student to identify and correct errors. Error analysis is useful, not only because it develops the student's self-checking skills, but also because it allows the tutor to check the student's understanding of how and where to punctuate, when a sentence structure is awkward etc. This leads to further explanation and practice where needed. It also helps boost student self-confidence, both by showing students that most of their errors consist of only a few main types and also by revealing to them how much they can correct themselves once they begin to identify errors. This frequently helps students to make the leap from writer to *reader* and to begin to become self-critical. Using the model of the teacher providing 'scaffolding' to prop up the student's learning process (Greenfield, 1984), it is at this point that the tutor can begin to dismantle the scaffolding.

References

BUZAN, T. (1974). *Use Your Head*. London: BBC Publications.

GREENFIELD, P.M. (1984). A theory of the teacher in the learning activities of everyday life. In: B. Rogoff and J. Lave (Eds), *Everyday Cognition: Its Development in Social Context*. Cambridge, MA: Harvard University Press.

KLEIN, C. and MILLAR, R. (1990). *Unscrambling Spelling*. London: Hodder & Stoughton.

PETERS, M. (1975). *Diagnostic and Remedial Spelling Manual*. London: Macmillan Education.

PRATLEY, R. (1982). The language experience approach to literacy teaching. *ALBSU Newsletter* insert.

Chapter 25
The Dyslexic Child's Transfer of Learning from the Individual Lesson to Work in the Classroom

ANN COOKE

Introduction

The special teaching systems in use with dyslexic children share many agreed and essential characteristics. These include a sequential multisensory programme of phonic structure in gradual steps. Pupils may have their lessons individually or in very small groups separately from the rest of their class.

The provision available for dyslexic children to have this kind of help varies widely across Britain. At one extreme there is the specialist school where all work takes individual needs into account; at the other, no help of any kind is available. In between are those systems which offer small group placement to very handicapped children, or support teachers who go into the classroom with selected individual pupils, sometimes for as many as 15 hours per week. Other authorities provide a limited number of lessons with a specialist teacher on a one-to-one basis or in a small group. Dyslexic children receiving this limited amount of help, usually have 1 or 2 hours a week; they are lucky if they get more.

Most dyslexic pupils spend the greater part of their school day in mixed ability classes, where the language part of the work is unstructured and there is little if any direct support for their attempts to cope with general classwork. Access to books and other printed material – worksheets and the like – is probably limited by underachievement in reading. Production of required written work is likely to be slow, with numerous mistakes.

There is thus a sharp contrast between the two learning situations. Individually, the pupil is carefully observed, supported and stretched appropriately; in class he is on his own for most of the time. It is expected and hoped that the phonic skills that he learns in the individual lesson will be used in the wider context of his general work.

From my own observations, and other teachers' comments, pupils find this application of phonic work in their general lessons very difficult indeed. When they have to convey all kinds of ideas and information in writing, with many different spellings, they can become very confused. In such situations they do not easily recall what they have learned, forgetting even words they can get right when the phonic context is controlled. Typically, the pupils are unable to use taught word structures in classwork because they are not able to formulate ideas with sufficient clarity to write them down. Supported, they can talk over what is wanted; when left in the class, they do not know where to begin. Children experience similar difficulties at all levels of schooling.

Some important points arise from this state of affairs. First, can we tell how efficiently and quickly pupils' new-found knowledge and skills are assimilated into general class work? Secondly, is it necessary to assist this transfer of learning in a direct way and, if so, how can it be done?

How do we Check Transfer?

There are a number of ways in which the process of assimilation can be seen and certain stages to watch for. Observation of the pupil in the classroom can give clues, reports from class teachers may note increased willingness to try, increased confidence and better concentration. All of these can happen quite soon after tuition begins, which suggest that they are a direct consequence of the individual help. Regular inspection of pupils' classwork will show effects of all kinds. First may come an increase in the amount of writing attempted. Next, pupils may make fewer major errors so that writing can be more easily understood, with improved handwriting. Greater involvement with books may be noticed. A gradual increase in accuracy of spelling and use of punctuation should follow. It should be possible to note the point at which certain stages are reached; for instance, the point when certain spelling mistakes cease to occur, or when full stops and capital letters begin to be used consistently. The pupil should be applying his or her knowledge automatically, rather than 'remembering to remember'.

How quickly this transfer occurs will vary according to the individual child and her particular circumstances. On the one hand, there is the age at which she is referred for help, the extent of her difficulty, and her intelligence and personality; on the other hand, there are the pupil's school placement, class size, the number of individual lessons, differing demands of schoolwork and how subject and class teachers respond to the dyslexia difficulty itself. How the pupil sees the connection between the two kinds of teaching is also important. All these can and do affect the rate at which work done in individual lessons leads to all-round improvement in attainment. In the long term, successful assimilation can only be tested by results: does the pupil's general work improve while special help continues, and does the improvement continue when help is withdrawn?

Follow-up testing and collection of information about later educational progress would be needed to show this.

Helping Transfer

Many teachers, of course, already do try and ensure that their work is put into practice. Consultation with class teachers, giving follow-up work to be done between lessons, inspection of pupils' classwork, help with learning essential subject vocabulary and spellings, helping older pupils with general English work: all these have been regular practices for many years. However, I suggest that there is an urgent need for more explicit work. Specialist teachers of dyslexic children, wherever possible, should take practical steps to help pupils use their structured lesson material in the wider context of the curriculum. The exact nature of these steps will, of course, vary according to the pupil's school year.

Helping Infant and Junior Pupils

At the infant and first junior level, basic phonic work should perhaps transfer into the classroom situation with the least difficulty because the gap between the individual dyslexic child and his or her age group is still quite small. The learning of sounds and letters, sound blending, rhyming, correct letter formation, could all be followed through by the class teacher; there could be others in the class who would benefit from the same kind of work. It is important that the dyslexic pupil has the right kind of reading book, and that someone hears reading regularly. He should be encouraged to write, applying his phonic knowledge wherever possible – but it is important that he should not be inhibited by frequency of mistakes. It would be necessary to provide suitable work material and games so that the class teacher or assistant could give appropriate help. Daily practice, for instance, of the sound–letter linkages could be invaluable.

In junior schools, it is common for work to be left for pupils so that they can follow up the phonic work during the week – perhaps a workbook exercise or some spellings to learn. They will probably be asked to read some pages from a particular book. The aim here is usually to ensure a revision session – in the gaps between lessons much can be forgotten. It is often difficult for a dyslexic pupil to complete work given in this way. It is often seen as an extra task, to be done when he has a spare moment – and it might be up to him to remember to do it. Can a busy teacher with 30 or more pupils be expected to take responsibility for this special work? The crucial question is, what is the work for? Is it an extra or a valuable part of the pupil's learning? I suggest that individual teachers should discuss the purpose of such work with class teachers, and when it should be done. Many junior school classes have a flexible timetable and special work can be done unobtrusively so the pupil is not made to feel different. Reading books left by the specialist teacher need to be used with the class teacher's help – or perhaps that of a voluntary reading helper – but this needs to be set up explicitly rather than left as a casual arrangement.

Some pupils seem to have difficulty in understanding that the work of their individual lesson should be used on other occasions; they tend to 'pigeonhole' their special lesson work. What may happen more often is that the very structured phonic approach of the dyslexia work is so different from the approach they meet in the classroom, that they are not able to make the transfer of strategies. If, in the classroom, the emphasis is on whole-word spelling, on finding words or getting them from the teacher, they may be unable to change to a new way of proceeding unless directly helped. If their phonological awareness is poor, they may have enormous difficulty in putting their new skills into practice and may give up rather than struggle unaided. Free writing in the individual lesson can help to bridge this divide. But it is not quite the same. Their teachers do not usually sit by and watch them struggle unaided; they support and encourage, give useful prompts and reminders to use their phonic knowledge and skills (What about magic 'e'?, What does the vowel say?). It is a different situation.

It is valuable for the individual teacher to go into the pupil's classroom from time to time both to observe and to help. Watching how he sets about ordinary written work can be very informative. How competently does he use spellings which seem secure in the structured context? Does he punctuate work? Is he able to frame thoughts and write them down without difficulty – leaving spelling mistakes aside? What about reading: does he turn to a book for information? Direct observation of this kind can be very useful in planning the next steps in the spelling and reading work.

In order to make the link between the two learning situations explicit for the pupil, he or she could be encouraged to apply in the classroom the structured work that has been done in the individual lesson. This kind of exercise would be particularly valuable in the third and fourth year of junior school, when demands on writing increase. It is obvious that careful negotiation would be needed before any such activity went ahead because the class teacher should not push far ahead of the spelling programme.

Contact with Class or School Teachers

Contact with teachers is a key factor at all stages. If we know what our pupils are doing for most of the school week, we may be able to help them more effectively. What subject material are they using, how much writing are they expected to do, how much reading and what kind of books or other printed matter do they meet? How difficult is their general class work? Is material specially adapted for those with learning difficulties and how is the individual dyslexic pupil expected to perform?

We can get some of this information from the pupils themselves, but it may be incomplete or even incorrect. It is better to get it from the teachers. The necessary discussions are often quite easy at junior school, where most of the work is done by the class teacher, and contact can be made every week. At secondary school, teachers are more difficult to reach. The key person here will be the special needs teacher, the head of the support team or the head of the year. They should be able to provide information about the curriculum and the pupil's general performance. There may also be classroom support teachers and contact with them is very important. Regular discussion, perhaps every half-term, should enable individual teachers to keep abreast with how the pupil is doing. In ideal situations, the dyslexia specialist will be seen as a member of the team.

Information can be given at such meetings as well as obtained. It is important that class teachers know the kind of programme the dyslexic pupil is following, the objectives of such work and how far it has proceeded at any time; reports can be given about how he or she is coping and his or her particular difficulties and strengths. Suggestions can be made, for instance about corrections, and where particular help would be useful. A realistic level of expectation could be set as a result of such discussions. This will be very important now that many secondary schools are organised in fully integrated, mixed ability classes.

Expectations vary about what dyslexic pupils can do − and should be able to do. Sometimes very little is expected of them − although they attempt the same work as the rest of their class. At other times, their failure to perform at the average pace and level may bring penalty and reprimand. The specialist teacher has an informed contribution to make to this discussion. We should aim, by negotiation, to reduce the gap between what is asked and what can be achieved, so that the pupil has a better chance of putting his or her new learning into practice. At the very least, a pupil may be encouraged to make a better effort if the demands made on him or her are realistic ones. Then he or she might be expected to get right at least the work done in the individual or small group tuition.

Explicit Help in the Secondary School

It is very useful if the individual lesson teachers are familiar with curriculum material: Is the pupil using test books or specially provided worksheets and typed material? If the former, does she make full use of the illustrative parts of the text, can she use an index efficiently, does she know how to 'read' a chart or a table? Class teachers are not able to check up on every individual's understanding, and an explanation given to the whole class may go over the head of the dyslexic youngster. Very often books are not allowed out of the classroom and dyslexic pupils will probably not have enough time to make full use of them.

Separate worksheets have their own problems for dyslexic pupils. Such material often takes the form of dense typescript, with few headings and little of the extra information that published books provide in the way of non-verbal, or non-text material. The great advantage is that pupils can at least have their own copies so they may be brought to an individual teacher for help – and taken home to be read at their own pace.

I suggest that full use should be made of such resources. Help with the spelling of technical words and other vocabulary is often given by the individual teacher. But this could be taken further. Part of the work in each lesson could be centred around a subject topic. Reading – word attack, fluency and comprehension – could be from subject texts or worksheets. The same material could provide sources for some of the phonic work.

Those pupils who reach secondary school with low reading and spelling skills are in particular need of help with assimilating special lesson work. They have a huge struggle to keep up in class and with completing homework. Clearly, the phonic work must take priority, but they should begin to apply this work as soon as possible. Ways of adapting very basic spelling work to meet the needs of secondary school pupils are described in the Bangor Teaching System (Miles, 1989) and in such programmes as Spellbound (Rak, 1972). By using such methods, e.g. proceeding early to two- and three-syllable words and the easier suffixing rules, we can help pupils who need this immediate boost to their skills. It could be very helpful if we were able to mesh such spelling work directly with their curriculum material. Pupils might more readily transfer the new phonic strategies to classwork if the link was made explicit in the first place through a factual subject. Where appropriate, in consultation with other teachers, curriculum material could also be used to help with written expression and study skills such as note-making. It can also be very motivating for pupils, particularly the older ones, to find that their reading and spelling work was immediately useful.

Many dyslexic pupils find their greatest difficulty in the area of English as a subject and dislike the tasks it involves. Passing the 'O' level English examination (and now the GCSE) has long been recognised as a major hurdle. This may be because they find the need to generate much of the content in 'English', to organise and write down ideas – a task of impossible dimensions. Structured help with English work, such as essay writing and the inferential reading necessary for comprehension of literary texts, can therefore be very valuable and is a well-established part of the work with older pupils.

Implications for Arrangement of Individual Lessons

All teachers working with dyslexic children are very conscious of time pressures. Pupils must be helped to catch up as quickly as possible and there is always a huge amount of work to be done. Yet haste is not productive; they will not learn if they are pushing along too fast. The available time must therefore be used in the most effective way. If the lesson time is very limited, this may restrict the opportunities for working in the classroom, or for using non-structured material. Where lessons are more frequent, I believe that it would be advantageous to divide them between work on the structured phonic programme, and helping with curriculum work in the ways I have suggested. By helping our pupils to put their new learning to efficient use with minimum delay, we can help them get greater benefit from every part of their education.

References

MILES, E. (1989). *The Bangor Dyslexia Teaching System.* London: Whurr Publishers.
RAK, E.T. (1972). *Spellbound. Phonic Reading and Spelling.* Cambridge, MA: Educators Publishing Service.

Chapter 26
The Use of Tape-recorders to Develop Speaking and Listening Skills

JEANNE REILLY*

It is broadly agreed that the dyslexic child has difficulty organising oral language output as well as reading, writing and spelling. Without an ability to organise ideas logically and express them in a sequential way, the dyslexic child has little chance of producing coherent written work. Poor auditory memory or sequencing can mean that the child does not have the means to monitor and modify his or her own oral language.

Taping the child's spoken language, and helping him or her to make judgements about it, giving suggestions for improving the sequencing of ideas and then providing further opportunity to try out the suggestions, can be a useful method of teaching.

Aims of Taping

Many of the aims of taping practice are features of the National Curriculum for English.

Specific aims of taping can be itemised as follows:

- To help develop an awareness of sequence cause and effect.
- To provide children with a means of listening to and evaluating their own work in a non-threatening way.
- To provide an opportunity for children to express their thoughts and ideas without the constraints of handwriting.
- To provide a means of trying out different styles of language to suit a variety of audiences, purposes and contexts.
- To give children an opportunity to describe their own personal feelings and thoughts.
- To improve the effectiveness and clarity of their spoken language in communicating messages to others.
- To encourage the sharing of and discussion of their efforts with others.

---

*The copyright for this chapter is retained by the author.

- To work out clearly defined requirements for some activities so that children can judge for themselves whether they have fulfilled task criteria.
- To provide a basis for written work in the classroom.
- To provide support for written work in the classroom.

Practical Considerations

A typical lesson lasts an hour, during which time a single activity can be discussed, planned, taped and listened to. Depending upon the activity, efforts can be improved upon there and then. It is not advisable to carry an activity over until the next week. Immediate feedback is best for making decisions on how to improve or change a piece of work.

The groups are no more than six children. This is big enough, because the support needed by each child is considerable. A group of six children can make a fair amount of noise and there is the possibility of interference on each other's tapes. It is not necessary to provide sound-proof booths. Taping can be carried out in a normal classroom. Older children are likely to be much more independent and helpful to one another – in this case the group can be larger.

Children tape using a condenser microphone and they listen back through headphones. A headphone distribution centre, where up to five children can listen at a time, is a useful investment, as are tape-recorders that can stack. It is important to spend adequate time teaching children the vocabulary of tape-recorders, as well as how to operate them. The whole operating process is a set of sequences, and provides practice in an area dyslexics find difficult. The activity needs, and indeed teaches, children to control the use of their voices. They soon learn that speaking out of turn is heard on everyone's tape and very quickly learn to inhibit inappropriate talk and to be aware of others in the group.

For the age range being discussed, taping and writing activities should be separate. Taping can support work in the classroom, but it seems to work best if only minimal writing is introduced during the taping lessons themselves. This can take the form of note-taking, for example.

Taping Activities

This is a selection of successful activities used and enjoyed by the children:

- Short story from a picture sequence.
- Description of an object or animal from a picture.
- Reading from a children's book.
- Incoming message on a telephone answering machine.
- News item in the style of a short radio news broadcast.

- A radio play devised by the group.
- A reporter describing a topical news event.
- A taped letter to a friend.
- A recipe from the last cookery lesson.

Example 1: What it's like to be a witch

Paul was 9.3 years old with an IQ of over 120 and, although comprehension of spoken language was average, reading and spelling well below expected levels and his ability to apply phonic strategies was very limited, he found reading in context was the best way of learning.

Paul found speaking in any group context an enormous trial. While he liked to write down stories, it was not until he started taping that a true picture of his verbal ability could be assessed, his confidence could be built up and so he could bridge the gap between his verbal and his written skills. The transcript of the tape illustrates this gap.

Transcript of Paul's tape

Now I'm going to tell you about my job. My job is that I'm a witch. Very nice job actually. How you start to be a witch, you have to get a lot of gear. I'll tell you what gear right now and you won't be afraid. I get a black hat and put it on my head. Dye your hair green or any other purple colour or anything like that. A black cape will be good, a dress that is black, a skirt that is black and some peculiar socks. Then a broom. That is all. A cat a cottage and that is what you need.

Now I'm going to tell you what I do. Well what I do in the afternoon, I get up for one hour, and walk around in my ladylike clothes and say my name and I look at all the children that are bad, fat, little podgy little childs and obedient silly stupid little childs at the school. The grand school of Podgy and Pandy and silly old children. And then I go back home. I mix up some spells, I set my alarm for midnight and then I go to sleep. And then I wake up the alarm gets ..... I go for something to eat. I get on my clothes, black cape, my black hat, I dye my hair put on my socks. I put my silly little shoes on, my broom and I look up. I get my 'postpan' and my cat and then I go to their house and I put a little spell on each person.

How I do that you ask is I get a blower thing, it's a bit like a trumpet, and then I put loads of medicine sort of stuff and blow on them. Then they turn into a frog or something. Then when I've done all that I just go to see my friend the werewolf, have a cup of tea and that's my breakfast and a bit of food, I go home and have a sleep then wake up and do the same. I hope you enjoyed the story.

(Recorded 21st March 1990)

When listening back to himself, Paul had a list of ten single words that had been discussed by the group and which he had attempted to use while taping. Playing them back became a listening activity to check how many of the ten words he had managed to focus on. Out of ten words, Paul had indeed used nine of them and was well pleased with his efforts.

Example 2: Telling a story from a set of pictures

Simon is a boy with considerable difficulties in both processing language and problem solving. He has average receptive vocabulary and language levels on standard testing, but weak auditory sequential memory. This tape shows how he struggles to keep a story going at times, but he has also used taping to improve his story telling. The transcription is one taken after a year in a taping programme. He is able to produce a story with some repetitions, hesitations and false starts but with a coherent sequence of events.

Transcript of Simon's tape, Autumn 1989, aged 9.1 years

The Robber and the Blind Man
One, one day this lady was, this lady was looking in the window of a hat shop and while she was looking in the window, a man came up behind her and stole her purse and then he ran away with it. And the lady was, talked to this, this policeman. So he he came and ran with the woman to get the, the person who stole the lady's bag. And there was an old man sitting on a bench with a walking stick and the man who stole the lady's bag got tripped up by the old man, because the man stuck out his stick and the old man said, the lady said to the old man 'That's very nice of you.' and the old, the robber wen to jail 'cos the policeman caught him. The End

Judging and Monitoring Taping

A variety of ways have been devised to help monitor the taping efforts of children, which are both non-judgemental and non-threatening. The principal rule is that, in listening back to a child's tape in a group, the first person to talk about the tape is the child who made it and the only person allowed to criticise the tape is that child. This works well and the other children, if they have something to say, must say something positive about the tape they have heard. In this way, there is no child who is afraid to have his tape heard by the group. A check-list is gradually developed over the year to include the items that need to be monitored and changed, such as reducing hesitations and repetitions, or the use of descriptive words on the check-list; improved intonation, stress and expressions can also be judged.

Children can listen to one another's tapes and learn from another approach to the same exercise. They can also offer positive feedback to each other at the same time as learning purposefully.

Chapter 27
Pupils' Self-evaluation as an Aid to Teaching Handwriting

JANE TAYLOR

Handwriting is an acquired physical skill which some pupils find difficult. Such pupils need constant attention and monitoring to prevent poor writing habits from developing. These requirements make demands which, for the teacher in the busy classroom situation, may be difficult to accommodate. A measure of the problem is that, even in a one-to-one situation, where expectation is higher, a pupil often finds it difficult to maintain his or her standard of handwriting when concentrating on written expression rather than on the mechanics of handwriting. The burden on the teacher could be reduced if procedures were developed which enable the pupil to cooperate more fully by assuming more responsibility for his or her own performance. It is postulated that the use of self-evaluation by the pupil provides him or her with greater insight into his or her difficulties and, when incorporated into a teaching programme, enables him or her to assess handwriting performance on a continuing basis.

A pupil is often aware that his or her handwriting is unsatisfactory, but appears to lack the necessary knowledge to improve the situation. To be in a position to effect a change, the pupil needs to be made aware of the many underlying factors that can affect handwriting and taught how to apply these to his or her own handwriting. These factors can be divided into three groups:

1. Handwriting hardware, which covers furniture, paper ruling and type of writing tool to be used.
2. The body in relation to handwriting, covering posture, paper position and tool hold.
3. The elements affecting legibility and fluency necessary for acquiring fast, fluent and clear handwriting.

Each of these factors will now be examined in some detail.

Hardware

The teacher can demonstrate to the pupil that a good writing environment can be created if attention is paid to the associated 'hardware'.

Furniture

Teachers should try to provide furniture of the correct height or to make the necessary adaptations. Ideally the table should be half the height of the pupil and the chair a third of his or her height (Brown, 1989). Furthermore, when writing on a single sheet of paper, on a hard surface, the pupil should have a piece of card on which to rest the paper.

Paper ruling

Many pupils with difficulties seem to find the use of lined paper helpful. All letters have a direct relationship to each other and to the baseline, i.e. real or imaginary line on which the body of the letter sits. Providing the pupil with at least a baseline helps him or her to establish this relationship. A second line to indicate the height of the mid-zone letters helps the pupil to achieve uniformity of letter heights. Some pupils may require a third line to indicate the height of ascenders and a fourth line to indicate the length of descenders. The width of ruling can be varied to suit the pupil's age and size of writing.

Type of tool to be used

A change of writing instrument can affect outcome; therefore the teacher should have a range of writing tools available. The width and shape of the barrel varies, as does the thickness of the lead or nib. These parameters have a direct effect on handwriting performance. A pupil should be encouraged to experiment with a variety of pencils or pens and to select the one which suits him and his style of writing. Whenever possible the use of ball-point pens should be discouraged.

The Body in Relation to Handwriting

As in many other physical activities, the ability to produce handwriting with ease and fluency is influenced by the correct use of the appropriate parts of the body. The teacher should be aware of any underlying physical difficulties a pupil may be experiencing. However, to obtain optimum conditions in which the pupil can work to best advantage, particular attention should be paid to the following points.

Posture

The pupil should adopt a good sitting position with the thighs well supported and feet flat on the floor. The forearms should be well supported on the table at all times. The non-writing hand should be placed on the paper to keep the paper steady. The left hander should be encouraged to place his or her non-writing hand above the line of writing so that it does not obstruct the writing hand.

Paper position

The paper should be tilted away from the mid-line. If the paper is put in the correct position, the writing arm will be more or less parallel to the paper's edge.

Positioning the paper correctly is particularly important for the left hander. If the paper is positioned with sufficient tilt, he or she is less likely to adopt an unconventional hooked grip. However, the left-handed pupil with a hooked grip should tilt the paper in the same direction as the right hander to prevent the writing hand covering the written text.

Tool hold

A dynamic tripod tool hold is desirable. The tool should be held at approximately 1.5 cm from the point for the right hander and at least 2 cm for the left hander. The left hander should place his or her writing hand below the line of writing so that he or she can see the letters as he or she writes them. A Stetro pencil grip may be used to assist the pupil to obtain an improved grip.

Elements Affecting Legibility and Fluency

The complexity of handwriting performance is addressed in this section. Performance often breaks down in only one or two areas but to affect a change, the pupil needs to understand where his or her difficulties lie. Precise teaching will need to be given on those areas to enable him or her to work on improving these specific aspects of his or her handwriting.

Letter names and sounds

The teacher must check whether the pupil knows the names and/or sounds of letters. A pupil who cannot identify or is confused by certain letters is less likely to have an automatic motor plan available to him when he comes to write the letter. He may have to hesitate for a moment to sort out in his mind which letter he wants to write and this will break the rhythm of his writing.

Numerals

The formation of numerals should be checked. Numerals should be the same size as capital letters and be started at the top.

Legibility

There are a number of rules relating to legibility (Jarman, 1979, 1988; Alston, 1990; Alston and Taylor, 1990; Taylor, 1990).

The rules can be divided into four groups. The first group is concerned with letter formation, shape and alignment:

1. All letters except 'd' and 'e' start at the top.
2. Round letters should be round and closed.
3. Straight letters should be straight and parallel.
4. The relative height of letters should be uniform.
5. Letters should align to the baseline correctly.

The second group is concerned with space:

6. The space between letters should be even.
7. The space between words should be even.

The third group is concerned with joins:

8. Letters which end on the baseline join diagonally.
9. Letters which end on the mid-line join horizontally.

The fourth group is concerned with punctuation:

10. A sentence begins with a capital letter and ends with a full stop.

These rules can be used in a number of ways. They can be:

- Used by the teacher to define areas of weakness.
- Incorporated into a self-evaluation check-list.
- Incorporated into teaching strategies.
- Used to monitor progress.

There are three stages in the development of this knowledge:

1. The ability to match letter with letter.
2. The ability to recall the letter name/sound when shown a given letter.
3. The ability to match a letter to the given letter name/sound.

The difficulties experienced appear to be two-fold. There may be confusion with the actual letter name or sound, e.g. g/j, u/y, or with the actual shape of the letter, i.e. the manner in which the letter is formed. A pupil may experience one or both of these difficulties.

Letter formation

The teacher must check that all small letters are being formed with the correct movement patterns, i.e. from the top (excepting 'd' and 'e'). The Letter Formation Assessment Sheet in the Handwriting File (Alston and Taylor, 1988) can be used for this purpose. The teacher should observe very carefully the precise manner in which the pupil has formed each letter.

Joins

Teaching letters with entry and exit strokes facilitates a natural progression from writing single letters to using a joined script. The teacher should observe carefully the manner in which joins are executed. Inconsistent diagonal and horizontal joins can affect the overall appearance of a piece of handwriting.

Capital letters

The formation of capital letters should be checked. Capital letters should be the same height as letters with ascenders.

The teacher should make sure that the pupil's name and the date are on the samples of the pupil's handwriting. An evaluation of the handwriting should be made and recorded. The Handwriting Checklist and the Class Record Sheet are provided in the Handwriting File (Alston and Taylor, 1988) for this purpose.

Self-evaluation

There are two main approaches to teaching handwriting: there is the direct approach whereby the pupil is generally told what he is not doing correctly, e.g. the comment 'Your writing is untidy' may be made but no strategies given as to how the pupil might improve the situation. Alternatively, there is the discovery approach which engages the pupil more directly. One way in which this may be achieved is for the pupil, who is experiencing difficulties with his or her handwriting, to use his or her critical abilities in the form of self-evaluation as a learning aid.

Self-evaluation can be built into a teaching programme in a number of ways. It can be incorporated into handwriting practice, used in the form of a self-evaluation check-list or used for monitoring progress.

Handwriting practice

In the initial stages of learning to write a letter, or at a later stage when working to improve the formation of a letter, the pupil can be asked to write out the letter three times and to evaluate the well-formed letters by giving them a tick – the first stage of self-evaluation. The number of well-formed letters is recorded. This exercise can be repeated using letter strings or words.

A well-formed letter, once mastered, needs to be written with greater speed and fluency. One way that this can be achieved is to ask the pupil to write out the letter repeatedly for 10–15 seconds. Again, the well-formed letters are evaluated and ticked. As before, this exercise can be repeated using letter strings or words.

This approach to handwriting practice begins to make the pupil more aware of his own performance.

Self-evaluation check-list

Figure 27.1 gives an example of a self-evaluation check-list. A check-list incorporating a number of statements relating to handwriting performance is drawn up.

The check-list is divided into three sections: the first section is concerned with posture, paper position and tool hold; the second with the formation of small and capital letters, their slant and alignment, spacing between letters and words, the formation of joins and numerals and the use of punctuation; lines are provided in the third section on which the pupil can list areas requiring practice.

Each statement is presented in a positive manner, e.g. 'I sit correctly'. This is followed by Yes [   ] and No [   ] boxes for the pupil's response.

The objective of the check-list is for the pupil to be able, with the help of the teacher, to define both the positive aspects of performance and to highlight the areas of difficulty.

Once the check-list has been completed satisfactorily, the teacher should encourage the pupil by making positive comments to all the 'Yes' responses. The pupil may be quite surprised and encouraged to see how many 'Yes' responses he or she has made. Frequently, there are only one or two points which are giving rise to difficulties.

The pupil may need guidance to decide on the order in which he or she should work. Goals should be set that can be attained. Some direct teaching will be needed so that the pupil is able to effect an identifiable change in his or her writing as quickly as possible. Accordingly, only one or two tasks should be specified and practised at any one time.

The teacher may observe a response which is incorrect. Such a response may indicate that a pupil is unaware of the implication of the statement. For example, the pupil may indicate that all his or her letters with descenders are the correct length when in fact he or she writes the letter j as a tall letter. The teacher may not wish to intervene immediately, but to raise the issue in a teaching situation.

STUDENT SELF EVALUATION CHECK LIST

Name .... Bobby ....   Date 25.10 91

	YES	NO
I sit correctly.	[✓]	[ ]
My writing hand is placed on the paper correctly.	[ ]	[✓]
My paper position is correct.	[✓]	[ ]
My tool hold is correct.	[ ]	[✓]
I need to use a pencil grip.	[✓]	[ ]

-===-

	YES	NO
My letter formation is correct.	[ ]	[✓]
My tall letters are the correct height.	[✓]	[ ]
My letters with tails are the correct length.	[✓]	[ ]
My midzone letters are the same size.	[ ]	[✓]
The straight lines of my letters are correct.	[✓]	[ ]
My letters sit correctly on the line.	[ ]	[✓]
The slant of my letters is regular.	[✓]	[ ]
The spacing between my letters is even.	[✓]	[ ]
The spacing between my words is even.	[ ]	[ ]
I use capital letters correctly.	[✓]	[✓]
I use full stops correctly.	[✓]	[ ]
My numerals are formed correctly.	[✓]	[9]
My horizontal joins are correct.	[✓]	[ ]
My diagonal joins are correct.	[✓]	[ ]

still learning to join letters.

-===-

I need to work on:-

1. .. pen grip ....
2. .. d f j k z a ....
3. ....

Figure 27.1 A self-evaluation check-list by Bobby.

Monitoring progress

The self-evaluation check-list can be used periodically to evaluate progress. The frequency with which it is used will depend on the speed with which the pupil manages to effect the change in the stated areas of practice.

Conclusion

A pupil is often aware that his or her handwriting is unsatisfactory but appears to be unable to improve the situation by him- or herself. The incorporation of self-evaluation techniques into a teaching programme enables the pupil to become self-critical. It enables the teacher to draw the pupil's attention to areas of his or her handwriting which he or she performs satisfactorily and to focus on the specific points on which the pupil needs to work. This system of self-evaluation can be applied to any piece of handwriting. However, the pupil will still need to continue to practise, but with practice he or she is more likely to attain the specific goals which he or she sets. Each successful achievement encourages further progress.

References

ALSTON, J. (1990). *Writing Left-Handed*. Manchester: Left-Handed Company.

ALSTON, J. and TAYLOR, J. (1988). *The Handwriting File*. Cambridge: Learning Development Aids.

ALSTON, J. and TAYLOR, J. (1990). *Handwriting Helplines*. Manchester: Left-Handed Company.

BROWN, B. (1989). *The Ergonomics of Handwriting. Handwriting Interest Group Seminar*. London: Institute of Education.

JARMAN, C. (1979). *The Development of Handwriting Skills*. Oxford: Basil Blackwell.

JARMAN, C. (1988). 12 rules for good handwriting. In: J. Alston (ed.), *Handwriting Review*. 7 Harrington Drive, Gawsworth, Cheshire SK11 9RD6.

TAYLOR, J. (1990). Handwriting practice can be fun. In: G. Hales (ed.), *Meeting Points in Dyslexia*. Reading: British Dyslexia Association.

Chapter 28
A Multisensory Approach towards Reading Music

MARGARET HUBICKI

Viewpoint

Shown the short tune in Figure 28.1 and asked what he sees, a non-music lover might well reply 'Oh! I can't tell you anything because I know nothing about music'.

Figure 28.1

In fact, he has immediately answered our question by telling us what he saw. He could not have mentioned the word 'music' if he had not *seen* music. He had no need to know anything *about* it to recognise that music was what he was looking at. However, in reading music, we not only need to glance at it but also to *notice detail*. This paper takes into consideration coordination of eye, ear and hand and how such coordination can help to broaden our awareness of what we 'see' in written music – and therefore we are more able to respond to what it tells us.

Some Difficulties for 'Dyslexic' Musicians

Initial observation

A quick glance at the illustration already seen (Figure 28.1) draws our attention to a number of points. To begin with, we notice the black lines and white spaces which form a musical staff representing the written places for high or low sounds – five horizontal black lines across the page from left to right with a white space in between each line.

Each line or space is placed on above the other – from the lowest line up to the highest one. If we look downwards, each line or space is placed one below the other – from the highest line down to the lowest one.

Words that can cause difficulties

So far so good! But already a possible problem has arisen. Four of the words 'left', 'right', 'low' and 'high' all have more than one meaning. Words with more than one meaning can easily create confusion, particularly for dyslexics! This is especially true when these words are used for referring to the abstract qualities of music.

'High' and 'low'

In everyday life a learner might often talk about a 'high wall' or a 'low wall'. He can see the difference between them with his eye and can also feel it with his hands and, if necessary, such sensory awareness could prove how these words 'high' and 'low' relate to something concrete – such as this wall. But when 'high' or 'low' is used to describe the intangible, unseeable and untouchable qualities of music, it becomes quite another matter. For anyone who has difficulty with those words, it is not the *differences of sound* that is the problem. It is the names that are given to the sounds' differences which seem meaningless. When this is the case, the learner needs to be invited to give his or her name for the sound he or she hears – a name which makes sense to him or her.

There could be many ways to offer help over this problem. One is to encourage the student to listen to non-musical sounds and name them – moving his hand in the direction in which he hears the sound moving – pointing upwards for what we call a 'high' sound and downwards for a 'low' sound. From his responses, we can discover what words he uses for the hand movement he has made for 'high' or 'low'. Initially, it is helpful to use the learner's own words whenever referring to a 'high' or to a 'low' sound. At a later stage, when he has gained some confidence, the more usual terms 'high' or 'low' could be substituted.

'High' and 'low' relating to the page

The words 'high' or 'low' can also cause difficulty when they are used for musical notation. We say 'high up on the page' or 'low down on the page' – or 'high on the staff' or 'low on the staff'. But the page and the staff written on it *look* flat. So whatever is meant? How can we help?

First of all, we should guide her hand to feel the page in the direction we mean by 'high' or 'low' – shown in Figure 28.2. The sensations of these movements and their directions 'up' or 'down' then begin to give sensory information – an awareness of direction – which the words themselves do

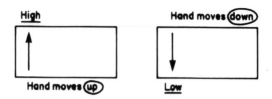

Figure 28.2

not have. As before, the learner is invited to give her name for the different movements (up or down) which she feels in her hands and sees with her eyes. When talking about these directions, use her names for them.

'High' and 'low' relating to the staff

Looking at the staff, this same method of help is valuable. Using his fingers encourage him to trace the lines and spaces which represent high sounds on the staff or low sounds. The aim is to coordinate what his eyes see with what his hands feel so that he can give his name for the sensation which these different directions make.

'Left' and 'right'

Time is represented in musical notation by the different black or white symbols seen on the staff. Both the symbols for time (black and white) and for pitch (placed high or low on the staff) have to be read from the *left* side of the page across it to the *right* side. To develop that sense of direction, it can again be a useful exercise to guide the learner's hands, this time *across* the page – similar to exercises in reading words.

These words 'left' or 'right' can cause trouble in many ways for dyslexics, of course, and many clues and mnemonics can help.

Awareness of Pattern

Reading music is not just a question of playing the right note in the right time and with a true sense of rhythmic purpose – vital though all that is! When a composer writes music he creates *patterns* of both time and pitch. We need to be constantly aware of this.

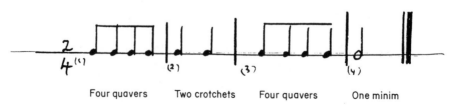

Four quavers   Two crotchets   Four quavers   One minim

Figure 28.3

The next section takes our simple tune for illustrating how useful our hands can be in tracing written patterns – both on the page and in the air. In doing this, we acquire the *sensation* of patterns quite apart from performing them. All the ideas below can be adapted and extended at every level of musical learning.

Time patterns

General observations

Reference to Figure 28.1 will help the reader make more sense of the examples given.

1. Glance across this whole tune.
2. '²⁄₄' at the beginning tells that there are two crotchet beats in a bar.
3. Decide on a speed for the crotchet beats.
4. Clap a bar or two of even crotchet beats at the chosen speed, or tap them with the foot, thus establishing the sensation of a clear, regular rhythmic beat as a background for clapping the about-to-be-detailed time pattern.
5. Count the number of bars: four bars.
6. Next, name all the details of the time pattern. Point to each note as you name its value – and notice the bar lines! (Figure 28.3).

Performance

1. Once again clap or tap a bar of crotchets for the feel of the beat.
2. Clap the time pattern.
3. Be very conscious of the sensation of *progression* from one bar to the next one. Clap with a sense of rhythmic purpose – that feel of purpose which is suggested by the look of those arrows moving from one bar to another – always *ON* across the bar-line. This is shown in Figure 28.4.

To become precisely aware of music's rhythmic progression in this way is a vital part of what causes the sound of music to 'live'.

Melodic line

Again, referring to Figure 28.1, notice the details of melodic patterns in the tune. There are two scales, both up and down, and some leaps. While

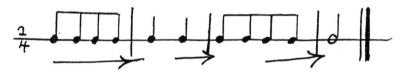

Figure 28.4

the eye follows each note, the hand should trace the sensation of the line made by the notes progressing across the staff.

General awareness

Bar (1)
Starting on C, the hand follows a scale up to G in bar (2) as in Figure 28.5.

Figure 28.5

Bar (2 and 3)
These bars contain two leaps in contrary motion. The hand movement can feel the sensation of this as it follows the shape: from G down to C then up to A in bar (3) (Figure 28.6).

Figure 28.6

Bar (3)
1. A scale of four descending notes.
2. The leap of a third moving on by step down to C which is the last note in bar (4) (Figure 28.7).

Figure 28.7

Musical awareness

Following the shape of the tune as a whole, it shows a climax point in bar (3), at A, its highest note – giving a sense of arrival there. Then, moving down by step and a small leap to C (the same note on which the tune began), the curve of the melodic line is completed.

In addition to following the melodic pattern with the finger feeling it on the page, the hand can trace its shape by 'drawing' it in the air in a similar fashion to dancers who use their hands for such expression of shape. This is an informative practice and well worth cultivating.

Looking for all such detail provides sign-posts and guidelines which can give security when in unknown musical territory. It offers an 'awareness' which is so much a part of communication in performance.

Some Reflections and Further Observations

So far we have been thinking about the position of musical symbols on the page, high or low, left to right – feeling their location and observing the patterns which they make and relating such observations to the movement of hand in appropriate directions and the clapping of time patterns.

Through noticing all these details, what we have *seen* with our eyes has led to *sensations* in our hands which are capable of suggesting to our ears how the written music *would sound* – even if this is only approximate. Such coordination of the visual, tactile and aural is an ability well worth cultivating. Not only does it lead to the accurate location of each written note, either on an instrument or in the voice, but it also leads to the performance of musical, rhythmic line instead of a mere string of isolated notes. It helps to create a sensitive response to a composer's written intentions.

Musical Notation: A Basic Problem

Musical notation uses only black or white symbols for representing both time and pitch. For some people, this uniform look of 'black or white' can cause a total block, creating a serious lack of confidence for anyone who tries desperately to remember what lies behind the fog (to him or her) of written musical symbols.

Pitch symbols

Relating colour to pitch can be of great help for identifying each letter-named musical sound, ABCDEFG, and its repeating pattern which forms the staff of black lines and white spaces.

It is outside the scope of this chapter to go into details of the use of colour, but one example of it is my own 'Colour Staff' material. This makes use of coloured, movable plastic pieces which can be placed on different boards provided for the purpose. Each letter-name is printed in a separate colour. The look of each colour and the letter-name printed on its plastic piece makes it possible for the learner to touch and feel the symbols of written music while positioning them in their appropriate places.

Time symbols

A great many time problems exist for learners who do not have a clear sense of a regular beat to which they can relate the different meanings of musical time symbols – especially the white one. For example, there can be a desperate haziness about the length of white minims or semibreves – as for tied, noted or dotted notes, their obscurity can be absolute.

Ideally, right from the start a regular beat should be developed through the sensation of walking, marching, clapping etc. Then the feel of these beats becomes a secure basis for understanding how the different lengths of sounds are represented in the black and white symbols of musical notation. The use of French time-names can be helpful, but any words or names that are meaningful to a learner for identifying note lengths should be used, provided that these are used in a consistent way and with a secure sense of beat.

Conclusions

Here it has only been possible to select a few examples of each point for illustrating a multisensory approach to reading music, but the principles within them can be applied and extended throughout the study of music. The great essential point lies in a wishful attempt to break through barriers which can exist and which are often caused by the uniform look of black and white symbols representing the sounds of music.

Index